SLAVERY AND SILENCE

SLAVERY
AND SILENCE

LATIN AMERICA AND THE U.S. SLAVE DEBATE

PAUL D. NAISH

PENN

UNIVERSITY OF PENNSYLVANIA PRESS

PHILADELPHIA

Published by
University of Pennsylvania Press
Philadelphia, Pennsylvania 19104-4112
www.upenn.edu/pennpress

Printed in the United States of America
on acid-free paper
10 9 8 7 6 5 4 3 2 1

Library of Congress Cataloging-in-Publication Data

Names: Naish, Paul D., 1960–2016, author.
Title: Slavery and silence: Latin America and the U.S. slave debate /
Paul D. Naish.
Description: 1st edition. | Philadelphia: University of Pennsylvania Press,
[2017] | Includes bibliographical references and index.
Identifiers: LCCN 2017012496 | ISBN 9780812249453
(hardcover: alk. paper)
Subjects: LCSH: Slavery—Political aspects—United States—History—19th
century. | Slavery—Latin America—History—19th century. | United
States—Race relations—History—19th century. | Whites—United
States—Attitudes—History—19th century. | Racism—Political
aspects—United States—History—19th century. | Conversation—Political
aspects—United States—History—19th century. | Political culture—United
States—History—19th century.
Classification: LCC E441 .N35 2017 | DDC 306.3/62098—dc23
LC record available at https://lccn.loc.gov/2017012496

[T]here are gentlemen, not only from the Northern, but
from the Southern States, who think that this unhappy
question—for such it is—of negro slavery . . . should never
be brought into public notice . . . Sir, it is a thing which
cannot be hid . . . you might as well try to hide a volcano,
in full operation . . .

—John Randolph, 1826

"Shadow," said he,
"Where can it be—
This land of Eldorado?"

—"Eldorado," Edgar Allan Poe, 1849

Contents

Publisher's Note

Sadly, Paul Naish died before finishing this book. His friend and former classmate, Evan Friss of James Madison University, assumed responsibility for seeing the work through the final stages of production.

Preface. Creatures of Silence

The early twenty-first century has been marked by a series of crimes and tragedies revealing, to the apparent surprise of many Americans, the longevity and pervasiveness of racism in the United States. Despite the fiftieth anniversary of important landmarks of civil rights legislation and the election of the nation's first African American president, a "postracial" future has not arrived. The bluntly discriminatory administration of justice reveals that the day-to-day lived experience of many nonwhite Americans differs significantly from that of whites. These sadly repeated discoveries of crude discrimination inspire equally regular calls for a "national conversation on race."

Considering how much the subject of race is openly debated at the beginning of the twenty-first century, it seems surprising that the need for further discussion is consistently invoked. But in the United States, race, for all its notoriety, is usually talked about in intimate contexts among people expected to hold roughly the same opinion. It is too loaded a topic to explore with strangers. Although it is a subject that affects the entire nation, there is nothing "national" about the conversation about race. In a society still much more segregated than we like to admit, it is difficult to talk freely, and frankly, about race.

In the thirty-five years before the Civil War, it was comparatively easy, for white people at least, to talk about race, to broadcast what today seems blindingly hateful and woefully ignorant and to present it as scientific fact.[1] "At least 3/5ths of the northerners *now* believe the blacks are an *inferior* race," estimated abolitionist Theodore Dwight Weld in 1836.[2] Not all white people declared blacks were less than human, but most believed they were decidedly less than whites. Even if people of African descent were free, declared Supreme Court Justice Roger Taney in the Dred Scott decision, they could never be citizens, and "the special rights and immunities guarantied to citizens do not apply to them."[3]

But slavery was harder to discuss. As Ralph Waldo Emerson said, "[Slavery] does not love the newspaper, the mailbag, a college, a book, or a preacher who has the absurd whim of saying what he thinks."[4] To talk about slavery was to explore—or deny—its obvious shortcomings, its inhumanity, its contradictions. To celebrate it required explaining away the nation's proclaimed belief in equality and its public promise of rights for all. To condemn it was to insult people who might be related by ties of blood or friendship or business, to threaten the very economy and political stability of the nation. The effects of the suppression of open discussion concerned thoughtful Americans: "Sooner or later [slavery] must be discussed," wrote abolitionist Amos Phelps in 1834. "Silence will never mend the matter. The very evil, that threatens us with such ruin, is in itself the creature of silence."[5]

There were certainly partisans who chose sides in the debate, and more and more people identified themselves as opponents or supporters of slavery as the Civil War approached. But there were many, many others who hesitated to express what they thought for fear of unpleasant or even dire consequences. And the partisans increasingly found themselves cornered—publicly championing one side in the debate over slavery, but privately doubtful and unable to ignore weaknesses in their position.

How these people talked about what they hesitated to say—how they had a national conversation about slavery by talking about nations other than the United States—is the subject of this book.

Introduction. Surrounded by Mirrors

In the winter of 1859 Julia Ward Howe, who would go on to write "The Battle Hymn of the Republic," stopped in Nassau en route to Cuba, where she was struck by something that had not particularly troubled her at home in Boston. Like many opponents of slavery, she was no great believer in racial equality. Nonetheless, she hesitated in making one observation because it effectively justified the human bondage she publicly deplored. Perceiving what she identified as the indolence and idleness of the free black population of the Bahamas, she guiltily indulged in an expression of doubt about black capacity; "you must allow us one heretical whisper,—very small and low," Howe confided in one of a series of anonymous articles published in *The Atlantic* beginning in May 1859 and collected in a volume called *A Trip to Cuba* in 1860. While she declared herself "orthodox" on the subject of abolition, the results of emancipation raised for her "the unwelcome question, whether compulsory labor be not better than none."[1]

In the thirty-five years before the Civil War, Howe was not the only person of apparently "orthodox" beliefs about slavery who made a guarded confession of uncertainty. Across the great divide that separated antislavery activists from defenders of human bondage, few people were more indefatigable in slavery's defense than the strident George Fitzhugh, who went so far as to argue in 1857 that so "natural, normal, and necessitous" was slavery that the enslavement of white people was justifiable.[2] Yet in an 1855 personal letter to his friend George Frederick Holmes he confessed, "I assure you, Sir, I see great evils in slavery, but in a controversial work I ought not to admit them."[3]

Howe's remark was made in a published text, Fitzhugh's in private correspondence. In confessing their guilty suspicions, neither was humiliated or persecuted. But both felt obliged to check their speech. In a political climate characterized by shouting, neither Howe nor Fitzhugh felt entirely at liberty to express a whisper of doubt about slavery.

Consider also Aaron Hulin, a Northern schoolteacher looking for work in Louisiana during this period. Upon beginning his trip south he wrote a

Figure 1. Most Americans had no firsthand experiences of life in Latin America and relied on a limited vocabulary of stereotypes about the region. But even those like William Meyers, a sailor who visited Cuba in 1838 and recorded his impressions in delightful watercolor sketches, often went looking for sights they had been primed to see and emphasized the most exotic, like this scene of enslaved musicians and smiling senoritas at a dance. William H. Meyers Diary/Diary: Voyage of Schooner *Ajax* from Philadelphia to Baltimore, Havana, Santiago and Cuba, n.d. Manuscripts and Archives Division, The New York Public Library, Astor, Lenox and Tilden Foundations.

friend in upstate New York, "they are so tenacious of their privileges in slavery, that were I, or any other man to disseminate the doctrine of Arthur Tappen [sic], or Murrel, I'd be killed, hung by public consent, without a hearing—SANS jury or trial!!!" Hulin went south at the moment of the "Murrell Excitement" in 1835, when suspicion of a slave conspiracy planned and financed by northern abolitionists terrified the white population along the Mississippi.[4] "It behooves those who come into the south, at this critical time, to be at peace, and attend to their own business," he wrote.[5] But the atmosphere of paranoia and suspicion he described was often reported by visitors to the South, who felt surrounded by spies on every railway platform and steamboat landing. They exchanged accounts of "persons who had expressed themselves too freely . . . [and] had been escorted to the station by a party of the inhabitants, and forced to take their departure."[6]

This book explores one instance of what happens when people hesitate to speak openly about a controversial subject—whether because they fear a kick under the table or a knife in the ribs—and resort to discussing it through metaphor. The people speaking behind this rhetorical mask were, like Howe and Fitzhugh, sometimes publicly associated with one side or the other of the slavery debate. They could not easily acknowledge the complexity of the situation, yet they were troubled by contradictions that threatened to dismantle their elaborate arguments. Just as often, they were ordinary Americans like Hulin, who saw discussions about slavery as volatile and destructive. The great mass of Americans who tried to keep their own counsel about slavery in the antebellum period were both black and white, male and female, northern and southern. They were bankers, farmers, politicians, merchants, publishers, preachers, and businesspeople. The majority kept silent because there was nothing to be gained by speaking up, and often a great deal to be gained by saying nothing.

But they found ways to talk about U.S. slavery without seeming to do so.

The impulse to indirection, to creative evasion, to criticism from a safe distance, has historically created rich and evocative political satire, children's fables that comment on grown-up concerns, and subversive theatre and fiction.[7] Sometimes the act of contextual substitution is obvious, even acknowledged. More often it is elusive, and the author's intention is open to interpretation. Partisans do not write manifestos in this form, although they sometimes allow themselves to engage imaginatively with their opponents' views. They playfully trespass into foreign territory, sampling the forbidden fruit.

The foreign territory invaded in this case was Latin America, a region most Americans had never visited and would never encounter directly but that they knew from news reports, travel accounts, commercial prospectuses, paintings, novels, and plays. The fact that most Americans had no firsthand knowledge of this area made it easier to reduce Latin America to stereotypes—sugar and coffee and gold; *volantes, senoritas,* and *machetes;* incense-clouded cathedrals, crumbling pyramids, and sultry jungles. It was a nearby world that was simultaneously and profoundly exotic: people spoke Spanish or Portuguese or African or Native American languages, practiced Catholicism, openly dined and slept with people of other races.

In this context Americans could—and did—say things about slavery that they would never utter when talking about the United States.

The suggestion that slavery was the subject Americans displaced on this region for the purposes of inspection and analysis is apt to sound surprising. Surely in the thirty-five years leading up to the Civil War there was little reticence about slavery and little need for indirection. This period, after all, resounded with rabid proslavery invective and radical (and in the words of its opponents, fanatical) abolitionism. Proslavery propaganda filled books and journals, and abolitionist handbills and pamphlets featured illustrations of slave auctions and grisly whippings. This strident conflict was, moreover, made striking by its historical novelty. Until the early 1800s the inevitability, if not the rightness, of slavery went virtually unquestioned. Before the 1830s abolitionists remained a tiny minority, and slave owners felt little necessity for defending human bondage as a positive good. Then after a period of relative calm following the American Revolution, a series of events in rapid succession provoked open debate. William Lloyd Garrison began publishing his virulent antislavery *Liberator* newspaper in January 1831. Nat Turner's rebellion roiled the South in August that same year. Britain abolished slavery in its colonies in the early 1830s, convincing many Southerners that their peculiar institution was besieged from without as well as within. For the next thirty years, with increasing vehemence, the United States rang with voices decrying and defending slavery.[8]

But in fact many people in the United States shrank from discussing the subject, or spoke about it in coded language. These people occupied the wide spectrum of opinion between fire eaters and immediate emancipationists, and they spoke about slavery much more circumspectly. Whether or not they were really prevented from speaking openly, Americans of many different backgrounds and in many different positions complained that they were. The sensation of being gagged was real enough. "We have various ways of covering slavery," remarked Frederick Douglass in 1846. "We call it sometimes a peculiar institution—the patriarchal institution—the civil and domestic institution."[9] For many people in the South the greatest danger attending open discussion was planting thoughts of revenge and rebellion in the minds of otherwise docile servants. For many Northerners, to challenge slavery was to undermine the stability of the Union and the foundations of American economic prosperity. So grave were the potential consequences of irresponsible words that at certain moments an unwelcome remark about slavery could lead to violence, and a public gathering to discuss its future could incite a riot.[10] But there were many other reasons why slavery proved a sore point and a source of conflict. Whether the subject could be debated publicly, whether greater danger attended its silencing or its open discussion, was almost as controversial as what was said. "The war of argument must come, or in its stead will come the war of arms," foresaw the abolitionist Amos Phelps in 1834. "Is discussion free, frank, and unrestricted, fraught with danger? Discussion smothered, rely upon it, is fraught with ten-fold danger."[11]

During this period the opposing positions were so polarized that there was little room for casual inquiry or unheated debate. On the vast middle ground between the two extremes, many Americans kept quiet. Some continued to leave unquestioned an institution they considered unexceptional. Some held opinions certain to be unpopular in their families or communities and did not wish to be shunned by speaking out. Some felt guilty or anxious about profiting from human bondage, or brooded uneasily about the expected results of emancipation. Some had the foresight to recognize the destructive power of the argument over slavery and forced themselves to hold their tongues. The defense of slavery traded heavily in politics and religion, those two subjects conventionally acknowledged as threats to polite conversation. Abolition was popularly associated with ideas shocking to the mid-nineteenth-century bourgeoisie: feminism, free love, and communism. As with the subject of race in the twentieth and twenty-first century United States, there was much about slavery that remained unspoken or at least unrecorded, discussed with like-minded friends sotto voce but not committed to paper for posterity to analyze.

The sense of constraint people experienced was sometimes quite real, though not so real as to prevent public discussion entirely (Howe, after all, ultimately published her "heretical whisper" under her own name). A climate of mandatory silence only encourages the reckless show-off and the attention-seeking politician. Plenty of radical abolitionists and self-justifying slaveholders felt at perfect liberty to say exactly what they thought. But their contributions did little to advance an honest dialogue about an intractable problem, and made others more determined to keep silent. The exaggerated theatrics of radical abolitionism and proslavery advocacy have obscured the degree to which slavery remained for many people an uncomfortable topic, its very unpleasantness arising from the hostility of the public volleys. Suppression of free expression and self-censorship existed alongside, and because of, the acrimony and viciousness that characterized speaking out. Historian David Grimsted captured this self-conscious silence amid shouting in his *American Mobbing*: "Political parties and majority populations in both sections saw the wisdom of avoiding discussion of slavery and were racist enough so that turning African Americans into property seemed small cost, or a nice bonus, for union. . . . Clear in the riot conversation of 1835 was the idea that the only national answer regarding slavery was not to think, or at least to talk, about it."[12]

Yet much of what people in the United States were unwilling or afraid to utter about slavery in their own country, they eagerly proclaimed in the context of Latin America. Thinking about the way Americans talked about Latin America reveals how people who would never have otherwise championed slavery or identified themselves as abolitionists meditated about the economic benefits and the flagrant injustice of the institution. In the thirty-five years before the Civil War, many Americans found an outlet for their doubts and concerns, fears and fascinations about slavery at home by talking about slavery south of the Rio Grande. Latin America, in other words, served as a proxy that allowed Americans to break many varieties of silence, from the studied tact of politicians who wanted to straddle both sides of a controversial issue, to the unspoken agenda of expansionists whose perception of the inferiority of blacks and Indians believed it justified claiming the land of a neighboring republic and instituting human bondage there, from the restraint of comfortable Northern white people who did not want to stir up trouble, to the rigorous self-censorship of proslavery Southerners who had no outlet for admitting the miscegenated realities of their own households. When they talked about Latin America, cautious and circumspect Americans of the 1830s, 1840s, and 1850s let down their guard and discussed slavery with candor. For example, Massachusetts historian William Hickling Prescott, though no radical abolitionist, used the history of the Spanish, who had sown the "seeds of the evil" in America to call for a national examination of conscience on the subject of the "wretchedness of the institution." Meanwhile, proslavery Southerners appraising slavery in Cuba and Brazil insisted that the U.S. version of slavery was superior to all others—perfect, in fact.

Indeed, in certain respects, Latin America served as the perfect metaphorical surrogate for its northern neighbor. The Spanish American republics shared many things with the United States: a colonial past, a heritage of relations with native peoples and African slaves, a hemisphere. With an emulation that could not fail to flatter the young United States, the emerging Latin American nations had followed the example of their republican predecessor, fought for their independence, and copied their constitutions from that of the United States. Besides these similarities, the United States and Latin America had other points in common. Europeans and creoles of European descent shared territory with indigenous people, with black slaves and free people, and with admixtures of these races. Native-born Protestant Americans uneasy about the rapid influx of immigrant Papists shuddered at Cuba and Brazil as models of societies with Catholic majorities. Haiti and Jamaica offered some observers a preview of post-emancipation South Carolina or Mississippi.

On the other hand, because Latin America seemed so different to many people in the United States, they could discuss aspects of slavery and race relations there without risking offense. The Spanish and Portuguese, with their long subjugation to the dark-skinned Moors, with their brutal Inquisition, with a system of slavery considered uniquely barbarous by those who subscribed to the Black Legend of Iberian cruelty, appeared very different from the European ancestors claimed by many white U.S. citizens. Latin America's casual race relations, unstable governments, and exotic Catholicism kept it at a secure remove from the United States. A safe distance separated the United States from its neighbors, even, ironically, as the imperatives of Manifest Destiny shrank that distance precipitously.

Other historical and geographical examples outside the contemporary Spanish- and Portuguese-speaking world south of the border served as points of reference as well. Both proslavery and antislavery Americans were especially obsessed with the former French colony of Haiti as a metaphor freighted with contradictory meanings—a symbol both of horror and destruction and of independence and autonomy.[13] Haiti, a topsy-turvy republic disavowing the plantation export economy, birthed in a bloody revolution and growing to maturity with blacks in the majority and in charge, was as different from the United States as could be conceived. "The first feature that strikes us, is the difference, the next the rivalry of races," summed up *Littell's Living Age* in 1844.[14] If Haiti was an "experiment of negro self-government," the English colony of Jamaica, where slavery had ended in 1838, was an "experiment of free negro labour"—one interpreted as a success but often as failure.[15]

Farther west and south, the Spanish American republics, including Mexico, Peru, and Argentina, as well as the monarchy of Brazil, occupied a place in the American imagination somewhere between the United States and Haiti, subject to endless reinterpretation. Their resources were expansively estimated, their commitment to republican government endlessly debated, their racial composition extensively probed. Through all this discussion, these regions served as an invaluable context for displacing national apprehensions about slavery when the cost of speaking out was high. Some of the people who participated in this conversation set policies that affected or even determined the lives of dozens if not thousands of others, but many had no greater impact than contributing to culture through their voting patterns, reading habits, and consumer choices.

The Americans engaged in the project of using these regions to displace discussion of U.S. slavery were not necessarily making calculated estimates or rational comparisons. They often based their conclusions on hearsay, assumption, and prejudice. Many of them should have known better, and perhaps they did. Their proclamations were sustained by repetition, but collapsed under the weight of serious investigation. Their purpose was first to vent their repressed anxieties, and ultimately to proclaim their safety because of the differences that separated them and the objects of their comparisons. They could not have failed to notice the ways in which their supposedly peculiar institution mirrored slavery in other places, but rather than proclaiming common cause, they often insisted on points of distinction. Their protestations of exceptionalism created a space in which they could freely say what was otherwise unspeakable.

The reasons Americans kept silent about U.S. slavery varied by context, geography, and historical moment. Politicians anxious to build national coalitions had different motives than merchants wary of offending customers or suppliers, and Northern tutors seeking jobs in Southern planters' families had still other concerns. But people with these varied agendas shared in common the release of geographical (and often temporal) displacement. In a multiplicity of cultural contexts, men and women from diverse backgrounds inserted critiques, vented objections, and acknowledged fears by proxy.

While countless histories have analyzed the noisy pronouncements of slavery's bombastic defenders and the searing cries of abolitionists, there exists a smaller body of literature about how the debate over slavery was silenced. Until the publication of papers by moderate abolitionists like Theodore Weld and James Birney in the 1930s, historians generally understood antislavery activists as a fanatical fringe movement.[16] Clement Eaton's 1939

Freedom of Thought in the Old South, among others, reframed the argument, proposing that the death of Jefferson in 1826 ushered in a repressive regime of censorship and thought control that stifled minority opinion below the Mason-Dixon Line.[17] Eaton made himself extremely unpopular with Southern historians in the process. "It did not seem to occur to Mr. Eaton that the abolitionists and their political allies were threatening the existence of the South as seriously as the Nazis threaten the existence of England," seethed Frank L. Owsley of Vanderbilt in a review in the *Journal of Southern History*.[18] When Eaton reissued his book as *The Freedom-of-Thought Struggle in the Old South* in 1964, he identified the anti-abolitionist crusade as the ideological antecedent of the white South's furious mid-twentieth-century pushback against the civil rights movement: "both the old and the new societies have suppressed freedom of speech and forced their moderate citizens to acquiescence or to silence."[19]

The very vocal protests and the acknowledgement of the therapeutic value of free discussion in the noisy 1960s made periods of enforced silence more difficult to imagine. Nonetheless, a number of works since 1970 have considered the way the subject of slavery was quashed in the antebellum era.[20] These studies demonstrate that free speech is not always restrained through riots and torchlight processions, nor is censorship always enabled by tyrannical fiat. In the nineteenth century as in the twenty-first, there were social and economic costs when uttering opinions against what was understood as the position of the majority. The consequences of running afoul of common wisdom included social shunning and neglect, and as a result self-censorship was often stunningly effective at shutting down minority opinion.[21]

In the antebellum period, outright violence was more characteristic of some years than others. During the period considered in this book, there were two moments when the tension between freedom of speech and the press and the hazards of discussing slavery did in fact erupt in hysteria. The first outburst, most severe from 1834 to 1838, included rioting by anti-abolitionists, the hindering of mail delivery, and the tabling of antislavery petitions submitted to Congress. The second period, awakened by the attack on Radical Republican Senator Charles Sumner in 1856, lasted until the Civil War. At these moments, even to pose questions about the peculiar institution was considered tantamount to undermining the safety of half the country.[22] So combustible did many Americans consider the South that outright criticism of slavery was deemed quite literally incendiary: "The torch of free speech and press, which gives light to the house of Liberty, is very apt to set on fire the house of Slavery," declared Republican reformer Carl Schurz in 1860.[23]

Why the spike in abolitionist agitation and proslavery suppression in the mid-1830s? Looking back from the vantage point of the late 1850s, northern antislavery journalist George Weston in *The Progress of Slavery* maintained that "1835 is the designated epoch of this outbreak of abolitionism," not because antislavery voices suddenly rose in shrillness, but because of Southern paranoia over despotic federal power. According to Weston, the tariff controversy made Southern legislators aware of how tenuous was their hold over national affairs, and imputations of Northern interference in the Southern political economy contracted to a narrow focus on slavery. And white Southerners clung to slavery because it was profitable, and becoming fabulously more so in the antebellum period.[24]

And yet, even if the abolitionism of the post-1831 period was a response to Southern proslavery hysteria rather than the cause of it, the face of abolitionism was assuredly changing. Abolitionists increasingly included blacks as well as whites, common people as well as elites, women as well as men.[25] Colonization—the project of sending emancipated slaves back to Africa— lost favor with many abolitionists, who now insisted free black people had every right to remain in the United States. Abolitionists were more outspoken—"I WILL BE HEARD" vowed editor William Lloyd Garrison in the first issue of the *Liberator*—and spoke out against a society they considered complacent and cowardly.[26] To amplify their message, they took advantage of new technologies like telegraphy and steam-powered presses that vastly increased the volume of their output and helped them broadcast their message more quickly: the American Anti-Slavery Society's production of 122,000 tracts in 1834 paled beside the million tracts, many of them lavishly illustrated, produced only a year later.[27]

Antislavery rhetoric from the North met a firm response from the South. Loose talk about possible slave insurrections could lead to violence—often perpetrated against the slaves themselves, executed on suspicion of malicious intent when nervous white people worked themselves into a froth of anxiety over rumors of wrath to come. Paranoia was particularly rife in areas where black people outnumbered whites or a put-upon class of nonslaveholders resented what it perceived as a local Slave Power oligarchy.[28] Indeed, as Frederick Douglass noted, by 1830, "Speaking and writing on the subject of slavery became dangerous."[29]

According to defenders of slavery, the prospect of abolitionist materials provoking insurrection justified censorship and the seizure of mail. Although naturally content, the slaves could be roused to revolt by the diabolical persuasion of canny traitors from the North who polluted the channels of the postal system with their libelous materials, including picture books and handkerchiefs printed with graphic depictions of abuse.[30] In Charleston, postmaster Alfred Huger, working with the cooperation of New York postmaster Samuel L. Gouverneur, established a *cordon sanitaire* that remained in force from 1835 to the Civil War to intercept the delivery of abolitionist materials sent through the mail.[31] In such a time of crisis, insisted former U.S. Representative William Drayton in 1836, "extra judicial" trials and punishments meted out according to the decisions of hastily assembled tribunals "composed of the best citizens" were perfectly defensible. He asked, "who dares say that such tribunals have, in a single instance, exercised the powers conferred upon them unjustly or improperly?"[32] Dismissing the implications of such interference with the free exchange of ideas in the American republic, Drayton declared that "it would be folly to hesitate in removing a great and imminent danger, in the apprehension of incurring a slight and remote one."[33]

Still more ominously, the U.S. House of Representatives passed a gag rule in 1836 in response to a perceived deluge of antislavery petitions directed to Congress.[34] Legislators in the Senate similarly protested the increase in petitions received. "They do not come as heretofore, singly, and far apart: from the quiet routine of the Society of Friends, or the obscure vanity of some philanthropic club," complained Senator William Preston of South Carolina, "but they are sent to us in vast numbers, from soured and agitated communities; poured in upon us from the overflowing of public sentiment, which, every where, in all western Europe and eastern America, has been lashed into excitement on this subject." Preston advised the Senate to be mindful of the precedents of Jamaica and St. Domingo and to follow the example of the House.[35] Keeping silent seemed to be the key to the safety and prosperity of the nation. In 1840 Representative William Cost, dissatisfied by the fact that the 1836 House rule had to be renewed at each session of Congress, pushed for the permanent rejection of antislavery petitions.[36]

Eclipsed by economic anxiety and the splintering of the antislavery cause into various reform efforts, these hyperbolic apprehensions subsided somewhat in the early 1840s (although mobbing, destruction of property, and personal attacks certainly did not disappear entirely).[37] The Wilmot Proviso, the acquisition of Texas, and the U.S. War with Mexico generated extensive debate in Congress about slavery in the mid-1840s. Then a second spike in calls for silence on the subject of slavery occurred between 1856 and 1860. In an 1856 speech called "The Crime Against Kansas," Massachusetts Senator Sumner likened South Carolina senator Andrew Butler to Don Quixote. Like that misguided would-be knight, Sumner said, Butler had dedicated his life to the honor of his mistress who, "though polluted in the sight of the world, is chaste in his sight:—I mean the harlot Slavery. For her his tongue is always profuse with words."[38] In retaliation, Butler's nephew, Representative Preston Brooks, beat Sumner unconscious with his gold-handled cane. Abolitionists characterized the assault as the suppression of free speech. However "profuse with words" Butler was in defense of slavery, the South would tolerate no utterance in its condemnation. The Slave Power demanded the concession of silence. An article in *The Independent* with the sarcastic title "Silence Must Be Nationalized" began, "Liberty of speech in a despotic government means a liberty of the despot to say what he pleases, and a liberty of everybody else to hold their tongues. This is the idea in the South now."[39]

John Brown's raid on Harpers Ferry in 1859 amplified the demand for silence. Proslavery members of the Thirty-Sixth Congress blamed Hinton Rowan Helper's 1857 *The Impending Crisis* for inciting Brown's activities and called for the book's suppression.[40] Heated exchanges in Washington in late 1859 and early 1860 confirmed that there were definite limits to freedom of speech in the South. Representative Owen Lovejoy, Republican from Illinois and brother of antislavery martyr Elijah Lovejoy who had lost his life in a raid on his press during the eruption of violence of the 1830s, demanded, "Has not an American citizen a right to speak to an American citizen? I want the right of uttering what I say here in Richmond. I claim the right to say what I say here in Charleston." Representative Elbert Martin of Virginia threatened that if Lovejoy made his remarks publicly in the South, "we would hang you higher than Haman."[41]

Attempts to regulate speech reached a climax in a resolution proposed by Stephen Douglas of Illinois in the Senate on January 16, 1860. Called "Invasion of States," the resolution called for the Committee on the Judiciary to prepare a bill for the "suppression and punishment of conspiracies or combinations."[42] Douglas indicated that he considered as "conspirators" those from the North who sent "agents" to "seduce" slaves to flee to Canada via the Underground Railroad.[43] Because of its potential for outlawing speech judged to be seditious, one scholar has called this proposal the culmination of "the slave interest's long battle to impose intellectual conformity on the Republic."[44] Although Douglas's resolution was tabled, it demonstrates both the way speech was regarded as an act of aggression and the hostility employed in quashing it.

At these dramatic junctures in the mid-1830s and late 1850s, provocative words about slavery were, with some justification, considered a matter of life and death. But throughout the thirty-five years before the Civil War, many people thought consciously about how to give the least offense while discussing slavery, and often decided that the best tack was not saying anything at all. In a letter to his cousin, Northern-born Zelotus Holmes, who had moved to South Carolina to study for the ministry, allowed that first-hand observation of slavery had altered his views, which had once been "perhaps somewhat ultra . . . [but] No logic can plead with the power of ocular demonstration." He admitted, "I have not written my northern friends freely upon this subject since in the South, knowing that no good could arise from it."[45] Opinions about slavery divided families, and the outspoken discovered there was no going back. "Thou knowest what I have passed thro' on the subject of slavery, thou knowest I am an exile from the home of my birth because of slavery," wrote Charleston-born Angelina Grimké to her sister Sarah after her antislavery views became public.[46]

Just as it is important to notice the temporal context of discourse about slavery, it is necessary to pay attention to the place where remarks were made and the audiences attending them. The hazards of discussing slavery differed greatly in the North and the South, and within the regions there were different accents and inflections. Nineteenth-century Americans thought of themselves in a global context and looked to Latin America, among other places, to understand themselves. They did not live in an autarky, but in a global economy where they needed to be conscious of available resources, changing markets, and foreign tastes and attitudes.[47] In particular, white Southern elites considered themselves cosmopolitans who understood their political and economic goals in relation to their slaveholding brethren in the Caribbean and Brazil. Whatever their expressions of superiority, they were tied to Latin America by both business and blood.[48] But this commonality of economic interests did not preclude expressions of distaste about conditions south of the border and an insistence that the ways of the United States were superior.

The Latin American context was invaluable for an American claiming to speak on behalf of the whole nation, particularly on a global stage before an international audience. In the 1850s, the South closed ranks around its defense of slavery, and white Southerners often presumed to represent the entire region. In such circumstances the temptation to disparage Latin America by highlighting the cruelty or lack of discipline in the slave systems of Cuba and Brazil proved almost irresistible.

There were "many Souths" and "many Norths" as well.[49] Talking about slavery exposed these fault lines. Since it was far easier to speak openly before a local audience than a regional or national one, politicians—especially those in national office—had to be particularly careful of what they said. As long as they were confident that they expressed the beliefs of the majority of their constituents, they could be boldly outspoken. But if they presumed to speak for a whole region rather than a particular locality, or if they aspired to national office, they needed to exercise more caution. Similarly, local newspapers dared say what national journals and books did not. Authors hoping to sell their publications to a broad audience resorted to more obfuscation than those writing for local consumption. Writers, editors, and publishers surveying a nation with many irreconcilable opinions about slavery consciously sought to commodify an "average racism" that was inoffensive (at least to white readers)[50]

Even in a small community, one could not always tell where an American stood on the subject of slavery. Geography could not be depended upon to determine opinion. By no means was every Northerner an abolitionist, nor was every Southerner a defender of slavery (the slaves themselves hardly rose to its defense).[51] Southerners doing business, making purchases, attending school, and escaping sultry summers thronged Northern cities and vacation spots.[52] Northerners sought business opportunities in the South. Journalist Jane Cazneau confidently predicted that all would be won over to the benefits of slavery, because American consciences "like that peculiarly useful article of which we make shoes and life preservers . . . stretch indefinitely when they come among cotton fields, and melt altogether in the ardent heat of sugar and rice plantations."[53] Northern transplant Tillson Harris, a mechanic who found work repairing cotton gins in Georgia, fulfilled Cazneau's prediction: he sounded like a true son of the South when he declared he was "gitting to hate the people of the North" and complained to his father in Maine that abolitionists "Dont look around them & see their own privations but must have something in somebodies business to shriek over."[54] Indeed, since many Northerners knowingly or unwittingly profited from the dominance of cotton in the U.S. economy, they wanted no interference with its production. Northern ships insured by Northern firms bore cotton to Northern factories capitalized by Northern banks.[55] Cotton had become the most important U.S. export by 1820, and accounted for half of all exports on the eve of the Civil War.[56]

Edward Neufville Tailer, a prolific New York diarist, expressed his ambivalence about slavery in seemingly contradictory reflections. He was not without sympathy for enslaved people: he avidly read *Uncle Tom's Cabin* and attended two stage versions of the novel, and on a trip to Baltimore he contributed to a purse for the manumission of a slave who worked in a hotel. But as a staunch Unionist, he saw abolitionism tearing at the national fabric by stirring up unnecessary dissent. He understood the 1859 raid on Harpers Ferry primarily in terms of the effect it would have on his own fortunes in the dry goods trade: "John Brown's foray in the South has created a bad feeling between North & South and it remains yet to be seen, whether the Southern merchants will buy goods from us at the North as liberally as formerly," he wrote. He was eager to see the whole affair hushed up and forgotten.[57] Talking about such an explosive issue could do no good.

The necessity of silence characterized much of the South. Publicly it was necessary for the proslavery faithful to insist that all slaveholders supported the institution; privately they knew that the commitment of the Upper South to slavery wavered. In written apologias they proclaimed the attachment of the enslaved laborer to the land where he or she was born; in private correspondence they arranged the sale of slaves whose presence was an inconvenience because of their insolence, their incorrigibility, or awkward suspicions about the identity of their fathers.[58] The dominant proslavery stance, insisting that the slaves were not merely patrolled but so content that they would not rebel, left little room for the articulation of doubts about white safety. Too much public airing of rebellion fears might lead Southerners, especially those who could not afford to own bond people, to question whether the benefits of slavery were worth the eternal anxiety.[59] Conversely, Southerners worried that too-frequent mention of slave revolts might somehow conjure these horrors into existence, presumably by awakening slaves to the possibility of their success. Southerners were not alone in their concern about the possibility of race war; European cotton manufacturers, who uneasily watched the growing dominance of U.S.-grown cotton during the antebellum period, worried about the potential interruption of supplies because of slave revolt or voluntary emancipation.[60] If it was impossible to stop the printing of inflammatory texts, it might be possible to prevent their being read: in the years after 1831 all slave states but Maryland, Kentucky, Tennessee, and Arkansas declared it a crime to teach slaves to read or write.[61]

Some settings and situations bred a particular aversion to frank discussion. The question of the morality of slavery tore at the unity of American churches, dividing Protestant denominations.[62] By 1857 the Baptists, Methodists, and New School Presbyterians had split into Northern and Southern branches.[63] In 1834 Weld and other students at the Lane Theological Seminary in Cincinnati debated slavery in public for nine days, concluding with a vote supporting immediate abolition. The seminary trustees summarily prohibited all public meetings on seminary grounds and ordered the dissolution of the school's Anti-Slavery Society, deploring the students' inciting of "civil commotion." Town/gown relations suffered as the citizens of Cincinnati feared the stirring up of trouble. "The scenes of France and Hayti recur to their imagination," shivered a trustee.[64]

Churches refrained from endorsing antislavery activities or declaring slavery a sin, fearful of driving congregants away and discouraging fundraising.[65] Anna Quincy Thaxter Cushing, a comfortably situated doctor's wife of Dorchester, Massachusetts, generally attended the First Church (Unitarian) twice on Sundays, hearing one sermon "in the forenoon" and another in the afternoon, the topics of which she dutifully noted in her diary. In August 1855 a sermon by a visiting divine stirred up trouble in the congregation. "Mr. Fred. Frothingham, of Montreal, . . . introduced the subject of slavery by way of illustrating the subject about which he was speaking, and spoke of it at some length," wrote Cushing that Sunday; "some twenty people saw fit to leave the church. A very undignified and illbred proceeding, to say no more." Congregants demanded whether the pastor had known what the visiting clergyman had planned to say: "some of his friends, most of them, probably, think that it will be better to let the whole affair pass over in silence," wrote Cushing—which is apparently exactly what happened.[66]

Sometimes silence on the subject of slavery signaled the despair Americans felt at the possibility of ever finding a remedy. Harriet Beecher Stowe, of all people (referring to herself in the third person), was later to recall, "It was a sort of general impression upon her mind, as upon that of many humane people in those days, that the subject was so dark and painful a one, so involved in difficulty and obscurity, so utterly beyond human hope or help, that it was of no use to read, or think, or distress oneself about it."[67] Stowe ultimately decided there was something she could do, and almost singlehandedly piloted the subject of U.S. slavery to the foreground of mainstream fiction in 1852 with the publication of *Uncle Tom's Cabin*. But before she put slavery front and center in her bestselling novel, most American literature aiming at a national audience kept slave characters on the periphery in the "plantation novel" tradition, where they bowed to their masters and joked merrily with each other.

Alternately, for people like Howe and Fitzhugh who had chosen sides in this most charged and vociferous of contexts, there were certain hidden doubts or buried suspicions that could be neither safely spoken nor entirely stilled. Among radical abolitionists, there was the guilty fear that blacks and whites were essentially different, that amalgamation was unnatural, and that emancipation might be a disaster. Among the proslavery faithful, there was the quiet knowledge that they shared more with their black slaves than they dared admit, and that enslavement of their fellow human beings was indeed inhumane, unjust, and sinful.

It should be pointed out that while Americans often kept dumb about slavery, they were quite vocal and unselfconscious in their expressions of racism. If they were reticent, it was not out of shame or discomfort so much as out of a reflexive sense that the superiority of whites and inferiority of blacks were so generally understood as not to need articulation. Two famous Americans—by any measure giants in the antislavery cause—demonstrate the way hatred of slavery coexisted with kneejerk racism in a way that is apt to make modern Americans wince.

After John Quincy Adams lost his bid for a second term in the presidential election of 1828 to Andrew Jackson, he began a new career in the U.S. House of Representatives. What might be seen as a significant demotion in status demonstrated a genuine commitment to public service. During his long career in the House, he butted frequently—and sometimes in amusing ways—against the strictures of the gag rule, finding ways to introduce antislavery petitions into the public record.[68] In 1841 he defended the rebels of the Spanish slave ship *Amistad* before the Supreme Court, and won his case.[69] But by twenty-first-century standards he is hardly a model of tolerance. In particular, he was revolted by the idea of sexual congress between the races, declaring that "the intermarrying of black and white blood is a violation of the law of nature."[70] In a dinner-table conversation with the

English actress Fanny Kemble about *Othello*, Adams, freely using what Kemble called "that opprobrious title" for a black person, diagnosed Shakespeare's play as flawed because audiences could never fully sympathize with Desdemona's love for her husband.[71]

Likewise, no American politician is more associated with the ending of slavery than Abraham Lincoln. The South's secession was occasioned by the expectation that he and his Republican Party would begin undermining slaveholders' rights to their human property.[72] His 1863 Emancipation Proclamation, if it was not in fact as immediately effective as is remembered in the popular imagination, certainly opened the door to universal freedom for slaves in the United States. But black voters were not among Lincoln's constituents, and the extension of equal opportunities to them was not one of his principal concerns. Lincoln enjoyed the music and comedy of blackface minstrels. He told "darky" jokes. He was not above using Adams's "opprobrious title" himself.[73] Inconsistency of opinion over a lifetime hardly makes someone a hypocrite. But these snapshots do suggest that racism and antislavery identities coexisted amicably in nineteenth-century white thought.

Although the battle lines between proslavery and antislavery were clearly drawn, there were no corresponding camps gathering racists and antiracists.[74] Expressions of intolerance generally went unchallenged. Claims of white superiority provided the underpinning of a system that rewarded a few plantation plutocrats at the expense of their exploited labor force, but those same claims also soothed poor whites who received no other benefits from slavery. One significant difference between racism and slavery is that while racism was a straightforward proclamation of supposed biological superiority, advocacy of or opposition to slavery erupted from a wide variety of impulses.[75] Many Northern and Western farmers opposed slavery because they perceived (correctly) that the Slave Power monopolized the best farmland. Factory operatives often opposed abolition because they believed free black labor undercut their wages. Slavery offended some people only when they had to see it, or its most troublesome aspects. A revealing letter from Northern educator and reformer Elizabeth Palmer Peabody encouraging a young friend to take a job as a governess in a slaveholding Baltimore family described the situation in a way that suggested the young woman's delicate sensibilities would not be compromised: "There never was a whipping while [the previous governess] was there. The severest punishment was shutting up in a closet in the entry and that happened but once or twice. [The slaves] are well clothed and fed and taken care of as children and in fact slavery is as much robbed of its evils as it <u>can be possibly</u>."[76]

Many Republicans abhorred slavery more for causing economic backwardness than because of its cruelty or injustice.[77] Poor whites moved from the South to the Northwest to escape economically devastating competition with slave labor. By any measure, they were antislavery. But they were also racist, bringing with them not only Southern prejudices but also fears that free blacks might compete with them in the socially fluid milieu of the fast-developing West. By the 1850s, the Democratic and Republican parties sometimes appeared to be in a contest to demonstrate which more stridently championed white privilege at the expense of black equality.[78]

Slavery's critics shared no common solution to the problem. Those who favored immediate abolition had little patience for those who favored gradual abolition, and still less with advocates of colonization.[79] While full-fledged abolitionists were not hated and vilified in the North to the same degree as in the South, they nevertheless inspired little admiration for most of the antebellum period. Although not always silenced, they were often ridiculed. Some Southerners regarded abolitionists as foolish but harmless. Maria Dubois of New Orleans, visiting her mother and sister in the canal town of Canastota, New York, spoke to participants at an abolition meeting in 1848: "one says it is true that when a slave gets to [sic] old or is otherwise disenabled that the Master kills him and sells his skin for shoe leather . . . it is very amusing to hear their ideas of slavery."[80] Their reputation was not a great deal higher in the North. "The Liberator is the most unpopular paper in New England," complained antislavery activist A. Sydney Southworth, who had charged himself with selling subscriptions. "The reason is obvious. The clergy are almost universally opposed to it, and of course the most of their people must follow them and do as they say, without inquiring whether they are right or wrong."[81]

The passion of abolitionists was generally received as unseemly enthusiasm, and they were associated with soiled collars, uncombed hair, and sexual irregularity. A matrimonial advertisement placed in the *Water-Cure Journal* in 1855 by a female devotee of hydrotherapy suggests how abolitionism was conflated with a number of unconventional interests: "[I] must be mated phrenologically and spiritually, or not at all. Should wish one who could do without tea, coffee, pork, beef, mutton, and feather-beds; a practical anti-slavery man, anti-tobacco, and I care not if anti-razor."[82] John

Humphrey Noyes, the founder of the utopian Oneida Community, probably did the abolitionist movement no favors when, in a pamphlet called
Slavery and Marriage. A Dialogue, he equated the liberating possibilities of
free love with antislavery. The dialogue concluded with a formerly equivo-
cating participant deciding that if slavery is a monstrous abuse, it shares
many characteristics with marriage: "I must either let Slavery alone, or go
for a revolution of society at the north as well as the south."[83]

Perhaps it is not surprising, then, that so many squelched impulses
should find expression elsewhere. Americans of the early republic spent a
great deal of energy trying to define the national character against foreign
models and gauging what other nations might say or think about them.
Through comparisons with other countries, the young United States
defined itself.[84] England, the mother country of the colonies that ultimately
became the United States, from which its inhabitants drew their language,
their conception of freedom, and the basis of their law, was the major
touchstone. France, England's age-old enemy, which had followed the
United States into the republican experiment, with less happy consequences
as it lapsed into violent revolution, dictatorship, empire, and finally a reestablished monarchy, provided a powerful but very different kind of comparison. Federalists admired England, while Republicans—notably Thomas
Jefferson—chose France as their *beau ideal*. The nation's early political parties slandered one another by applying the most reviled characteristics of
these respective countries to their opponents—thus Federalists reviled
Republicans as dangerous Jacobins and Republicans condemned Federalists
as would-be aristocrats.[85]

Just as they did with England and France, Americans tried to understand their identity and national character by considering themselves in
relation to Latin America, a region with which they had essential commercial and diplomatic ties, whose territory they traversed in order to reach the
Pacific, in which they fought a major war. During the thirty-five years
before the Civil War, between the jubilee celebrating the fiftieth anniversary
of U.S independence and the year the Union broke into pieces, people in
the United States cast the nations of Latin America in a variety of roles.
The countries to the south were promising disciples of republicanism following in the footsteps of the path-breaking United States; cautionary
examples of democracy subject to foreign domination; lurid cultures in the
thrall of Roman Catholicism; and fertile fields for mining, discovery, and
conquest. Latin America was at once a destination and a gateway through

which white America's unwanted black and Native American populations would pass on their way out of a nation purged of its racial cast-offs.

While Americans understood themselves in relation to other nations, foreign visitors—especially Europeans—were busy observing them, describing the new republic in travel accounts that were eagerly consumed on both sides of the Atlantic. These foreign visitors showed no reserve in analyzing the peculiar institution—increasingly peculiar as slavery was progressively shunned by the rest of the world.[86] Northerners suffered torments in the face of European excoriations. Southerners found themselves called upon to apologize for an institution branded backward and barbaric. Nationalists in the young republic were especially concerned with setting the United States apart from its European origins. They saw their country setting off on a grand and conspicuous experiment, but it was certainly not for slavery that they wanted to be exceptional. If, in the company of foreign visitors, Americans were reticent about human bondage, their motive is understandable enough: they instinctively recognized slavery not only as an issue that held the potential for tearing apart the new nation but also as a magnet for foreign censure: "foreigners heap [reproaches] upon our national character on account of the existence of this stain upon it," brooded the *North American Review* in 1835.[87]

European travelers to the United States not infrequently observed that the self-proclaimed free society maintained a tight-lipped reserve about topics that might provoke controversy or depict the nation in a less-than-flattering light. "I do not know any country where, in general, less independence of mind and genuine freedom of discussion reign than in America," proclaimed Alexis de Tocqueville in 1835.[88] Similarly, Charles Dickens's 1844 novel *Martin Chuzzlewit*, written after the author's American tour, includes among its pompous, self-absorbed American characters only one, Mr. Bevan, who is capable of honest analysis. "I believe no satirist could breathe this air," he says, in words that echo de Tocqueville. "If another Juvenal or Swift could rise up among us to-morrow, he would be hunted down."[89] Americans were capable of censuring those who deviated from the will of the majority, maligning members of rival political factions, and readily identifying the splinter in their neighbor's eye. But they refrained from speaking openly about the shortcomings of the nation as a whole.

Europeans ridiculed this willful ignorance: "one of the most remarkable traits in the national character of the Americans," wrote Frances Trollope, "[is] their exquisite sensitiveness and soreness respecting every thing said or written concerning them."[90] With laser-like sharpness, her 1832 *Domestic Manners of the Americans* lacerated U.S. pretension to justice and gentility; her scathing criticisms were all the more damning for being so barbed and witty. "At every table d'hôte, on board of every steam-boat, in every stage-coach, and in all societies, the first question was, 'Have you read Mrs. Trol-lope?'" reported a British traveler.[91] Sensitivity to the opinion of foreign visitors persisted throughout the antebellum period: Swedish novelist Fre-drika Bremer, who toured the United States twenty years later (and also turned her experiences into a much-discussed travel narrative) everywhere met anxious natives who pestered her with questions, trying to make sure her impressions were positive. On one occasion she was denied passage on a boat because the captain "did not wish to have any authors on board his ship who would laugh to scorn his accommodations, and would put him in a book. . . . And for this I have to thank Mrs. Trollope and Dickens," Bremer added drolly.[92]

Descriptions of Latin America written by U.S. travelers can be read as a response to these European snubs. As American patriots discovered in the 1830s through the 1850s, descriptions of their southern neighbors worked as a way to present issues of race and slavery before both foreign and domestic audiences without striking too close to home. By asserting the differences between the United States and the Latin American nations, U.S. nationalists hoped to ascribe the worst abuses of the slave system to others. If foreign critics commented on the brutality of labor in the cotton fields, they needed to compare it to the sugar plantations of Cuba. If European visitors remarked on the Quadroon population of New Orleans, writers in the United States hoped to distract them with the mixed-race chaos of Peru: "Instead of resulting in one common uniform race, [amalgamation] has multiplied races to such an extent as is hardly conceivable," sniffed the *Democratic Review* in 1853. "The state of these colonies, both before and since their independence, so different from that of the United States, may be in a great measure traced to the amalgamation of different races in one, and the purity of blood in the other."[93]

In some ways the limitations of knowing the region only secondhand, or allowing it to be mediated by familiar stereotypes, allowed Americans the freedom of uncritical and highly selective use of particular tropes.[94] They often emphasized what made the United States different (and better). Many Americans spoke confidently about conditions in Latin America with absolutely no direct acquaintance with the region. But even those who did encounter the region firsthand relied on common ways of seeing and interpreting what they saw. No matter how foreign and unfamiliar Latin America seemed on first glance, U.S. visitors fell back on a vocabulary that prescribed its own deterministic taxonomy. Mary Gardner Lowell left Boston for Cuba when her husband's business took him there in 1831–1832. "I came upon deck just after the custom house officers were there, and never shall I forget the astonishment & delight experienced at the scene which burst upon my view. Every thing [—] buildings, trees, boats, men, costumes, were unlike any I had ever seen; the whole had the effect of magic," she marveled. But upon reaching shore and settling in, she was soon describing the indolence of the women, the cockfights, and the mummery of the Catholic mass where "blacks and whites kneel together promiscuously"—all staples of the travel literature.[95]

To maximize its potential as a screen upon which portrayals of U.S. slavery could be projected, Latin America had to be characterized as incapable of living up to the U.S. model. Describing Latin America as a region of profligate racial mixing and political instability suggested a United States that was by contrast pure and well regulated. That this determined effort intensified in 1826 is perhaps not coincidental: only fifty years old, the country was nostalgic for a primal innocence and a racial integrity that had never existed. In the 1820s it could no longer be imagined that slavery was dying out in the United States; the abolition of the African slave trade did little to arrest the growth of the flourishing slave economy, and the profits from cotton cultivation promised no easy waning of enslaved labor in the future. If slavery could not be suppressed, it could perhaps be kept out of sight, banished from the nation's capital, moved ever farther west while displacing the Indians.[96]

The assertion of U.S. preeminence colored discussion of Latin America throughout the 1830s, 1840s, and 1850s. Latin America served as a negative example by which the comparative integrity and achievement of the United States was thrown into sharp relief. Latin American revolutions were smudged carbon copies of the U.S. war for independence; Latin American governments were unsteady and corrupt. From similar beginnings, the United States quickly vaulted ahead of Latin America economically. Preening comparisons with its southern neighbors defined a nation that, however fragmented by politics or sectional interest, was unified by its superiority.

But complicating this easy display of difference was the fact that even as its people scorned Latin American culture, the United States progressively laid claim to Latin American land. No modern reader can escape the conclusion that, when people in the United States discussed Latin America in this, the age of Manifest Destiny, expansionism was frequently the subtext. From the earliest days of the republic, people in the United States looked to the eventual acquisition of territory south of its borders. "Our confederacy must be viewed as the nest from which all America, North and South is to be peopled," Thomas Jefferson had written in 1786. "We should take care to not . . . press too soon on the Spaniards. Those countries cannot be in better hands. My fear is that they are too feeble to hold them till our population can be sufficiently advanced to gain it from them peice by peice [sic]. The navigation of the Mississippi we must have. This is all we are as yet ready to receive."[97] When the navigation of the Mississippi—as well as the control of the vast Louisiana territory—fell unexpectedly into Jefferson's grasp seventeen years later, the nation faced the task of absorbing not only land but people they immediately understood as foreign. Massachusetts Federalist Fisher Ames described them as a "*Gallo-Hispano-Indian omnium gatherum* of savages and adventurers" who could hardly be expected to "sustain and glorify our republic."[98] In Louisiana, Washington politicians worked out—often through a process of improvisation—a blueprint for the future addition of non-English territory and non-English people into the national polity. In this project they were aided on the ground by federal administrators and local white Louisianans who saw benefits in incorporation rather than separatism or resistance.[99]

Louisiana similarly established an early precedent of Pandora's box disguised as fabulous bargain. Rather than sating the desire for further acquisition, the purchase of this territory from France seemed to stimulate the nation's greed for additional real estate.[100] And out of every acre of newly acquired ground sprang up the same question about its disposition. "The United States' purchase of Louisiana and the expansion it engendered made slavery *the* issue of American politics—trumping partisanship, nationalism and nativism, and the tariff."[101]

Yet until territory was actually absorbed by the United States, Americans focused not on overcoming the differences they perceived, but expressing and reifying those differences. If anything, comparisons with Latin America in the antebellum republic served to unify and reassure rather than to fracture and provoke. Even as the displacement of domestic conflicts over slavery onto Latin American society provided a safe context in which these issues could be explored, the disparagement of Latin America proved to be something about which many disparate groups could agree. Writers from old families that had settled the original thirteen colonies and immigrants on the western edges of white settlement, black Northern abolitionists and anxious white Southerners, scholars hungering for fame and scribblers trying to earn the cost of their next meal, all found Latin America a convenient tablet upon which to inscribe their ideas about U.S. preeminence. The output of these Americans extended across a variety of disciplines, from sermons to scientific inquiry, from the well-rehearsed speeches of lawmakers to the dashed-off screeds of newspaper squibs, from the low doggerel of third-rate versifiers to the blank verse of five-act dramas. In the antebellum period, congressmen quoted poetry and scientists cited the Bible as evidence; novelists and historians tackled political subjects in their fiction that they knew intimately from their work in politics. The audiences that received this material were similarly diverse.[102]

This book describes the process by which Americans from many backgrounds and with varying agendas redefined their image of Latin America from an immature and somewhat hapless younger brother to an estranged and finally unrelated alien. Latin America's likeness to the United States could not be entirely denied—its colonial past, its struggles for independence, its efforts at republican reinvention. Some common elements, like the contiguousness of territory, were indeed emphasized; others, like its ancient past, were effectively invented. But the crushing weight of difference was more useful than what was shared, providing the necessary cover for Americans to speak about themselves.

Latin America provided a staging area for dramas that people of the United States preferred to rehearse out of town. Here they tried out in the 1820s the racial attitudes usually associated with Democratic politics of the 1830s. The Panama Congress debates of 1826, for example, included articulations of white arrogance and black unworthiness heard more loudly in the strident 1830s and 1840s. Within this context, the challenges of absorbing a free black population became possible to imagine. Similarly, acknowledging that Manifest Destiny pushed south as well as west, appropriating the property of a fellow sovereign republic as well as the territory occupied by Indian tribes, necessitates a reinterpretation of antebellum expansionism. From this perspective the Texas land grab anticipates the imperialist ambition the United States would demonstrate in the late nineteenth century.[103] Indeed, the chauvinistic confidence in the rightness of U.S. approaches expressed by the rejection of foreign models is much more characteristic of twentieth- and twenty-first-century America than the apologetic inferiority complex the United States assumed in its comparisons with Europe in the early national period.

Considering the ways Americans discussed their southern neighbors illuminates and complicates many frameworks for understanding the early republic with which historians would do well to engage. Although slavery is the primary concern here, this project necessarily has implications for other historical perspectives of the antebellum United States. Because slavery was so integral to the economy, diplomacy, and reform efforts of the first half of the nineteenth century, recognizing the role played by Latin America in the national imaginary raises new questions and suggests new approaches toward our understanding of the period. Thinking about how Americans displaced their anxieties and conjectures upon Latin America clarifies some of the paradoxes of the Jacksonian era, reveals neglected aspects of the politics of Manifest Destiny, and enriches the modern picture of antebellum nationalism and transnationalism.

In more than one way, this book is all about boundaries. It is most obviously about the physical lines on a map that separated Anglo America from Spanish America, as well as the political and social differences that made Mexico and Cuba and Peru and Brazil so exotic to travelers from the United States. It is also about the boundaries between races and national groups: how did U.S. nationalists insert the *hidalgo* of obviously mixed race, or the Brazilian soldier of color, into the limited dichotomies of white/ black, slave/free with which most people in the United States were comfortable? The period covered in this project is one in which the physical boundaries of the United States were constantly being negotiated, with much of the new territory—Texas, the Mexican cession, the Gadsden Purchase—the former property of Mexico. Just as the mapmakers of the 1820s, 1830s, and 1840s were busy drawing and redrawing borderlines, Americans of the early republic had to reconsider where their counterparts south of the border belonged in relation to them.

During this period, among the many roles Latin America played for its U.S. neighbors, the most useful was as a window through which could be viewed the vexed and volatile reality of slavery many Americans did not want to discuss openly. Through this window they gazed with condescension at their counterparts failing to live up to the United States standard even as they beheld something at once familiar and foreign, a simulacrum both exotic and uncomfortably recognizable.

Yet sometimes in the unstable reflection of the glass, Americans glimpsed themselves. "The people of the United States are like persons surrounded by mirrors. They may catch their likeness from every quarter, and in every possible light, attitude, and movement," declared *The North American Review* in 1838. "Turn we as we may, we catch our reflected features; the vista seems to lengthen at every sight."[104] Whether the reflection of the United States in the mirror of Latin America was flattering or unsettling, whether it was heeded or ignored, depended upon the circumstances. But in the thirty-five years before the Civil War it consistently served as a measure by which people in the United States judged themselves.

Chapter 1

Never So Drunk with New-Born Liberty

"Sir, I know there are gentlemen, not only from the Northern, but from the Southern States, who think that this unhappy question—for such it is—of negro slavery . . . should never be brought into public notice," John Randolph of Virginia admonished the Senate in 1826. But, he warned, slavery "is a thing which cannot be hid—it is not a dry rot that you can cover with the carpet, until the house tumbles about your ears—you might as well try to hide a volcano, in full operation."[1] Yet at the time Randolph chided his colleagues for ignoring the ominous rumblings of discord produced by slavery's foes and defenders, increasing numbers of Americans hoped that slavery was a subject that could be shut away and concealed.

Randolph was generally considered eccentric if not actually crazy (attended by slaves and accompanied by hunting dogs, he delivered rambling speeches well lubricated with alcohol, punctuated by snaps of his riding whip against his boot, and seasoned with Greek quotations and venomous outbursts), but he proclaimed what his colleagues hesitated to say.[2] The problem was that he proclaimed it in a national forum. His fellow Southerners in Congress sought particularly to prevent federal interference in what they called a local institution: Congress's ability to discuss slavery, they feared, was dangerously proximate to the power to regulate it.

Randolph spoke on the occasion of the debates over U.S. participation in the 1826 Panama Congress, a proposed gathering of the republics of North and South America. It was five years after the Missouri crisis, which exposed, to the horror of both participants and spectators, the breadth and depth of a national fissure over slavery that had been growing wider and deeper since then. There had been disputes in Congress about slavery before, notably around the 1787 Northwest Ordinance that prohibited human bondage in the future states of Ohio, Illinois, Indiana, Wisconsin,

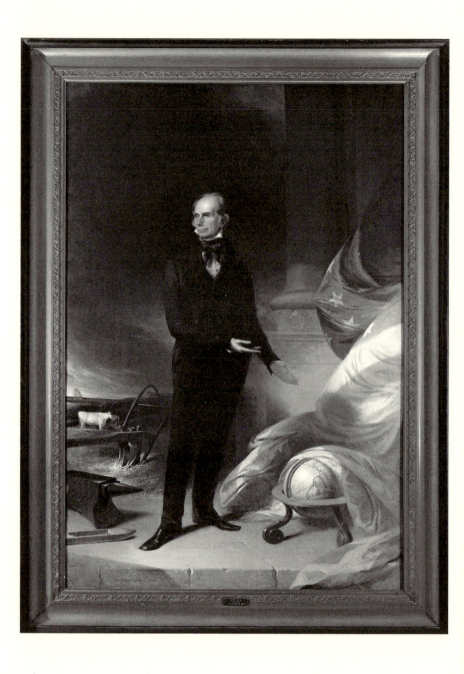

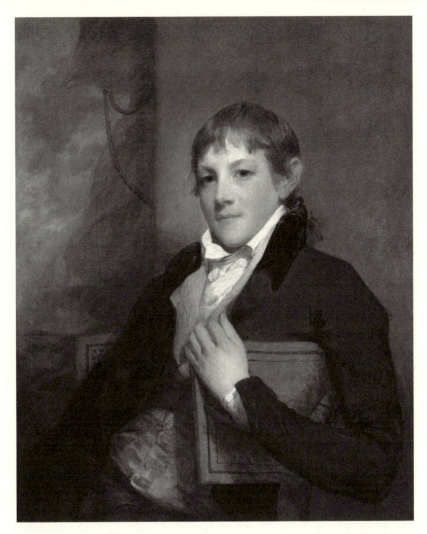

Figures 2 and 3. Henry Clay—in this portrait indicating a globe turned to show South America—advocated the American System of internal improvements and commercial relations between the United States and its southern neighbors. But when in 1826 the United States received an invitation to participate in Simón Bolívar's Panama Congress, Virginia's John Randolph pointed out that U.S. delegates might well be seated "beside the native African, or their American descendants, the mixed breeds, the Indians, and the half breeds." The disagreement between Clay and Randolph escalated into a duel, which ended without serious harm to either opponent, but in the following years Randolph's characterization of Latin America as marked by racial difference trumped Clay's understanding of shared republicanism. *Henry Clay*, 1843, John Neagle, American, 1796–1865. The Union League of Philadelphia, gift of Henry Pratt McKean, Courtesy of The Abraham Lincoln Foundation of The Union League of Philadelphia; *John Randolph*, 1804/1805, Gilbert Stuart, American, 1755–1828, Courtesy of the National Gallery of Art, Washington, D.C.

and Michigan, and around the 1808 abolition of the African slave trade. But nothing had reached the extremes of bitterness occasioned by the question of whether the federal government had the right to restrict slavery in Missouri—or indeed to regulate slavery at all.[3]

From the beginning of the republic, politicians both within and outside the United States had sensed the wisdom of sweeping the subject of slavery under the carpet. The insistence that words do not mean what they seem to mean, the recourse to coded language when discussing difficult topics, goes back to the founding documents of the United States. Thomas Jefferson's "all men are created equal" was a declaration subsequent generations took considerable pains to explain away. The Articles of Confederation and the Constitution usefully referred to "interstate commerce" and "property" and "other persons," circumlocutions whose meaning was transparent to those who could interpret them. Foreign visitors attuned to the subtleties of national politics knew to shun this controversial subject: Edmond-Charles Genêt, hoping to win U.S. support in France's wars with England and Spain in the 1790s, kept his opposition to slavery to himself on a fundraising tour of the U.S. South.[4]

In retrospect it is quite easy to understand why, early in the second quarter of the nineteenth century, a subject that had been successfully relegated to the shadows for so long suddenly seemed to pop out from every unlikely corner. In the years following the invention of the cotton gin and the purchase of Louisiana, slavery had become an economic lynchpin of the South and, indirectly, the North as well.[5] Meanwhile, the abolition of slavery in Northern states proceeded apace, and audible anti-slavery voices both at home and abroad grew louder. In the years after the Missouri Compromise, avoiding the contentious subject became increasingly difficult.

Then an unexpected opportunity for safely airing concerns about race and slavery appeared. In 1825 the United States received an invitation to Panama to participate in a congress of all the republics of America. Mexico, Peru, Chile, Buenos Aires, Colombia, Venezuela, and Bolivia had recently emerged from prolonged wars of independence with Spain. Simón Bolívar, aware that the infant nations were still vulnerable to Spanish attacks, and eager to solidify trading treaties with England, proposed an assembly to discuss a defensive alliance and to forge commercial relationships. Bolívar was disinclined to jeopardize the arrangements recently established with Britain, which was sending an observer to the conference, by having the

United States present. But Mexico and Colombia, who hoped for better trading relations with Washington, extended an invitation to the United States to attend the assembly when it would be held in the spring of 1826.[6]

Like many issues in the thirty-five years before the Civil War, the Panama Congress apparently bore only a tangential relation to slavery. Stated objections to U.S. participation in the congress touched on a variety of issues, from despotic overreaching by President John Quincy Adams to the dangers of implied foreign commitments. But as members of Congress held forth in an extended period of debate about the implications of participating in this gathering of all the American republics, they frequently emphasized everything about the populations of Latin America that made them seem unfit to participate in the republican project. In proclaiming these differences, congressional leaders discovered that they could talk about slavery in the most national forum imaginable without dire consequences.

That the Panama Congress debates would lead to American perceptions of Latin America as a second-rate region defined primarily by aspects of racial difference was not foreordained. The years before the announcement of the Panama Mission had been characterized by popular enthusiasm for the former Spanish colonies' struggles for independence and embrace of republican government as well as canny, acquisitive expectation about how a liberalization of trade policies might benefit producers and exporters in the United States.[7] Americans following the debates in their local newspapers did not always pick up on the racist cues their representatives were supplying, responding instead out of interests that were alternately idealistic or economically shrewd.

But much of the testimony marked a decided shift in the way Latin Americans were described and the limitations imposed by the characteristics they embodied. Rather than partners in the global republican project who happened to speak Spanish, practiced Roman Catholicism, and sometimes had African blood, Central and South Americans appeared in Congressional speeches as knaves and fools playing an absurd and possibly dangerous game of dress-up. After U.S. Senators and Congressmen finished their harangues in opposition to sending ministers to Panama—and even defenses of the idea—the eager, hopeful sense of republican fellowship yielded, if not to active disdain, certainly guarded hesitation.

The shift in national attitudes was neither immediate nor universal. As with many historical turning points, this one is easier to recognize in retrospect than it was at the time. It did not mark a shift as abrupt and complete as some historians assert.[8] But the widely publicized congressional characterizations of Latin America established a vocabulary of difference, and both domestic and international developments made it easy to fall back on this vocabulary. A new way of understanding the identity of the United States through its relations with its southern neighbors took hold of the national imagination. Members of Congress referred directly or obliquely to the complexion of the republicans in whose company the U.S. ministers would convene and the effect this association might have upon white slaveholders' ability to manage their bond people. This perception of racial difference, and the way slavery was understood, would prove pervasive in the way the United States would define itself against a Latin American foil in the coming decades.

The aspects of race and slavery that figured in the debates assumed an importance in the context of the time. It might not have been irreversible without the rise of the second-party system, the explosive importance of the slave economy in the United States, and the abolition of slavery in the West Indies. It corresponded, significantly, with a transition to a second-generation nationalism in the United States, from a colorblind one that invoked the universalizing possibilities of political ideology to one more narrowly connected to race. Most important, as slavery assumed a new role in the nation's social and economic identity, Latin America provided a context—and the Panama debates set the tone—for the way slavery would be discussed for the next thirty-five years.

Writing in 1854, at the end of a thirty-year career in the Senate, Thomas Hart Benton recalled the 1826 Panama Congress as an "abortion" "long since sunk into oblivion."[9] At the time, however, the debate over U.S. participation in this now-forgotten assembly dominated much of the business of the Nineteenth Congress. More than sixty legislators participated, at length, in a debate that had far-ranging implications for future foreign policy and relations between the United States and its southern neighbors.[10]

In the United States, the debates over the implications of sending ministers on the Panama Mission coincided with the anniversary of the Declaration of Independence, when citizens had occasion to reflect on the accomplishments of half a century.[11] The Fiftieth Jubilee was marked everywhere by patriotic speeches, poems, and a series of thirteen toasts (one for each of the original thirteen colonies). Mixed with the cheers of festivity was not a little nostalgic awareness that the revolutionary era was fast fading away. "That was not the Lafayette that I remember!" mused eighty-nine-year-old John Adams when the last surviving general of the Revolutionary War, now an elderly visitor, appeared in Quincy, Massachusetts, on his 1824–1825 tour of the United States.[12] The founding generation was in eclipse. "Columbia's sires have gone to rest," mourned the poet "Zero" in the *National Intelligencer* on the anniversary of the Declaration of Independence.[13] As if to underscore the passing of the old order, on the Fourth of July, 1826, Thomas Jefferson and John Adams died within hours of one another.

The termination of the independence struggles by the former colonies of Spain that occurred just in time for this U.S. anniversary added poignancy to a national atmosphere that was at once triumphant and tinged with melancholy. Spain's former colonies had followed the example of the United States in declaring themselves republics and producing written constitutions, in many cases copying whole passages verbatim. These were heady days: what stains of religious bigotry, superstition, and cultural backwardness could republican government and free trade not erase? Why should not the Spanish or Portuguese American, living in a modern, enlightened state, become the ally who would help defend the United States against European aggression? Why should Latin America not serve as the great supplier and market of its northern neighbor? The independence of the new nations held out the possibility that they would come to favor (in both senses of the word) the United States. Republicanism promised to replace the lockstep submission and deference of the former Spanish subjects and turn them into thoughtful, responsible citizens. Liberalism would open Central and South American ports to U.S. exports and offer in return minerals and agricultural products to which the United States did not have access within its own borders. That these new nations imitated their northern neighbor demonstrated that U.S. ideals were imitable and exportable. While still a raw and callow nation in many respects, in its relation as an elder sibling to the growing family of republics, the United States assumed a kind of venerability: "we sowed the seed, and others are also reaping the fruits of it. On this continent we have witnessed the establishment of five new Republics, animated by our example and enlightened by our precepts," exulted the *Richmond Enquirer* in a July 4 editorial in 1826.[14]

Simultaneously, the emergence of these new Spanish-speaking Catholic republics also necessitated national stock-taking in the United States. The freedom-fighters of Central and South America called themselves Patriots,

and they championed liberty, established republics, and now assembled a
congress. But what, asked the senators and representatives of the Nineteenth Congress, did those words mean in an area geographically contiguous with the United States and yet foreign? In the course of the debates
over the Panama Congress, both in and out of the Congress of the United
States, the essence of many words came up for consideration: liberalism,
liberty, republic, equality, nation. Now that they were being applied in new
ways, their universal application could no longer be assumed. Was a black
republic a republic? Were the oppressed subjects of a Spanish despot ready
for the same prerogatives as a people with a heritage of English freedom?
Could equality really stretch to accommodate everyone? The year 1826 was
hardly the first time Americans asked these questions, but there was a new
resonance, if not a new urgency to them. These words, and the ideas behind
them, were claimed by people who were neither white nor Protestant nor
of English descent.

Before the Panama brouhaha, American attitudes toward the independence of Latin America as expressed in newspaper coverage and in political
discourse were generally positive. If the number of U.S. cities and counties
named for Bolívar and other Latin American heroes and places, or the
number of toasts to Spanish American independence, are a measure of
popular support, Americans certainly cheered the wars of independence
against Spain and the establishment of republican governments in the
period 1810 to 1822.[15] Even when newspaper accounts made clear the race
of the republicans in the pre-Panama Congress period, they were more
inclined to praise their bid for liberty than shudder at the color of their
skin.[16] Southern newspapers were no less likely to run positive accounts of
these revolutionary struggles than Northern ones, even though Bolívar was
using Haiti as a staging ground for his attack on the royalist forces in Venezuela and accepted military and financial assistance from the island's
mulatto president.[17] To be sure, there were qualifications to this rule: news
accounts were quicker to blame the race of the insurgents when they suffered defeat than to mention it in celebrations of their victories. The nearer
their struggles to the United States, the more the racial identity of the rebels
became a problem, so, for example, journalists noted the race of the revolutionaries in Spanish Florida in 1817 and 1818.

Geography similarly illuminates the complex reactions to Haitian independence a generation earlier. Northern Federalist Rufus King saw the revolution in Saint Domingue as the first step to "accomplishment in South

America to what has been so well done in the North."[18] Even Southern Federalists respected the revolutionary goals of the island's oppressed and saw an independent Haiti as a useful threat to despised France.[19] Americans toasted Haitian independence in 1804 and continued their trade with the citizens of the new black republic—including trade in arms.[20] On the other hand, in 1793 many Southerners were convulsed with fear of rebellion inspired by the Haitian precedent, particularly if French refugees brought their slaves, infected with dangerous ideas of liberty, to U.S. shores.[21] Free Africans in Saint Domingue were not threatening in the way free African Americans in South Carolina or Virginia were.[22]

There was a limit to the nation's support for Haiti, the second republic of the Western hemisphere, which existed beyond the pale of official American diplomatic recognition.[23] The transition from John Adams's Federalist administration to the Democratic-Republican presidency of Thomas Jefferson in 1801 signaled a chilling of U.S.-Dominguan relations, not exactly warmed by the violence perpetrated against the island's whites in the early nineteenth century. Although the former French colony seized its independence in 1804, the so-called "black republic" did not win recognition from the United States until 1862. On the other hand, the United States recognized Chile, Argentina, Peru, Colombia, and Mexico in 1822, with additional nations joining their company in the next few years.[24] What made Haiti unique and prevented its official recognition was effectively summed up by Missouri Senator Benton in 1826: "the peace of eleven states in this Union will not permit the fruits of a successful Negro insurrection to be exhibited among them."[25] Slaveholders came to fear the influence the Haitian template might have among their enslaved population. In Louisiana in 1811, Haitian native Charles Deslondes organized a short-lived reign of terror.[26] Haiti actively inspired the slave revolts led by Denmark Vesey in 1822, and quite possibly Gabriel in 1800. Although Nat Turner was not directly motivated by Haiti, the Turner Rebellion was quickly linked with the island in the popular white imagination.[27] As Benton pointed out, other Latin American nations had "already put the black man upon an equality with the white, not only in their constitutions but in real life," but this equality had not been achieved through a terrifying race war, as had happened in Haiti.[28] This difference was important enough to determine political recognition, but cultural acknowledgement would be another matter.

If until this moment Americans tacitly accepted what Scottish Enlightenment philosopher Adam Ferguson in 1767 called "civil society" and what is today called civic nationalism, the national venting of racial and religious prejudices against neighboring republics forced a reconsideration of what being American meant.[29] In 1826, the invitation to the Panama Congress that implied a shared political identity among the United States and the republics of Latin America led to the expression of all the ways the United States differed from its neighbors. The claiming of commonality from abroad provoked cries of distinctiveness—indeed, exceptionalism—at home. The Panama Congress served as a kind of test to see whether Spanish America, which had achieved its independence without a Jacobin blood-bath, which imitated U.S. precedents in such a number of flattering ways, came close enough to the U.S. paradigm to join its company. The answer was, apparently not close enough.

Possibly the popular enthusiasm for Latin American achievement never had run deep; it was based on minimal information if not outright misinformation concerning conditions in the new republics, particularly the fact that many of the citizens Americans claimed to admire were not entirely white. As they toasted "The Patriots of South America," nationalistic Americans celebrated themselves, rejoicing in independence and self-government, ideas by which they identified their own nation.[30] Commercial prospects also drove much of the enthusiasm for the independence of Latin America from Spain in the 1820s.[31] "The commerce of Spanish America is very interesting to all nations, on account of two essential considerations," noted Manuel Torres in a pamphlet published in Philadelphia in 1816. "First, Because that country consumes yearly, the value of one hundred millions of dollars in articles of foreign manufacturing industry. Secondly, Because it is there, and only there, that all nations can obtain, with facility, those precious metals, which have become so necessary to trade throughout the world, and particularly with Asia."[32]

Independent nations not under the thumb of Spain promised the possibility of liberalized trade (although many U.S. exporters resentfully expected that Britain would corner uniquely favorable privileges). As if by magic, trade in free Latin American ports would stimulate the manufactures so necessary to what Henry Clay called the American System. Hoping to promote national unity in a country of clearly defined sectional differences, Clay insisted in 1820, "It is in our power to create a system of which we shall be the centre, and in which all South America will act with us. In respect to commerce, we shall be most benefitted: this country would become the place of deposit of the commerce of the world."[33] Clay predicted this American System, by encouraging better transportation and more robust domestic commerce, would foster mutual economic dependence among regions with different social and economic interests.[34]

The Panama Congress debates followed in the wake of the divisive four-way presidential race of 1824—in which there had been no clear winner—which had been resolved when Clay threw his support behind John Quincy Adams, spoiling the chances of Andrew Jackson, the popular favorite. Adams subsequently appointed Clay secretary of state, an arrangement Adams's pro-Jackson adversaries branded a "corrupt bargain." (John Randolph, already quoted at the beginning of this chapter, characterized the relationship between the president and his secretary of state as "an alliance, offensive and defensive, . . . got up between Old Massachusetts and Kentucky, between the frost of January, and young, blithe, buxom May—the eldest daughter of Virginia—young Kentucky—not so young, however, as not to make a prudent match, and sell her charms for their full value."[35]) But the new president scarcely acknowledged his lack of a mandate. His first message to the Nineteenth Congress in December 1825 presented a startling presumption of presidential power. He proposed that the national government take the lead in constructing canals and turnpikes, fund a national university, and build astronomical observatories (the latter immediately pilloried with his own locution, "lighthouses of the skies"). Europe was harnessing the power of government to effect similar ends, and the United States ought not to fall behind. Adams's mention that the United States had been invited to participate in a Pan-American conference, and his request for congressional approval of the designated plenipotentiaries and funding for their trip, should have been the least contested of Adams's proposals. Richard C. Anderson of Kentucky, who would be tapped to be a minister plenipotentiary, predicted in July 1825 that "probably some more specific statement of the questions to be discussed there is required, before a decisive step is taken."[36] Anderson seriously underestimated the obstacles that lay ahead. In fact, Adams's proposal for participation in the Panama Mission blew up among accusations of secrecy and continued for much of the Congress's first session, to expose serious reservations about the universal applicability and potential exportability of American ideals.

Adams had an agenda for participating in the Panama Congress that he acknowledged in his diary: cementing good relations with the nation's southern neighbors might help facilitate the eventual purchase of Texas and smooth the way for an interoceanic canal through the Isthmus of Panama.[37]

In his public defense of attendance at the Panama Congress, however, Adams focused on three other themes: the duty to extend a neighborly hand to the new republics, the wisdom of providing a good example and steering the infant nations from self-inflicted hazards and external dangers, and the practical benefits of neutrality and commerce to be gleaned from participation in the meeting.[38] When they were not actively engaged in deflecting the attacks of Adams's critics, his supporters in the Senate and the House of Representatives amplified each of these points.

First, the argument seemingly most colored by goodwill and least tainted by self-interest was that the United States ought to acknowledge the great accomplishment of the Spanish republics in winning their independence and recognize them with what Representative Charles Miner of Pennsylvania called "parental regard."[39] The invitation to the congress had been tendered in a spirit of friendliness and sincerity, with no hidden conditions the president's supporters could discover; to refuse the outstretched hand of amity was to risk offense.[40] Francis Johnson, Representative from Kentucky, pointed out that there was no shame in being called a friend of liberty.[41]

Second, many of the politicians who spoke in Adams's defense alluded to the ways the United States might help Latin America avoid pitfalls in establishing republican governments. "Let us be first to meet them, and, if in our power, afford them useful advice as to the improvement of their condition, and in perpetuating their independence and liberty," urged Representative John Reed of Massachusetts.[42] It was in the best interests of the United States, so long as it could avoid active involvement in foreign military affairs, to help position the new republics on a footing secure enough for them to be free of threat of reconquest by Spain or the Holy Alliance of Catholic countries in Europe. Furthermore, as the president himself had suggested, a gentle nudge from the United States might encourage the new nations to turn away from a policy of established religion, specifically Roman Catholicism.[43]

Third, the potential profits of trade played no small part in the calculations of those who advocated sending representatives to Panama. "These South American States contain twenty millions of freemen: they will require the supply of manufactured goods to the amount of one hundred millions of dollars," predicted Representative Silas Wood of New York.[44] If American industry needed a goad to expansion, here it was. The vast market would stimulate American manufacture better than any tariff. Senator Asher

Robbins of Rhode Island estimated the population of South America still higher, at thirty million, and pointed out that nations of freemen were energetic and prosperous—a natural market for the products of the United States.[45]

Even among the administration's supporters there was a limit to assertions of fellowship with Latin America. In their defense of attendance at the assembly, they refrained from suggesting that ministers from the United States would sit down with their equals. Despite their calls for friendliness and courtesy, in the remarks of the mission's advocates a damning-with-faint-praise undertone hinted that the emerging Latin American nations were unformed if not slightly foolish. Representative Daniel Webster of Massachusetts spoke firmly in favor of attendance in the congress of "sister Republics," among the "great American family of nations," but at the same time he made clear their lowly status: they were "pupils" in a school from which the United States had presumably graduated with honors.[46] Rejecting the opposition's refrain that the United States might somehow be contaminated by association with its neighbors south of the border, the Adams men suggested that their superiority would prevent their being flecked with pitch even if they touched it. The upstart republics existed not simply at an earlier stage of political development. They belonged to a wholly distinct order. The problems that might plague them and the diseases to which they might succumb represented no danger to the United States, a member of another species entirely and therefore not susceptible to infection.

Far more colorful than the defenders of the Panama Mission were speakers from the opposition. The objections to the Panama assembly were striking in their variety. Among the charges were these: Adams's actions bore the hallmarks of the tyrant. There were no precedents for attendance at this congress. By appearing at Panama, the United States would find itself committed to undesirable, expensive, or dangerous policies. The United States would be drawn into war with Spain. The Panama Congress would encourage instability in the strategically significant—and nearby—Caribbean. And perhaps most damningly: the abolition of slavery in Latin America would exert a demoralizing effect on white Southerners and a dangerous influence on U.S. slaves.

Actually the opposition was more organized than it appeared. The forging of a unified coalition out of these assorted objections was the work of New York senator and future president Martin Van Buren, who took it up as a convenient Adam's rib around which to fashion a new political coalition made up of the enemies of John Quincy Adams.[47] Besides the outrageous John Randolph of Virginia, Van Buren's allies included Thomas Hart Benton of Missouri, Robert Hayne of South Carolina, John Holmes of Maine, John Berrien of Georgia, and Adams's own vice president, John C. Calhoun of South Carolina, a geographically assorted group, each member of which addressed a critical aspect of an opposition position that Van Buren skillfully stitched together. In Van Buren's efforts to unify Adams's enemies, it is possible to see him erecting the foundation of the nation's second party system, to achieve through political organization what Clay attempted through his integrated economic program. One of many people who understood and feared the growing sectionalism exposed by the Missouri crisis, Van Buren believed party politics might distract the citizenry from sectional fragmentation over the issue of slavery.[48] Later in 1826 Van Buren would begin his party-building project in earnest, but he laid the groundwork here. The irony of his attempt to escape sectional animosity was that among the assorted agendas he hoped to reconcile, whether aversion to potential military commitments or entangling alliances or John Quincy Adams himself, many masked support for slavery and resistance to interfering with its profitability. As with many issues of the antebellum era, slavery was frequently the unspoken subtext and could not so easily be escaped.

Despite the fact that the agendas of Adams's enemies were so varied— "It is not identity of *principle*; it is merely identity of *feeling* that forms the bond of their association," scoffed former New Hampshire representative Salma Hale in an 1826 pamphlet—what most of them shared was an abhorrence to associating with people so clearly different from themselves.[49] The United States ought not submit to anything that looked like an alliance with Latin America because such a union would be an unnatural one, a kind of political miscegenation. Although there were too many parallels with the North American situation for the most skeptical critic to overlook them entirely, the proclamation of republicanism was not enough to make the entire hemisphere one.

Not all these differences were specious. Whereas in North America the Continental Congress had coordinated the actions of the thirteen British colonies long before their independence, the Latin American states were coming together for the first time. The original thirteen British colonies emerged as one nation (admittedly one loosely bound together at the beginning), while the former Spanish colonies took another route, with the erstwhile viceroyalties declaring independence on different schedules and as wholly separate nations. Although many of the new states enthusiastically copied the U.S. Constitution, they departed from it in telling ways. They built in provisions for what one historian calls "regimes of exception,"[50] making constitutional provisions for the suspension of civil rights during periods of political unrest and allowing for domestic control by the military. And they elected not to follow the U.S. practice of disestablishing religion, retaining Roman Catholicism as not merely the sole state-supported church but the only faith tolerated by the government.

On the other hand, they took a more enlightened approach to slavery, in some cases providing for its eventual elimination and in others abolishing it totally. In many cases these nations took much more literally, and embraced much more inclusively, the language of liberty and equality employed by the Founding Fathers of the United States. And if Haiti offered any preview, subsequent interpretations might be even more generous. In a series of decisions culminating in its constitution of 1816, the Republic of Haiti radically broadened the idea of freedom and redefined the concept of property familiar in the United States. Property included the right of the individual to control the disposition of his or her work, effectively forestalling understandings of "property" that allowed the ownership of human beings. Further, President Alexandre Pétion's interpretation of the constitution in an 1817 case in which fugitive slaves from Jamaica were given freedom characterized slavery as a form of oppression for which asylum should be granted. While the notoriety of these decisions was limited and their influence circumscribed, they suggest the challenge Latin American manifestations of republicanism could pose to the existing order of the U.S. South.[51] By elevating people of mixed race, people of full African descent, and Catholic clerics to positions of political authority, the Latin American nations were already implicitly challenging the United States to realize its self-proclaimed ideals.

Religion and national origin provided immediate markers of foreignness for both sides of the debate in the U.S. Senator Thomas Hart Benton of Missouri attempted to startle his auditors into understanding just how different a nation with an established church looked: "Who is the negotiator contending with our Minister in Mexico for this doctrine of exclusive privileges? Is it not *Don Ramos Arispe*? And who is Don Ramos? A Catholic Bishop; (and I do not mention this in derogation of his character . . .)."[52] The gulf between Catholicism and Protestantism, between established religion and the separation of Church and State, was an easy one to understand. Seemingly just as vast a divide, though somewhat harder to describe succinctly, characterized the European ancestry of North Americans and South Americans. James Hamilton of South Carolina, citing common language, philosophy, religion, and letters, claimed that people in the United States felt more "real sympathy . . . for the People of Old England, than any States of Spanish origin, whether miscalled or rightly named Republics. . . . Rest assured, moreover, if free principles are ever in danger—if a combination of despots should endeavor to put out the light of liberty—we shall be found fighting by the side of England against the powers of blood and darkness, whatever may be the alliances the Spanish Republics may form."[53] Republicanism was not so transformative a rebirth that it could wash away one's European origins, however distant: there was a fundamental, even an essential, difference between Americans of English stock and Americans of Spanish descent. And simply speaking the right words—republic, congress, independence—did not suffice: it mattered whether those words were uttered in English or in Spanish.

But opponents of the Panama Mission, going beyond a comparison of the European ancestors of the North and South Americans, went much further when they vilified their southern neighbors for the fact that too much non-European blood ran in their veins. The racism expressed by Adams's enemies in 1826 anticipates the assumption of white supremacy that would underlie Jacksonian democracy a few years later. Senator John Holmes of Maine coyly suggested that "When our fresh and fair Ministers shall enter the hall of that Congress, and look round on their associates, I apprehend that they will deem it invidious and indelicate to talk about *color*."[54] As usual, John Randolph was the most direct: should U.S. delegates go to Panama, they might well be seated "beside the native African, or their American descendants, the mixed breeds, the Indians, and the half breeds." Indeed the racial purity of all Latin America was suspect: Randolph pointed out that plenty of African blood ran in the veins of the peninsular Spanish; and Guatemala, adjacent to the province in which the congress would be held, he believed, "was considered as much a black Republic at this time as Hayti itself."[55]

Some of the congressmen were more discreet in admitting that the true barrier to hemispheric solidarity was a racial one. A certain amount of reading between the lines is required, but the lines are sufficiently far apart to permit an unobstructed view. Opposition Senator John Berrien of Georgia employed a policy of indirection in talking about race and slavery, though his tack was more to assume the whispered complicity of racial supremacy than to threaten and terrify. Berrien suggested that there were certain loyalties that sent all political ones into eclipse: "I have been educated in sentiments of habitual reverence for the Constitution . . . The feeling is no where more universal, or more strong, than among the People of the South. But they have a stronger feeling. Need I name it? Is there any one who hears, and does not understand me?"[56]

Once this insistence on racial differences between the United States and Latin America was established, it was possible for senators and representatives to mention slavery without violating the informal ban on its discussion in the federal arena. Ever since the debates over the Missouri Compromise had exposed the fateful fault line between Northern and Southern interests, a tacit understanding had made raising the issue of slavery in the federal Congress an unofficial taboo. While no formal embargo existed, the memory of the acrimony of 1819 and 1820 was still fresh enough to make legislators think twice before raising the subject of slavery: "deeply shocked by the volcanic anger and potential for sectional division revealed by the Missouri debate, Congress would rarely discuss slavery without recourse to euphemism and circumlocution," wrote Robert Pierce Forbes.[57] With memories of the rancor still fresh, Southerners in particular insisted that the very mention of slavery had no place in Congress; it was an issue for state legislation only.

While there would be no formal gag rule in Congress until 1836, the ritual of tabling resolutions and petitions dealing with slavery was common in the early 1820s. The professed refusal to talk about slavery reached absurd extremes. In the Senate in 1825 Rufus King of New York introduced a resolution to establish a fund for the emancipation and colonization of slaves. The resolution was tabled, removing it from debate, much to the consternation of Robert Hayne of South Carolina, who submitted a counter-resolution "intended as a *solemn protest*" against the very suggestion of federal interference in slavery. Hayne's counter-resolution was similarly tabled.[58]

But in the context of Latin America, legislators could express themselves with uncharacteristic bluntness. Though they often approached the dangerous subject of slavery in a roundabout way, they discovered they could shed much of their customary caution. Representative John Floyd of Virginia stated his objection to the Panama Mission thus: "Shall we not be told by this Congress that *every* man, on this Continent, is entitled to liberty?"[59] That representatives of the South American states might point out the contradiction of slavery in the United States was problematic enough; but one of the stated objectives of the congress was to discuss the fate of Cuba and Puerto Rico, still under Spanish rule and still flourishing slave societies, enriching their mother country with slave-generated wealth and supplying a staging area for counterrevolutionary activities. Looking at the future of Cuba, Senator James Hamilton of South Carolina predicted revolution followed quickly by servile revolt, threatening both the Southern states specifically and U.S. access to the Gulf of Mexico more generally.[60] Hamilton, who had served as mayor of Charleston when the city's Vesey conspiracy was exposed in 1822, had particular reasons for suspecting connections between free discussion of abolition and rebellion.[61]

Representative William Brent of Louisiana used the same Southern fear of abolition in Cuba and Puerto Rico in support of the Panama Mission, arguing that U.S. involvement might prevent the colonies' precipitous liberation from Spain. He likewise spoke about race through indirection, pointing out that while of course his sympathies lay with any people still in the thrall of a monarch, Spain's islands presented a special case, one a Southern man must "*feel*," though "I need not refer to the population of Cuba, to justify my fears."[62] Brent proceeded to sketch for Congress various scenarios that would follow in the wake of the liberation of islands with black majorities, scenes of "ruin, horror, and desolation, too painful to be portrayed" all indicated through suggestion, intimation, and artful rhetoric. Like the narrator of a ghost story who achieves his effects through dramatic pause and innuendo, letting the imagination of the hearer supply the details, Brent allowed his listeners to make associations with Haiti and the resulting threat for neighboring Louisiana: "the very thought of the consequences flowing from such a state of things, excites feelings too heart-rending to be dwelt upon for one moment. I must turn from them."[63]

Race clearly trumped professed republicanism even more explicitly in some of the testimony. Without a shadow of hesitation, Georgia's John Berrien defended colonial status for colonies with a black majority. Should the United States participate in the congress, it would be expected to assist in freeing Cuba and Puerto Rico from Spanish control, spawning two new states with black majorities and insufficient white supervision. In such a case Berrien could imagine no other possibility than that "*these Islands [would] pass into the hands of bucaniers, drunk with their new born liberty*" who would reenact "the horrors of St. Domingo." There was but one course: "Cuba and Puerto Rico *must remain as they are*."[64] The safety of the

South—by which he presumably meant the white South—depended upon prevailing over those so literal-minded as to insist that "he who would tolerate slavery is unworthy to be free."[65] But in championing colonialism over republicanism, Berrien only seconded John Quincy Adams. Owing to the "peculiar composition of their population. . . . It is unnecessary to enlarge upon this topic, or to say more than that all our efforts in reference to this interest, will be to preserve the existing state of things," Adams had admitted.[66] However much the defense of European colonization in the Western Hemisphere and the limitation of liberty would seem to be inconsistent with U.S. ideals, the complexion of Latin America demanded a new and more limited understanding of liberty than that proclaimed in Boston in 1776—or even Buenos Aires in 1826.

One way around this conundrum—in which liberty was not available to everyone—was to define liberty in a particular way. The fulfillment of the promise of freedom—from the standpoint of the abolition of slavery—would seem to be one area where the South American students had vaunted ahead of their so-called teachers. But this mark of superiority depended entirely on what liberty signified. "The fundamental principle of all liberty, Mr [Samuel] H[ouston of Tennessee] said, in his opinion, was equal rights, equal privileges, laws that give protection to individuals, to their lives, persons, and property: where the People are represented, and where every man has liberty of conscience guarantied."[67] "Liberty of property" presumably included slave property, a right denied in nations with universal emancipation; "liberty of conscience" was code for the absence of established religion. The Spanish American republics failed to make these vital distinctions.

Liberty to African slaves, insisted some congressmen, threatened the entire social order. Representing the grain-growing state of Pennsylvania, James Buchanan made a remarkable attempt to characterize the United States in a way that would transcend both party division and section. "The cause of liberty in South America is the cause of the whole American People, not of any party," he declared.[68] The investment of the United States in the republicanism of its Southern neighbors was something upon which the whole country had to agree. On the other hand, added Buchanan, the entire country could find benefits in the continuation of Cuba's colonial status. Cuba accounted for both one-seventh of the imports and nearly as much of the exports of the United States—a greater proportion than the new southern republics. Particularly if it assisted in Cuba's struggle for independence, Mexico would represent a potential rival for this trade, and its liberation of the island would hurt the West.[69] For the South, the threat of Cuban liberation was even more obvious, involving "a subject to which I have never before adverted upon this floor, and to which, I trust, I may never again have occasion to avert. I mean the subject of slavery." Though slavery was an evil, Buchanan insisted, its elimination would involve dangers to the prosperity and even safety of the "high-minded, and the chivalrous race of men in the South" that could not be permitted. "For my own part I would, without hesitation, buckle on my knapsack, and march in company with my friend from Massachusetts (Mr. Everett) in defense of their cause."[70]

Where the subject of slavery in Latin America was concerned, Southerners, who were usually the most strident in insisting the federal Congress had no business discussing the matter, were often more eager to speak than Northerners. Sometimes they spoke out even as they insisted on silence. "Let us then cease to talk of slavery in this House; let us cease to negotiate upon any subject connected with it," directed Senator Hugh Lawson White of Tennessee, before immediately taking up the thread again: "One word more upon this point, Mr. President, and I will dismiss it. If there be any gentlemen in the United States who seriously wish to see an end of slavery, let them cease talking and writing, to induce the Federal Government to take up the subject, because by the course now being pursued, by some, they are protracting a measure which they profess a wish to hasten the accomplishment of."[71] So great was the relief he evidently felt in being allowed to violate this taboo, however, White proceeded to discuss Haiti and the possibility that the abolition of the slave trade would be brought up in Panama.[72] Similarly, Senator Robert Hayne of South Carolina insisted that all questions of slavery, because of their "extreme delicacy," "belong to a class, which the peace and safety of a large portion of our Union forbids us even to discuss." Yet he supplied a detailed description of the likely effect on U.S. slaves that might be produced by any formal association of the U.S. participants at the Panama Congress with "men of color" from Haiti. One of the proposed U.S. ministers, Hayne suggested darkly, was "a distinguished advocate of the *Missouri restriction*—an acknowledged abolitionist."[73]

Some Southern congressmen expressed the fear that complicity with Latin America would force emancipation upon them. Would participation in the congress signify recognition for Haiti? asked Hamilton of South Carolina.[74] "Is this Congress to tell the gentleman from South Carolina, and all of us from the Southern States, that 'all men are free and equal;' and if you join us to command the Emperor of Brazil to descend from his throne, we shall then turn round to you, and say to the United States, 'Every man is free; and if you refuse to make them so, we will bring seven Republics, in full march, to compel you . . .?' " demanded Representative John Floyd of Virginia.[75]

In their discovery that no one tried to abort discussion of emancipation in Cuba or colorblindness in Guatemalan society, these legislators had stumbled upon a kind of outlet, a safety valve: talking about nations next door to the United States allowed the airing of proscribed subjects in public. The debates over the Panama Congress supplied an occasion for public figures to speak at length and in detail about slavery, sometimes with the kind of circumlocution Forbes talks about but sometimes with startling directness, with the audible sound of relief as bottled-up opinions were at last vented. That Latin America *was* perceived as foreign, that their commitment to republicanism could not quite erase their singularity, made this frank discussion possible, and even allowed the bolder congressmen to address U.S. slavery directly.

On Van Buren's initiative, those in opposition to Adams and his Panama proposal settled on a strategy of delay. First Adams's enemies in the Senate demanded a review and publication of the correspondence related to the Panama Congress and then stalled the nomination of delegates. For their part, Van Buren's allies in the House of Representatives subsequently held up the appropriation of monies to fund the U.S. delegation.[76] Finally, on March 14, 1826, the Senate confirmed the nominations of Richard C. Anderson and John Sergeant as ministers plenipotentiary, and appropriations for their remuneration were approved by the House of Representatives in mid-April. In the event, however, Anderson, setting out during malaria season, died on the way, and Sergeant did not arrive until after the congress had adjourned.

The Panama Congress has been read as an abrupt coup de grace for the exuberant glorification of Latin American independence and the popular enthusiasm for universal republicanism and fellowship with the region. For the first time, congressional discourse about Latin America emphasized what was dangerous, unsavory, and different about the region.[77] After the widely published debates exposed newspaper readers to the mixed-race reality and rampant Catholicism of the once-admired republics, popular enthusiasm gave way to reserve. According to this analysis, many Americans lost interest in the future of their southern neighbors after 1826.[78]

Although it was difficult to be oblivious about the racial and religious composition of Latin America after the Panama debates, it took a bit longer for public opinion to catch up with political discourse than this reading suggests. Americans remote from Latin America, and from the center of discussion in Washington, were slow to relinquish their expectations of shared republicanism and their dreams of commercial benefits. The romance of Latin American exoticism continued to hold their fascination, with both towns and babies christened in tribute well after the immediate postrevolutionary period. Simon Bolivar Hulbert, a Union private whose Civil War experiences were published as *One Battle Too Many,* was born in 1833.[79] Peru, Indiana, birthplace of the Broadway lyricist and composer Cole Porter was founded in 1834, and Bolivar, Missouri, in 1835. Migrants from Peru, Illinois (established 1838), settled in Peru, Nebraska (1857).

During the semicentennial celebrations in 1826, immediately after published reports of congressional testimony had presumably awakened newspaper readers to the many ways Latin America differed from the United States, toasts reflected popular ambiguity rather than wholesale repudiation. Even among toasts reported by one Southern newspaper, the *Richmond Enquirer,* at celebrations in various Virginia communities, these references included the frankly cynical ("The Panama Mission; An egg laid in our Federal Cabinet by the political crusader H. Clay to hatch popularity. In the nest has been found executive corruption, let its offspring beware of Randolph the Virginia falcon") but also the enthusiastic ("The Republics of the South! The bright example of the Republics of the North, has not been lost upon them!").[80] These toasts reflect political faction at home and awareness of the particulars of political organization abroad, but they by no means universally ignore or condemn the new republics.

In the U.S. Congress, the most national forum imaginable, the advocates and opponents of the Panama Congress had had a national conversation about slavery. Latin America, having been established as racially and religiously distinct from the United States, proved its worth as a setting in which issues like abolition could be safely discussed. But in more local settings, where there were established trading relationships with Latin American ports, for example, it took more than simply pointing out the racial composition of Latin America to transform the perspectives of U.S. observers. It fell to the nation's newspapers, rather than to Congress itself, to explain what the Panama debates actually meant, and they often expressed more nuanced—because more local—analyses of the situation.

Editors did not immediately fall in line with the relentless racial understanding that characterized the speeches of many of the politicians, instead
continuing to celebrate the possibility of bountiful trade and rapprochement with neighboring republics. When they did connect attendance at
Panama to the slavery issue, they could not always be counted upon to say
exactly what the party wished. The *Liberty Hall and Cincinnati Gazette*, for
example, recognized, and condemned, the way Southern congressmen let
their own fears of abolition influence their recognition of the new republics.
From Washington, Clay noted in a letter to Cincinnati publisher Charles
Hammond that the "Panama articles in the Liberty Hall are able and highly
useful" but expressed a wish for "mutual forbearance" on the subject of
slavery, particularly from the "Non-slavery holding states, as the stronger,
safer and happier party."[81]

In New York, the pro-administration *New-York Evening Post* viewed
the growing excitement of the congressional debates with a weary hauteur,
declining to work up either any enthusiasm or any consternation over an
issue it considered much ado about nothing and presuming that its readers
were likewise uninterested in the whole subject.[82] The *Post* suggested that
the United States might do good by spreading the benefit of republican
government, and it might do itself some good in the process. The way the
Post conflated these two objectives suggests a reinterpretation—or at least
a decidedly economic inflection—of the U.S. revolutionary goals of fifty
years earlier. Rather than seeking liberty from despots, the former Spanish
colonies were casting off the fetters of mercantilism. Using slavery-to-
freedom imagery, the *Post* predicted, "Great principles are now about to be
adopted; a great experiment is making in the world, by which freedom is
given to commerce, and the shackles are about to be removed from the
enterprise of all nations."[83] The United States might claim a share in this
good fortune.

For the Old Northwest, the Panama Mission also held out the enticing
possibility of enhanced trading opportunities, and western papers worked
themselves into more of a lather over the importance of participation than
the languid *New-York Evening Post*. In roughly equal measure, the *Liberty
Hall and Cincinnati Gazette* protested the Southern distaste for associating
with nations that had abolished slavery, expressed good faith for the republican intentions of the new states, and speculated about the consequences
for western prosperity if new commercial possibilities were not adequately
exploited or, worse, if relations with South America soured because of

Southern prejudice. "This subject is one of first importance to the United Sates generally, but particularly to the Western country," avowed the pro-Adams *Gazette* on February 17, 1826. "It would not be extravagant to say, that their commerce may become, in less than a quarter of a century, of more consequence to the valley of the Mississippi, than that of all the world beside."[84] Although on the face of it this prediction of prodigious trade would seem dubious, an article published a month later quoted statistics to back up this claim with specific regard to Haiti, the locus of much Southern disapprobation. In 1824, the *Gazette* stated, U.S. exports to Haiti amounted to nearly two million dollars, with flour, pork, and beef, the products of the West, making up nearly half the total. Sharp-eyed residents of Cincinnati, nicknamed Porkopolis with good reason, would notice that exports of pork totaled $378,000 and soap and candles (made from the byproducts of pork processing) $158,000.[85]

In such a case it would seem more in the interest of the West to mute its objections to the proslavery forces; after all, the intensive cultivation of cash crops in regions dominated by slave societies created markets for the products of free farmers and industrialists, but here the *Gazette* took the high road, condemning Southern arguments and pointing out the hypocrisy of their position. The *Gazette* even went so far as to approve of the potential invasion of Cuba by liberating forces from Mexico and Colombia, a possibility so unpopular with the South that even Adams warned against it.[86] "However the policy of our government, regarding chiefly the security of the slave property of the Southern states, may unite with the views of European governments, in retaining Cuba as a colonial appendage of Spain, we think it very clear that, in all other respects, its independence would be of advantage to itself and to this country," the *Gazette* noted dryly, appending another chart showing the value of exports to Cuba.[87]

At New Orleans, the Mississippi port into which South America-bound produce from the West flowed, attitudes about participation in the Panama Congress were lukewarm, at least in the pages of the *Louisiana State Gazette*. A bilingual newspaper (English and French), the *Gazette* emphasized regional news; it took two to three weeks to get dispatches from Washington, New York, or Philadelphia. Its maritime register mentioned cotton more than Cincinnati hams, and it reflected the interests of the slave South more than the grain-growing West. Its objections to the Panama Mission focused less on the fate of Cuba or executive overreaching than the threat of entangling alliances. "If South American independence is threatened, this government can give to our neighbors aid and succor, without alliances."[88] Explicitly disavowing antiadministration motivations for its opposition to the mission, the *Gazette* maintained a consistent reluctance against "intermeddling" in Latin American affairs.[89] Andrew Jackson's providential victory in the Battle of New Orleans had occurred only eleven years earlier; perhaps the *Gazette*'s lack of enthusiasm for anything that suggested a military commitment also reflected that recent experience in which disaster and dishonor had so narrowly been avoided. The *Gazette* recognized that one difference between the United States and the republics of Latin America was the reliance among the latter on standing armies. "An unemployed army in sight of our coast, flushed with victory, and panting for future conquest, may create no alarm at Boston—but it will excite deep and painful thoughts to the reflecting inhabitants from the mouth of the Sabine to the mouth of the Potomac."[90]

After the Senate confirmation of Anderson and Sergeant as ministers plenipotentiary to Panama, "P. Henry," writing in Thomas Ritchie's *Richmond Enquirer*, decided that the results of the votes were "curious, and ominous."[91] "By reference to the map . . . it will be seen, that the whole country south of the Pennsylvania Line, and of the River Ohio, to the Gulph of Mexico, [save Maryland, immediately in the focus of Presidential influence, and Little Delaware, who, I apprehend, is about to fall from 'her high estate,'] is opposed to this novel, if not dangerous scheme of international diplomacy."[92] What was "ominous" was not the fact that the vote had broken on clearly sectional lines, but that the kind of intelligent statesmen (at least in "P. Henry's" estimation) who dominated the slave-holding regions were so obviously absent from the North and West.

Actually the situation was a bit more complex than "P. Henry" suggested. The interests of the South further diverged according to geography. Maryland and Louisiana, with port cities heavily invested in South American trade, endorsed the Panama Mission. Meanwhile, the North and West were even less solid in their support: while the Northeast was relatively firm in backing the administration, in the West, the Susquehanna and Ohio River valleys demonstrated more interest in the potential benefits of the congress than rural areas remote from water-born trade.[93] But the protection of slavery and increased opportunities for commerce, more than other, more abstract causes, determined voting patterns.[94] In extending actual assistance to the Latin American revolutionaries generally, and in backing the Panama Congress more specifically, national self-interest figured as a prominent motive.[95] A young republic, its resources tied up in its own defense and development, the United States concentrated on ways of "helping" its neighbors that would bring about better opportunities for itself. Americans were willing to overlook race where money was involved.

Yet this analysis may be unnecessarily cynical; at any rate it hardly tells the whole story.[96] Let one example of a less than purely self-interested popular response suffice. On July 4, 1827, "Philanthropos" published a book called *Essays on Peace and War, Which First Appeared in the Christian Mirror*.[97] "Philanthropos" was William Ladd, a Maine antiwar activist who was shortly to establish the American Peace Society. He devoted one of his essays to the Panama Mission, writing, "I view the Congress of Panama as one of the links in the great chain of events, by which Providence designs to bind all the nations of Christendom,—which will be, finally, all the nations of the world,—in one grand bond of permanent and universal peace."[98] Ladd also noted a correspondence between the opponents of the mission and the supporters of slavery. "Thus, in this case, as in all others, we find a natural alliance between liberty and peace, slavery and war."[99] At the Panama Congress, Ladd saw a remarkable confluence of opportunities not for profit but for the complete abolition of the slave trade; the end of privateering; a system of international law that would, at a minimum, define contraband and the right of blockade; and the ultimate extension of religious liberty. He beheld the gathering as a potential prototype for the eventual establishment of something that sounds very much like the United Nations.[100]

On the surface, it seems clear that in 1826 Americans at home analyzed the Panama situation from many perspectives, not simply racial ones. They had to be coached to pick up on racial cues, and they did not pick them up immediately. But the often-repeated refrains of the Panama Congress debates, that Latin America was different from (and therefore inferior to) the United States, that the most important difference concerned race, and that Latin America was therefore safe ground upon which to consider slavery, indeed penetrated regional consciousness over the next decade. What happened?

The main selling points of the Panama Congress—that Latin America would complete the work of bringing republicanism to the hemisphere, and that the new nations would form a vast market—evaporated. By the time Ladd's *Essays on Peace and War* was published in 1827, it was becoming clear that the vision of Pan-Americanism proffered by the Panama Congress would ultimately come to naught. Although Buenos Aires and Chile refrained from attending, ministers from Peru, Mexico, Colombia, and Guatemala did meet and approved tentative agreements providing for a common army and mutual defense, adjourned, and agreed to reconvene in Tacubaya, Mexico, after their governments had ratified the treaties. But only Colombia went so far as to take that step. With considerably less fanfare than in 1826, Congress approved the posting of John Sergeant and Joel Poinsett to Tacubaya in 1827, but that convocation never took place.[101]

By any measure, in the years following the Pan-American conference in Panama, the new republics of Central and South America experienced growing pains. U.S. politicians and diplomats sent home damning accounts of encounters with their counterparts in the fumbling young nations and their failure to realize republican ideals. Joel Poinsett, minister to Mexico, wrote in 1828, "I had a lonely time in this Babylon . . . this country is doomed to experience a long & disastrous civil war, which I should have preferred hearing of rather than experiencing."[102] Mexico was to undergo some fifty changes of presidential administration between 1821 and 1857.[103] In 1832 Francis Baylies, a former Federalist congressman serving as the U.S. chargé d'affaires in Argentina, wrote to Gulian C. Verplanck in New York, "I wish our moonstruck, imaginative romantic politicians who have deluded themselves with such notions of South American liberty and South American greatness could stay here one-week—I think their hallucinations would be dispelled." The Argentines had no aptitude for creating a republic: "I have no hesitation in saying that I think that any well regulated tribe of Indians have better notions of national justice—national dignity—and national policy than the rulers of this Sister Republic of ours."[104]

To the extent that high hopes for the Panama Congress were inflated by dreams of a mighty commercial coup, Latin America soon enough proved disappointing.[105] On a typical day in 1826 a port city advertised a dozen ships preparing to sail for Buenos Aires, Valparaiso, Havana, and Montevideo.[106] But what commercial advantages could be obtained at the Panama Congress were scooped up by Great Britain's Edward Dawkins, who represented a nation with products and credit the United States could not supply and who refrained from speaking out against the invasion of Cuba.[107] Meanwhile, the vision of Latin America as a vast marketplace conjured by Buchanan and the *Liberty Hall and Cincinnati Gazette* proved elusive. There was a reason Cuba was such a good market for American products: its colonial economy had not been devastated by a war for independence. Mexico, by contrast, took a long time to recover economically. "There is no cash in the country except in the hands of a few individuals, who are already supplied with more goods than they can consume in two years," complained the *National Intelligencer* in 1825.[108] A Latin American population swelled by European immigration never quite materialized: European immigrants expected greater economic opportunities in the United States. And as the years went by, the north-south routes made imperative by riparian and maritime transportation were supplanted or at least rivaled by west-east canals and railroad routes, which turned the U.S. West into a breadbasket for the industrializing East. By the early 1840s the value of exports to independent Mexico still amounted to less than half of those to colonial Cuba, leading Representative Archibald Lin of New York to propose saving the expense of sending a minister there.[109]

The so-called Transportation Revolution also had an effect on perception by collapsing the distance that had separated far-flung locations. But in this case the strangeness of Latin Americans in the U.S. imagination was little reduced by propinquity, while their presence in the neighborhood now seemed undesirable. Fellowship with republicans regardless of complexion became more problematic when they suddenly seemed to be living next door. Unflattering reports of the laziness and prodigality of Spanish Americans reached the United States more quickly and were disseminated more widely. Adrian R. Terry's *Travels in the Equatorial Regions of South America, in 1832*, advertised as being available in Boston, New Haven, New York, Albany, Philadelphia, Baltimore, Richmond, and Charleston, reported that "internal commotions, and a disjointed and precarious state of society; and . . . a low standard of morals and education" counteracted the natural advantages of the port of Guayaquil, Ecuador, resulting in the paralysis of industry and the stultification of trade.[110]

Similarly dramatic changes were afoot on the domestic scene. Most importantly, the boldness and vigor of the slave-based economy in the United States exceeded all expectations. Critically, U.S. slavery in the post-1826 period was a dynamic new institution. In defiance of all the predictions of the revolutionary period, human bondage was in no sense withering away. The institution needed fresh fields of operation, which conveniently opened up throughout the antebellum period. It needed new technologies to facilitate its spread, also appearing in the form of steel plows, railroads, and steamboats. It needed manpower, which was forcibly marched from the Upper South where slavery was moribund to the Black Belt where all was speed and sweat. New financial instruments facilitated the movement of capital. The corn and wheat of the West, the calicos and brogans of the northern factories that were supposedly destined for Mexico and Colombia found eager buyers in the U.S. South, where they filled the bellies and shod the feet of slaves.[111]

Because of the remarks made about race and slavery in Latin America, the Panama Congress debates ultimately cast a long shadow. As alarm over real and supposed threats from the federal government to the peculiar institution grew, many Southerners remembered Adams's presumption in accepting the invitation to Panama. The kind of power he wielded could be used to wrest control of slavery from the states. The emergence of the Democratic Party under Andrew Jackson became for his supporters a safeguard of their rights as slaveholders.[112] Opponents of slavery in the North had an even longer memory. In an 1847 pamphlet published during the U.S. War with Mexico, Massachusetts abolitionist Loring Moody quoted Senator Berrien's remarks in the Panama Congress debates to show just how far short of the example set by the Latin American republics the United States fell in its commitment to liberty: "In what respect did the United States differ from 'these new republics,' which this sturdy democrat here [Berrien] stigmatized as 'Bucaniers?'" asked Moody. "Certainly there is a broad difference,—the United States—whether bucaniers or not—never got so 'drunk with their new born liberty,' as to demolish their human flesh shambles, in the boisterous merriment of their intoxication. They were always sober enough to keep the watch-dogs of their plantations well trained."[113]

Something of the complexity of the initial post-Panama reactions is revealed in Timothy Flint's *Francis Berrian, or, the Mexican Patriot*, a fictional work that appeared in American bookstores "in the fifty-first year of the Independence of the United States of America," as the publisher noted.[114] It was the first U.S. novel with a Spanish American setting.[115] Published even as the Congress of Panama assembled sans representatives of the United States in 1826, the novel documents the shifting meanings of race and nation, fraternity and foreignness during that memorable summer, demonstrating that wariness and ambiguity concerning the implications of future U.S.-Latin American relations were expressed in many varying contexts. In the novel the two regions do not share the blood of brothers, but their ultimate marital union becomes much more intimate than the fraternity invoked by U.S. congressmen. Yet Flint refrains from promising the success of this marriage.

Flint was a New England native like his hero, who traveled to Cincinnati as a minister but became a novelist, short story writer, and editor of the short-lived journal *Western Monthly Review* (1827–1830). His novel depicts the creation of the new Mexican republic through the eyes of a Massachusetts native who plays a pivotal role in the war for Mexican independence in 1821 and 1822.[116] This character becomes in effect an American Lafayette, a foreign visitor swayed by the vision of independence and singularly efficacious in its realization.[117] On the surface, *Francis Berrian* is a story of battle, romance, and upward mobility, resolved by marriage at the end of the second volume. On another level, the novel can easily be read as an allegory, informed by the hopeful prediction that republicanism will bind the United States and Mexico in a union of well-matched partners.[118] But beneath its adventure-story veneer lurks skepticism about the heroics of revolution, the hardiness of republicanism, and the future of relations between the United States and Latin America.

Francis Berrian, off to seek his fortune, heads from New England to the southwest where he rescues a Spanish captive, the noble Dona Martha, from a band of Comanches. Martha becomes Berrian's love interest, and consistent with the conventions of the typical nineteenth-century novel, differences of background and temperament must be overcome. Martha is the titled daughter of a Conde committed to suppressing the incipient rebellions for independence throughout Mexico—a foil for Berrian's intrepid republicanism. Her nobility sets her on a social plane above Berrian, who despite his Harvard education is only a farmer's son. Her Catholicism contrasts with Berrian's sober Protestantism. But Flint takes care not to let the differences between the central characters stray too far. Romantic alliances between people of different races are out of the question (Berrian is bothered by advances of one of the "copper-colored daughters of the savages").[119] When Berrian rescues her, Martha throws herself upon his mercies, citing their common background: "Stranger! you are of our race."[120]

Although Martha does not renounce her religion, she becomes a devout convert to republicanism. She instinctively understands and appreciates the political ideals Berrian takes for granted, if anything, surpassing him in her enthusiasm. People of Spanish origin do not lie beyond hope of republican redemption, Berrian recognizes: "Enlighten their ignorance;—break their chains;—remove the threefold veil of darkness with which your priesthood has hoodwinked them. My heart tells me that nothing can be more amiable than the Spanish character," he says.[121] Unfortunately, those of Spanish character do not form the majority of the Mexican population. When Berrian is drawn into the Patriots' struggle for independence, he musters little sympathy for the Indian, mulatto, and Creole "rabble" that makes up the Patriot army; indeed it is suggested that they are not worthy of liberty.[122] The select group Berrian looks forward to incorporating into the polity seems to be a tiny minority.

Two celebrations bookend Berrian's adventures (even as the national jubilee served as the context of the novel's publication). Early in the story, after Berrian's rescue of Martha, the Conde has a party to celebrate her safe return.[123] Berrian disapprovingly observes that during a fandango, titled guests smile upon the Terpsichorean efforts of the humble, and servants share the dance floor with the great. When Berrian turns up his nose at this demonstration of unexpected democracy, Martha challenges him, not out of noblesse oblige but out of a more inclusive interpretation of his own political creed: "Our national manners call for all this, and allow strangers privileges here, which would not be tolerated in any other place," she says. "I should think it would be conformable to your republican notions to see the rich and the poor mixing together in the same sports, in which their ancestors mixed in the generations of the past. Will you have the goodness to walk this dance with me?"[124] To Martha's annoyance, Berrian stiffly refuses. After a sleepless night of torment, however, he accepts the justice of her rebuke and begs her forgiveness.[125]

Then at the end of *Francis Berrian,* Flint's hero takes his new bride on a visit to his family in Massachusetts. What impresses Martha is the level of prosperity enjoyed by the general population, but her new husband wants her to see his family occupying a position above the common herd. Berrian sends Bryan, his clownish but loyal Irish servant, ahead of the bridal party "with a good round sum of dollars" to be invested in "plenty of wine, turkies, and pies for a sociable visit of a whole winter" as well as new clothes for his family and a fresh coat of whitewash for his father's stone fence.[126] Bryan, a veritable Potemkin preparing a village for the state visit by the empress, does his work well: Berrian finds his mother decked out in "false 'everlastings,' false teeth, and every thing false but her maternal heart" and his father suitably unrecognizable in a "long-tailed wig."[127] Berrian's whole village proceeds to partake in an extended orgy of "invitations, and dinners, and parties without number" where his less fortunate neighbors vie with one another in their degree of fawning adulation.[128] "The people there all possess, at least, a most accurate sense of the real and practical utility of dollars; and much as they look down upon all assumption of every sort, they think none the less of a man for being rich."[129]

A curious contrast, to be sure: two festive occasions, the one in aristocratic Mexico where "old and young, parents and children, masters and servants, on these occasions . . . join in the same dance;" the one in the United States characterized by whitewash, false hair, and envy, where "merits" are equated with dollars.[130] Martha's kindness has a surprising allegorical significance. Much the way she cited "republican notions" to justify the inclusion of the unwashed masses in a dance, Mexico's new government took seriously the era's professed commitment to liberty. In 1821 the Patriots issued a provisional constitution called the *Plan de Iguala* extending citizenship rights to Indians, mestizos, and free *afromestizos*. The Constitution of 1824 began a process of gradual emancipation of slaves.[131] Meanwhile Berrian supports not only the separation of the races—no "copper-colored" maidens for him—but also the reinforcement of an economic hierarchy. Looked at from one perspective, Hispanic "amiability" bodes well for the future relations of the United States and the Spanish republics. But from another angle, some troubling ambiguities emerge. The relationship points up ways in which the United States falls short of its own professed ideals—as it did in working to oppose the independence of Cuba for fear of immediate emancipation. Is Flint suggesting that it is in this failed goal of republican equality that the success of the project of independence is marred? Except for Martha's challenge concerning Berrian's fastidiousness about the fandango, there seem few suggestions that Flint regards Berrian's segregation by class as unnatural or undesirable. Still, Martha's censure hangs in the air.

Her compatible political ideals do not seem to explain Martha's suitability as a partner for Berrian. Republicanism is easy. Seemingly more relevant are the essential characteristics of her pedigree. First, she is white. As the undisputed daughter of Gachupin (European-born) parents, Martha's racial background is above suspicion. (In marked contrast, nine years later the novelist Robert Montgomery Bird would acknowledge that even "among the southern provinces of Spain and Portugal . . . the blood of Europe has mingled harmoniously with the life-tides of Africa."[132]) But almost as important is her breeding and secure upper-class status. What Berrian champions about Martha is not her empathy for the hoi polloi (which is suspect), nor her harmonious political inclinations, but her refinement and dazzling fortune. It is the ignorance and laziness of the mixed-race majority, not the aristocratic expectations of Martha's family and the other members of the elite, that present the greater threat to the new order.

Analyzing Martha's suitability as a fit spouse for Berrian suggests one more reason why U.S. suspicion of the Latin American population grew during the early nineteenth century. The fading confidence that mastering the lessons of republicanism would bring Latin America into fellowship with the United States reflects a turn away from the late eighteenth-century faith in the effects of culture and improvement to a nineteenth-century emphasis on heredity and ultimately race.[133] The Enlightenment had promised that inborn skills and talents could be developed and twisted habits straightened out; nineteenth-century thought tended to see determinism in bloodlines. The French Revolution and its aftermath (which included its echo in Saint Domingue) did part of the work of discouraging faith in human perfectibility.[134] Race and "blood"—noble or otherwise—would increasingly be credited with an unopposable power that no subsequent training could correct.[135] White fear of pollution by the nonwhite races contributed as well to an awareness of genetic difference that would reach its zenith (or nadir) in scientific racism.[136]

That Flint himself became increasingly conflicted about the probable future of republicanism south of the U.S. border (and increasingly able to see Latin America as a context for discussing U.S. slavery) is demonstrated a few years later among the pages of his journal *The Western Monthly Review*. In September 1829, supplying his readers with a digest of Robert Owen's visit to Mexico, Flint mentions the "ignorant, factious, bigoted and versatile inhabitants, who seem as little fitted to enjoy that liberty, for which they are struggling through revolutions, as the slaves of our southern country would be, if they were at once emancipated."[137] Flint also produced "Paulina, or the Cataract of Tequendama," a short story set in Colombia that reprises in eight pages many of the situations of the 600-page *Francis Berrian*. Published in 1830, its hopes for the proximate progress of republicanism were decidedly tepid, amid "the heavy, monotonous and sickening chronicle of politics, and Bolivar, and what knave of to-day has supplanted the fool of yesterday."[138]

In the years following the Panama Congress debates of 1826, many of the new states of Latin America failed to live up to the rosy predictions of U.S. optimists. Some of the republics slipped into a period of *caudillismo*, where local strongmen and petty dictators snatched the reins of power over separate territories. At the same time, some took the concepts of liberty and republicanism to an extreme to which the United States would not follow. Democratic politics in the post-1826 United States would furnish a dance floor where different classes might "mix together" as long as the dancers were white. In the United States the meaning of the newly emerging democracy was trimmed to exclude men of color and women generally. In the years that followed, the franchise was increasingly withheld from black freemen, and the possibility of manumission for individual slaves was similarly circumscribed. The Nat Turner Rebellion of 1831, demonstrating how sorely slaves chafed under bondage, was met not with a less burdensome yoke but with heavier chains. The new republics of Latin America had extended an invitation to attend a congress, but also challenged the United States to accept an enlarged definition of its own ideals. Like Francis Berrian answering Martha's invitation, the United States refused, instead erecting higher barriers between slavery and freedom.

The multivariate nature of U.S. responses to the Panama Mission both in and out of Congress suggests that what happened in 1826 was not an abrupt change in attitude by citizens of the United States concerning their southern neighbors. But the proclamations of difference, particularly racial difference, began crowding out expectations of fellowship and communion. The debates laid the groundwork necessary for displacing representations of slavery: they established Latin America as essentially different from the United States. In 1826 the understanding of race and slavery was only one of the ways the United States differed from Latin America, but it would come to be the most conspicuous because of changes taking place in the United States. That difference made Latin America the perfect proxy for the United States in a variety of situations.

In the years that followed, the United States continued to hold up its southern neighbors for purposes of comparison. But with the rise of Jacksonian democracy, scientific racism, and virulent abolitionist and proslavery rhetoric, the differences between Latin America and the United States became more useful than the similarities. A national print culture enabled by steam presses and cheap postage that could reach large sections of the country—indeed the nation as a whole—fostered a rhetoric that presumed to speak for the United States, and that rhetoric was often racist and xeno-phobic. Americans in many situations discovered what the legislators in the Panama debates had realized: Latin America provided an excellent cover for the discussion of their apprehensions and anxieties about slavery before a vast audience. In the process of redefining the relationship between the early republic of the United States and the new republics of Latin America, the definition of republicanism became more limited, and the exceptional-ism and racial composition of U.S. nationalism became more pronounced.

Chapter 2

"Our" Aborigines

While pro- and antislavery Americans used Latin America in their own ways to suit their own interests, Americans of all stripes sought to distance themselves from the modern Indians, proving, pseudoscientifically, that the ancient Americans—those of Mexico as well as the great mound builders of North America and the civilized makers of South America—must have been white.[1] By linking themselves to the ancient, early nineteenth-century Americans distanced themselves from the modern, further enabling a safe space from which to project uncomfortable political discourse. Indeed, just as open discussions of Latin American slavery served as a means to say things about domestic bondage otherwise left unspoken, these archaeological speculations also operated as a form of displacement, a way of talking about the early republic by projecting modern attitudes back upon the ancient American past. "It would seem that the White race alone received the divine command, to subdue and replenish the earth! . . . thus the youngest people, and the newest land, will become the reviver and the regenerator of the oldest," crowed Missouri Senator Thomas Hart Benton in 1846.[2]

As Americans displaced their qualms about slave societies by attributing all manner of deformities onto living, breathing Latin Americans, they were simultaneously finding much to admire in ancient civilizations of Mexico. The American response to the discovery of those civilizations offers an intriguing counterpoint to prevailing stereotypes. Here contempt gives way to admiration and in so doing throws the dominant pattern of displacement into sharper relief. Long dead Mexicans were the archaeological exception to the living rule.

By turning back the clock, archaeologists used a distant time *and* space in order to make contemporary political arguments, to justify the removal

Figure 4. Although there are few mid-nineteenth-century visual representations of aboriginal earthworks in North America, a fascinating exception is the *Panorama of the Monumental Grandeur of the Mississippi Valley* by John J. Egan (1850). First exhibited in Philadelphia, the artwork was featured as the centerpiece of a lecture series delivered throughout the Mississippi Valley. Archaeologists tried to establish a connection between the people who had built these mounds and the monuments of Mexico and Peru. John J. Egan, American (born Ireland), active mid-nineteenth century; Scene 24 from *Panorama of the Monumental Grandeur of the Mississippi Valley*; distemper on cotton muslin; overall: 90 in. x 348 ft. (228.6 x 10607.1 cm). Saint Louis Art Museum, Eliza McMillan Trust 34:1953.

Figure 5. Artist Frederick Catherwood illustrated John Lloyd Stephen's accounts of
his explorations of the Yucatan in the early 1840s (the 1844 illustration above
depicts a pyramid at Tulum). His sketches, drawn in situ with exacting detail, made
clear that there was little resemblance to North American mounds. *Views of Ancient
Monuments in Central America, Chiapas and Yucatan*, plate 24. Frederick
Catherwood, 1844, Rare Books Division, The New York Public Library, Astor,
Lenox and Tilden Foundations.

of Indians, and to reconceive the relationship between Americans and their
southern neighbors. The stakes were never higher. Countless lives were lost.
And the fate of slavery, inextricably tied to the question of expansion, hung
in the balance.

In the decade following the Panama Congress, the risk of publicly
opposing—even discussing—slavery rose higher and higher. The Nat
Turner Rebellion in 1831 convinced many white Americans of a direct connection between increasingly radical abolitionist agitation and servile insurrection. Silencing national disagreements over slavery seemed imperative.
By 1835 an era of mob assaults on antislavery activists had begun and would

continue to nearly the end of the decade. Horrified by this climate of suppression, the poet John Greenleaf Whittier expressed his outrage at Southern attempts to mute voices raised against the injustice of human bondage in the 1835 "Stanzas for the Times." Complaining that he was forced to "speak but as our masters please," Whittier protested that he was made a slave himself. To make his portrait of Southern depravity particularly vivid, he used imagery recalling the bloodthirsty Aztecs of Mexico to represent the desecration of the nation's altar of liberty:

> Of human skulls that shrine was made,
> Round which the priests of Mexico
> Before their loathsome idol prayed;
> Is Freedom's altar fashioned so?
> And must we yield to Freedom's God,
> As offering meet, the negro's blood?[3]

Many Americans had, by the 1830s, learned to scorn and despise the inept, mixed-race, would-be republicans south of the border and the native tribes—the Aztecs in particular—renowned for their cruelty. But one group of Latin Americans retained the admiration of antebellum Americans. They had been dead for hundreds of years.

In the 1810s and 1820s independence liberated Latin America from the absolutism and secrecy of Spanish rule, inviting the curious to dig for buried treasure. Accounts of discoveries almost forgotten since the time of the Spanish Conquest trickled out of Central and South America. Ruins of ancient temples and pyramids encountered in the Yucatan—often decorated with intricate carving—excited the interest of both scholarly and uneducated Americans fascinated by the nascent field of archaeology. Who could have built the wonders in Tulum, Copan, and Palenque? Certainly not the ancestors of the disreputable natives of the nineteenth-century Americas, reasoned U.S. nationalists.[4] The brutal Aztecs encountered by the Spanish could not have been responsible, nor the alternately treacherous and lazy tribes of North America. The nineteenth-century Indians being rapidly displaced from their homelands were nomadic and improvident; they drifted from place to place, warring savagely with other tribes. The long-vanished builders of America's ruined monuments—the great mounds of the Ohio and Mississippi valleys, the pyramids of Central and South America—had been settled and civilized . . . by whites.[5]

From the accounts of the conquistadores, U.S. readers knew that the Aztecs had displaced an earlier nation called the Toltecs: the nineteenth century would understand these Toltecs as migrants from Israel, Carthage, Wales, Egypt, or Scandinavia.[6] According to early nineteenth-century theories, these people had crossed the Atlantic or Pacific in boats. In North America they built fortifications and serpent-shaped earthworks first glimpsed by nineteenth-century Americans as they moved west. In Central and South America the genius of these ancient peoples reached its apex in the great cities of the Yucatan and Peru. Then across the Behring Strait from Asia swarmed another race, the ancestors of modern Indians, like latter-day barbarians descending on Rome, massacring and driving off the people who first settled the continent.

However prolifically this remarkable assumption flourished in the reflexive racism of Jacksonian America during the 1830s and 1840s, it could not ultimately withstand the harsh sunlight of systematic observation nor the storms of serious scholarship. But for a period of twenty or twenty-five years, variations of this useful myth fit neatly into a historical moment when Americans intensively dispossessed Indians and mixed-race Mexicans from their land and installed in their place white settlers and their enslaved workforce. Great triumphs of past civilizations were considered de facto proof of the whiteness of their populations rather than demonstrations of nature's democratic distribution of brilliance among all her people.[7] With extraordinary economy, this line of analysis at once vindicated white supremacy, established an ancient connection between the inhabitants of North and South America, justified the appropriation of land occupied by nonwhite peoples, and mapped upon that land a space for immediate or potential cultivation by enslaved labor. Historian Sven Beckert refers to the conjoined forces "resting on the violent expropriation of land and labor" as "war capitalism."[8] Making clear the connection between Indian removal and the spread of slavery, Beckert writes, "The coercion and violence required to mobilize slave labor was matched only by the demands of an expansionist war against indigenous people."[9] Along with slavery, white Americans' ability to obliterate Native American claims to the land, giving cotton planters total control over land and resources, set the United States apart from suppliers like India in the global marketplace.[10] These linkages established a claim to the land now so unworthily occupied by usurping Indians.[11] Turnabout was fair play: in the dim past the Indians had driven off the original white settlers of the ancient world; in modern times the valuable patrimony would be reclaimed. If this story rested on the flimsiest of evidence, it gained credibility through endless repetition in a variety of formats.

The connections between early archeological studies, Indian removal, and racial pseudoscience were more often assumed than explicitly drawn. Analyzing the way these ideas intersected in support of one another reveals much about U.S. understandings of race at midcentury, ideas that would in turn inform views about slavery. But whereas many remarks about slavery were deliberately silenced in national conversation because they were too volatile, assumptions about the race of ancient Americans often went unmentioned because they were considered self-evident, hardly worth the trouble of defending.[12] Beliefs that racial differences were essential and unchangeable, that land occupied by inferior races might be conquered and cleansed, that the race-based, slave-dependent economy of the Market Revolution signaled not the emergence of a new stage of capitalism, but the restoration of an order rooted in and justified by history, all supported the status quo.[13]

Like so many other issues of the antebellum period, the nation's steady absorption of land in the southwest was intimately connected to the expansion of slavery, though the connection was not always explicit.[14] "[T]he expansion of slavery in many ways shaped the story of *everything* in the pre-Civil War United States," writes historian Edward Baptist. "Scholars and students talked about politics as a battle about states' rights or republican principles, but viewed in a different light the fights can be seen as a struggle between regions about how the rewards of slavery's expansion would be allocated and whether that expansion could continue."[15] Expelling the Indian inhabitants was justified by prevarications, fanciful arguments, and occasionally legitimate concern for their welfare, but much of the mania was driven by the lust for their land. Eager for more senators who would dependably promote the peculiar institution, the South particularly welcomed the addition of new states invested in the plantation economy ("this cotton argument, as it is called, is a strong inducement with me for desiring the acquisition of Texas," said U.S. representative Thomas Bayly in 1845. "It will give us the entire control of that great staple").[16] New England opposed southern expansion for a related reason: it feared the waning of its political influence as its densely populated states lost migrants to the west.

The process of occupying southwestern territory—first through the enforced removal of native peoples, then through the annexation of Texas, and finally through the spoils of the war with Mexico—was riven with controversy. During the 1830s politicians, particularly in areas where Indians were long gone, railed against the injustice and its inhumanity of driving the tribes from their homes. Citizens organized petition drives to protest.[17] A glance at the way the centers of opposition overlapped with centers of abolitionism—among New Englanders and Pennsylvania Quakers particularly—confirms the connection between expansionism and the diffusion of slavery. As the equally controversial possibility of annexing Texas and fighting a war with Mexico seized the attention of the American public in the 1830s and 1840s, opponents of slavery criticized Southern expansionism. Abolitionist Theodore Sedgwick understood the annexation of Texas, whatever the reasons given in its defense, as "but another name for the *perpetuity of slavery*."[18] One Isaac C. Kenyon wrote ruefully in the *North Star* in 1848 that the United States "is at this moment spending an enormous amount of treasure and blood for the purpose of establishing in Mexico that singular kind of freedom which is the lot of her colored people at home."[19]

Recent scholarship offers a corrective to the popular notion that the "Old South" was languorous and archaic; rather, it was restless and expansive, exploiting new technologies of transportation and communication to extend its social and economic system.[20] Opponents of slavery perceived the threat that undergirded southern designs. In 1851 essayist Ralph Waldo Emerson warned his fellow New Englanders of the South's aggressive imperialism, making it sound as determined as the heartless go-ahead capitalism of the North: "But will Slavery lie by? I fear not. She is very industrious, gives herself no holidays. No proclamations will put her down. She got Texas, and now will have Cuba, and means to keep her majority."[21] A parasitical organism, slavery could not thrive—indeed, could not survive—without spreading. Slavery's demand for new territory was insatiable. The way to control and ultimately to abolish it, its enemies understood, was to check its growth.

In the 1820s and 1830s Indians blocked the way of southern expansion. Their presence on the land interfered with the purposes for which nature seemed to have destined it. Indians were distrusted because of their failure to plant cotton (and regarded with jealousy when they did) and suspected of giving refuge to fugitive slaves.[22] Tensions erupted whenever U.S. settlers, demanding the privilege of growing cotton, pressed into areas reserved for Indian nations or belonging to the Mexican republic. They expected their representatives in Washington to defend their rights. Andrew Jackson, who was not without a patronizing sympathy for his "red brothers," was more inclined to support his white constituents. Indian removal emerged as a cornerstone of Jackson's administration.

Once the Indians were gone, slavery secured the land for white ownership. Involuntary labor cleared, cultivated, and made the land profitable. Slavery's spendthrift exploitation of natural resources, and its crude designs on new territory, ever pushing against the frontier, served U.S. expansionist interests well. Borders were most effectively held not by armed patrols but by settlers plowing fields and making roads. Unlike Mexico, which had to advertise for immigrants to settle on and hold the vulnerable northern areas of Texas, Southern pioneers in the United States brought along involuntary immigrants, their enslaved workforce whose labor effectively marked territory as a U.S. possession.[23]

On occasion Southerners acknowledged their motives in coveting southwestern territory. In the wake of the U.S. War with Mexico, Albert Gallatin Brown, soon to be a U.S. senator from Mississippi, demanded, "what were we battling for, but a country to which southern slavery could be carried?" Furthermore, he continued, "if I go for the acquisition of Cuba, or for any other territory in the South, let it be distinctly understood now, and through all time, that I go for it because I want an outlet for slavery. I am for extending the area of slavery. . . . When [slaves] have become profitless or troublesome, we, too, want a South to which we can send them. We want it, we cannot do without it, and we mean to have it."[24]

Although the link between territorial acquisition and the spreading of slavery was no secret, provocative justifications for expansion like Brown's stirred up conflict.[25] Employing questionable archaeology to justify white possession of land held by Indians or Mexicans not only reflected the unapologetic racism of Jacksonian America; it was also less contentious than explicitly invoking the goal of slavery's growth. Claims of ancient white settlement of the land added a veneer of scholarly respectability and political neutrality to policies fraught with potential for disagreement. The fanciful theory that white people had once occupied the entire hemisphere continued to provide justification for conquest; once again, Latin America figured prominently in how Americans understood and talked about the politics of expansion and, by extension, slavery. Citizens of the United States annexed large tracts of land in Texas, and then went to war with a neighboring republic to acquire even more Mexican territory, while amateur archaeologists supported the proposition that the once and future United States was a white man's country.[26] By this reasoning, Manifest Destiny reestablished the integrity of a land that had been temporarily mired in chaos under Indian and then Spanish ownership.

In the 1830s and early 1840s, archaeology was just one of the expressions of this self-confidence that might have had a distinctly less bombastic tone had Americans felt the need to be more respectful of their neighbors. Patriotic Americans had an obligation to take pride in the antiquities of the continent, chided *The Knickerbocker* in 1837. "Aside from the historical interest of American antiquities, the ingenuity and magnitude of these specimens of art already discovered, are well calculated to inspire national admiration." Apparently untroubled by the fact that citizens of the United States could not take national pride in the archaeological remains of Mexico, or perhaps anticipating a not-far-off day when Mexico would be part of the United States, the author of this article included as "proof of this position" not only sites in Ohio, Illinois, Missouri, Wisconsin, and Arkansas, but also "the stupendous pyramids of ancient Mexico and Tultica, some of which exceed in dimensions the largest of Egypt; and the vast ruins of immense Tultican cities."[27] Nineteenth-century borders faded and disappeared as nationalists imagined a hemispheric empire stretching not just from ocean to ocean but from pole to pole under the control of its original inhabitants, the "Tultican" people—the Toltecs. The land formed one integral whole, awaiting reunification. "And who will say that the West shall remain dismembered and mutilated, and the ancient boundaries of the republic shall never be restored?" demanded Senator Robert J. Walker of Mississippi in a pamphlet of 1844.[28]

Politicians quickly recognized the practical value of archaeology in justifying their agendas, which often related to slavery. Many early theorists either dabbled in politics or were employed by the government. With the new presidential administration of Andrew Jackson came an excellent example of this usefulness. In 1828 voters rejected what the opposition to John Quincy Adams termed "splendid government" and elected a candidate who embodied the power of the people, the triumph of democracy.[29] The Democratic Party drew support from groups as disparate as Northern immigrant laborers and wealthy Southern planters by championing the rights of white men at the expense of blacks and Native Americans.[30] Jackson, who hailed from the West, promised to represent the interests of a constituency that felt hemmed in between the established settlements of the

Atlantic coast and threatened by the Indians of the frontier. In 1829, four years after Adams had proposed to harness the power of government for internal improvements and educational initiatives, Jackson in his first address to Congress outlined one of the proposals that would define his presidency: Indian removal to allow western settlement by white citizens (and the spread of African American slavery).

Jackson's Indian policies manifested a growing attitude that redefined the way white Americans understood not only their republican counterparts in Latin America but also the nonwhite peoples within their own borders. Whether one dates the turning point to the Panama Congress debates of 1826—the moment when Latin America was declared irremediably foreign, despite its republicanism—or to the election of Andrew Jackson in 1828, or to the utterances of the proslavery argument around 1830, white Americans began exhibiting a racially exclusive rather than politically defined nationalism in this era. In the urban North and on the western frontier, no less than in the rural South, skin color was a subject of furious conflict.[31] Historians often point to expanded access to the franchise as the pivot point when U.S. nationalism ceased being grounded in an ideological commitment to republicanism and became increasingly defined by race. A democracy that disregarded property qualifications as a prerequisite for voting also began privileging white male voters at the expense of all other members of the polity. Researches into dubious science and history justified racism and celebrated an ambiguously defined Anglo-Saxonism. A vigorous defense of slavery extolled it as a positive good rather than a necessary evil.[32]

Distinguishing the ancient peoples of Central America from contemporary Indians, much like novelists setting their stories about slavery in Latin America, allowed U.S. expansionists to put distance between their imagined New World ancestors from the people they were in the process of displacing from their homes in the Southeast.[33] The progress made by the "five civilized tribes"—the Cherokees, Creeks, Choctaws, Chickasaws, and Seminoles—who attempted to accommodate themselves to American practices had to be disparaged. Despite the fact that the Cherokees had adopted a form of government based on the consent of the governed with a written constitution inspired by that of the United States, and followed such practices as house-building, cotton-growing, and slave-owning, when white Americans looked at them their first impression was still of difference. If republican government had not been enough to make brothers of the European-descended peoples of Latin America in 1826, it was certainly not enough to render the Cherokees any less foreign to the white people of the United States in 1830.[34]

The imperative for Indian removal reveals with striking clarity the political implications of archaeological speculation. In his first address to Congress in 1829, Andrew Jackson invoked the Indians' membership in separate nations as the justification for expelling them from states that were already part of the Union. He cited the Indians' project of forming "a foreign and independent government" within the boundaries of existing states as a practice in no one's best interest. Having encountered prompt condemnation in the *North American Review*, among other places, Jackson tried another tack a year later.[35] His defense of the removal policy before Congress in 1830 had a different inflection and invoked archaeology as an explanatory tool. A racial definition of the Indian nations replaced a merely political one. Philanthropy, Jackson acknowledged, had long sympathized with the fate of the Indians. "But true philanthropy reconciles the mind to these vicissitudes as it does to the extinction of one generation to make room for another," Jackson advised. "In the monuments and fortifications of an unknown people, spread over the extensive regions of the West, we behold the memorials of a once powerful race, which was exterminated or has disappeared to make room for the existing savage tribes."[36] The Indians had themselves displaced an earlier people. Now Fortune's wheel had turned again and in the fullness of time they, the interlopers, needed to depart in order to make room for "our extensive Republic, studded with cities, towns, and prosperous farms."[37]

Quite possibly the source for Jackson's theory of cyclical displacement was political operative and archaeology enthusiast Caleb Atwater, whose "Description of the Antiquities discovered in the State of Ohio and Other Western States" had appeared in the very first *Transactions and Collections of the American Antiquarian Society* in 1820.[38] Atwater had included a copy of the *Transactions* in a letter to Jackson on June 24, 1824.[39] He speculated that ancient civilizations in Mexico and Peru might have established colonies as far north as Lake Ontario, or early civilizations in New York might have migrated to Central and South America where their civilization reached its zenith.[40] "But one fact is, I suppose, quite certain, which is, that all our antiquities belonged to the same people whose posterity was found in Mexico and Peru, by Cortez [sic]. That this people were not the ancestors of our present Indian race in the United States, seems to me a well established fact," Atwater concluded.[41] Some of his conclusions would be disputed in the 1830s, among them the idea that Aztecs were a true remnant of the earliest peoples in Mexico. But for Andrew Jackson, the "fact" that the present-day Indians were not the original inhabitants of the area but were instead transients in a long history of migration, established an invaluable defense for their displacement. "The present policy of the Government is but a continuation of the same progressive change, by a milder process," soothed Jackson.[42]

Although it is not surprising that Jackson would find Atwater's supposition useful, the Whig Party, emerging in opposition to Jackson's Democrats, was not far behind in exploiting this theory. While Democrats are generally associated with the policy of Manifest Destiny, Whigs also dreamed of a more extensive United States during the antebellum period.[43] Perhaps nowhere are the twin efforts of sundering the ties of ancient aborigines and modern Indians, and connecting the Toltecs and Mayas with the early inhabitants of North America, all in the service of vindicating U.S. proprietorship over land, so economically expressed as in a short discourse prepared by Whig William Henry Harrison in 1838 and reprinted numerous times.[44]

Two years after preparing this discourse, Harrison would ride to power as the first Whig elected president—and then sink into semi-obscurity as something of a historical footnote, dying of pneumonia on his thirty-second day in office, serving as president for a shorter time than anyone before or since. In composing his *Discourse*, Harrison drew on his experiences negotiating with Indians and his knowledge of military tactics.[45] He had a relevant background making connections with Latin America as well, having served as minister plenipotentiary to Gran Columbia in 1828–1829. (His tenure there was little longer than his presidency, arriving just before Christmas and being removed by Jackson as soon as the latter took office in March—but he made an impression, reproaching Simón Bolívar for his dictatorial tendencies in no uncertain terms.[46])

"Fifty-five years ago," Harrison explained, "there was not a Christian inhabitant within the bounds which now compose the state of Ohio."[47] Neither, aside from a few wandering tribes, were there many Indians—and yet there were earthen remains, which Harrison had examined in the 1790s, that indicated that Ohio had once been populated by a considerable number of people. Harrison projected a vision of contemporary Ohio back onto this ancient past. As described, the builders of Ohio's mounds sound remarkably

like the white pioneers of Harrison's own state—devout in religious observance, industrious in agriculture, inhabiting dwellings "ample and convenient, if not neat or splendid."[48] Harrison identified the surviving remains
as forts, with "a military character stamped upon them which cannot be
mistaken," built by engineers who "appear to have known the importance
of flank defences."[49] These people, Harrison declared, were the "Astecks."
Attacked "by a race of men, inferior to the authors of the great works we
have been considering," the Aztecs made a last stand near what is now Cincinnati, and then fled south, over time losing "in the more mild and uniform
climate of Anhuac, all remembrance of the banks of the Ohio."[50]

Having argued that the native Aztecs were driven off by a wholly distinct race of barbarous usurpers, Harrison turned to the modern Iroquois
claim to "all the country watered by the Ohio" and showed, in an argument
not fundamentally unsound, why this claim could not be sustained. He
challenged Iroquois pretensions with rhetoric of stunning ruthlessness,
seeking to prove, through the sheer accumulation of facts, that their claims
were unsupported by evidence other than their own assertions, that they
exhibited ignorance of the land they claimed to occupy, that they played
fast and loose with dates in order to strengthen their authority. Setting
the claims of other tribes in opposition to those of the Iroquois, Harrison
rhetorically carved up their empire and dispossessed them. "[T]he favored
region which we now call our own, as well as that possessed by our immediate contiguous western sisters, has been *for many centuries* as it now is, 'The
land of the free and the home of the brave,'" he concluded.[51] In his hands,
history was a deadly weapon.[52]

Harrison presented his case for white ownership of the land as a military
strategist and a politician. But his argument was one of many that came
from different perspectives and dovetailed, overlapped, and sometimes
butted up against each other in fascinating ways. A diverse assembly of
early nineteenth-century philologists, historians, scientists, and theologians
gathered around the problem of explaining the origins of the native peoples
of the New World. Not all of them were consciously proslavery, but many
of them produced arguments that were used in support of the spread of
human bondage. Some were gentlemen scholars from well-heeled
families—physicians, jurists, or professors who made a hobby of the study
of antiquities and who published their monographs for the edification of
their friends.[53] Some were amateur archaeologists who apparently hoped to

profit from their work, and presumably the more entertaining or outrageous their speculations, the larger the market share they could corner.
Thus some of the material on the aborigines was written by giddy enthusi-
asts who relied more on inspiration than observation or study. They published books that they clearly hoped would sell.

But the gentlemen scholars and the cranks shared some characteristics.
In many of their works there is a curious combination of gullibility and good
sense. Their speculations alternately drew on the authority of scripture and
on acute powers of critical observation and scientific methods. They applied
new theories they found useful, heedless of their sources, and ignored what
was discomfiting or distressing. What was posited by one antiquarian was
not infrequently applied or misapplied by someone with quite another
agenda. Most importantly, they directly or implicitly supported claims to
white legitimacy based on an assumed racial superiority. In their estimation,
their self-confidence not only vindicated their takeover of territory but their
deployment of enslaved labor. Thus, popular prejudices antedated the "scientific" racism of the 1840s and 1850s, but scientific arguments for separate
creations and new understandings of what constituted a species were eagerly
picked up by Western frontiersmen and proslavery rhetoricians.[54]

Twenty-six-year-old New Yorker Alexander W. Bradford was one of the
more respectable amateurs. After producing *American Antiquities and
Researches into the Origin and History of the Red Race* in 1841, he would go
on to become a lawyer and then a judge active in Whig politics.[55] He concluded that the ancient inhabitants of North and South America were "all
of the same origin, branches of the same race, and possessed of similar
customs and institutions. . . . [and that] the only indications of their origin,
to be gathered from the locality of their ruined monuments, point toward
Mexico."[56] The spottiness of his evidence, curiously, did not bother him:
the connection he established between burial mounds in the Ohio Valley
and pyramids in Mexico was that both are high, and manmade. Variations
between the stone pyramids of Mexico and the earthen ramparts of Ohio,
he decided, could be explained on the basis of the different construction
materials available in each location.

On the other hand, Josiah Priest was one of the amateurs who clearly
hoped to benefit from his hobby. He evidently saw no advantage in cautious
scholarship, so he made good use of a fertile imagination. The ancient
Americans he invented came from Greece and Rome. In 1837 he speculated
that the Romans might have built a fort at Marietta, Ohio, "however strange

this may appear."[57] He reported the discovery of an engraved stone that proved that "a contemporary of Aristotle, one of the Greek philosophers, has dug up the soil of Brazil and La Plata, in South America"[58] which, according to the title of his book, provided "evidence that an ancient population of partially civilized nations differing entirely from those of the present Indians peopled America many centuries before its discovery by Columbus."[59] To profit from his researches, he dispatched a team of door-to-door salesmen who unloaded more than twenty thousand copies of *American Antiquities* in thirty months.[60] A through-line connects Priest's assumptions about white superiority with his declarations of black inferiority (and the fitness of Africans for slavery). In 1851 he published *Bible Defence of Slavery; or, The Origins, History and Fortunes of the Negro Race* in which he argued, among other things, that the "pyramids [were] built by the shepherd kings, a race of copper-colored men of the blood of Shem, and not by the blacks of Egypt."[61]

In their use of archaeology to buttress the project of Manifest Destiny, white U.S. nationalists of the 1830s and 1840s thus engaged in a two-part process: drawing parallels between the geographically separated aborigines of North and Central America, the Mound Builders, and the Toltecs, and establishing that those people had been white. First, they argued that the ancient people who had left the spectacular monuments they discovered as they pushed westward were related to the people who built the great empires of Central and South America but were unrelated to modern Indians. Second, they attempted to establish racial connections, if not genetic continuities, between themselves and the original inhabitants of the continental West, and even the territory they did not (yet) control in Mexico and Peru. What had to be sundered in the present needed to be laced together in the past. These two related projects—collapsing the distance between the Ohio Valley and Central America, and severing the connections between ancient and modern Indians—were not the result of idle speculation. They provided a background for both Indian removal and the acquisition of territory in Texas and Mexico. The conclusions drawn by both scholarly and popular archaeologists frequently served the political imperatives of Indian removal and the extension of slavery no less than those of politicians like Jackson and Harrison. And so, yet again, Central and South America (and in this case the Ohio Valley too) figured prominently in the politics of slavery in the United States. This time, though, the stories were set not in the present, but rather in the ancient past.

The first of the two parts of the early nineteenth-century archaeological project reimagined the ancient continents of North and South America controlled by a common group of people. In the process, Americans found themselves looking at another map, one both familiar and strange.[62] The map of the early nineteenth-century United States was divided into East and West, the East more densely settled and broken into states, the West vast, sparsely populated, and still relatively unexplored. It was also divided into North and South: a North increasingly urban and rapidly industrializing, a South agricultural and dependent on its slaves. Boundaries running east to west separated the nation from its northern and southern neighbors. The ancient nation, on the other hand, was concentrated in the middle of the continent, its settlements stretching from the Great Lakes in the North to Chile in the South, petering out on the edges past the Alleghenies and the Cordilleras. Migrants had once pressed from the Ohio and Mississippi Valleys not west but south. To look thus at America was to see a rather different world—one that disregarded the national boundaries that circumscribed territorial migration. Nineteenth-century eyes had to be trained to look at geography this way—by excavating the earth, exploring another dimension.[63] But for those eager to see the spread of chattel slavery, the exercise was liberating.

The project of linking the Mound Builders and the Toltecs, articulated as early as the 1780s, reached giddy heights in the 1830s, boosted by access to new data.[64] Even when sources of information about ancient ruins were inaccessible, printed in Spanish in limited editions, priced beyond the means of most readers, or locked away in manuscripts in European archives, American audiences eagerly consumed the limited information they were able to sample. Notwithstanding the cost and rarity of texts like Lord Kingsborough's 1820 *Antiquities of Mexico* and Frederic Waldeck's 1838 *Voyage pittoresque*, the U.S. popular press recognized the interest in American antiquities and supplied a reasonable means of gratifying it through excerpts and reviews.[65] Newspapers and journals ran articles, both singly and in series, about antiquities in the United States and in Latin America.[66] The 1830s and 1840s brought cheaper, more accessible American efforts drawn from these sources and often trading in the outlandish or sensational.

What strikes the modern reader is not only what these early nineteenth-century antiquarians got wrong but also what they got right. There was a widespread acceptance of a migration from Asia across a land bridge at the Bering Strait, for example. But what is also striking is the felt need to justify hypotheses with textual sources rather than the geologic record. Positing the timetable generally accepted now—with the peopling of North America between ten thousand and thirty thousand years ago—was impossible for scholars trying to reconcile their theories within a biblical framework. The seventeenth-century chronology of Anglican bishop James Ussher went so far as to hazard an actual date of creation—October 23, 4004 B.C.E.—but both Johannes Kepler and Isaac Newton independently formulated chronologies with creation dates around that time, and these timetables were still accepted in the 1800s.[67] Many assumed the veracity of Noah's flood (dated to 2348 B.C.E. by Ussher), with the emergence of distinct races occurring through his three sons, Ham, Shem, and Japeth.[68]

Using human remains, some early scholars managed to pioneer new methods of observation and experimentation that subtly challenged Ussher's chronology without radically upending a worldview based on belief in the Bible. For example, by the 1830s and 1840s the new study of craniology supplied additional linkages between North and South America.[69] In the 1830s John Collins Warren, a member of the faculty of Harvard Medical School, came into the possession of a skull unearthed from a mound on the banks of the Ohio River that led him to posit that "The ancient race of the mounds is identical with the ancient Peruvians."[70] Warren was credited with being probably the first to use anatomical evidence to demonstrate the existence of "another and more advanced race having existed in the Western country previous to those who were found there at the time it was discovered and explored by the Europeans."[71]

But much better known than Warren is Samuel George Morton, a Philadelphia physician and president of the Academy of Natural Sciences, who in 1839 published *Crania Americana*, an illustrated study of skulls found in America to argue for the essential unity of race and species among all the native inhabitants of the hemisphere.[72] Morton measured hundreds of human skulls, studying and recording their dimensions and angles and filling them with peppercorns to ascertain their capacity.[73] Like many other scientists of his era, Morton, despite his hands-on techniques, was hampered by his understanding of historical time and his reliance on textual sources. Defending what would today be called essentialism, he maintained the unchanging characteristics of race through history, dating the emergence of races to the period after Noah's flood.[74] Admittedly, he insisted on the unity of human species and seemed to find "race" a somewhat problematic term for the five divisions of humanity he identified—

Caucasian, Mongolian, Malay, American, and Ethiopian.[75] The American race had not come from anywhere else; it was native to America.

Using his cranial investigations, Morton argued that the paragons among ancient Americans in both North and South America—the Peruvians, the Toltecs, and the Mound Builders—shared the same cranial characteristics "from the confines of Chili to the shores of Lake Superior."[76] Nonetheless, even in maintaining the essential unity of these people, he found it necessary to divide them into the American family and the Toltecan Family—the former debased and primitive, the latter advanced and civilized.[77] While not denying that modern Indians were related to the ancient aborigines, their Toltec blood had been adulterated with that of inferior peoples: "the mixed and motley people who now bear their names, are as unlike their ancestors in moral and intellectual character, as the degraded Copts of Egypt are unlike their progenitors of the age of Pharaoh."[78]

Morton's scholarship thus combines relatively progressive strategies of research and unapologetic, standard issue racism of the nineteenth-century variety. The kind of study he pursued and the evidence he collected would ultimately help discredit Ussher's chronology. Morton's theory even suggested the possibility that human beings had arisen in different parts of the world, an idea called polygenesis. To make such an assertion was to challenge the biblical account of creation—a challenge apparent to writers arguing from a Christian perspective.[79] Morton's theory, which unshackled science from a literal reading of the scriptures, in certain contexts appears like progress. But his conclusions about all three groups—the Caucasians, the Ethiopians, and the Americans—served to reinforce the existing order. Morton's measurements of the crania of different human types bolstered the assumption that the white race was destined to dominate the nonwhite races.[80] His concept of separate creations proved useful to proslavery authors arguing for the innate inferiority of the Africans.[81] Furthermore, these elaborate classification systems, establishing rigid racial hierarchies reaching far back into human history, clouded any vision of potential change through acculturation or instruction. The constant presentation of the race of people of color as "inferior and degraded," wrote Lydia Maria Child in the *Anti-Slavery Catechism*, "effectually rivets the chain on [their] necks," precluding the possibility of them ever becoming useful citizens.[82]

The second part of the American archaeological project, making the Toltecs white, and declaring modern Americans their legitimate offspring and true heirs, necessitated finding Old World origins for America's ancient peoples. This presumption became an essential and nearly universal premise of archaeological thought by the late 1820s and held sway for the next twenty years. The speculation that American Indian tribes were descended from Bible peoples (often the Ten Lost Tribes of Israel) already had a venerable history. Casting America as the antitype of the biblical Israel had several benefits—among them, providing a scriptural precedent for Manifest Destiny in the Exodus story's emphasis on territoriality and taking possession of the land of Canaan.[83] (The Bible also provided ammunition to the opponents of expansionism, as in David Lee Child's 1845 *The Taking of Naboth's Vineyard; or, History of the Texas Conspiracy*.[84] "Every body will understand that Naboth is Mexico, and the Vineyard Texas," wrote Edgar Allan Poe in a review.)[85] What was new was the theory that modern Indians were not simply degraded remnants of these biblical refugees but were an entirely different race whose ancestors drove off the earlier settlers. "Whatever may be our uncertainty, in regard to American antiquities, it is scarcely possible to resist the conviction that we owe them to a race, or races, other than the red men who were found by the Spaniards in the country," wrote editor William Gilmore Simms in an article tellingly titled "The White Man,—Northman or Irish,—in America."[86] According to the reasoning of the time, the very existence of their advanced civilization was proof that they could not have been the Indians' ancestors.

White Americans, whatever their hesitancy about disturbing a hornets' nest through an unwelcome discussion of slavery in the antebellum period, felt absolutely no embarrassment in discussing race, particularly in proclaiming themselves at the top of the racial hierarchy. From slave owners who automatically ascribed the uncooperativeness of their enslaved workforce to their lack of intelligence—"after being eyes ears & *head* for eight or nine stupid negroes for ten hours I feel as if my intellect could never soar above their dull incapacity," complained one Mississippi planter's wife—to scholars attempting a methodical analysis—"How else can we account for the fact, that from the earliest periods of which history presents any record, to the present day, the Caucasian variety has invariably held the same undisputed and enviable superiority over all the other races?" asked Harvey Lindsly in *Southern Literary Messenger* in 1839—white Americans unashamedly proclaimed their own preeminence.[87] U.S. law made racism legal. In the North, where slavery had been abolished, free blacks were denied the franchise. In the Old Northwest, where slavery had never been

permitted, so-called Black Laws aimed to exclude free blacks entirely.[88]
While the major political parties trod carefully around issues related to
slavery, there was nothing to be lost in exploiting their constituents' racism.
Likewise, whether those who pondered human origins argued from a biblical cosmology with a single Edenic creation and the separation of the races
after Noah's flood, or rejected the Bible for polygenist theories of human
emergence on separate continents, they were far more likely to defend
assumptions of black inferiority than to question them.[89]

The variety of contexts in which the story of the white aborigines was
repeated added to its credibility. The poet William Cullen Bryant deftly
described the eclipse of the ancient Mound Builder civilization by invading
hordes of barbarians in his 1832 poem "The Prairies," composed on a visit
to his brother in Illinois:

> . . . Are they here—
> The dead of other days?—and did the dust
> Of these fair solitudes once stir with life
> And burn with passion? Let the mighty mounds
> That overlook the rivers, or that rise
> In the dim forest crowded with old oaks,
> Answer. A race, that long has passed away,
> Built them . . .
> . . . The red man came—
> The roaming hunter tribes, warlike and fierce,
> And the mound-builders vanished from the earth.[90]

After describing the heaps of corpses resulting from the epic encounter of
the Mound Builders and the red men, Bryant's concluding lines predicted
the subsequent eclipse of the red trespassers with a new race of "Sabbath
worshippers." He omitted scenes of carnage in describing this second
encounter, or any suggestion of compulsion in the Indians' search for "wilder hunting-ground." Instead, the Agent in this second removal was divine,
as innocent of conscious intention as the act of breathing, and as full of
destiny as the inspiration of heaven: "Thus arise / Races of living things, /
glorious in strength, / And perish, as the quickening breath of God / Fills
them, or is withdrawn."[91]

Searching for forebears among the ancient inhabitants of North
America was a pastime popular enough that it could even be parodied for

its absurdity. In the short-lived journal *Arcturus*, editor Cornelius Mathews (best known for coining the soubriquet "Young America" in a speech of 1845) inquired of the Mound Builders, "Who was their great man in their palmiest day? Was he, Webster-like, of huge thews and sinews; or did he steal upon the nation in the dwarfish shape and guise of a Van Buren? Or were their politics, their parties and political divisions, based on some tomb-building question?"[92] Mathews proceeded to sketch a picture of ancient life preoccupied with nineteenth-century concerns, a sort of Jacksonian-era *Flintstones*. Although the humor was broad, the author suggested an indigenous past that corresponded with the modern Market Revolution present, down to the particulars of stock markets, charter elections, and auctions. "Tread lightly, therefore, on the fair fields of the west; for you know not what ancient and cherished echoes may be slumbering in its cliffs and riversides, nor how gently the fore-parents of us all are sleeping there!" Mathews concluded.[93] Needless to say, these fore-parents were white.[94]

Romantic speculation about "Western Antiquities" surfaced even among the female factory operatives of Lowell, Massachusetts. In the May 1841 issue of *Lowell Offering*, Louisa Currier ("Lisette") interpreted the ancient peoples as prototypes of English America's pioneers: "Were they a colony from Greece? . . . Did they, too, seek a home across the western waters, because they loved liberty in a strange land better than slavery at home?"[95] While admitting that imagination must supply what is lacking in the historical record, Currier did not hesitate to declare that "they were not the ancestors of the race which inhabited this country at the time of its discovery by Columbus, [as] appears conclusive from the total ignorance of the Indian tribes of all knowledge of arts and civilization."[96]

Backyard archaeology exploded in the 1820s, particularly wherever farmers' plows turned up bones and arrowheads. On land made suddenly accessible to white settlement by the Erie Canal, everyone turned into an amateur antiquarian.[97] Some of the most active myth-makers were Westerners on the borders of white settlement who were most apt to benefit from Indian displacement.[98] In 1825 Joseph Smith, hunting for buried treasure, announced that he had dug up curiously inscribed golden plates near his home in Palmyra, New York. According to Smith's translation of these plates, America had been settled by a group of Israelite refugees who escaped Jerusalem at the time of that city's capitulation to the Babylonians in 586 B.C.E.[99] Guided by a divine compass, they arrived at the "promised land" where they were further divided into two tribes, the Nephites, who were God-fearing and honorable, and the Lamanites, who were cursed for their disobedience with dark skin.[100] There they encountered the Jaredites, an even earlier group of immigrants, who had made an ocean crossing after the destruction of the Tower of Babel. The Book of Mormon, in other words, repeats the trope of several migrations of people distinguished by their physical characteristics and accomplishments or lack thereof. The Book of Mormon itself refrains from making a connection between the migrants from Israel and the modern Indians; nineteenth-century readers did that.[101]

In their first attempts to boost sales of the Book of Mormon, Joseph Smith and his brother Samuel promoted it as a history of the Indians. Historian Richard Bushman, Joseph Smith's biographer, finds this decision—what an early twenty-first-century entrepreneur might call branding—somewhat surprising given that "The question of [Indian] origins was not a pressing issue for New York's rural population in 1830."[102] By this moment the farmers around Palmyra encountered few living Indians in their neighborhood. On the other hand, Fawn Brodie, in her 1957 biography *No Man Knows My History*, quotes Smith's mother, who recalled how as a teenager Smith entertained his family with speculations about "the ancient inhabitants of this continent, their dress, mode of travelling, and the animals upon which they rode; their cities, their buildings, with every particular."[103] Characterizing the Book of Mormon as an account of the origin of America's indigenous peoples situated it in a familiar body of literature in the 1830s and 1840s. During a period when ideas about race were undergoing a rapid change, the Book of Mormon clung to an older view that emphasized skin color as simply a mark on the body—one that could be applied or removed—rather than an essential difference. The book of Nephi identified dark skin as a curse for disobedience, although the curse could be lifted.[104]

To rally his struggling church, Smith continued to draw upon the ancient aborigines as predecessors of his community. In 1834 when he led a group of Mormons into Illinois, they discovered an Indian mound that they proceeded to excavate, disinterring a skeleton with an arrowhead lodged in its ribs. The prophet announced that the skeleton belonged to a "white Lamanite" named Zelf killed in the last great confrontation between the Lamanites and Nephites. Heartened by this fortuitous discovery of a connection between the landscape and their sacred text, Smith's followers took these relics with them on their journey.[105]

The credibility and sophistication of American archaeology made a major advance in the 1840s through the work of travel writer, political operative, and amateur archaeologist John Lloyd Stephens, ably assisted by illustrator Frederick Catherwood. Where Stephens's predecessors studied skulls in their back bedrooms or dug up arrowheads in their backyards, Stephens made a series of comprehensive visits to the areas he studied, analyzing artifacts in situ and comparing them to the antiquities of the Old World, which he had also encountered firsthand. Although his fieldwork could be sloppy and his intentions unabashedly commercial, Stephens brought a new, less speculative approach and a more modern outlook to the study of ancient monuments in the New World. The dual projects of territorial and scholarly appropriation of the region south of the U.S. border reached a kind of culmination in Stephens's work. But by the time he completed the second of his hugely popular accounts in 1843, he began to cast doubt on some of the underlying assumptions concerning the ancient unity of the race that overspread both North and South America, and their whiteness.

Like many nationalists with an interest in the aboriginal past, Stephens, a well-connected Jacksonian, made use of his political alliances.[106] In 1839, Secretary of State John Forsyth appointed him special ambassador to Central America. This assignment was of particular interest to Stephens, who had been looking for an opportunity to explore the ancient ruins of the Americas, and who teamed up with Catherwood, an architect and draftsman who proposed to travel with him to illustrate the journey. In his official duties Stephens failed entirely; he was unable to even identify the legitimate government of the area, which was embroiled in civil war during his residence.[107] But Stephens and Catherwood were much more successful in their exploration of forty-four pre-Columbian sites with a dizzying pace that suggests latter-day tourists on a tight schedule.[108] When the publishers Harper and Brothers set a two-volume edition of *Incidents of Travel in Central America, Chiapas, and Yucatan* priced at $5 before the public in 1841, readers purchased twenty thousand copies.[109] "We know that the public expectation has been generally awakened in relation to this work; that people are prepared to find it wonderfully curious, entertaining, and instructive: such was our own anticipation; and we cannot praise it more highly than by saying that the anticipation was realized and satisfied to its full extent," enthused *The Knickerbocker* in its review.[110] Stephens and Catherwood followed this success with *Incidents of Travel in Yucatan* in 1843.

It is little wonder that Stephens's books proved tremendously popular. They dramatically convey the exhilaration of sweeping aside a veil of obscuring foliage to reveal treasures hidden for centuries. The indecipherable hieroglyphics proved, "like newly-discovered historical records, that the people who once occupied the Continent of America were not savages."[111] Catherwood's illustrations, subtly shaded and finely detailed, even now strike the viewer with their strange mystery. But if the ruins were the most memorable aspect of the books, they were set in a now-familiar context that emphasized the foreignness of Latin America, a travel narrative describing cockfights, corrupt officials, and Catholics. Any hopes left over from the days of the Panama Congress for a progressive, republican Latin America were here fully laid to rest. While Catherwood remained at his drawing board, attempting to capture the impact of the carvings in two-dimensional sketches, Stephens raced tirelessly through Guatemala and Mexico, reporting on lazy Indians, well-fed prelates, and the horrors of a "sanguinary" civil war.

If Catherwood fits the picture-taking tourist stereotype down to his omnipresent camera (which was a cumbersome daguerreotype model), Stephens can be cast as a U.S. traveler of an equally familiar stamp, the pitiless souvenir hunter. He no sooner caught a glimpse of the exotic than he expressed the urge to possess it. So acquisitive was Stephens that he conceived the idea of buying an entire ancient city, shipping it home, and reconstructing it in New York.[112] In the name of saving ancient remains he pried them from their original contexts, destroying much of what he discovered and carelessly smearing the archaeological record. When one particularly fine example of a stone mask did not yield to his attempts to dislodge it from its setting, he left it, not particularly improved by his exertions, in situ.[113] Greedily he snatched the best preserved and most perfect specimens, packed them in straw, and sent them to New York to be displayed in Catherwood's Panorama, a museum of curiosities the artist operated on Broadway. Fate itself seemed to mock the pretensions of the would-be saviors: the priceless artifacts, after surviving so many eons' exposure to the elements and a sea journey to North America, were all lost one night soon after their arrival in a devastating fire.[114]

Although the fact that so many writers investigating aboriginal origins south of the U.S. border dabbled—or immersed themselves—in politics at a time of aggressive expansionism might suggest that the projects of claiming a past and staking out territory were not entirely unrelated, the ambitious historian should no doubt take care not to suggest too definite a causal relationship between archaeological fieldwork and ruthless appropriation.[115] The elaborately worked-out myth of Anglo-Saxon superiority that eclipsed Enlightenment hopes for the assimilation of savages did not provoke Indian removal. Quite the opposite: in the nineteenth century, scholarly science caught up with the racism of South Carolina planters and Tennessean and Georgian frontiersmen.[116] In a similar fashion, archeological speculation fed on the expansionist impulse of the 1830s and 1840s as much as it nourished that impulse.[117] The repeated assertions that the Mound Builders could not have been the ancestors of the modern Indians, and that the ancient inhabitants of the Ohio Valley were one people with the inhabitants of the valley of Mexico, sounded not so much as a rallying cry as a faint but perceptible hum in the background of westward and southward migration.[118]

Except sometimes the hum erupted in a shout, or even a roar. Some outbursts, in which the claims of ancient inheritance and contemporary ownership are explicitly connected, command attention. Territorial conquests, expressions of racial or ethnic superiority, and invocations of ancient history dovetail too perfectly to be entirely coincidental. The same rhetoric that argued for the whiteness of the Toltecs justified the mastery of Caucasians over their darker-skinned slaves.

This insistence on the whiteness of the earliest Americans and the need to dispute the claims of their nonwhite usurpers arose at the same time settlers from the United States, led by Stephen Austin, began arriving in the Tejas region of Mexico. Initially responding to an invitation from the Mexican government to immigrants who could help secure the republic's northern border, the new arrivals began introducing black slavery into a region where it was officially outlawed and encouraging a movement for independence in Texas. Even as they spun fictions that supported their dubious claims to Central and South America, white politicians undermined or reversed existing policies that were more tolerant of people of color and less apologetic for slavery.[119] The irony was not lost on black Americans. In 1828 *Freedom's Journal* made the point by juxtaposing two squibs: a quote from *Ward's Mexico* headed "Slavery in Mexico" noted that the new Mexican republic outlawed importation of slaves, allowed manumission, and set a policy of gradual abolition, while a quote from the *Philadelphia Daily Advertiser* titled "Slavery at Home" described a coffle of twenty-eight slaves passing a farmhouse in rural Pennsylvania en route to Mississippi.[120]

When Mexican General Manuel de Mier y Terán made an expedition to the lands settled by Stephen Austin's Anglo migrants in the late 1820s, he made a prescient analysis of the situation, providing a striking description of the way mythmaking proved as effective as open warfare in establishing claims to territory. The Americans, he wrote, avoid "armies, battles, or invasions, which make a great noise and for the most part are unsuccessful." Rather, they simply moved in and insinuated themselves, making claims at once exaggerated and provocative that insisted on their lawful ownership of the land.[121] Lúcas Alamán, Mexican minister of the interior (and a historian himself), echoed this assessment in 1830. "[I]nstead of sending conquering armies, [North Americans] . . .begin by introducing themselves in a territory that they desire and establish colonies and trading routes," Alamán observed. "Then they demand rights that would be impossible to sustain in any serious discussion, and basing their claims on historical facts that nobody admits . . . little by little these extravagant ideas, out of repetition, become sound proofs of ownership."[122] Archaeology became the most scholarly and apparently scientific of these fictions.

U.S. settlers in Texas allied themselves with the non-Indian Tejano elite and disparaged the Indian natives and mestizos in the region. When the Mexican army led by Santa Anna (and composed, it was pointed out, primarily of Indians) tried to reassert control of the region, it was routed by Samuel Houston and his U.S. forces in 1836. Texas became an independent nation. In his inaugural address as first president of the Lone Star Republic, Houston cast the Mexicans (not the Americans) as "the base invader."[123] Although the independent Texas sought annexation to the United States, Jackson feared international condemnation for the expansionist behavior of the United States and Van Buren drew back from potential conflict with the Northern states over the extension of slavery into the region.[124]

Meanwhile, the Yucatan described by Stephens was in turmoil, a ripe fruit ready to fall into open hands. Some of his readers undoubtedly thought those hands should be American. Texans may have been most interested in his descriptions of unstable governments and officials ready to sell their patrimony or switch loyalties for the right price. In 1841, the year *Incidents of Travel in Central America, Chiapas, and Yucatan* was published, some Texans tried to lure Yucatecan rebels into secession, and contracted with them to supply three ships from the Texas navy to help keep the sea lanes open between Yucatan and Vera Cruz while they carried out the proposed war of independence. Meanwhile Mirabeau Buonaparte Lamar, president of the Republic of Texas, aided rebels in New Mexico in their breakaway project, hoping to consolidate more Mexican territory into the new Texan nation.[125]

Similarly, adherents of Mormonism found the latest archaeological findings useful in the vindication of their sacred text and land claims. The very year that Catherwood's illustrations produced graphic evidence of ancient civilization in the Yucatan, Mormon apologist Charles Blancher Thompson associated the Maya people with the Nephites in *Evidence in Proof of the Book of Mormon*.[126] A year later the Mormon newspaper *Times and Seasons* stopped just short of identifying the ruins of Quirigua as the site of Zarahemla, mentioned in the Book of Mormon.[127] Brigham Young, successor to Joseph Smith after the latter's death at the hands of a mob in 1844, led his people farther west.[128] When the Mormons finally reached the Salt Lake Valley in 1847 and Young declared, "This is the place," Utah was still part of Mexico, not incorporated into the United States until the Treaty of Guadalupe Hidalgo ended the war with Mexico in 1848. Like the Indians, the Mormons treated modern national boundaries as irrelevant, migrating according to another map.

The ultimate expression of the justification for the U.S. takeover of supposedly ancestral land is contained in the Democratic platform calling for the "reannexation" of Texas in James Polk's 1844 presidential campaign. The term has an echo of the Spanish policy of *reconquista*, through which the Iberian Peninsula was taken back from the Moors on the eve of Spain's New World exploration. (Spain's use of this term is no less dubious, since the area supposedly restored to its former glory had been a backwater inhabited by Visigoths before the Muslims arrived in 711.[129]) It also recalls a series of articles in the *St. Louis Beacon* in 1829, when Thomas Hart Benton spoke of the "retrocession" of territory improperly awarded to Spain in 1819.[130] Senator Robert J. Walker of Mississippi published a pamphlet calling for the "Reannexation of Texas" in early 1844.[131] Polk argued that he simply wished to take back what John Quincy Adams had ineptly surrendered to Mexico in the 1819 Adams-Onis Treaty that established the boundaries of the Louisiana Purchase.[132] "Natural borders"—so went the Democratic argument—trumped political ones, and made inevitable the U.S. possession of land occupied by unworthy Mexicans who were nothing like those long-dead, white Mexicans.[133] But in the U.S. context, the term reannexation would have had an even more venerable justification for Americans convinced that white aborigines had once populated the middle of the continent, only to be driven south by invading hordes of red savages.

The U.S. War with Mexico was conducted with an unquestioning sense of the nation's fitness for rule that began in the White House with James Polk's experience as a slaveholder. His determination to exact compensation in the form of land for violation of U.S. honor exposed to many Americans his motivation for going to war in the first place.[134] The Americans' ability to drive off hostile Indians sufficed to justify their conquest of Northern Mexico.[135] Particularly among regiments of volunteers who had gone to Mexico with dreams of acquiring real estate, the inferiority of the Mexican natives and their apparent racial difference served to excuse repeated atrocities.[136] If the archaeology of Manifest Destiny supplied a handy myth that would explain the presence of white Americans in Mexico, those white Americans brought with them their black slaves. In whatever disguise it was dressed, the land grab was generally nothing more or less than claiming more territory for the cultivation of cotton by an enslaved population. "Ask not my vote for peopling a new continent with slaves," wrote "One of the People" to the *Brooklyn Eagle* in 1848, then tellingly adding, "The gaze of the world is on us."[137]

But then the myth that seemed so durable began crumbling just at the moment of its seemingly greatest utility. Beneath the surface of the nation's apparent assurance, cracks appeared. Stephens's two books, for example, describe a journey not simply through the Yucatan but to a new understanding of the people he was studying. His earlier book begins with frequent references to the "mystery" of a race who "vanished," but by the end he was prepared to hazard that "opposed as is my idea to all previous speculations, . . . [the abandoned cities] were constructed by the races who occupied the country at the time of the invasion by the Spaniards, or of some not very distant progenitors."[138] His second book, *Incidents of Travel in Yucatan,* goes further: it can be read as an extended argument for the connection of the present to the past. The doggedness of the conquistadores in obliterating all traces of native history suggested to Stephens that there was a direct link between the ancient and the modern Indians that the conquerors felt a need to destroy; their very thoroughness in erasing traces of the past attested to the native vitality the Spanish had confronted.[139] Although Stephens pointed out that the Indians had degenerated from their former glories, he was the first to argue that ancient and contemporary

Indians were in fact one people.[140] A measure of his theory's controversy was its reception in contemporary reviews: *Arcturus*, for example, took him to task for inconsistency in imagining that contemporary Mexicans could have any relation to the builders of Copan and Palenque.[141]

By the 1850s, archaeologists were increasingly ready to concede the possibility that modern Indians were the descendants of the builders of the mounds and that the latter were unrelated to the Aztecs.[142] Theories linking the builders of the Ohio mounds and the Mexican pyramids did not disappear entirely, and in corners of the popular imagination Americans clung to the myth that the Mound Builders were a lost race for another half century.[143] It was not until the end of the century that the popular understanding of the ancient Americans as a race essentially distinct from modern Indians was exploded at last by Cyrus Thomas in his *Report on the Mound Explorations* of the Bureau of Ethnology published by the Smithsonian Institution.[144] But after the war with Mexico, what historian Robert Silverberg called the "great debate" over the probable origins of the Indians became less one-sided.[145]

This shift in attitude would seem oddly timed, occurring just at the moment the United States was taking possession of its vast new Mexican holdings. Several factors explain this change. Led by Stephens and Catherwood, the archaeological discipline was becoming more professionalized, making theories of scholars more cautious and the ravings of hobbyists less believable. Doing the kind of research that modern archaeology involves was costly, with some of the funding provided by the federal government. Because Congress had to vote on appropriations of funds, even well-connected writers and artists had to tread carefully and compete fiercely with one another. The resulting scholarship could be dull and badly organized, but it tended to avoid the fanciful and controversial.[146]

Furthermore, in the 1850s new printing technologies made possible the wider dissemination of visual images. News about archaeological discoveries in Latin America had previously been available chiefly in written description. "Artistic images of the Mound Builder culture of the Ohio and Mississippi Valleys are rare," asserts art historian Angela Miller.[147] Catherwood's extraordinary illustrations were singular not only for their faithfulness to their subjects but their novelty. In their wake came illustrated weekly magazines like *Frank Leslie's* (1852) and *Harper's Weekly* (1857), which brought pictures of exotic scenes, historical episodes, and current events into every living room.[148] Henry Rowe Schoolcraft's multivolume

Historical and Statistical Information Respecting the History, Condition and Prospects of the Indian Tribes of the United States (1851–1857) was illustrated with plates by Seth Eastman and other artists; Ephraim Squier and Edwin Davis's *Ancient Monuments of the Mississippi Valley* (1848) was illustrated as well. As access to graphic representations of both North and Central American antiquities became more readily accessible, a comparison of views of the ancient cities of the Yucatan and the mounds of Ohio revealed as many differences as similarities.

The U.S. War with Mexico itself, giving thousands of Americans first-hand exposure to the Mexican landscape, also made an impression. John Russell Bartlett, hired by the Mexican Boundary Commission to survey the two thousand miles between Mexico and the United States, had ample opportunity to inspect antiquities in southwest. The more he saw, the more he became convinced that the people that had produced them had not migrated from as far north as the Great Lakes.[149] He declared himself mystified about the origins of the claim that peripatetic Aztecs had made stops in North America. In an unconscious echo of Lúcas Alamán, he observed that the repetition of misinformation compensated for a lack of evidence: "This is another idea which has been so widely promulgated that it has settled down into an acknowledged fact, although I confess I have seen no satisfactory evidence of its truth. . . . No analogy has yet been traced between the language of the old Mexicans and any tribe at the north of the district from which they are supposed to have come; nor in any of the relics, ornaments, or works of art, do we observe a resemblance between them."[150]

Perhaps the best case for the connection between the needs of Manifest Destiny and politically expedient archaeological theories is the fact that alternate perspectives did not gain a foothold in the popular debate until after the War with Mexico. The heyday of Mound Builder-Toltec connections was the 1830s and early 1840s, when figures as diverse as Samuel Morton, Josiah Priest, and Cornelius Mathews were writing.[151] Only when the hazards of southwestern expansion became manifest in the late 1840s did new theories begin gaining ground. The practical problems of absorbing southern territory soured the taste for expansionism by 1846, when Northerners and Whigs protested the entry of the United States into war with Mexico.[152] In these areas the natives could not so easily be removed, and the presence of Hispanic and mixed-race people could not be explained away. "I think I should be pretty well pleased with this country if there was white folks here but there is nothing in the world could induce me to stay here among these molatto [sic] Mexicans," complained soldier William King to his mother in Virginia.[153] Since no American had ever seen a Toltec, it was possible to picture them as white, but no corresponding process of the imagination could transform the living Mexican population. As Mississippi Senator Robert J. Walker warned, "Five-sixths of the whole, by the latest estimate, are of the mixed races, speaking more than twenty different languages, composed of every poisonous compound of blood and color—Indians, Africans, mulattoes, Zambos, Chinos, and Mestizos."[154] These qualities could be invoked by both annexation's advocates—who argued that statehood would redeem these unfortunates from the tyranny of the Church (and presumably assign them to their proper social sphere)—and annexation's opponents, who despaired of incorporating such foulness into the American republic.[155]

Added to the problem of race was the problem of religion. Dislodging the stubborn roots of Catholicism in the new territory discouraged Milton Braman, pastor of the First Church in Danvers, Massachusetts, who warned that the task of annexing Mexican conquests would involve another war, "a war not against steel and military array, but a war against ignorance, irreligion, Romanism and the most formidable foes that ever assailed freedom."[156] The Catholic Church, advised Braman, stood ready to send priests and nuns to spread its errors. Were the people of New England prepared to send missionaries and pay higher taxes to foster Protestantism and republicanism?[157]

It would be difficult to establish slavery in heavily populated areas of Mexico where it did not already exist.[158] In 1848 John C. Calhoun argued that although the United States had conquered many Indian tribes, it had never incorporated into the polity "any but the Caucasian race. To incorporate Mexico, would be the first departure of the kind . . . I would consider such association as degrading to ourselves, and fatal to our institutions." Echoing remarks made at the Panama Congress debates twenty-two years earlier, Calhoun demanded of his colleagues, "Are any of you, Senators, willing that your State should constitute a member of a Union, of which twenty odd Mexican States, more than one-third of the whole, would be a part, the far greater part of the inhabitants of which are pure Indians . . . ?"[159]

With the end of the War with Mexico, the Manifest Destiny impulse stumbled.[160] The movement to acquire all of Mexico collapsed the wake of the combined Northern distrust of perpetuating the Slave Power and Southern distaste for mixing with native Mexicans.[161] The Rio Grande marked the boundary beyond which it was impossible to imagine the land as empty, where the U.S. urge for possession was forced to butt up against another group of free people who would have to be absorbed rather than dislodged. Proslavery advocates might have recognized the accuracy of the analysis of black abolitionist Henry Highland Garnet, who estimated that out of seven and a half million Mexicans, 40 percent were Indians, 40 percent were black or mixed-race, and the remaining white 20 percent were "ultra Abolitionists." White Southerners, however, would not have shared Garnet's enthusiasm: "For one I would welcome my dark-browed and liberty-loving brethren to our embrace. Aye! let them come."[162]

However fallacious, the narrative of ancient America that tied the continents together and made their original inhabitants white was repeated in countless contexts in the 1830s and 1840s. As Alamán so perceptively stated, repetition anchored fiction in the American imagination and gave the weight of fact to a story based mainly in fancy. Because so many mobile and ambitious citizens benefitted from these archaeological speculations, they showed little humility or embarrassment in their insistence that the legends were true. A good story, endlessly repeated, gave these expansionists an undeniable power. Conversely, recognizing the power of a good story also helps explain why both Northerners and Southerners dreaded open discussion of slavery. Archeologists peddled their own fiction about the Americas, North and South, in ways that spoke to, but that also differed from, those who used Latin America as a means to discuss slavery in the United States. Talking openly about a subject—framing compelling narratives, seducing with enchanted words—lent skillful storytellers great authority. To describe, to estimate, to posit origins for ancient America assisted in the U.S. project of continental domination. That same power, when applied to slavery, could destroy and divide. It was not only discussion of slavery by the federal legislature that could preserve or threaten the continuation of slavery. In 1852 Stowe's *Uncle Tom's Cabin* would demonstrate the power of convincing fiction to form opinion. But in the years before this watershed, as the next chapter will show, other novelists and dramatists would present tales of slavery in Latin American dress.

A more obscure novel suggests the way the failure to convincingly possess the past helped doom the Indians. Just as Flint's *Francis Berrian* suggests some of the ways a hoped-for relationship between the U.S. and

Mexican republics were subject to doubt and anxiety, a novel of 1829 fore-grounds issues involved in interpreting America's natives and original inhabitants. The themes of history, antiquity, and proprietorship are treated in *Tokeah, or, the White Rose* by Austrian immigrant Charles Sealsfield (né Carl Anton Postl).[163] In this fascinating, prescient novel published just three years after *Francis Berrian*, and the year Jackson proposed Indian removal, Sealsfield attempts to reconcile Indian legitimacy and the inexorability of white dominance. *Tokeah* is set in the North American Southeast, in terri-tory that has recently passed from French and Spanish ownership into U.S. hands, and depicts a universe in which whites and Indians live in worlds of divergent customs and loyalties, the map of one world overlaid upon the geography of the other. Although the distinctiveness of various Indian tribes plays a crucial role in the plot, the outline of the Indian world is inscribed with only vague boundaries: their empire stretches from Canada to Mexico and beyond. The whites are much more aware of crossing national borders; it is they who give names to the landmarks the Indians refer to only as "the big river" and "the saltlake." The lines drawn by the white men, however, both determine and circumscribe the movement of the Indians.

Sealsfield's transatlantic output was prodigious, but reliable information about his background remains elusive: his identity as Carl Postl did not emerge until after his death. Born in 1793 and ordained a priest at twenty-one, he left Europe in 1823, emigrated to New Orleans, and began publishing works, including novels and books of travel in both German and English (*Tokeah* was subsequently issued in an expanded version in German in 1833 under the title *Der Legitime und die Republikaner*). After the publication of *North and South; or, Scenes and Adventures in Mexico* in 1844 (originally published in 1842–1843 as *Süden und Norden*), Sealsfield abruptly stopped writing, dying twenty years later.[164] In his lifetime Sealsfield was compared to James Fenimore Cooper—to the latter's disadvantage—but he has since slipped into obscurity.[165]

The first volume of *Tokeah* depicts a white minority in the U.S. South-east outnumbered by Indians; the second, treating a period just a few years later, shows the Indians boxed into a white cosmos from which they fer-vently desire to escape. "The white men want only the skies and the lands of the red men," complains the title character.[166] An acute observer of politics, Sealsfield uses the rise of Tecumseh and William Henry Harrison's humili-ating 1809 Treaty of Fort Wayne as set pieces, and includes the pirate Jean

Lafitte and a clearly recognizable but unidentified Andrew Jackson as characters.

The title *Tokeah, or, the White Rose* is suggestive of two appellations for the same character; in fact, Tokeah is the Miko of the Oconees, and Rosa is the white infant he adopts. Having taken part in Tecumseh's abortive pan-Indian movement, Tokeah chafes under white treaties over which he has had no control that shut off access to his people's native lands.[167] Hope for the Indian future is represented by the vigorous young El Sol, native of Mexico and chief of the Cumanches, to whom Tokeah has promised his daughter in marriage. It is in the South, birthplace of ancient strength, that the Indians will find future refuge: "From the prairies of the Cumanchees . . . will spring the tree of liberty for the red people, . . . and the tomahawk will be buried for ever between the men of Mexico, and the Cumanches," predicts El Sol, evoking images of both interment and regeneration.[168]

Up to the end of the first volume, Sealsfield narrates *Tokeah* from the Indian perspective. To a contemporary reviewer in *The Critic: A Weekly Review of Literature, Fine Arts, and the Drama*, this volume contained "some very trashy writing. . . . The part of the story which transpires in the Indian village of Tokeah is decidedly the poorest—for it lacks the interest of proba-bility, and the style is burdened with mawkish attempts at sentiment, amus-ing only as they are ridiculous."[169] To modern readers, however, Sealsfield's treatment is notable for giving the Indians sympathetic characteristics. As Sherry Sullivan has written, such early nineteenth-century treatments are common but often overlooked in favor of portrayals of Indian barbarism and bloodlust. "At the very least, such literature reveals that in the nineteenth-century quest for national identity, the Indian's symbolic func-tion was two-fold: not only as an anti-image against which Americans dis-tinguished themselves, but also a positive image with which they sought to be associated."[170] Tokeah is more to be pitied than condemned for his hatred of the whites, and his majestic taciturnity is increasingly mistaken for a lack of anything important to say. Sealsfield writes, "his better feelings would have made him, under other circumstances and in a brighter sphere, a hero or benefactor to a greater nation."[171]

Volume 2 advances the plot to 1814 and shifts to the white perspective. Sealsfield inserts assorted justifications for white—or, more specifically, American—control of the land. In a curious scene between the Indians and an unidentified but apparent Andrew Jackson, who is preparing the defense of New Orleans, Jackson defends the conduct of the whites who are, he says, equally lawful possessors of the land as the Indians—at any rate, they are stronger. And unlike the Spanish, they did not make slaves of the Indians. Tokeah replies that the whites are spiders who have gummed up the land with their webs.[172] Though their fathers' land is fairer, the Indians prefer to find less hospitable territory far from the whites, who jealously guard their own territory but do not respect the property rights of their neighbors.[173] Tokeah and the broken remnants of his tribe will go into exile in Mexico. In Sealsfield's tale, the Indians voluntarily choose removal rather than confrontation or accommodation.

But Tokeah never escapes the United States. Sealsfield describes his end in the penultimate chapter, where Tokeah feels himself called to return once more to his ancestral lands to exhume the bones of his mother and father by night ("The light of heaven must no more behold them—they were given unto the dark, and they must be lifted in the dark"[174]). Sealsfield does nothing to mitigate the horror of this scene, where the burial ground, now passed into white ownership, has been dishonored by the plough. A barking dog indicates the proximity of the white man; a rail fence domesticates the scene; and stalks of Indian corn—apt symbol of a native plant tamed by white cultivation—lie strewn on the ground.[175] Desperate to rescue the remains of his ancestors from desecration, the elderly Indian digs furiously in the earth with bleeding hands. Sealsfield actually renders the scene with more restraint than might be expected, and it remains an affecting, if melodramatic, image. The Indian burial ground has become a cliché of modern horror movies, but here Sealsfield insists on showing it from an Indians' perspective. Even in death, the Indians are not safe from white encroachment.

Tokeah dies not of heartbreak but in a tribal skirmish that follows quickly on this scene—the Indians are killing each other. He is pierced through with an arrow while clutching a pitiful coffin crafted of pine bark and containing his parents' bones: "the author very judiciously places a hostile tribe in ambuscade, by whom he is killed in the very nick of time, just as he was found to be greatly in the way," remarked a sarcastic reviewer in *The Ariel*.[176]

Sealsfield was a Jacksonian who presumably expressed his own views as he acknowledged the inevitability of U.S. dominance.[177] Still, he was not unaware of the cost of American ambition. The last glimpse of *Tokeah*'s title character frantically trying to preserve his own link to the past makes a compelling contrast with the white settlers leveling Midwestern mounds for farming and white archaeologists breaking open hidden tombs in Mexico. The last miko of his tribe tries to properly honor the bones of his parents, disinterring them by moonlight, even as white explorers throw open ancient tumuli to the searching light of day, seeking to fabricate their own histories out of the remains they disinter. Yet Tokeah's claims ultimately stretch back no further than one generation.

With considerably less legitimacy, white U.S. nationalists reached much further back into the past, and claimed the ancient world—and the future nation—for their own. The course of slavery would be forever changed.

Chapter 3

The Problem of Slavery

"But mercy!" recalls the character Lydia Brainard on her first visit from New Hampshire to South Carolina at the turn of the nineteenth century in Sarah Josepha Hale's 1827 novel *Northwood*, "here the negroes are thick as bees . . . I trembled all over, for I began to remember the stories I had read of slaves murdering their masters and mistresses, and many such bloody things."[1] The harrowing texts described by the fictional Lydia date from the late 1700s, but by the time Hale was writing it was uncommon to encounter "slaves murdering their masters" in fiction written in the United States for a national audience of general readers. Beginning in the 1830s, enslaved characters began disappearing from mainstream American literature.

The dramatic situations in which fictional bond people might engage— falling in love or falling victim to sale, suffering abuse or rebelling, indeed any circumstances that humanized them beyond their role as willing servants—were simply too provocative for publishers to handle. Slavery's remarkable absence from American fiction between 1832 and 1852 suggests its toxicity.[2] But geographical displacement did provide an outlet for the presentation of these situations. Nowhere more strikingly than in the U.S. novels and plays of the 1830s and 1840s does the usefulness of Latin American settings as a context for the discussion of slavery come into focus.[3]

Until 1852, when Harriet Beecher Stowe's *Uncle Tom's Cabin* fundamentally transformed the literary landscape of the United States not only through its phenomenal and unprecedented sales figures but also through its graphic, if often mawkish depiction of slave life, fictional outlets for the presentation of U.S. slavery fell into two categories.[4] So-called plantation novels like John Pendleton Kennedy's 1832 *Swallow Barn* presented a mostly charming picture of Southern life that pushed African American characters to the margins, while abolitionist tales like those that ran from

THE PROCESSION.

Figure 6. Joseph Holt Ingraham's *Montezuma, the Serf; or, The Revolt of the Mexitili* was a popular pulp novel of 1845 that imagined life in Mexico a millennium before the Spanish Conquest (hence the anachronism of the horse is particularly ludicrous). The novel told the story of a slave, Montezuma, who is distracted from his rebellious activities by falling in love with a princess. By situating his novel in both a long-ago and far-away context, Mississippi author Joseph Ingraham could depict both servile rebellion and amorous relations between slaves and masters.

1839 to 1858 in the annual series of gift books called *The Liberty Bell* produced by the Boston Female Anti-Slavery Society foregrounded the conflicts of their slave characters but never reached more than a niche
audience.[5] In an era in which even Americans might have grudgingly
echoed Sydney Smith's famous challenge of the *Edinburgh Review* of
1820—"Who reads an American book?"—no author aiming for a wide
readership would intentionally alienate a sizable portion of his or her
potential audience by extensively describing, much less criticizing, U.S.
slavery.[6] If American readers brooded about the possibility of slave rebellion
or race war, if they were repulsed or fascinated by miscegenation, they did
not encounter these set pieces in U.S. literature set in the United States.[7]

But by relocating their situations from the U.S. South to Cuba or
Peru—or even to the sixteenth-century Carolina coast under Spanish
control—U.S. authors could break their silence. And they did. The caution
with which American authors avoided presenting the realities of slave life
in U.S. contexts was matched only by the enthusiasm with which they foregrounded slave revolts, doomed love affairs between slaves and masters,
and fugitives making successful escapes in stories with Latin American settings. A Latin American background supplied fiction writers with a toy
stage upon which the titillating, lurid, and shocking side of slavery could
safely be enacted. In marked contrast to the circumspection with which
they treated dramatic incidents and everyday realities of slave life in Virginia or Alabama, U.S. authors treated the cruel, the barbarous, and the
sordid aspects of slavery and race relations in Cuba and Peru with prolix
abandon. Furthermore, even ultra-Southern writers who would never
express thoughts outside the approved proslavery rulebook took up their
pens to depict whippings, rapes, and grisly murders. By the 1830s, Latin
America was so recognizably foreign territory that writers discussing slavery
were on safe ground when they set their plays and novels there.

Yet if fiction made possible subversive, or at least unguarded, critiques of
U.S. slavery, it does not follow that the impact of these texts was minimal.[8]
Citing *Uncle Tom's Cabin*, slavery's defenders were horrified when a "wholesale attack on the institutions and character of the people of the United States
is in a great measure founded on a romance, having not the slightest pretensions to truth, and no authority whatever to sustain it."[9] The antebellum
period was an era in which novels and plays served as platforms for the
examination of serious social problems. British and American literature of
the 1840s and 1850s depicted women striving for autonomy, workers seeking

opportunity, poor people struggling for survival.[10] Fiction swayed public opinion, and, as abolitionists well understood, "Public Opinion is the engine by which we hope to destroy the grievous evil that exists in our land, and to efface the foul blot of slavery from our national escutcheon," as Edwin Hubbell Chapin declared in a speech to the Anti Slavery Society.[11] Debates about contemporary problems gained resonance by being associated with compelling (if fictional) characters and exciting (if frequently sentimental) situations. Lincoln's apocryphal remark to Harriet Beecher Stowe—that she had started the Civil War through her fiction—does suggest the power literature was understood to have in forming opinion and fomenting change.[12]

It is possible to trace the indirect route by which American authors came to recognize the advantages of the literary displacement of the explosive subject of slavery into a foreign context. American authors first responded to the attractions of Latin American backgrounds because they desired to enter the international literary game when European writers seemed to be holding all the cards. The anxiety expressed by Thomas Jefferson in his 1787 *Notes on the State of Virginia*, in which he angrily responded to Abbé Raynal's charge that "l'Amérique n'ait pas encore produit un bon poëte," had grown to a chorus by the 1820s and 1830s, when U.S. intellectuals fretted about the absence of native writers good enough to be read in Europe.[13] Novels and plays would serve as ambassadors to the rest of the globe and, further, would help Americans understand themselves. "To write from a people, is to write a people—to make them live—to endow them with a life and a name—to preserve them with a history forever," declared Southern novelist William Gilmore Simms in 1844.[14] Literature was capable of containing that most evanescent of substances, the distilled essence of the American character, in a form that could be exported for worldwide consumption.

One impediment to the proliferation of American letters was feeble U.S. copyright law, which seemed purposely designed to thwart writers hoping to earn a living by their craft. Although the American Copyright Club (formed in 1843 by William Cullen Bryant and Cornelius Mathews when they were not writing poems and stories about ancient Americans) helped encourage a sense of literary patriotism, publishers who wanted the opportunity to exploit English imports proved a more effective lobby against copyright restrictions than struggling authors who argued in their defense.[15] During the antebellum period, cheap editions of English novels flooded the American market. On the other side of the Atlantic, European pirates printed American works without fear of legal retribution.[16] Many authors, discouraged by poverty, turned to professions other than writing.[17]

Furthermore, although their intention was to put their nation on the literary map, many American writers of the early nineteenth century felt compelled to follow European formulas. Unfortunately for them, the favored fictional genre in the 1820s and 1830s was romanticism, and writers were judged not on innovation but on how closely they could approximate the style of Sir Walter Scott.[18] "We little fiddle-dee-dees, his children, that are fighting for the rags of his mantle, must cut our coats according to the measure of the cloth bequeathed to us," complained U.S. novelist Robert Montgomery Bird.[19] Scott's master plot (Samuel Taylor Coleridge, in an 1820 review of Scott's work, said his subject was always the same) was the conflict between progress and reaction, which translated well during the wrenching dislocations of the Market Revolution.[20] In Scott's romances, the future always prevailed over the past, but he acknowledged the disappointments of the losers. Because the romance captures something of the complexity of social transformation, the formula resonated with American readers struggling with forces of change that seemed even more arbitrary and abrupt than those unleashed upon the contemporary Scottish Highlands.[21] But the materials from which to assemble an American romance were scarce.

James Fenimore Cooper, "the American Scott," was the first to recognize the potential of setting a romance in the New World.[22] But many reviewers overlooked the romance's thematic concerns and focused instead on more superficial conventions of setting and situation where U.S. backgrounds fell short. The crumbling castles, feudal lords, picturesque peasants, and courtly dialogue that formed Scott's stock in trade were all notably lacking in the United States. "But where are your materials for the higher order of fictitious composition? What have you of the heroic and the magnificent?" lamented W. H. Gardiner in the North American Review of 1822.[23]

Apparently the answer to Gardiner's query lay in sixteenth-century Latin America. Just as early nineteenth century archaeologists claimed Mexico and Peru for "America," writers of American fiction eagerly colonized land settled by the Spanish. The most enthusiastically reviewed romantic fiction written by Americans concerned the cavaliers and courtly manners of the Conquest. When Bird produced his novel Calavar; or the Knight of the Conquest in 1834, the North American Review reported triumphantly,

"If there is any portion of modern history, fertile in romantic and exciting interest, it is that of the conquest of Mexico by the Spaniards."[24] According to *American Quarterly Review*, Bird was the first author to recognize the possibilities of the Spanish Conquest of Mexico as a subject for romantic fiction in *Calavar*.[25] He was a Philadelphia doctor whose literary output provides a rich mine of material that demonstrates how Spanish-American contexts could be used to reflect on U.S. concerns.

Among the figures of American letters, Bird is not a giant. Nonetheless, his popularity in the nineteenth century is evidenced by his works' multiple editions, including English ones. "The general opinion of the public, judging not solely from the sale of his works in our cheap form (which in itself is a good criterion), has stamped its approbation on our judgment, that as a writer of both novels and historical romance, he is inferior only to Sir Walter Scott," enthused the London editor of a cheap anthology of abridged fiction called *The Novel Newspaper*. Bird's work appeared in this English digest alongside other new American work, all of it free of copyright.[26]

In *Calavar* (1834) Bird tells the story of a young knight who accompanies Cortés on his attempt to retake Tenochtitlan—the site of the future Mexico City—after it is lost by the Spaniards, on their calamitous retreat from the city on the *Noche Triste*, and on their final, seemingly providential victory over the Aztecs when a depleted band of three thousand Spaniards and Tlascalan allies overcame an army of fifty thousand Aztecs in the valley of Otompan. From the same events with which the historian William Hickling Prescott would construct his triumphant 1843 *The Conquest of Mexico*, Bird assembles a tale of conquest haunted by doubt. A cloud of uncertainty broods over the Spanish scramble for domination; the self-assurance of the soldiers, most of them veterans of the wars with the Moors, is scratched thin in the deserts of Mexico. Knocked from his pedestal, Cortés is not so much inspiring as manipulative, less prescient than shrewd. Don Amador de Leste, the novel's protagonist, retreats to Spain at the end of the book, chastened by the warfare in which he has engaged.

The sourness of *Calavar* hints at how the American perception of Mexico has slipped from the cautious optimism of *Francis Berrian* in 1826. Rather than introducing the rudiments of English freedom to the New World, the Spanish establish systems that will ensnare the Indians in superstition and bondage. Bird has the Spanish soldier De Morla recognize the republican instincts of the Tlascalans, a tribe of Indians who flee their subjection to the Aztecs and voluntarily ally themselves with the Spanish.

DeMorla says ruefully, "For my part, I think them rogues to love *us*, their truest enemies, better than their domestic rivals, the people of Tenochtitlan. Wo betide them, who help us to conquer their foes, when their foes *are* conquered!"[27] He predicts, with some evident shame, that the Spanish will turn the Tlascalans into slaves as soon as their usefulness as soldiers has passed.[28]

In *Calavar* Bird does not fully realize the possibilities of a Latin American setting as a way of displacing American anxieties. Despite its concerns about slavery, freedom, and tyranny, Bird does not consistently use the Mexico of the Conquest as an allegory for the early-nineteenth century United States. His evident purpose is to show that a credible romance can be assembled from American materials. In his achievement of that goal, critics of the time celebrated Bird's success in using an American setting for a romance that followed the template of Sir Walter Scott.[29] But this attempt demonstrated the viability of a setting that other novelists would use to more powerful effect.

Bird produced one more romance set in Mexico, *The Infidel* of 1835, before becoming disheartened by his inability to make a profit and abandoning the project of writing his once-contemplated series of eight Latin American novels. But Southern novelist Simms picked up the thread. Within the parameters of the romance structure, he began using the Latin American setting to comment on realities not usually discussed in fiction by Southern novelists. If Bird, a Delaware native who lived in Philadelphia, glanced at the issues of slavery and freedom in *Calavar*, Simms, a South Carolinian, treated them more directly. In his fiction with Spanish American settings, Simms rendered an extraordinary vision of slavery, threatening and explosive, more remarkable because he was a Southern author writing at a time when most of his contemporaries maintained a defensive, proslavery posture when they spoke about slavery at all.

Born outside the easy, well-to-do world of Charleston he desperately wanted to enter, Simms penned panegyrics to the Southern way of life throughout his career. He wrote not as an outsider with a clearness of vision but outsider eager for approbation.[30] His prodigious activities included authorship of dozens of novels, speeches, and essays, as well as editorship of *Southern Quarterly Review*.[31] He was, in short, an unlikely figure to frankly express his doubts about slavery, but he found an outlet for doing so in the Latin American context. In 1839 Simms published the first of his books with a Spanish American setting, *The Damsel of Darien*. The novel

focuses on the late Conquest period and Balboa's successful search for the
Pacific, what Simms (and the Spanish) referred to as the Southern Sea.
Despite the fact that Simms said that to follow European models was "to
enslave the national heart" and claimed that "it is a sort of patriotism,
amounting almost to a duty, that the American author should confine himself exclusively to the boundaries of his own country,"[32] several efforts featuring south-of-the-border backgrounds appear in Simms's extensive
oeuvre. Admittedly, Simms often wrote about the colonial period, and territory that was south of the border at the time of the events described had
already been incorporated into the United States. Simms was nothing if
not prolific, and perhaps more prolific than exacting in his craftsmanship.
Obscure now, he was heralded in his own day as a major figure of American
letters by Edgar Allan Poe, among others.[33] Simms relied on considerably
less primary research than did Bird, finding much of what he needed in a
secondary source, Washington Irving's *The Voyages of the Companions of
Columbus*.

Where Bird was unable to break out of the straitjacket of courtly dialogue to reveal realistic personalities, Simms succeeds in making his Spanish
characters more human—but to a man they are narrow-minded, craven,
and superstitious. Their lack of empathy for their fellow creatures particularly affects their treatment of the Indians they enslave. Only his protagonist
in *The Damsel of Darien*, Vasco Nunez de Balboa, while no paragon, has
enough human kindness to pity the natives of Santo Domingo, where the
novel opens. These Indians have been doubly abused, first robbed of their
land and then forced into the system of *repartimiento*, in which they must
render labor to their European overlords.

Balboa loves the scornful maiden Teresa. His hated rival for her
affections is Jorge Garabito, who administers the land of its absentee owner.
Garabito's harsh treatment of the Indians establishes his villainy. Sensing
no particular benefits in preserving the human property of his offshore
employer, Garabito exploits the Indians mercilessly, eager for immediate
profit rather than the preservation of long-term investment.[34] Lest the
reader overlook the U.S. parallels three hundred years later, Simms notes
that Garabito's position, with its opportunities for abuse, is "not unlike
that of an overseer in our own country."[35] Even defenders of U.S. slavery
acknowledged that overseers—especially Northern ones—did not always
have the best interests of the slaves at heart, but Simms goes out of his way
to draw the parallel here.

While Balboa is preparing a voyage of exploration to the Southern Sea, the Spanish settlement is convulsed by fear of a possible rebellion by the legendary Caonabo, "the cassique of one of the most valorous of all the Haytian tribes."[36] Consumed by vengeance for the wrongs suffered by his people, Caonabo slips out of Santo Domingo and goes into hiding to plot his attack on the Spanish. If Simms expected his readers to recognize intimations of contemporary overseers in long-ago Spanish slave drivers, he knew they might make even more explicit connections with descriptions like this: "There were hundreds of fastnesses among the mountains of Hispaniola, which the feet of the invaders had never yet explored, and into the recesses of which, no opponent could be found sufficiently courageous to follow a fearless band who valued liberty more than life."[37] The Haitian rebel willing to risk all for the liberty of his people: here was a figure to trouble the slumbers of the U.S. South, a terrorist to be discussed in hushed tones, not a figure for a novel. Even Stowe tiptoed around the presentation of slaves in open revolt, cloaking a scene of rebellion in the conventions of minstrelsy.[38] Writing more than a decade before Stowe, Simms dares to depict a scene of coolly calculated vengeance. Furthermore, Simms's invocation of the island from which Caonabo set out on his mission of retaliation would have sent a shiver down the backs of his Southern readers, for whom "Santo Domingo" would have stood in metonymically for the Jacobin carnage of half a century earlier.

How then did Simms manage a fictional depiction of such a touchy subject? He was a full-throated advocate of slavery and the Southern way of life.[39] Yet he introduced this terror into a work of fiction for nearly gratuitous effect. Indeed, his presentation of the possibility of servile revolt is almost casual, occurring halfway through the first volume but not finally suppressed by Balboa until halfway through the second. Evidently Simms trusted that he could present the motivations and mechanics involved in a slave revolt without so intimidating Southern readers that they boycotted his fiction.

Simms accomplishes this feat by emphasizing the foreignness of the Spanish. He begins by rejecting Irving's backhanded slap to the conquistadores who, according to The Voyages of the Companions of Columbus, were chivalrous and urbane with their fellows and only cruel to the unavenging and weak (i.e., the Indians). No, Simms says, their rascality extended to everyone; he excepts only Columbus himself from censure.[40] Spanish colonialism, writes Simms, is a "heartless tyranny that destroys where it cannot enslave"; he notes that the Indian population of Hispaniola has declined to eighty thousand from more than a million at the time of the Spanish arrival.[41] As a final indication of just how different are the Spanish from U.S. Southerners, with their fastidiousness about race, Simms has Balboa reject the haughty, treacherous (but white) Teresa in favor of the loyal Indian woman Careta, the damsel after whom *The Damsel of Darien* is named.

Simms goes even farther in depicting the patient bloodlust of slaves in another work of fiction, his "historical nouvellette" of 1842, *Lucas de Ayllon*.[42] This piece of fiction begins with a raid on what is now the Carolina coast by the Spanish in 1520. Conquistador Lucas de Ayllon, engaged in a thriving trade in slaves among the Indian population, lures the tribal leader Chiquola and his queen, Combahee, onto his ship. The queen manages to throw herself into the ocean and swim to the canoes of her subjects, who rescue her. Her husband Chiquola, denied this opportunity, jumps into the sea far from shore without hope of survival and drowns. But his widow sets her heart on revenge. She waits months until de Ayllon's ship is wrecked and he is washed ashore; then she captures him and burns him at the stake.

Simms scholar John Caldwell Guilds speculates that this tale "may well be the earliest slave-ship narrative in American literature" and points out that the depiction of experiences on board anticipates *Benito Cereno*, Herman Melville's post-*Uncle Tom's Cabin* masterpiece, by more than a decade.[43] Simms makes his slave trading villain Spanish, and inserts into the narrative the usual reproaches about the Spanish cruelty and greed for gold. The enslaved people are Indians, not Africans. But his setting is, after all, the Carolina of which Simms was a partisan, and he undergirded *Lucas de Ayllon* with enough universal truths about the horrors of slavery, the longings of slaves for liberty, and their thirst for vengeance that it is still somewhat shocking that it was published by someone so eager to say what Carolina wanted to hear. Here is Chiquola, bound on the deck of the slave ship, perceiving a route of escape: "[His eyes,] when he had concluded his unobtrusive examination of the vessel, were turned upon the shore, with the expression of an eager joy. His heart spoke out its feelings in the flashing of his dilating and kindled eyes. He was free. That was the feeling of his soul!"[44] The irony of fate that brings de Ayllon back into the power of Combahee at the end of the story is portrayed not as horror but as the working of "an overruling and watchful justice" with even nature cooperating in retribution against the slaver, the breakers seizing "upon the doomed ship, as the blood-hounds seize upon and rend the expiring carcass of the stricken deer."[45] (The bloodhounds, it need hardly be pointed out, unconsciously anticipate the most famous scene in the dramatized version of *Uncle Tom's Cabin*, when Eliza crosses the ice-choked Ohio River to escape her pursuers.)

The patient mania of slaves for freedom, and the skillful deliberation with which they might plan to secure it and take vengeance on those who deprive them of it, are hardly the usual concerns of proslavery authors. In general, Simms's work does not suggest a struggle to utter repressed home truths about slavery. But in this "nouvellette" and in some of his essays he explicitly declares that the glory of fiction is in expressing what cannot be expressed in other formats. History itself, though concerned with facts, can paint a skewed picture of reality because of what it leaves unsaid. "It is the true purpose of fiction to supply [history's] deficiencies, and to correct her judgments," he writes.[46] In this particular tale, a Conquest-era, Spanish-controlled setting allows him to comment on slavery in a fashion he would not have dared to follow if writing about the United States.[47]

Pre-Columbian Latin America also provided a context in which the less violent but no less shocking amorous relations of slaves and masters could be presented. The pulpier the fiction, the more prurient the possibilities— provided the setting was offshore. One of the more colorful examples is the work of Joseph Holt Ingraham, a Maine native transplanted to Mississippi who revered the slave society of his adopted home with the zeal of a convert (a few months before his death he published an epistolary response to *Uncle Tom's Cabin* called *The Sunny South*).[48] A writer of formidable output (in 1846 Ingraham claimed authorship of more than eighty novels and an income of three thousand dollars per annum), his short story "A Legend of the Mountain of Burning Stone" appeared in *Southern Literary Messenger* in 1839 and in a much-padded novelistic version called *Montezuma, the Serf; or the Revolt of the Mexitili* six years later.[49] Ingraham's tale imagines the foundation of the Aztec dynasty a thousand years before the Conquest through the union of a princess and a net-maker. The novel's title designates Montezuma a serf and describes an economic system in which vassals are attached to the land and owe military service to their feudal lords. But the members of this degraded class consider themselves slaves and so refer to themselves, particularly resenting the *droit de seigneur* assumed by the nobles who lord it over them. Ingraham's slaves do what U.S. slaves were feared to do: they plot rebellion with positively Garrisonian rhetoric. In the novel-length version of the tale, one slave leader points out that a million slaves need not submit to a mere thirty thousand nobles: "They have no right over our lives and liberties. Let us, then, assert them, and break those chains that shackle us. As for me, I am resolved to be free. The first blow will soon be struck. The time is ripening; and, then, when you hear me call upon you—rise, freemen!"[50]

Resolution arrives not in a bloodbath but a shower of rose blossoms: the slave and the princess fall in love. Given the dime-novel nature of the prose, the eroticism is more flimsily veiled than in fiction with higher literary aspirations. Snowy bosoms heave and fall, eyes flash with defiance, breath comes rapid. The princess deceives her father by sneaking her slave beloved into her boudoir night after night (for earnest conversations only, of course). Love between people of unequal degree is a staple of fiction through the ages ("Cupid is a true democrat," Ingraham writes), but the author goes out of his way to insist on Montezuma's status not simply as lowborn but as a slave—a seemingly deliberate choice considering the setting is clearly fanciful.[51] But it is this setting that allows Ingraham to present something truly unspeakable—an affair between a female noblewoman and her enslaved lover, which invites readers to luxuriate in contemplation of forbidden relationships of domination and submission. Here the master/slave relationship is not explicitly defined by race, although the possibilities of racial amalgamation were clearly on Ingraham's mind: in his 1841 novel called *The Quadroone* a "Maiden of a race accursed and outcast" finds "*true love* to me is but *dishonour*."[52] (And again, the backdrop for this story was not and could not be the United States—although it was New Orleans. It took place in 1769.)

In a highly original argument in *The Making of Racial Sentiment*, Ezra Tawil suggests that frontier romances of the 1820s and 1830s by James Fenimore Cooper, Catharine Maria Sedgwick, and Lydia Maria Child anticipate the racial politics of the 1850s by providing a language in which new ideas about race could be expressed. Fictional treatments of relationships between Euro-Americans and Indians, particularly those set in the colonial period, provided a less confrontational way to discuss relations between whites and blacks. And within the format of the novel, with its concerns of love, family, and inheritance, American authors could explore new concepts of the implications of racial difference. Working within the frontier romance structure, Tawil suggests, novelists demonstrated the inexorability of nature and the impermanence of culture in defining what it meant to

belong to a particular racial group. While Indians were the ostensible subjects of Sedgwick's *Hope Leslie* and Child's *Hobomok*, slavery was always an
"off-stage voice."[53]

Tawil's argument might apply in a related way to the use of Spanish-
American characters and settings as a less hazardous context for discussing
racial and religious relations that characterized the United States. Simultaneously, the distance of a Latin American backdrop or a Conquest-period
setting could provide opportunity for all kinds of experimentation. Writers
could portray native peoples who sat on jaguar thrones or battled for control of the Inca Empire with more complex shadings than what was possible
using the type of the North American savage (noble or otherwise), and
could indict Catholics more for their foreignness than for their Catholicism.
Most strikingly during a period of virulent proslavery apologias, authors
like Bird and Simms could make subversive presentations of slavery in a
South American context.

Calavar and *The Infidel* were not the first of Bird's literary efforts featuring Latin American settings; by the time he completed his novels he had
already collected extensive research on Latin America and employed this
material in preparing a script for a playwriting contest. In November 1828
he had noticed a squib in William Leggett's weekly newspaper *The Critic*
announcing that actor and producer Edwin Forrest, "feeling extremely
desirous that dramatic letters should be more cultivated in my native country, and believing that the dearth of writers in that department is rather the
result of a want of proper incentive, than of any deficiency of the requisite
talents" proceeded to offer a five-hundred-dollar prize to "the author of the
best Tragedy, in five acts, of which the hero, or principal character, shall be
an aboriginal of this country."[54]

Forrest, exactly Bird's age, had already been singled out as a national
prodigy, having made his New York premiere as Othello before his twenty-
first birthday and, according to the *New-York Mirror*, "while we were complaining that our stage was lighted only by the borrowed luminaries of
Europe, a star has arisen in our own hemisphere, which promises, ere long,
to be hailed as the cynosure of the dramatic horizon."[55] Forrest was to make
a career of defending homegrown plays, native heroes, and domestic acting
styles against those of "borrowed luminaries." His audiences rallied to his
call for national honor, most notoriously in the 1849 Astor Place Riot when
they tussled in the streets with devotees of the English Shakespearean William Macready in a brawl over rival portrayals of *Macbeth*.[56] Forrest's

nationalism had a strong flavor of Jacksonian democracy: his persona was bombastic, hypermasculine, even misogynistic, and opposed to a European acting style dismissed as fussy, dandified, and effete. He appealed to workingmen as a good fellow, and favored roles in which his character rose from obscurity to defend the people against oppression; yet the vehicles in which he appeared were always mounted to draw attention to him at the expense of the rest of the acting company, and generally presented him as leading a rabble that did not know how to act in its own best interests—in this he was a perfect type for Andrew Jackson, the man of the people who had the tendency to rule like an autocrat.[57]

Although Bird did not win the playwriting contest in 1828, his second effort, *The Gladiator*, featuring the rousing part of the rebel slave Spartacus, was more successful, winning Forrest's competition in 1831. So popular was the result—Forrest went on to play Spartacus more than a thousand times before 1854—that when Forrest's contest was held again in 1832, Bird won by submitting a play with a similar theme.[58] This time his play had an American setting—Latin American. His play was *Oralloossa, Son of the Incas*, set shortly after the conquest of Peru, a period the *New-York Mirror* claimed was familiar to every reader.[59] Although *Oralloossa* offered a variation on the *Gladiator* plot by centering on an Inca leader rallying his people against Spanish oppression (surefire with American audiences), and opened to strong reviews, with several of its speeches singled out for praise (two scenes were reproduced thirteen years later in an elocution textbook called *The American Speaker*), *Oralloossa* achieved nothing like the wild success of Bird's *Gladiator*.[60]

In choosing Conquest-era Peru for his play *Oralloosa*, Bird may have been drawing on a familiar source, August von Kotzebue's *Die Spanier in Peru oder Rollas Tod* (1796), which had been translated into English both by the American playwright William Dunlap and, much more famously, by William Brinsley Sheridan under the title *Pizarro* (1799). The central role in *Pizarro* is the valiant, self-sacrificing Rolla, leader of the Incas—a role also associated with Forrest, who appeared in productions of both the Dunlap and Sheridan translations of Kotzebue.[61] The Spanish conquistador is depicted as a brutal, heartless thug whose trusted lieutenant, Alonzo, has defected to the Indian side. Alonzo wins the heart of Rolla's beloved, Cora, the daughter of the Incas, but Rolla nobly preserves the life of Alonzo and Cora's infant—while sacrificing his own—in the climactic battle scene. The clash between the Spanish and the Peruvians forms the backdrop for the central triangle of the Indians Rolla and Cora and the Spaniard Alonzo, who in assisting the "People who never wronged the living Being their Creator formed" has "not warred against my native land, but those who have usurped its power."[62]

Now almost entirely forgotten, *Pizarro* was the second most popular play on the London stage in the eighteenth century and remained popular in both England and America in the nineteenth, performed as late as 1878.[63] (When it was presented in the social hall in Nauvoo, Illinois, in April 1844, it was the first play staged in a Mormon theater, with Brigham Young in the cast as an Inca priest who called down fire from heaven to light the altar.[64]) *Pizarro*'s theme of challenging tyranny sold well on both sides of the Atlantic, and using Spanish invaders as the heavies against an aboriginal people repeatedly described as "innocent" was a safe choice for both American and English audiences—perhaps preparing the way for audiences who would side with a put-upon Metacom/Metamora against the traitorous English colonists in countless popular plays about King Philip's War.[65]

Composing a variation on such a well-known product might be seen as an act of sheer presumption, and Robert Montgomery Bird's effort could not equal the success of Sheridan's drama. In *Oralloosa*, his version of the Pizarro story, Bird retains Kotzebue's characters—at least in their rough outlines—but keeps little of the Kotzebue/Sheridan plot (which Kotzebue had made up anyway). But what he adds, in the context of 1832 race relations in the United States, is fascinating. First, he moves the plot forward in time, to some fifteen or twenty years after the Conquest, after the Spaniards have subdued the Peruvians and submitted them to the system of *encomienda,* or forced tribute. Oralloossa (the Rolla character, his name lengthened by five additional letters and his role padded out with considerably more lines, played by Forrest) is still the main character, facing off against a corrupt Pizarro. But Oralloossa's sometime ally (the Alonzo character, here called Almagaro) is the mixed-race offspring of a conquistador and an Inca woman. Neither entirely trusted by the Spanish, with whom he is officially allied, nor the Indians, Almagaro is torn between competing desires, alternately joining the Inca and the Spanish sides. Finally, the Cora part in Bird's play is Ooallie, Oralloossa's sister and Almagaro's lover. Almagarao's love for her sways him to the Peruvians, but his attraction to the power of the Spanish leads him to betray her ("Why weigh the value of a poor maid's life/Against the golden balance of a crown?").[66]

The play opens with the arrival of Vaca de Castro, a representative of the Spanish monarch, alarmed by rumors of Indian rebellion. Having heard about "The pagans rising from their servitude," de Castro asks about "the Indians,—/ Their mountain risings?" Francisco de Alcantara, Pizarro's uncle, reassures him that "our slaves [are] submissive and contented." Oralloossa, rightful heir to the Inca throne, indeed had plotted an insurrection.

> Millions of brown barbarians join'd his standard,
> And fear beset us in our citadels:
> Scarce could our strongest garrisons resist him;
> And, with his war-word ringing in our ears,
> *Extermination for the Whites*, he rush'd
> Like a swoll'n torrent, roaring from the hills
> Upon our fear-throng'd city.[67]

But the danger has past, de Alcantara assures de Castro, because Oralloossa died, the rebellion evaporated, and the Indians were left leaderless.

This identification of the Indians as "brown barbarians," this racialization of a people their enemies in Sheridan's *Pizarro* refer to only as "heathens," and innocent ones at that, this grim evocation of incipient conflict between slaves and masters, are new with *Oralloossa* in 1832. The period in which Bird was writing was still reeling in the wake of Nat Turner's Rebellion, in which the slave leader similarly called for the extermination of the whites in rural Virginia in August 1831. Turner's conspiracy, rather than inspiring the reformation and limitation of slavery, catalyzed strongly repressive regulations to suppress uprisings through the silencing of any speech or text deemed incendiary. Bird was certainly aware of the Turner Rebellion—it occurred shortly before the premiere of *The Gladiator,* and he mentioned it in his private diary, reacting to the indiscriminate massacre of whites with condemnation and noting the contrast between his own hero and Nat Turner.[68] In *Oralloossa*, Bird conjures an atmosphere, thick with treachery and paranoia, that evokes the contemporary United States. "We have been slumbering on a volcan's brink," says Almagaro.[69]

Undated notes and drafts of *Oralloossa* reveal that Bird considered various positions for the "Extermination for the Whites" speech in the text (in one draft it appears in two places), assigning it to various characters, apparently to gauge the effect. In some versions the rumor of Oralloossa's planned revolt is a fabrication of Almagaro to weaken Pizarro's power; in other drafts the conspiracy is real.[70]

Within this context, and despite his ambivalence about the nobility of a slave rebel, Bird provides a complex and compelling portrait of slave psychology. Despite the assurances of de Alcantara, Oralloossa is not dead. He lives in the viceregal palace in the guise of Pedro, slave to Pizarro. Playing the role of trusted chargé d'affaires for the viceroy involves particular indignities. As Pedro, Oralloossa is assigned a most unsavory task: Pizarro has imprisoned a Coya, daughter of the Incas, and wishes to make her his mistress. He gives Oralloossa a chest of jewels to win the Coya's love. "What, for her love!" exclaims Oralloossa. "Is she not then your slave?"

"Let her not think so," begs the besotted Pizarro. Oralloossa quickly realizes the Coya for whom he has been asked to play pimp is his sister, Ooallie.[71] Bird's insight in imagining this situation—the humiliation of a male slave forced to act as go-between in the sexual submission of his sister, the concupiscent master who demands not simply sexual submission but love—is remarkable. No doubt variations of this scene, at once horrific and matter-of-fact, played themselves out on countless real-life plantations in the antebellum United States, but could seldom be so frankly represented in literature. The extraterritorial setting made it possible.

Life in the palace does give Oralloossa access to useful skills like literacy and secrets like the recipe for gunpowder (an interesting detail, as Nat Turner also mentions experimenting with its manufacture).[72] He awaits the moment he can throw off the guise of a servant and assume his rightful status as a leader. He lives for the shedding of Spanish blood and the destruction of the Spanish city. When his dreams of revenge are finally thwarted, and he acknowledges that he must surrender his natural feelings of self worth, he concedes: "I was an Inca once, and should be yet; / That was a dream: I was a man, and should be; / But that was madness." Bird imagines the inner turmoil of a slave caught between illusion and reality: "Like the fool, that lies / On earth and rags, and dreams his soul inhabits / The golden-canopied chambers of a palace,—/ So lay I on my bleak and flinty floor, / And built me gorgeous nothings."[73]

The role of Oralloossa must have been a challenging one to play; certainly it would have demonstrated Forrest's virtuosity if he could carry it off convincingly. Oralloossa cringes before Pizarro, rebukes his sister, fulminates in soliloquies. He prevaricates, he hesitates, he changes his mind and shifts his strategies. Feeling always superior to the base-born Iberians before whom he must kowtow, proclaiming his loyalty to Spain and his belief in Christianity even as he tries to subvert the Spanish regime, the tormented Oralloossa embodies what W. E. B. Du Bois will call double consciousness. Almagaro, son of a Christian father and Indian mother, would seem to have more cause for dramatic schizophrenia, but it is Oralloossa who, forced to assume the guise of a slave, rages with humiliation at his servitude and betrayal by his own people. At the end of the play, traduced by Almagaro, who had promised to help him recover his throne, he murders his betrayer near the corpse of his sister Ooallie. His words give no hope of racial rapprochement. "Thy blood is mixed with mine," he cries, not because both he and Almagraro literally share Peruvian blood, but because he kills Almagaro and then dies himself; their mingled blood runs together on the stage.[74]

What did audiences make of this drama of a royal prince reduced to the status of a slave? Did they make the connection between U.S. slavery and the fictional world of *Oralloossa* that seems so transparent now? Did Bird intend this apparent subversion? Sometimes the use of metaphor to discuss an otherwise taboo topic seems so obvious as to be unmistakable. For example, few Americans could have missed the contemporary overtones about interracial sex in Shakespeare's *Othello*. Nonetheless, the play was staged twenty times in Memphis and forty times in Mobile in the twenty-five years before the Civil War, though it dropped out of sight after 1865.[75] "In a nation wrestling with great issues, Shakespeare's works allowed Americans to express views that may otherwise have been hard to articulate—or admit to," writes theater historian James Shapiro.[76] Similarly, it appears neither author nor audiences were unaware that they were watching what was called a "servile war" in *Oralloossa*. Certainly the racial identity of the Peruvians was apparent. The epilogue of the play refers to the Incas as "brown children of the sunbeam."[77] One reviewer remarked on the incongruity of fair-skinned actress Mrs. Barrett playing Ooallie: "How comes it, however, that she is so 'passing fair?' her brother Oralloossa is certainly a little dingy."[78]

While other evidence related to the conception and reception of *Oralloossa* is scanty, telling clues survive for Bird's earlier play, *The Gladiator*, also with a set piece of servile revolt. While anxiously awaiting the premiere of *The Gladiator* in 1831, Bird wrote the following paragraph among his private musings. It is usually excerpted to highlight Bird's racism and apprehension about slave insurrection.[79] Racist Bird certainly was, but when quoted at length, his meditations have a different emphasis:[80]

Our theatres are in a lamentable condition, and not at all fashionable. To write for, and be admired by the groundlings! villains, that will clap most, when you are most nonsensical, and applaud you most heartily when you are most vulgar! that will call you "a genius, by G . . . ," when you can make the judicious grieve, and "a witty devil," when you can force a woman to blush! Fine, fine, fine, fine. But consider the freedom of an American author. If *The Gladiator* were produced in a slave state, the managers, players, and perhaps myself into the bargain, would be rewarded with the Penitentiary! Happy States! At this present moment there are 6 or 800 armed negroes marching through Southampton County, Virginia, murdering, ravishing, and burning those whom the Grace of God has made their owners—70 killed, principally women and children. If they had but a Spartacus among them—to organize the half million of Virginia, the hundreds of thousands of the states, and lead them on in the Crusade of Massacre, what a blessed example might they not give to the world of the excellence of slavery! what a field of interest to the playwriters of posterity! Some day we shall have it, and future generations will perhaps remember the horrors of Haiti as a farce compared with the tragedies of our own happy land! The *vis et amor sceleratus habendi* will be repaid, violence with violence, and avarice with blood. I had sooner live among bedbugs than negroes.[81]

Bird here slips from frustration to cynicism to deep irony to fear and finally to what appears to be simple racist hatred. As an American author writing for popular audiences, he complains, he cannot express his concerns directly. His frustration arises from his awareness that he cannot tell the truth ("consider the freedom of an American author"): slavery is a horrifyingly dangerous enterprise, promising profit but concealing the real probability of destruction. Bird understands slavery as evil not because it victimizes slaves but because it threatens masters and white people generally. But the stupidity of the groundlings, who wish only to be entertained, and their unwillingness to recognize how they themselves slumber "on the volcan's brink" proscribe what he can say. Bird lacks the "freedom" to depict slavery's horrors directly. He must present them through metaphor.

Nineteenth-century art and music indulged in what historian Charles Sellers, in a particularly memorable phrase, referred to as a "romantic orgy

of self-indulgent evasion."[82] As a way of denying the soulless reality of marketplace economics, Americans of the Market Revolution whitened the sep-
ulcher of capitalism with the chaste and godly through their taste for
hymns, sentimental poetry, and gothic architecture. On the other hand,
they were hardly strangers to the subtleties of reading art as allegory, particularly where slavery was concerned; Sculptor Hiram Powers's fabulously
popular 1844 nude statue of *The Greek Slave* and John Greenleaf Whittier's
1843 poem "The Christian Slave" drew parallels between Turkish and
American bondage.[83] At least one reviewer recognized *The Gladiator*'s contemporary relevance. In the *Brooklyn Eagle* in 1846, Walt Whitman
remarked, "This play is as full of 'Abolitionism' as an egg is of meat. It is
founded on that passage of Roman history where slaves—Gallic, Spanish,
Thracian and African—rose against their masters, and formed themselves
into a military organization, and for a time successfully resisted the forces
sent to quell them."[84]

A final strong connection between rebellious Incas and U.S. African
Americans should be mentioned.[85] Besides Forrest, another notable inter-
preter of Rolla, the Oralloossa figure in *Pizarro*, was the "African tragedian"
Ira Aldridge. It was in this role that he made his debut in 1822 in an all-
black production of the play in New York and in which he continued
appearing until at least 1860.[86] Aldridge's biographers Herbert Marshall and
Mildred Stock did not hesitate to propose that "Aldridge must have identified the conquered Peruvians with his own conquered and enslaved people."[87] Aldridge performed for white audiences in London, but in the
United States he typically appeared at black theaters like New York's African
Grove—not part of the circuit of entertainments generally patronized by
white audiences the way Harlem Renaissance nightclubs would be a hundred years later, but not entirely unknown to whites, either.[88]

On the other hand, it is possible that audiences for the kinds of dramas
Forrest favored—which featured underdogs battling a corrupt system—
were seeing parallels with their own wage slavery, not identifying with their
brothers of color. When they cheered a bondman's revolt, they cheered the
destruction of government by the elite. They were good Jacksonians, and
they applauded Forrest, their surrogate and favorite actor, when he
appeared in roles that featured him stripped to the waist like a prizefighter,
battling tyrannical masters.[89] After all, the same working-class audiences—
not otherwise sympathetic to Indian removal—roared their approval for
Forrest's denunciations of the white man in his role as Metamora.

This argument, however, partakes of a surprising degree of snobbery, suggesting that, because of their working class affiliation, Forrest's claque could not see beyond its own narrow interests. Although most of Forrest's roles shared a common denominator of working-class patriotism, the character of Oralloossa does not fit this category easily.[90] What motivates him is less love of his people than furious personal indignation and ambition, and when his duplicitous uncle tries to steal his thunder he actually plots with the Spanish to have his revenge on his Peruvian enemies. Moreover, in *Oralloossa* Bird insists on the racial specificity of the Peruvians, who are not simply set apart by their lack of Christianity, literacy, or European civilization, but by their complexions. De Castro, the royal visitor determined to suppress the slave rebellion in *Oralloossa*, claims the "authority to rule" like a proper tyrant, but his enemies are explicitly characterized as "brown assailants"; there is no overlooking the fact that this slave rebellion has been carried out by dark-skinned forces.[91] However much the "slavery" of the Peruvians seems like an ambiguous sign, there is no mistaking their color, particularly in a period increasingly attuned to racial difference.

In the United States of the 1830s there were real rebels like Oralloossa, and rumors of others. Most terrifying of all, perhaps, after Nat Turner, was David Walker, who published *An Appeal in Four Articles, together with a Preamble, to the Coloured Citizens of the World* (1829). Walker wrote in the time-honored American tradition of the jeremiad, in which he mourned slavery as an evil blot that stained American society. Surely God would punish a people who did not recognize in their slaves their common brotherhood in Christ. Yet Walker did not scruple to encourage slaves to act on their own behalf, and with impunity. "[M]y object is, if possible, to awaken in the breasts of my afflicted, degraded and slumbering brethren, a spirit of inquiry and investigation respecting our miseries and wretchedness in this Republican Land of Liberty! ! ! ! ! !" wrote Walker.[92] Spanish America figured into Walker's argument as proof that God's wrath would not slumber forever. Once the envy of the other nations of the earth, Spain and Portugal had been reduced to irrelevance.[93] "[One] can easily recognize the judgments of God among the Spaniards. Though others may lay the cause of the fierceness with which they cut each other's throats, to some other circumstance, yet they who believe that God is a God of justice, will believe that SLAVERY is the principal cause."[94]

Walker, an educated free black man living in Boston, had died under mysterious circumstances in 1830, but his provocative tract lived after him, particularly after the abolitionist William Lloyd Garrison began discussing it in the *Liberator*, proposing to send it to influential residents of the South in the mid-1830s. It took little to persuade Andrew Jackson's postmaster general, Amos Kendall, to intercept copies of Walker's inflammatory work that were sent through the U.S. mails. Despite the fact that these "incendiary" and "seditious" materials were addressed to whites, and most slaves were illiterate, the call to revolt was too charged a sentiment to be circulated freely.

American novelists generally seemed no more inclined to foreground slavery in their fiction than Amos Kendall was to distribute critiques of it through the mail. Abolitionist literature was another story, but its agenda was considerably different and its market obviously narrower. Lydia Maria Child, for example, wrote a series of short stories for an abolitionist publication called *The Liberty Bell*, including "The Quadroons" (1842) and "Slavery's Pleasant Homes" (1843) depicting exploitative relations between white owners, black slaves, and their mixed-race offspring. (In 1851 Harriet Beecher Stowe launched serial installments of her novel in a similar publication, *The National Era*, before its notoriety allowed it to cross over into the mainstream.) Antislavery poet Whittier went so far as to make Toussaint Louverture the subject of a flattering poem published in the *New-England Magazine* in 1833.[95] But both Northern and Southern novelists hoping to avoid controversy and appeal to a national audience tended to keep their discussion of slavery bland and polite, and slaves in minor roles.[96] These mainstream depictions of slavery are in stark contrast to the situations depicted in Latin American settings.

By contrast, European novelists surveying the American scene of the 1830s and 1840s felt none of this constraint. Slavery often figured as the very pivot of the plot of their U.S.-situated fiction. Three of the best-known visitors of the period, most famous for their travel accounts, also wrote novels in which slavery appeared with all its wretchedness. Their narratives turn on the vexed issues of abolition, torture, miscegenation, and slave rebellion. Frances Trollope, whose much-hated but much-read bestseller *Domestic Manners of the Americans* (1832) sold thousands of copies, anticipated *Uncle Tom's Cabin* by fifteen years in her virulent abolitionist effort *The Life and Adventures of Jonathan Jefferson Whitlaw* (1837, reissued under the title *Lynch Law* in 1857 after the publication of Stowe's novel). Harriet Martineau's more measured and less sensational travel account *Retrospect of Western Travel* (1838) did not win the popularity of Trollope's work, but her novel *The Hour and the Man* (1841) matched Trollope's in abolitionist fervor: it was a piece of fiction that presumed to represent the rebellion of Toussaint Louverture in Saint Domingue. Finally, Gustave de Beaumont, the traveling companion of Alexis de Tocqueville, produced *Marie; ou, L'Esclavage aux Etas-Unis, Tableau de Moeurs Americaines* in 1835, a novel that featured a white man in love with a light-skinned woman of color. None of the three books, which give centrality to the theme of slavery, achieved wide readership in the United States (*Marie* was not translated into English until 1958, and only *The Hour and the Man* was published in the United States or widely reviewed at the time of its publication).[97]

U.S. fiction particularly avoided discussion of slave revolt.[98] The most significant exception is Richard Hildreth's 1836 *The Slave or Memoirs of Archy Moore*, which Hildreth published as a first-person slave narrative. In the novel two victimized slaves shoot an overseer in cold blood and establish a fugitive colony with some other runaways. Though they are subsequently captured, Archy manages to escape to the North where, rather than being "conscience stricken" by his role in the overseer's murder, he lives secure "with that lofty feeling of manhood vindicated . . . which animated the soul of the Israelitish hero."[99] But Hildreth's work is the exception that proves the rule. He presented it as a slave narrative rather than a work of fiction and printed it himself since no publisher would touch it (some seven thousand copies were sold).[100] Reviewers ignored it except where they condemned it for "sustaining and impelling dangerous excitement."[101]

In the United States, servile insurrection could easily be imagined as race war, its horrors engulfing not only the slave South but the free North. In his *Liberator* editorials, Garrison painted slavery as a national crime, and imminent slave revolt as a national peril.[102] His editorial on Turner's Rebellion, published in the *Liberator* on September 3, 1831, just a few weeks after it occurred, suggests how easily the incident could be painted in lurid colors: "The first drops of blood, which are but the prelude to a deluge from the gathering clouds, have fallen. . . . You have seen, it is to be feared, but the beginning of sorrows. All the blood which has been shed will be required at your hand," wrote Garrison. "Wo to this guilty land, unless she speedily repent of her evil doings! The blood of millions of her sons cries aloud for redress!"[103]

Even moderate Americans feared such rhetoric would inflame the enslaved populace and took steps, both legal and extralegal, to silence it. Publishing texts critical of slavery became increasingly difficult in the

South, and was discouraged in the North as well. In 1833 James G. Birney, at that time a slaveholder in Alabama, submitted a series of eight essays to the *Huntsville Democrat*. Although he recommended colonization rather than immediate abolition, his opposition to slavery was clear: he described it as a hydra crushing the manhood of the United States. The first few articles were reprinted in other slave-state newspapers, but editors soon began declining to publish them, and finally the *Democrat* refused them as well. "The Alabama press was closed to Mr. Birney," recalled his son.[104]

When Birney moved north and began publishing his own antislavery paper called the *Philanthropist* in Cincinnati, concerns other than the possibility of slave rebellion motivated a group of local merchants and hoteliers to demand its muffling in 1836. If the city acquired the reputation for abolitionist activity, Southern visitors who had once escaped the oppressive heat of their plantations for Cincinnati hotels might fear that their enslaved attendants would run away. Three of Cincinnati's four newspapers, with varying degrees of implicit threat, urged the silencing of Birney's paper and its supporters, some of whom were numbered among the city's elite: "*A word of advice to Messrs. Ludlow, Price, Donaldson, &c.*—Publish no more cards or addresses about midnight invasions. Eschew the society of James G. Birney. Avoid him as you would a viper. Mind your affairs. . . . If any of you are foreigners we would advise you, most especially to be silent on the subject of slavery." The squib concluded darkly with the admonition, "*Verbum sat.*"[105]

While the slavery apologists contented themselves with a word to the wise, Birney and the executive committee of the Ohio Anti-Slavery Society framed their response in terms of freedom of the press. "To discontinue such a paper under existing circumstances, would be a tacit submission to the exhorbitant [sic] demand of the South, that Slavery shall never more be mentioned among us."[106] A year later, in Alton, Illinois, a vigilante group threw the printing press of abolitionist Elijah P. Lovejoy into the river and then murdered him.[107] Meanwhile, a mob in Philadelphia, outraged over antislavery speeches by abolitionist women, torched Pennsylvania Hall in 1838.[108]

But these proscriptions against publicizing the realities of slavery could be safely evaded in the production of U.S. fiction as long as Latin American slavery was the ostensible subject. Veiled comments about nineteenth-century slavery and race relations set in Latin America at the time of the

Conquest were twice removed from contemporary realities, both geographically and temporally. The romantic setting of the Spanish Conquest both allowed U.S. authors to compose fiction in the dominant style of the 1820s and 1830s and to make comments about contemporary U.S. slavery while doing so. The pastness of the Conquest setting, besides seeming tailor-made for the fashionable genre of romance, made even potentially volatile subjects like revolt less immediate.[109]

But by the late 1830s and 1840s the romance was, if not falling out of fashion, certainly competing with other forms of fiction, primarily novels treating social problems and everyday situations.[110] Meanwhile novelists of the so-called American Renaissance—Herman Melville, Nathaniel Hawthorne, and Edgar Allan Poe—pioneered developments in themes, storytelling, and effect that bore a recognizably American imprint.[111] But even as American literature matured in the 1840s and 1850s, and writers began producing work native in style as well as in setting, they continued to set works dealing with the realities of slavery in Mexico, Peru, and Cuba. Some writers dared to approach the realities of their own time simply by moving the location of their fiction offshore without simultaneously drawing the veil of history. A decade after the Panama Congress, Latin America was considered so different from the United States as to make temporal displacement unnecessary.

Even Americans intimately familiar with Latin America were prone to disparaging generalizations. Former chargé d'affaires in Colombia Beaufort Taylor Watts, asked about the people of Mexico in 1841, admitted he had never been there. "I can only reason therefore from analogy, and draw conclusions from having resided in Colombia," he wrote. While his impression of the Colombians was of a "mild and courteous" people, he did not hesitate to assume that the Mexicans were "jealous, vindictive, and without moral honesty."[112] Complimentary descriptions alternated with scurrilous ones: naval officer Allen Izard called Lima "one of the finest cities I ever saw . . . far superior to any of our cities in the United States," but dismissed Rio as "one of the filthiest places that I ever saw the streets are lined with monkey's & negro's, they are so much alike that you can hardly tell them apart."[113]

Published descriptions of Central and South America in travel accounts were similarly unflattering. Despite their aboriginal antiquity, these regions appeared raw and unfinished to American visitors. Governments were

shaky and leaders unstable. Authors of fiction fell back upon these characterizations constantly. "[Y]ou know the proverb all along this coast—
'Corrupt as Lima.' It but bears out your saying, too; churches more
plentiful than billiard-tables, and forever open—and 'Corrupt as Lima,'"
complains a Peruvian ruefully in "The Town-Ho's Story" in Herman Melville's *Moby-Dick* (1851).[114] Americans internalized these images: in a
Thanksgiving reflection, nineteen-year-old New Yorker Edward Tailer
noted in his journal that he was grateful for living in the United States
rather than in "distracted Mexico" or "those stagnant solitudes, the republics of South America."[115]

A major trope for distinguishing contemporary North and South
America was religion: Protestant United States was orderly, logical, and
law-abiding; Catholic Latin America was venal, emotional, and messy.
Rosamond Culbertson's *Rosamond: or, a Narrative of the Captivity and Sufferings of an American Female under the Popish Priests, with a Full Disclosure
of their Manners and Customs, in the Island of Cuba* (1836) provides a good
example of the way the foreignness of Latin America was presented in religious terms.[116] It can also be read as a slave narrative.

While anti-Catholicism was expressed in American letters before the
Jacksonian period, it increased markedly in virulence after 1830 when,
thanks to growing immigration from countries with large Catholic populations, nativists began to perceive Romanism as more of a threat to American values.[117] Anti-Catholic tracts had a strong flavor of xenophobia,
offering a nightmarish vision of nations where Catholicism reigned and
conjuring foreign conspiracies reaching out to strangle American democracy.[118] Maria Monk's *Awful Disclosures*, set in Canada, was the giant of the
genre, possibly the most widely read contemporary pre-1852 imprint in the
United States.[119] Having these narratives take place within a foreign country
permitted authors to cite specific locations that could not easily be checked
by American readers and quote witnesses not easily contacted for corrobo-
ration. Cuba proved particularly effective as a setting that allowed readers
a vicarious wallow in the luxury of institutionalized decadence, providing
access to the exotic aesthetic pleasures for which sober Protestants have
traditionally condemned and envied Catholics: deep-dyed velvets and gauzy
silks, shadowy cloisters echoing with Gregorian chant, guttering tapers,
attar of roses and clouds of incense.

Rosamond Culbertson's *Rosamond* did not ascend the giddy heights of
notoriety reached by *Awful Disclosures*, but it was popular, first appearing

in serialized form and then as a book, with a second edition issued only weeks after the first to satisfy reader demand.[120] Culbertson's narrative draws extensively from the common midcentury stereotypes of Cuba, trading in descriptions of "the ball room, the masquerades, the gambling tables, and the tea-parties."[121] Her captivity begins with her straying from the strict upbringing of her New England Protestant family and moving to New Orleans, Louisville, and finally Cuba, her respectability suffering with each stop on her journey south. Once in Havana, "I became acquainted, through one of my female friends, with a Spanish priest, named Manuel Canto, and commonly called Father Canto, who . . . made me an offer to take me under his protection; and I consented to live with him, not knowing, at the time, that he was a Priest."[122] Canto sets Culbertson up in a house and has her instructed in "the *Champara* language, which is a sort of Creole Spanish, half Spanish and half African," and a fitting metaphor for the mongrel existence to which he introduces her—luxurious and penitential, clerical and secular, promiscuous and repressive.[123] The picture she paints of Cuba is of all-pervasive hypocrisy where everything is performance. When Canto has to travel, he takes Culbertson along with him as a companion, also engaging "an *Alcowater*," (which Culbertson helpfully translates as "a pimp") to travel with them and disguise the true nature of their relation.[124] The most lurid revelation of *Rosamond* concerns the efforts of a priest who, in exchange for a hefty pay-off, wins a reprieve for a gang of Spaniards, Frenchmen, Italians, and Portuguese who have been kidnapping black slaves and grinding them up for sausage meat.[125]

Rosamond Culbertson's narrative echoes a venerable American genre. Indeed, her title gives a clue to an inspiration for this class of literature: her *Narrative of the Captivity and Sufferings* owes a great deal to the narratives of Indian captivity, like Mary Rowlandson's *Narrative of Captivity and Restoration*, which had been so popular in the eighteenth and early nineteenth centuries.[126] Again an unprotected female is subjected to the terrors of a hostile culture, threatened with various depravities and hardships, and released at the end. Not coincidentally, the captivity narrative is, finally, another way of talking about slavery. Culbertson is a sex slave. Although it is highly unlikely that she wrote with any abolitionist intention, she would not be the first author to represent slavery within the kidnapping-and-captivity context of sexual bondage. The theater historian Heather Nathans posits that Bird's 1828 *The City Looking Glass* includes the character of a white woman sold into an undesired union "as a substitute for the city's

[Philadelphia's] free blacks, who, like her, were victimized by unscrupulous villains and who also lacked legal protection and recourse."[127] In any event, the carnivalesque inversion of white slavery was conceivable only in an upside-down world like that south of the U.S. border.

This geographical difference worked as well as historical distance in rendering a discussion of taboo topics acceptable. Even in the present, it was unimpeachably established that Latin America in no way resembled the United States. Therefore, books published in the United States could present even the inflammatory subject of slave rebellion so long as it featured Spanish American characters or took place offshore. (Recall that it was Harriet Martineau's novel of Saint Domingue, rather than Trollope's or Beaumont's fictions set in New Orleans, that Harper and Row chose to publish.) For example, while literary treatments of the Turner revolt were hushed up in 1831, within a few weeks of the Spanish slave ship *Amistad* being discovered off the coast of Long Island under the control of its African rebel crew in August, 1839, a play appeared at the Bowery Theatre called *The Long, Low, Black Schooner*.[128] While little survives of this "Nautical Melo-Drama" except its playbill, the exclamation point-scattered sheet, with its list of characters and scenes, probably gives a pretty fair idea of its contents: "The slaves, led by Zemba Cingues, force the hatchway! Mutiny and Murder! . . . Inez [daughter of the ship's captain] the captive of Zemba Cingues—Her terrible doom . . . 'No you don't,—the Yankees are on board of you—Boys and all, here they come!' "[129]

The Slaver: A Tale of Our Own Times, a novelette that appeared in *Graham's Magazine* in three installments in 1847, seemingly demonstrates the outermost limit to which it was possible to present slavery in a mainstream publication (as it happened, one that featured light literature aimed primarily at a female audience).[130] With enough plot developments to fill a work twice or three times as long, *The Slaver* features not one but two slave rebellions, one onboard a slave ship and one on a plantation, complete with attempted rape (as well as two shipwrecks, two marriages, and a duel). The author insists on an up-to-date context for his tale (or relatively up-to-date; it is set in 1835). While fiction writers who go back to the sixteenth or seventeenth century "have a more widely extended field for the play of their imaginations," he writes, they lose in the process the immediacy of a story set in the present. But significantly, while the author eschews the distancing device of a period setting, he moves his story offshore, to the island of Cuba, where the African slave trade was acknowledged to continue. The events he describes are as near as the shores "of the same ocean, that laves with its salt waters the shores of our own happy land," and the slaver of the work's title is in fact one Charles Willis, a U.S. citizen, but the Latin American setting provides scope for the kind of events not usually presented in North American settings.

Willis's profession is frankly presented as despicable, but perhaps as much for its lack of respectability as its inhumanity. (Willis is untroubled by the slaves' plight. After a run-in with a man-of-war, "several of her men, and a number of the negroes, who had suffered from their compact position, had been killed. Willis was so rejoiced to find his masts safe that he did not mind the other damage.")[131] The squalid conditions of the factory and slave ship are duly presented, but Willis himself is cast as no worse than the classic bad boy of sentimental fiction, disowned by his rich family and determined to go to the devil until he falls in love with a good woman whom he saves from the aforementioned attempted rape ("struggling violently in the grasp of two huge, swarthy, and half naked negroes, armed with machetas, or sugar-knives, [was] a young girl, in white . . . their aim did not seem to be murder").[132]

While clichés about Cuba are kept to a minimum—there is a scene in a gambling house but not at a cockfight, and fewer prayers to the Holy Virgin than are common in this type of literature—the author presents enough details to estrange his story from the U.S. experience. It is clear, for example, that the sugar plantation where the rebellion occurs is not a model of U.S. efficiency and benevolence. The plantation owner has left it insecurely supervised. Furthermore, the slaves, by virtue of being African natives, are clearly wilder and more vengeful than those, like the slaves in the U.S., reared in the condition of servitude. Willis finds the overseer bound "and gagged with his own whip . . . [he] said the only reason they spared his life was because the Obi man wanted to have a grand Feteesh that evening, and offer him up as a sacrifice." The American Willis has no difficulty taking matters in hand. "Accustomed to deal with refractory negroes, [he] soon restored order on the plantation."[133]

The author, "A Son of the Late Dr. John D. Godman" (Godman *pere* had written an 1826 book on natural history), was Stuart Adair Godman, a Cincinnatian by birth who grew up in Baltimore.[134] Anointed by *Graham's* a successor to Cooper and "one of the best, if not the best writer of Nautical Romances now living," the *Southern Literary Messenger* eulogized him on his death as "a martyr to the cause of Southern Letters."[135] Yet in the *Slaver* his attitude toward slavery is inconsistent to say the least. The horrors of the middle passage figure, but the hero is also allowed an exculpating speech: "'Tis true, I have been guilty of bringing negroes from Africa to this island. But wherein am I thereby more guilty than you? Do you not eagerly buy them as soon as landed; and so hold out the temptation to bring them?"[136] In fact, what appears inconsistent in this presentation of slavery may be an accurate representation of the antebellum period's clumsy compromises and overreaching justifications, to wit: slavery is bad, but so are other labor systems; slave trading is a dirty business, but the profits of slave labor are clean enough; slave rebellions threaten the institution, but arise from African troublemakers rather than American-born bond people.

But consistency was not apparently of much concern to this author, nor to his readers, who according to *Graham's* "warmly received" the story.[137] The Cuban setting allows the presentation of an it-can't-happen-here perspective. In ways that would be developed much more extensively by apologists for slavery in the 1850s, Godman suggests that the precariousness of the slave system in Haiti, Brazil, and Cuba proved nothing about the risks slavery posed in the United States. Through better organization and more merciful treatment, the U.S. South had conquered the potential hazards of the system. The South was safe. Spanish America had always been different.

After the Compromise of 1850 the possibility of maintaining the silence about slavery became more difficult. The Fugitive Slave Act and the publication of *Uncle Tom's Cabin* opened the floodgates of antislavery literature. In quick succession appeared Frederick Douglass's *The Heroic Slave* (1853), William Wells Brown's *Clotel* (1853), and Martin Delany's *Blake* (1859). Melville's haunting *Benito Cereno*, published in installments in *Putnam's Magazine* in 1855, concerns an American sea captain who fails to understand that the Spanish slave ship he encounters in the open sea is under the control of the slaves.[138] Southerners raged that the works of Stowe and her successors stirred up hostility and disturbed the national peace.[139] Further, by airing the nation's differences, they damaged the reputation of the United States in the eyes of the world.[140] In response, Southern authors aggressively marketed "anti-Tom" fiction that, no less than the object of their criticism, moved the institution of slavery and the enslaved character out of the wings and onto center stage. The search for anti-Toms even led *The Southern Quarterly Review* to extol the memoir of a real-life refugee from Saint Domingue who had accompanied his former mistress to New

York and supported her: "Pierre Toussaint was better than Uncle Tom, for he was a good man, and a good christian, and not a sable saint or angel, sent to mock humanity with such virtues as it can never reach."[141]

But in the pre-*Uncle Tom* days of the 1830s and 1840s, the need for nationalists to avoid frank discussion of subjects like the mistreatment and sexual exploitation of slaves, the threat of rebellion, and the possibility of amalgamation was considered imperative. Under these constraints, Latin America served as the perfect screen on which to project the secret fears and fantasies of the antebellum United States. Here was an area that shared its colonial past, its mix of Europeans, indigenous peoples, and African slaves—but a very different place, whose very lack of definite shape lent it to all sorts of imaginings. Setting novels and plays in Latin America allowed a thorough exploration of the unthinkable to hide in plain sight. In her study of the way artists from the United States represented the Latin American landscape during this period, the art historian Katherine Emma Manthorne describes Latin America in its relation to the United States as "its surrogate or underground self."[142]

At the same time, the foreignness and exoticism of Latin America, whether explicitly declared or implicitly assumed, served as a distraction from the growing sectionalism of the period. The superiority of the United States to Latin America was a unifying bond stretched over the fracture between North and South. The fragility of that bond, however, was apparent to anyone paying attention. Two speeches given within a year of each other—one by the novelist William Gilmore Simms in Alabama and the other by the politician Daniel Webster in Massachusetts—illustrate the way Latin America was held up as an example of real difference, to remind citizens of the United States how much they had in common. Meanwhile, both Simms and Webster uneasily attempted to define the characteristics of the entire nation in terms of their own particular sections. Their characterizations anticipate the regional inflections Northerners and Southerners would use in talking about themselves through Latin America in the late 1840s and 1850s.

In December 1842 Simms was invited to Tuscaloosa, where he gave an address called *The Social Principle; the True Source of National Permanence* before the Erosophic Society of the University of Alabama, then only eleven years in existence.[143] The "university" where he spoke was at the time little more than a few slave-built structures housing a total student population of fewer than one hundred perched on the Alabama frontier, the ragged selvedge of the Cotton Kingdom, where it must have been quite a coup to secure the presence of the well-known author.[144] Curiously, considering its setting, Simms chose as his theme "national permanence," at once a denial of the inexorable imperative of expansionism and a condemnation of it. After dutifully acknowledging the ability of the early Tuscaloosa pioneers to wrest order out of chaos, and to quickly adorn their rude new settlement with the institutions of civilization, Simms proceeded to characterize the U.S. identity as defined by its love of home. He did not understand home as something an American carries with him or her, like a turtle its shell: he meant one's native soil, and he insisted that it was their devotion to that soil that made Americans who they are.

Simms found the source of this devotion in the English origin of the early colonists. Not so very long before, three powerful nations, England, France, and Spain, had contested for the rights to the North American continent, but two had utterly failed. Why was English the language of the United States, rather than the "sonorous language of the one nation, or the courtly dialect of the other"?[145] Why were U.S. churches not filled with the "gorgeous and imposing rites of their peculiar religion"?[146] The three nations crossed the Atlantic, said Simms, in quest of different ends, the French and Spanish for gold, or slaves, or conquest, but the English only for a home.

The French and Spanish had failed in their quest not because their designs were too grand but because their goals failed to unify the colonists. On the other hand, the English social principle, shared and acknowledged from Vermont to South Carolina, was this "domestic feeling," this commitment to the "humble processes of comfort."[147] *The Social Principle* fused together the colonies without government backing or money, indeed in the very absence of these resources.[148] A man's homestead was "*his own* . . . his little *peculium*," said Simms, using the Latin word for private, as opposed to common, property.[149] The Declaration of Independence, he argued, was more concerned with "the repose and security of society, rather than . . . that elementary principle of human equality, which the instrument begins with declaring."[150]

What makes Simms's oration such a curious text is its sentimental characterization of English colonies united, despite their apparent differences, by a common love of home. In *The Social Principle* Simms seems to be visibly struggling to construct a past that denies both national expansion and the rise of sectionalism. Delivered in a raw settlement in Alabama in the restless 1840s, his invocation of sacred home ties seems a lovely lie. Nor was this contradiction lost on Simms's contemporaries: in a review of the speech, *Southern Quarterly Review* noted dryly, "Had the ruling passion of our ancestors been the love of home, they would have remained where they were."[151] Simms's very choice of word for the private property to which, in contrast to their Spanish and French peers, all English settlers were so devoted—their "little *peculium*"—is likewise freighted with its association to the English cognate "peculiar," applied to that very institution that was stirring up sectional controversy.

In the 1840s, Simms was moving from national allegiance to ardent sectionalism.[152] Whereas at the beginning of the decade he was insisting on a common heritage for all the United States, by the end he would be increasingly committed to Southern nationalism. In 1849 Simms would become the editor of *Southern Quarterly Review*, the South's answer to New England- and New York-based journals like the *North American Review*. Even the idea of a common English ancestry for the original thirteen colonies would be questioned: increasingly, Southerners like Simms insisted that they were the descendants of chivalrous, generous Anglo-Normans, as opposed to the cold-hearted and calculating Anglo-Saxons who begat the unscrupulous Yankee strain of tinkers and peddlers.[153]

Some six months after Simms delivered his address on the Alabama frontier, Daniel Webster, fresh from serving as U.S. secretary of state, delivered a far more famous oration on Breed's Hill on the Massachusetts coast—the 1843 Bunker Hill oration.[154] Eighteen years earlier he had spoken at the groundbreaking ceremony; now the 221-foot granite obelisk was complete. Here sixty-eight years earlier the first shots of the American Revolution were fired, a year before the goal of separation from England was articulated in the Declaration of Independence.

Webster's theme was that America's past was all Americans' common property. After acknowledging the contributions of the great and the lowly to the erection of the monument, Webster inserted a curse: "Woe betide the man who brings to this day's worship feeling less than wholly American!" Webster insisted, "Union, established in justice, in patriotism, and the most plain and obvious common interest,—union, founded on the same love of liberty, cemented by blood shed in the same common cause,—union has been the source of all our glory and greatness thus far, and is the ground of all our highest hopes. This column stands on Union."[155] Webster's words recalled his Second Reply to Hayne of South Carolina during the period of the nullification crisis thirteen years earlier.[156] Yet Webster implicitly denied the intent to provoke, preferring instead to find a common identity among the colonists of the area that became the United States. Nonetheless, his characterization, consciously or not, privileged the New England stereotype over the Southern: the settlers of North America, he recalled, came looking for liberty and made sure it applied everywhere; came in family groups, bringing a love of home, and, in words that must have waved a red flag before any Southern listeners or readers, facility for "arts and manufactures" and a "middle class" sensibility.[157] Webster attempted to fit Sir Walter Raleigh halfheartedly and unsuccessfully into this paradigm and acknowledged that there may have been variances between the settlers of New England and Virginia, "but only enough to create a pleasing variety in the midst of a general family resemblance."[158]

Before becoming detained in the mire of equivocations, Webster clambered onto firmer ground by detailing how such insignificant differences paled beside those between the Spanish and the English colonists. As opposed to the individual initiative that had settled North America, he said, it was royal decree, enabled by force of arms, that had brought the Spanish colonies to heel. Settlers came lusting for gold, "not produced by industry, nor accumulated by commerce, but gold dug from its native bed in the bowels of the earth, and that earth ravished from its rightful possessors by every possible degree of enormity, cruelty, and crime."[159] Three hundred years later, Webster claimed, the differences were still visible in the contrast between an industrious, liberty-loving people in the United States who "govern themselves by reason"[160] and a collection of countries south of the border held together by force and characterized by ignorance and disparity of wealth. Webster focused on the ways Latin America fell short of the U.S. ideal. His words of 1843 contrasted jarringly with those of the oration he delivered eighteen years earlier, in honor of the beginning of the monument's construction. In 1825, just before the Panama Congress, he had looked on the new republics full of hope of a "new creation": "The southern hemisphere emerges from the sea. Its lofty mountains begin to lift themselves into the light of heaven; its broad and fertile plains stretch out, in beauty, to the eye of civilized man, and at the mighty bidding of the voice of political liberty the waters of darkness retire."[161] By contrast, in 1843 the light of republicanism guttered in South America: "Yonder is a volcano, flaming and smoking, but shedding no light, moral or intellectual. . . . The city is filled with armed men; not a free people, armed and coming forth voluntarily to rejoice in a public festivity, but hireling troops, supported by forced loans, excessive impositions on commerce, or taxes wrung from a half-fed and a half-clothed population."[162]

For both Webster the Northerner and Simms the Southerner, casting about for a unifying principle to acclaim on behalf of the entire nation, the division wrought by over-rapid expansion was difficult to deny. In the face of growing sectional differences that would only intensify over the next decade and a half, both speakers realized the value of contrasting a superior United States—free, rational, home-loving—to an inferior Latin America, held back by force and bigotry. Even as other regional differences widened, the idea that the English settlers had in them something that made them different from, and superior to, their Spanish (and French) contemporaries, would continue to operate in the 1840s and 1850s. Nationalists in both the U.S. North and the U.S. South would still define themselves against a foil of credulous, tyrannical, chaotic Latin America with its adulterated racial composition. But as the United States moved closer to civil war, the language in which the North and the South expressed their respective comparisons with Central and South America would fall on the ear with noticeably regional accents.

Present in the audience at the dedication of the Bunker Hill monument in 1843, specifically acknowledged by Webster, was William Prescott, a Massachusetts judge of great local renown. Sixty-eight years earlier his father, Colonel William Prescott, had built a "redoubt" and commanded the fort against the soldiers of the Crown. Webster did not mention Prescott's forty-seven-year-old son, William Hickling Prescott, who was quietly making a name for himself as a historian, having published *The History of the Reign of Ferdinand and Isabella* in 1837. The summer of Webster's oration, Prescott was getting ready to publish his second book, which would bring him an international reputation and allow him to easily eclipse the fame of his father and grandfather. That book, *The History of the Conquest of Mexico*, applied the romantic conventions of fiction to the writing of the past to stunning and indelible effect. It was immediately recognized as an immortal work of American history, though its subject was not the United States. But like the fiction writers he admired, Prescott would comment on the United States even as he wrote about Latin America.

Chapter 4

Conquest and Reconquest

In February 1846 the *American Whig Review* took notice of a new novel, *Montezuma: The Last of the Aztecs*.[1] A curious conflation of the romance-of-the-Conquest and the veiled anti-Catholic genres, *Montezuma* depicted an Aztec priest who conspires with Hernán Cortés in the overthrow of native Mexican rule.[2] Its author, Edward Maturin, had dedicated it to historian William Hickling Prescott, whose *The History of the Conquest of Mexico* had taken the United States by storm three years before and whose scrupulous research had provided invaluable background for the novelist. (With a dedication to Prescott that typically collapsed the distinction between the United States and Spanish America, Maturin expressed the wish that "the history of your country may long continue to be enriched by your pen."[3]) The *Whig Review*, along with many other reviewers, was enthusiastic.[4] Maturin's choice of subject "has introduced his readers to what should be claimed by approbation, as an exclusively American field—for, in a *Literary* sense, at least, 'The whole boundless continent is ours.'" The *Whig Review* went on to exult the Manifest Destiny of the United States to claim the cultural past of the whole New World: "The legendary and historical wealth of this entire hemisphere should be made ours by the bloodless conquest of the Pen. It is a duty we owe to our literature, and each pioneer in a new field should be greeted with kindness."[5]

The "boundless continent" quote, originally from a 1788 epilogue written by American Jonathan Mitchel Sewall to Englishman Joseph Addison's Revolutionary-era blockbuster drama *Cato*, was something of a cliché in the mid-1800s.[6] Park Benjamin had appended "The Whole Boundless Continent is Ours" to the masthead of his paper *The New World* in the early 1840s.[7] John O'Sullivan cited the line in a February 7, 1845, *New York Morning News* editorial called "More! More! More!"—demonstrating that

Figure 7. William Hickling Prescott depicted Cortés's conquest of Mexico in the glowing tints of romantic fiction, and many of his readers rushed to enlist in the U.S. War with Mexico in order to participate in the "Second Conquest." Prescott himself grew increasingly glum about the war. "We ride on conquering and to conquer, as you see, right up to the very halls of Montezuma," he wrote R. C. Winthrop, 30 May 1847, "and many, I should think from the positive manner they speak of them, expect to find the palace of the old Aztec still standing." Print Collection, Miriam and Ira D. Wallace Division of Art, Prints, and Photographs, The New York Public Library, Astor, Lenox and Tilden Foundations.

Figure 8. "Like Cortez, finding myself isolated and abandoned; and again like him, always afraid that the next ship or messenger might recall or further cripple me—I resolved no longer to depend on Vera Cruz or home, but to render my little army 'a self-sustaining machine,'" wrote General Winfield Scott, comparing himself to his *conquistador* predecessor. Carl Nebel's illustration for George Wilkins Kendall's 1851 book *The War Between the United States and Mexico, Illustrated* shows Scott entering the central square of Mexico City. Milstein Division of United States History, Local History & Genealogy, The New York Public Library, Astor, Lenox and Tilden Foundations.

the rallying cry of Manifest Destiny, which O'Sullivan first called by name in the July–August issue of the *Democratic Review*, drew upon a long tradition of expansionist self-confidence.[8] By limiting the possession of "the boundless continent" to the "*Literary* sense," the *Whig Review* in effect thumbed its nose at the ham-fisted, jingoistic cries of the Democrats, who were at that moment preparing to engage in a war with Mexico that would extend the territory of the United States by some 30 percent. Nevertheless, the *Whig Review* was not quite prepared to surrender all applications of Manifest Destiny. Episodes from the Mexican past furnished excellent sources for U.S. fiction that could be tapped without pangs of conscience. The *Whig Review* insisted that the "Literary" sense of conquest was justifiable. The vast wealth of the historical record of the first Europeans in America (although they happened to be Spanish and dominated an area far from that occupied by the United States in the era of the early republic) ought to be "claimed by appropriation, as an exclusively American field."[9]

But the implied distinction between the bloody lust for land and the "bloodless conquest of the Pen" was not quite as clear as the *Whig Review* would have it. The reprehensible snatching of territory and the apparently acceptable seizing of ideas were not so easily disassociated.[10] One type of conquest bled into the other. U.S. appropriation of the story of the sixteenth-century Spanish Conquest coincided with a second conquest of Mexico by the United States three hundred years later at Vera Cruz, Monterey, Buena Vista and finally Mexico City itself in the U.S. War with Mexico that began in 1846, the year the novel *Montezuma* appeared. That Whig William Hickling Prescott most memorably achieved the North Americanization of these events from Spanish history is just one of the ironies of the situation.

Another is that for nearly a century after his death, Prescott was considered above the fray of vulgar politics.[11] "Of Mr. Prescott's political opinions there is little to be said," declared George Ticknor, Prescott's friend and first biographer, in 1864.[12] Ticknor characterized his subject as more of a leftover Federalist than a member of any contemporary party. The biographer pointed to Prescott's friendship with Whig Edward Everett, Democrat George Bancroft, and abolitionist Charles Sumner, figures from three points of the political compass, as evidence that Prescott was apolitical.[13] An alternate, and equally valid, interpretation might consider that Prescott was in fact deeply interested in political issues even if he was not a strident member of one particular faction. For his part, Ticknor, while filling his biography with Prescott's correspondence, avoided quoting exchanges that dealt with issues like slavery and territorial acquisition.

Prescott was a quintessential example of a well-bred, well-read, well-informed Northerner who never raised his voice when airing his anxieties about slavery in public. In private, he was not above occasional expressions of the prevailing racialist assumptions and prejudices of his age. But his inquiries into the history of Latin America freed him from the constraint that ordinarily bound him and allowed him to say what would otherwise have made him enemies, or at least lost him readers. Even more, he sometimes went out of his way to draw connections between race relations and slavery in the era of the Conquest and in his own time. Prescott's predecessor in writing about the Conquest was Washington Irving, who produced the 1828 *History of the Life and Voyages of Columbus* and its sequel, the 1831 *Voyages and Discoveries of the Companions of Columbus.* Irving had made his reputation with *Knickerbocker's History of New York*, which went much further than Prescott in presenting characters and situation from contemporary politics in the Dutch accents of seventeenth-century New Yorkers.

In fact, Prescott's three great works, *Ferdinand and Isabella*, *The Conquest of Mexico*, and *The Conquest of Peru*, can be read as an extended meditation on the career of the early American republic, with admiration for the bravery and resourcefulness of the first settlers and disgust with the internal disagreements that propelled them toward civil strife. Prescott actually encouraged this kind of analysis: he often described situations of nation-building and conflict and then stepped out of his narrative to point out parallels with the present, particularly in relation to issues of race, slavery, and religion. Examined in this way, the reader recognizes the arc of Spanish florescence and fading, from the consolidation of Spain under the *reyes catolicos* to civil war among their contentious subjects in their far-flung colonies, as prefigurations of the achievements and potential perils of the United States. Prescott's mood, as evidenced by his literary memoranda and correspondence, reflected a similar darkening as the implications of U.S. expansionism become apparent between the early 1830s and the early 1850s.

Despite his protestations that he "dealt with political discussions only when they related to events and persons at least two centuries old," Prescott kept up-to-date with current events.[14] In 1852 he wrote to an English friend, "A book has come out here lately which has made a good deal of noise, from the picture it gives of slavery in our Southern & Western States, by a lady, the wife of a Calvinist clergyman, who lived many years among these people. I have myself read rather more than a hundred pages, & found it very interesting—and I think you will find it difficult to read it with a dry eye."[15] That he was moved by the injustices of slavery depicted in *Uncle Tom's Cabin* did not make him an abolitionist. But even as he was writing his history of Peru in the mid-1840s, he betrayed a growing restlessness about the failure of the United States to address the expansion of slavery. During the years when Prescott published his best-known books, the vicious suppression of slavery talk that characterized the late 1830s subsided somewhat, perhaps because Americans were distracted by other concerns, perhaps because they did not need reminders of the high price of raising such a sensitive topic. As Prescott charted the career of the Spanish empire in America, with its absorption of land and its effacing of native populations, his histories reflected a growing distress about the path trod by his own country.

Prescott can even be understood as a personification of the unwillingness of the Whig party to confront the issue of slavery head on, particularly as such reticence became increasingly difficult to maintain in the 1850s.[16] His brooding disenchantment with the mechanics of conquest and the ability of the Slave Power to withstand opposition surfaced forthrightly in his work between 1843 and 1847—but not so forthrightly that they troubled readers with opposing political views. His graceful, seductive prose allowed his critiques of contemporary slavery to be accepted, or perhaps overlooked.

A final irony is that just as Prescott wrote at a particular moment when the United States seemed to be fulfilling the destiny anticipated by its earliest explorers and, more troublingly, repeating some of their errors, his reading audience interpreted his work in the evolving climate of the breathless Second Conquest of Mexico, finding in his history precedents that he himself would not have sought. They ignored the devotion to "principle" espoused by the conquistadores and identified too readily with their quest for plunder. But Prescott's readers also cultivated some of his tolerance and argued, in the sense of the word most gratifying to historians, with some of his conclusions.

Hundreds of thousands of Americans have become conversant with the history of the Spanish in America through Prescott's masterpiece, *The History of the Conquest of Mexico* (1843), and its successor, *The History of the Conquest of Peru* (1847).[17] In the journal *Hispania*, scholar John E. Eipper credits Prescott with legitimating the study of colonial Latin America in the U.S. academy and for identifying the central texts in its canon.[18] In a 2009 edition of selections from Prescott, historian J. H. Elliott acknowledges Prescott's limitations—over many of which he had no control—but concludes he turned many of them into sources of strength, "reducing the story to an epic drama with poetic and melancholy overtones, [and making] it unforgettable for generations of readers."[19] The flowery prose can seem overblown today—all of "Prescott's forests have a tendency to be 'verdant' rather than green"—but his work has an undeniable dramatic power and visual impact.[20]

Although Prescott's histories are quintessential products of their time, they are still in print. He anticipates trends in history that would not fully develop for another century: long before the social history of the 1960s and 1970s, he attempted to include the common people as agents in his narrative.[21] Though lacking the cliometrical tools used to tell the story of voiceless groups, he created space on his stage for Indians and women.[22] He never heard of the cultural turn of the late twentieth century, but he attempted to include literature as evidence ("Could not the war of Granada be much vivified by drawing the popular opinions, attachments, sufferings &c, &c of the Moors, from the old ballads? Poetry itself becomes unexceptional testimony in regard to these circumstances."[23]) Like an environmental historian, he considered the role of diseases like malaria and smallpox in the Conquest; he lamented the exploitive impact of colonizers on the well-husbanded landscape of the natives.[24] And as Eipper notes, his self-conscious deployment of sources—footnotes at the bottom of the page offering contending interpretations, biographies of his predecessors set off in agate type at the end of chapters testifying to their subjectivity—"create a parallel narrative which enters into a dialogic relationship with the main text—in effect, metahistory deconstructs history."[25]

Through a past overgrown with tall tales and dubious evidence, Prescott is the ideal guide: broadly knowledgeable, generous, self-assured. The grandson of a hero of the American Revolution and the son of a judge, he grew up knowing security and comfort. His confidence is clearly born of privilege; his Back Bay Boston breeding and Harvard education seep through every syllable. He is a gentleman accustomed to being listened to and taken seriously; there is none of the pleading self-importance that sometimes creeps into the writings of William Gilmore Simms, for instance. Yet for all Prescott's noblesse oblige, he displays no smugness. Prescott assumes his readership shares with him a receptive rationality, an absence of prejudice or superstition. While it is true that he writes with a kind of omniscience that presumes that there is no higher type of man than a Boston Brahmin, he makes clear that he will welcome all into his library, though he may reserve the perusal of the rarest manuscripts and the consumption of the rarest sherry for men of his own class.

The reality of William Hickling Prescott is a bit more nuanced. The easy grace with which he writes, the wealth of sources he cites almost casually, betray the crabbed labor that went into the composition of his work, for Prescott suffered from a serious visual impairment. Nearly losing sight in one eye after being struck by a crust of bread in a Harvard food fight in 1813, he experienced compromised vision for the rest of his life.[26] (One of the doctors he consulted was John Collins Warren, the amateur archaeologist whose pioneering studies of skulls linked the Mound Builders to the aborigines of Peru.[27]) He depended on a series of hired and volunteer secretaries who read aloud to him and took notes. To write, he employed a device called a noctograph, a frame strung with wires running in parallel lines and placed over a sheet of carbon paper.

His biographer C. Harvey Gardiner insists that Prescott's vision problems form a compelling legend, but the actual dragon he had to slay was not blindness but indolence and surrender to social temptations.[28] Although his biography is studded with references that are code for a specific kind of privilege—a grandfather in the consular service, membership in Harvard's Porcellian Club, summers at Nahant—he lived a life of rigorous discipline. As with John Milton, the blind poet who undertook the similarly ambitious task of writing a Christian epic, the breadth of knowledge he commanded and the felicity of expression of which he was capable were achieved through steady Puritan exertion.

Although the fanatical, superstitious conquistadores would not seem congenial company for a historian of Prescott's background, the past of the Spanish and the Aztecs proved an ideal subject for a romantic historian for the same reason it did for writers of historical romances. It was studded with extraordinary situations and larger-than-life characters. In contrast, the Puritans of Plymouth and the junior entrepreneurs of Jamestown were dishwater dull. In *The History of the Conquest of Mexico*, Prescott partakes of the ambition and audacity of his subject, Cortés. Both conquistador and historian, handicapped by seemingly formidable limitations, pressed on in their quest to explore, to subdue, and ultimately to control. Both attempted something relatively untried—respectively overcoming a nonwestern empire and writing a scrupulously researched, psychologically complex history from an American perspective—and, working against seemingly impossible odds, both succeeded. Cortés had few resources and fewer men; Prescott was physically incapacitated and easily distracted. But Cortés redefined conquest just as Prescott revolutionized historiography. And the object of both men was similarly parallel: proprietorship and possession. Later encomiums of Prescott's achievement acknowledge his goal of conquest, even when they do so unconsciously. In a foreword to an annotated bibliography of Prescott imprints prepared for the Library of Congress in

honor of the centennial of Prescott's 1859 death, Howard Cline, director of
the Hispanic Foundation, called Prescott "a national author whose writings
in the middle of the nineteenth century formed a significant part of the
expanding intellectual frontiers of the United States."[29] Prescott himself had
a distaste for Manifest Destiny, but he practiced its intellectual equivalent.

Prescott noted his intention of writing the history of the "Spanish subject" in his diary on January 19, 1826, only a month after the Panama
Congress was announced ("A fortunate choice," he penciled in the margin
in May 1847[30]). *The History of the Reign of Ferdinand and Isabella* finally
appeared in print in 1837. Next Prescott turned to *The History of the Conquest of Mexico* in 1843 and *The History of the Conquest of Peru* in 1847. He
was at work on a history of the reign of Spain's Philip II when he died in
1859. His purpose, announced unapologetically and with great frequency,
was to recover the history of the Spanish in Spain and America from their
original chroniclers, whose writing was marred by silly delusions and naked
political expediency. Despite his visual impairment and inability to travel,
he would sift the wheat from the chaff by the most scrupulous research,
procuring and comparing original sources, many of which he ordered copied from archives in Spain and Latin America.

One of the salient themes of his first effort, *The History of the Reign of
Ferdinand and Isabella*, is the role of nationalism in the emergence of Spain
as a world power. A formidable enemy helped forge national purpose: the
kingdoms of Castile and Aragon united not only through the marriage of
their sovereigns but also through conflict with their common enemy, the
Moors. "Hence the national character became exalted by a religious fervor,
which in later days, alas! settled into a fierce fanaticism."[31] But Prescott was
similarly aware of the role of culture. As important in fostering a sense of
patriotism, according to him, was the popular enthusiasm for "traditional
minstrelsy" like the epic *El Cid*, which provided a superhero who stirred
the imagination of "common people" to national identification.[32] The valo-
rization of both literature and nonelite consumers of it strikes a democratic
note in Prescott's often Whiggish analysis.

Although today *Ferdinand and Isabella* remains in an obscure corner of
historiography, in the shadow cast by *The Conquest of Mexico*, the boldness
of an American tackling a European subject with such evident erudition
and sensitivity secured Prescott's reputation in Europe, where he was forever associated with his first effort. (When he was presented to Queen Vic-
toria in 1850, it was as the author of *Ferdinand and Isabella*.[33]) His friend

George Ticknor, a professor of Spanish and French languages at Harvard, made sure copies of the American treatment of the Spanish subject were placed in the hands of European authorities.[34]

But it was *The History of the Conquest of Mexico* that made Prescott's reputation timeless. Prescott divided *The Conquest of Mexico* into seven books, the concluding remarks of each book except the last devoted to discussion of the Spanish historians and chroniclers who were his predecessors. Wherever possible, Prescott consulted original sources, chiefly some eight thousand folio pages from the Royal Academy of History at Madrid and the archives of the Indies at Seville, and additional materials from numerous private collections.[35] His footnotes are filled with tales of sources lost for centuries and miraculously recovered.[36] He learned how to interpret texts related to the pre-Columbian past whose "dark and doubtful nature"[37] still mystify scholars, reports of early missionaries like Tomás de Torquemada displaying "a full measure of the bigotry which belonged to his order at that period,"[38] and later accounts of those with Spanish ancestry like Francisco Javier Clavijero whose "national zeal"[39] colored their reliability. He consulted tiresome annals where occasional gems of historical value lay buried under piles of repetitive trivia, and reports of the fantastic and marvelous that might nonetheless contain an occasional fact.[40] He waded through political dispatches that burnished the reputation of the conquerors, flattered the interests of the powerful, and minimized the outrages committed against the subjugated. And without false modesty he appeared quietly confident that he had "the philosophic spirit fitted for calmly weighing [their] doubts and difficulties."[41]

Yet the history Prescott wrote, for all its piled-up evidence, dutiful notes, and shimmering nineteenth-century prose, looks nothing like history written today. Prescott presumes to penetrate the inmost thoughts of his characters and does not hesitate to ascribe to them a variety of motivations that make them memorable, that humanize them—but at the same time that plumb their consciousness without apology. Here is his portrait of the embarrassment of Diego Velásquez, governor of Hispaniola, at his failure to prevent Cortés from setting out on his voyage of conquest: "Velásquez rode back to his house to digest his chagrin as he best might; satisfied, probably, that he had made at least two blunders; one in appointing Cortés to the command,—the other in attempting to deprive him of it. For, if it be true, that by giving our confidence by halves, we can scarcely hope to make a friend, it is equally true, that, by withdrawing it when given, we shall make an enemy."[42]

Here Prescott sounds less like a historian than—a novelist. He himself was conscious of this strategy. "I must make the mere narrative very interesting," he noted to himself in his diary November 3, 1828, while plotting out *Ferdinand and Isabella*. "This is to be done by selecting facts that have novelty & interest, & such as will particularly display the character of the actors. Indeed it is to this dramatic effect given to history that it owes its principal charm."[43] In Prescott's prose, historical figures scheme and worry and brood and dream; they suffer remorse and anticipate pleasure exactly like the fictional creations of Simms or Robert Montgomery Bird. As a matter of fact, Prescott, who had some experience writing fiction, mastered the skills of the storyteller.[44] "I cannot make my history profound. I have neither the knowledge or talent for this. I can make it *entertaining*," he wrote in his diary in 1830.[45]

The fiction-writer's approach also surfaces in *The Conquest of Mexico*, which can be analyzed from the perspective of the typical courtship plot of boy meets girl, boy loses girl, boy gets girl—with the girl in this case being Mexico. The manner in which the events are described, from the first encounter to the "battles and negotiations . . . retreat . . . rally and final siege," apply as well to sexual as territorial conquests.[46] But in this context the siege and surrender look more like rape than romance. The boy-loses-girl section of *The Conquest of Mexico* corresponds to the Noche Triste, during which, while Cortés is away from the city, the zeal of the soldiers to secure their takeover leads to a reaction from the Indians, who drive them out. The final surrender of Tenochtitlan requires its destruction, so that by the end of the Spanish occupation of the city scarcely one stone is left standing on another, and the Aztecs are decimated by famine and disease. No marriage in the novelistic vein concludes the story: the victory and possession of the Spanish is achieved at the price of the horrific violation of the Aztecs.

Indeed, drawing from even more ancient literary models, Prescott composed what the romancers of the time called "an epic in prose," with Cortés as pious Aeneas and wily Ulysses in one. He employed such devices as the epic simile and epic catalogue and divided his work into a series of books.[47] His limited eyesight even led him to resort to the technique of the ancient epic poets, that of declaiming his work aloud before it was written down. "Never take up my pen until I have travelled over the subject so often as to be able to write almost from memory, not from invention as I go along," he instructed himself in 1829.[48] This discipline gives his history a sonorous authority and a felicitous prose style.

Despite his devotion to primary sources, fiction and history were not for Prescott such dissimilar disciplines. A great mania for classification marked the Enlightenment and its aftermath, but the categories were not always defined as they are today. Simms, for example, insisted on the significant differences between two distinct varieties of fiction ("the standards of [romance] are as different from those of the novel, as its characteristics are," he chided a critic who had judged his *The Damsel of Darien* for its improbabilities[49]). On the other hand, Simms insisted, the true historian was an artist, using all the materials of literature for his work. But he was not hindered by preoccupation with pedestrian facts. "It is really of very little importance to mankind, whether he is absolutely correct in all his conjectures or assertions, whether his theory be true or false, or whether he rightly determines upon the actor or the scene," Simms insisted. "We care not so much for the intrinsic truth of history, as for the great moral truths, which, drawn from such sources, induce excellence in the student. . . . That moral truth, educed by thought from conjecture, is one wholly independent of details."[50]

What made Prescott's work so extraordinary was his ability to evoke the transcendent without sacrificing the "absolutely correct." He wrote a national myth with footnotes. Like Cortés on his journey to the heart of Mexico, he proceeded without a map, relying only on mumbled directions and half-hidden hieroglyphics. His sources were like Cortés's Indian guides, his predecessors as fallible as the medieval fairy tales to which Cortés listened, but out of them he constructed a model for others to imitate; he conquered—indeed, defined—a discipline as Cortés conquered an empire.

From its opening book, depicting the New World and its inhabitants rather than Cortés's departure from Europe, Prescott's *The Conquest of Mexico* is clearly doing something new. Long before the conventions of ethnohistory were worked out, assembling the pre-Columbian history of the natives of Mexico was no mean task. (Casting about for a term for what he was doing, Prescott wrote that his opening book on indigenous civilizations was "occupied with the antiquities and origin of a nation, as somewhat the character of a *philosophic* theme."[51]) He estimated that half of the labor he expended to complete the book was consumed in the sections on the natives and their origins, which make up only about a sixth part of the whole.[52] Nonetheless, he accounted for his decision to begin with the people of Mexico with a respect that should be acknowledged:

"Although the subject of the work is, properly, only the Conquest of Mexico, I have prepared the way for it by such a view of the Civilization of the ancient Mexicans, as might acquaint the reader with the character of this extraordinary race, and enable him to understand the difficulties which the Spaniards had to encounter in their subjugation."[53] Just as the enslaved characters in fiction after the publication of *Uncle Tom's Cabin* were suddenly endowed with recognizably human characteristics, both admirable and objectionable, Prescott allowed his Aztec and Inca characters to show human nobility and weakness.

But one may entertain the suspicion that he could be as evenhanded as he was about the native Mexicans because he had no particularly elevated opinion of their Christian conquerors. His New England assumptions are never far below the surface. Here, for example, is Prescott's paean to the success of Catholic evangelization, which manages to heap scorn on both Catholic and native religion at once: "The Roman Catholic communion has, it must be admitted, some decided advantages over the Protestant, for the purposes of proselytism. The dazzling pomp of its service and its touching appeal to the sensibilities affect the imagination of the rude child of nature much more powerfully than the cold abstractions of Protestantism, which, addressed to the reason, demand a degree of refinement and mental culture in the audience to comprehend them."[54]

Yet the Catholic Church, in Prescott's hands, manages to come off surprisingly well. That the principal aim of the Conquest was the conversion of sinners Prescott never questions: he allows the reader to doubt the strategies employed in achieving this end and the effectiveness of the process, but never the sincerity of the conquistadores. According to Prescott, they took seriously their mission to save the heathen from damnation. "However much it may have been debased by temporal motives and mixed up with worldly considerations of ambition and avarice, it was still active in the mind of the Christian conqueror," he writes.[55] Cortés, it is true, tries to collect souls the way a Casanova takes lovers. No sooner does he arrive in a new town than he heads for the nearest temple, from which the idols must be stripped. But his confessor Father Olmedo counsels a more deliberate method, preparing the soil in which the seed of faith will be planted. The Church has many such gentle and patient missionaries, Prescott adds kindly.[56] In private, Prescott was seemingly amused that Catholic readers and translators could not decide if he was a generous advocate or an irrecoverable heretic.[57] But he protested strongly against the charge that he expressed an anti-Catholic bias. Forwarded a notice from the *Catholic Review* by Brantz Mayer, he wrote, "I shall not plead guilty to the charge of *bigotry*. Universal toleration has always been my creed, and I have strictly endeavoured to make myself one of the age and nation of which I wrote."[58] This empathy stands in sharp contrast to much of the post-Panama Congress analysis of historical and contemporary Latin America, which tended to highlight anything that encouraged expressions of disgust or superiority.

Indeed, Prescott insists on a sort of indulgence even for Cortés's most indefensible behavior. Prescott refuses to find anything intrinsically more inhumane in the conduct of the Spaniards than "the most polished nations of our time; by the British at Badajoz, for example,—at Taragona, and a hundred other places by the French." The Spanish actions were certainly not worse for being motivated by religious fanaticism. "It is far from my intention to vindicate the cruel deeds of the old Conquerors. Let them lie heavy on their heads. They were an iron race, who periled life and fortune in the cause; and, as they made little account of danger and suffering for themselves, they had little sympathy to spare for their unfortunate enemies," he writes. "But, to judge them fairly, we must not do it by the lights of our own age. We must carry ourselves back to theirs, and take the point of view afforded by the civilization of their time. Thus only can we arrive at impartial criticism in reviewing the generations that are past. We must extend to them the same justice which we shall have occasion to ask from Posterity, when, by the light of a higher civilization, it surveys the dark or doubtful passages in our own history, which hardly arrest the eye of the contemporary."[59]

David Levin, in his 1959 *History as Romantic Art*, read Prescott's assurance of human progress as typical of the mid-nineteenth-century confidence that human destiny spirals upward to the culmination of Unitarianism and democracy.[60] Yet Prescott's faith is as characteristic of Whig historians as romantic ones. The present is more enlightened than the past, and the future will reach a brighter civilization yet. But there is sufficient shadow to make the thoughtful reader wonder to just what "dark and doubtful passages" of the nineteenth century Prescott alludes. Because of Prescott's sensitivity to the injustices visited on the indigenous people of the Americas, it is natural enough to assume that slavery is one of the contemporary world's unmentioned offenses. The study of history can evidently not only teach forgiveness for the errors of the past, but also inspire penitence for the sins of the present.

Like the novelists who found in Latin American settings the liberation of discussing controversial topics, Prescott also used the context of the Conquest to raise views of slavery that might have offended some of his readers. Prescott was neither abolitionist nor racial progressive. In a letter to his wife from Washington in 1828, he referred to people of color with an offensive epithet (and suggested Susan Prescott share the word with their daughter). "You can hardly open your eyes without seeing a score of them. They are so civil and attentive, however, that I begin to think better of slavery," he added.[61]

But fifteen years later in *The Conquest of Mexico*, the light tone is gone, as he reflects on the effects of slavery upon the enslaved rather than upon the comfort and convenience of the master. The bondage he considers is that of the Indians, but the lesson is clear for those who will heed it. In fact, he goes out of his way to relate the past to the present. Having glorified the achievements of the pre-Columbian Aztecs in governing their empire, he anticipates the objections of readers who, having read about the inferiority of their descendants, will not believe the portrait he has sketched:

> Those familiar with the modern Mexicans will find it difficult to conceive that the nation should ever have been capable of devising the enlightened polity which we have been considering. But they should remember that in the Mexicans of our day they see only a conquered race. . . . The difference is not so great as between the ancient Greek, and his degenerate descendant, lounging among the masterpieces of art which he has scarcely taste enough to admire— speaking the language of those still more imperishable monuments of literature which he has scarcely capacity to comprehend. Yet he breathes the same atmosphere, is warmed by the same sun, nourished by the same scenes, as those who fell at Marathon, and won the trophies of Olympic Pisa. The same blood flows in his veins that flowed in theirs. But ages of tyranny have passed over him: he belongs to a conquered race.[62]

In this extraordinary passage Prescott responds to those that suggest it is impossible to "forget" civilization.[63] Modern Indians, according to those who embraced the Mound Builder myth, could not be descended from the ancient aborigines. Similarly, according to proslavery thinkers judging by the condition of American slaves, Africa must have been always and everywhere in the savage state. The onward march of civilization could not be put in reverse. To these claims Prescott stands opposed. The example of Greece was shrewdly chosen. The outrage of white slavery there would inspire American sculptor Hiram Powers to carve *The Greek Slave*, the nineteenth century's most famous statue, in 1844, a year after Prescott wrote *The Conquest of Mexico*. The effect of the Turkish conquest of Greece was a powerful instance of how quickly the benefits of civilization could be stripped away. The brutality and hopelessness of slavery would efface them fast enough.

In taking this position, Prescott echoes eighteenth-century thinkers like the Comte de Buffon more than the increasingly essentialist theorists of his own day. Buffon had argued that animals, including those of the human family, can most definitely "degenerate" while remaining part of the same species: "Nothing can be a stronger proof that they belong to the same family, than the facility with which they unite to the common stock. The blood is different; but the germ is the same."[64] Both climate and quality of food can cause degeneration of animals.[65] But in human beings, wrote Buffon, a third factor can produce this result: slavery: "we will be astonished at the degree to which tyranny can degrade and disfigure Nature; we will perceive the marks of slavery, and the prints of her chains; and we will find, that these wounds are deeper and more incurable, in proportion to their antiquity."[66]

Although there is no evidence that Prescott had this passage of Buffon in mind as he wrote *The Conquest of Mexico* (where he was scrupulous about footnotes), the coincidence of certain words and ideas is striking, as is the way the texts diverge. If anything, Prescott gives more precedence to slavery as the cause of degeneration. Where for Buffon "the blood is different," among Prescott's ancient and modern Greeks "the same blood flows." While Buffon included climate as a cause of change, Prescott's contemporary Greek slave "breathes the same atmosphere," and "is warmed by the same sun" as his superior ancestor. For both writers it is "tyranny" that imprints the most ineffaceable marks of degeneration.

Still more pointed comments about slavery, and the relation of sixteenth to nineteenth century bondage, come late in *The Conquest of Mexico*. In the ultimate, "biographical" section of the book, which treats the last days of Cortés, Prescott mentions this "remarkable" clause that Cortés inserted into his will: "It has long been a question, whether one can conscientiously hold property in Indian slaves. Since the point has not yet been determined, I enjoin it on my son Martin and his heirs, that they spare no pains to come to an exact knowledge of the truth; as a matter which deeply concerns the conscience of each of them, no less than mine."[67]

Prescott could have let this quotation stand somewhat innocuously without explication; his Southern readers might have been mollified by the fact that Cortés wrote only about Indian servitude, although Prescott noted just five pages earlier that Cortés had attempted to plant a colony in California with "*three hundred negro slaves,*" and his will refrains from questioning the justice of African slavery.[68] But Prescott insists on relating Cortés's uneasy meditations on slavery in 1547 to the U.S. slavery debate three hundred years later. Stepping out of his consideration of the past, as he did previously when he appealed for a sophisticated analysis of pre-Reformation religious enthusiasm, Prescott delivers this measured, but still critical, take on slavery: "The state of opinion in respect to the great question of slavery, in the sixteenth century, at the commencement of the system, bears some resemblance to that which exists in our time, when we may hope it is approaching its conclusion." He compares the Dominican reformer Bartolomé de las Casas to the most vociferous of the nineteenth-century abolitionists, with the "great mass of proprietors" corresponding to slaveholders who merely sustain the status quo. "In one important respect, the condition of slavery, in the sixteenth century, differed materially from its condition in the nineteenth. In the former, the seeds of the evil, but lately sown, might have been, with comparatively little difficulty, eradicated. But in our time they have struck their roots deep into the social system, and cannot be rudely handled without shaking the very foundation of the political fabric." To pretend that the solution to the problem requires only good intentions is foolhardy. "It is easy to conceive, that a man, who admits all the wretchedness of the institution and its wrong to humanity, may nevertheless hesitate to adopt a remedy, until he is satisfied that the remedy itself is not worse than the disease. That such a remedy will come with time, who can doubt, that has confidence in the ultimate prevalence of the right, and the progressive civilization of his species?"[69] Prescott is unnecessarily generous to slaveholders, who by 1843 were less willing to "admit all the wretchedness of the institution" than to claim for it benefits not only for society but for the slaves themselves. And his assurance that slavery will somehow sink under the weight of its own turpitude while civilization climbs triumphantly skyward sounds more like a relic of eighteenth-century thought than the suspicions of his own age. But perhaps

Prescott's predictions about slavery are informed by a Whiggish belief in progress. Prescott had all the confidence in the onward march of society common to the Whigs.

Though Prescott did not publicly champion the Whig Party, he had no very high opinion of Democrats (or democrats). Encountering them in the close quarters of a brig bound for the Azores on a visit to his grandfather in 1815, the nineteen-year-old Prescott had written home that he "banished *ennui* by battling with Democrats and bed-bugs, both of which thrive on board this vessel."[70] Thirty-two years later he sounds scarcely more sympathetic to democracy when in *The Conquest of Peru* he calls "the good of the people . . . a suspicious phrase, usually meaning the good of the individual."[71] Nonetheless, if Prescott's Cortés, to whom Prescott *is* sympathetic, were an American politician, he would not be a Whig to the manor born; he would be a Democrat, more Andrew Jackson than John Quincy Adams. Cortés personifies the people's will when he is able to do so, presents his own decisions as the people's choice when necessary, and bows to the will of the people against his own better judgment when he cannot avoid it. Although every inch a leader, Cortés never for an instant forgets that his authority is based on the support of the soldiers and the Indian allies of the Spanish: he governs with a combination of rough camaraderie and Olympian prerogative. He does not punish if he can persuade; he does not condemn the full battery of malefactors if he can achieve the same effect through the censure of one prominent example.

Prescott's Cortés does not need instruction in wringing sweetness out of adversity. The historian describes the terrible rout of the Spaniards and their expulsion from Tenochtitlan in the magnificent Book V of *The Conquest of Mexico*. Montezuma having capitulated to the Spaniards, the Aztecs turn on him and the invaders with savage fury, cutting off their escape by destroying the causeways that separate the island city from the mainland. As the soldiers frantically try to flee, the Aztecs drive them to the canals, which are full of warriors in canoes. The greedy soldiers, having loaded themselves down with stolen gold, drown in agony. The treasure they hoped to win in the Conquest is sunk beneath the waves. Horses, guns, crossbows—everything that separates Spaniard from savage—is lost in the catastrophic retreat. Cortés escapes with a mere remnant of his army and their Indian allies, taking refuge at the top of a pyramid outside the city. Prescott imagines him still restless, wakeful, faced with the likelihood that the vast project he had undertaken lies in ruins. "Yet these agitating and gloomy reflections, which might have crushed a common mind, had no power over that of Cortés; or rather, they only served to renew his energies, and quicken his perceptions, as the war of the elements purifies and gives elasticity to the atmosphere. He looked with an unblenching eye on his past reverses; but, confident in his own resources, he saw a light through the gloom which others could not."[72] Cortés is never so resourceful as when he is reduced to calamity, as when he has nothing but "shattered relics" out of which to build an empire—for he retains his power as a leader. That power is in his words.

The soldiers want to retreat to the safety of the Spanish settlement on the Mexican coast, but Cortés persuades them instead to go back to Tenochtitlan and prevail. He has no money to pay them wages, but he promises them eternal glory. Their numbers are depleted, but he persuades the Aztecs' enemies to join their number. Soldiers come from the governor of Cuba to arrest him for insubordination, but he convinces them to join his army. This is the way a nation is constructed, Prescott suggests: people hear a compelling story, and believe it is about them.

As the little army returns to Tenochtitlan, it encounters the Aztecs in far superior numbers on the field of Otompan. Cortés rallies his band with a desperate strategy, telling them to seek out the Aztec leaders and move in for the kill. He himself with his "eagle eye" identifies a particularly important enemy commander, and dispatches him with such ferocity that the Aztec army collapses in panic and terror.[73] Prescott tacitly admits that the number of the enemy forces—whom the Spanish reckoned at two hundred thousand—is an exaggeration, yet without equivocation he calls the result of the contest "undoubtedly, one of the most remarkable victories ever achieved in the New World."[74] He credits not simply Cortés's rhetoric: "they had discipline on their side, desperate resolve, and implicit confidence in their commander." They were also lucky. Cortés was fortunate in getting close enough, in such a crowd, to the Aztec commander whose death caused such a stampede.[75]

The ease with which readers accepted or overlooked Prescott's remarks on slavery and politics suggests the timeliness of his conquest narrative in the 1840s. The tale he tells suited a lusty nation with imperial ambitions. The Europeans triumph despite their inferior numbers and lack of familiarity with an exotic landscape. While superior technology, immunity to disease, and simple good fortune aid them, Prescott credits their success to strategy, tenacity, and discipline. When Cortés has nothing left but courage he remains formidable. Despite the frequent cliffhangers and hairbreadth escapes, it is his destiny to prevail and he never swerves from it. Prescott considers rhetoric and discipline as Cortés's two essential strengths. Although the careers of Prescott and Cortés would appear to share few similarities, the two characteristics Prescott identifies in the conqueror define the historian as well. "[T]he history of the Conquest, as I have already had occasion to remark, is necessarily that of Cortés," he concludes.[76] Prescott would come to be associated no less completely with the history of the Conquest.

The History of the Conquest of Peru, published in 1847, only four years after *The Conquest of Mexico*, tells a different story. Though it followed its predecessor's template, even Prescott acknowledged that the stars of its composition did not align quite so perfectly, and no dramatic meteor shower accompanied its reception. As with many copies, the tracings, though firm and straight, lack the energy and boldness of the original lines. Francisco Pizarro—who had been portrayed as a thug in Bird's *Oralloossa*—is no Hernán Cortés. While Cortés left a record of his own actions in the form of letters to his sovereign (dramatic and well-composed of themselves), Pizarro was illiterate, leaving a hole in Prescott's depiction of his character not easily filled. Cortés was a pioneer, always backed into a corner but improvising his way out. Pizarro succeeded Cortés, and even when he was not imitating the latter's example, his strategies appeared derivative.[77] Prescott had an easier job in assembling sources and writing about Peru; as he mentioned in his introduction, there are more extant sources on Peru, and many of them had already fallen into his hands in his earlier researches. The sense of providential solutions to impossible problems in both research and military affairs, of eleventh-hour rescues and fortuitous coincidences that make reading *The History of the Conquest of Mexico* like reading an adventure story are lacking in *The History of the Conquest of Peru*.

Similarly, the Incas were not the Aztecs, neither in their fierceness nor their spectacular fall. The complex Mexican Montezuma is a more compelling figure than the Inca Atahualpa. The Aztecs built vertiginous pyramids crowned with gore-encrusted temples; the Incas constructed roads—practical and serviceable, but not appealing to the imagination in quite the same way. The Aztecs were vicious tyrants, the Incas resourceful bureaucrats. When cornered, the Aztecs mowed down the flower of Spanish chivalry and tossed their severed heads in Cortés's direction. When the execution of Atahualpa was imminent, he begged pitifully for his life.

But more troublingly, the central conflict of *The Conquest of Peru* concerns not the spectacular warfare of Christians against heathens but what Prescott considers an unworthy squabble for power among the Spanish themselves. Real religious feeling, admittedly pushed to the extreme of fanaticism, motivated Cortés and his band of conquerors, Prescott insists. By contrast, Pizarro and his men made gold their goal, with the result that they fought ignobly for land, titles, slaves—anything that could be converted to gain, where their true loyalty lay. "Bigotry is the perversion of religious principle; but the principle itself was wanting in Pizarro."[78] In the place of Cortés's good Father Olmedo, counseling patience and tolerance, Pizarro's department of conversion was headed by the ambitious Fray Vicente de Valverde. Atahualpa's rejection of Valverde's offer of baptism provided a convenient excuse for the Inca's arrest. Pizarro shared the original commission to conquer Peru with one Diego de Almagro—a relationship that dissolved quickly and led to power struggles between the two men and various members of their extended families that Prescott does not hesitate to call a civil war.

In *The Conquest of Peru* Prescott continues to emphasize the situations that anticipate the social conditions of his own day. It is possible to read his description of the Inca Empire as an extended comment upon the United States at midcentury. In Peru, the aborigines encountered natural obstacles in developing their country: Peru is a strip of coastline bordered to the east by mountains. Industrious with internal improvements, the Incas terraced the hillsides to permit agriculture, and constructed canals, aqueducts, and roads, the hallmark of their realm. Their roads allowed rapid communication over an area some 1,500 miles long. If Peru seems to anticipate the United States of the Market Revolution, in its version of Manifest Destiny it seems to do the United States one better. The Incas, in their acquisition of new territory, demonstrate foresight and patience: they do not gobble it down, like the Aztecs, who in the process of extending their power created legions of the dispossessed and disaffected. The Incas' goal is the cultural absorption of the conquered people into their empire, and to that end they move the subject gods into the imperial pantheon in Cuzco (where they are effectively held hostage, a guarantee against a siege of the Inca capital). The sovereigns of the conquered nations are similarly brought to Cuzco to be instructed in the Inca ways. And the incorporation of the new people is effected through their education in the lingua franca of Quichua.[79] While Prescott explicitly compares the Incas with the Aztecs, who in the process of extending their reach made many enemies, easily won as allies of Cortés, there is an implicit but more immediate comparison to the United States, about whose policies in Texas Prescott was anxious.

Similarly, when Prescott writes about a contented, orderly system of self-sufficient communities that operated on a cooperative model in Peru, it is possible to imagine him thinking of the experimental utopias dotting his native New England in the 1840s. But the Whig in Prescott emerges here: how were these communal Peruvians kept so content, or at least so passive? It was by denying education to everyone but the most privileged, so that there was no inducement to self-improvement. Just so in New England: as David Levin notes, Prescott had little respect for the "she-philosophers" of Brook Farm.[80]

Finally, Prescott describes the treatment of the Indians in ways that anticipate the mistreatment of enslaved people in the nineteenth century. Young women are "torn without remorse from the arms of [their families]" to gratify the lust of the Spaniards; bloodhounds are set upon the natives.[81] In 1535, a party of conquistadores set off to claim Chile for Spain. Their progress is checked by fierce cold and starvation, but Prescott notes that they are not moved to compassion for the "weaker natives." Instead, as they march through mountain settlements, they set them on fire and force the inhabitants to serve as bearers. "They were chained together in gangs of ten or twelve, and no infirmity or feebleness of body excused the unfortunate captive from his full share of the common toil, till he sometimes dropped dead, in his very chains, from mere exhaustion!"[82] Prescott could be describing a coffle of slaves headed from the Chesapeake to Mississippi. And again Prescott cannot resist driving home the parallel. "There is something in the possession of superior strength most dangerous, in a moral view, to its possessor," he writes. "Wherever the civilized man and the savage have come in contact, in the East or in the West, the story has been too often written in blood."[83]

In *The Conquest of Peru* the Spanish actions are held up for censure. Prescott can barely contain his disgust for this internecine conflict over gold and power in a land where both are so lavishly accessible. He deplores the senseless waste of lives in a situation where the conquerors have only recently taken control over a huge native population. He tells of soldiers murdered in the act of surrender or while recovering from wounds on the battlefield. "Such anecdotes, revolting as they are, illustrate not merely the spirit of the times, but that peculiarly ferocious spirit which is engendered by civil wars,—the most unforgiving in their character of any, but wars of religion," says Prescott.[84] Of a later conflict he writes, "It was a fearful struggle, not merely of man against man, but, to use the words of an eyewitness, of brother against brother, and friend against friend."[85] Although his turn of phrase anticipates the disunion of the United States fifteen years later, Prescott presumably was not writing with second sight. Nonetheless, he understood, and dreaded, the cost of civil war.

And he makes a connection between the last and most problematic civil war in *The Conquest of Peru* and the intractable problem of slavery. In 1542, explains Prescott, Dominican friar Las Casas presented to the Crown his report on the evils perpetrated against the Indians. Although Prescott has been straightforward in his presentation of the evils of slavery, he presents Las Casas as short-sighted, inflexible, prone to exaggeration, and blind to his own hypocrisy—the abolitionist as fanatic.[86] Again, Prescott inserts an editorial comment reflecting directly on the 1840s: "For Las Casas was the uncompromising friend of freedom. He intrenched [sic] himself strongly on the ground of natural right; and, like some of the reformers of our own day, disdained to calculate the consequences of carrying out the principle to its full and unqualified extent."[87] The result of Las Casas's report was a system of ordinances regulating the treatment of the Indians that Prescott presents as a kind of nightmare scenario of immediate abolition: "this remarkable code, which, touching on the most delicate relations of society, broke up the very foundations of property, and, by a stroke of a pen, as it were, converted a nation of slaves into freemen."[88] What interests Prescott is not the reaction of the Indians to their liberation—he acknowledges that their bondage to the Spanish was of a completely different order of rigor from what was due their Inca masters—but rather the effect on Spanish society.

The Crown sends a viceroy to enforce the ordinances, which he does, with a high-handed arrogance. The colonists, angry at the Crown's lack of gratitude for their subjugation of the country, furious at the loss of their slave property, and "astounded at the prospect of ruin that awaited them," need little incentive to turn into a mob.[89] In a grim counterpoint to Cortés's ability to use narrative to unify, the chaos of Peru is characterized by the flight of rumor from one city to another. The former soldiers of the Conquest turn to Gonzalo Pizarro, younger brother of the conqueror, who seizes power. An armed confrontation between the disaffected colonists supporting Gonzalo and the viceroy's forces results in the death of the viceroy. The rogue commander Gonzalo, assuming the title "Procurator General," finds himself running the colony. "No such rebellion, within the memory of man, had occurred in the Spanish empire."[90] Only the Crown's recruitment of a more effective representative in the colony finally restores order. Where *The Conquest of Mexico* had ended with the farsighted and efficient government of Cortés, *The Conquest of Peru* concludes with the lid of royal authority placed uneasily on a seething cauldron of rebellion.

In stern New England fashion Prescott presents not a parable to be imitated but a species of jeremiad: woe to the nation cursed with slavery. It is easy to deplore the evil of the institution, but dangerous to root it out without considering the consequences. Like amputation and bloodletting, the cure may be more deadly than the disease. In the case of Peru, the threat to peace comes not from the suddenly liberated Indians but the wrathful Spanish colonists deprived of their enforced tribute. What results from royal emancipation is not the vengeful retribution anticipated by U.S. southerners, but something that looks much more like the Civil War in the United States: a bloody conflict between two groups of white people, one fighting the other to the death over their right to keep slaves. Although *The Conquest of Peru* ends with a vision of a horror to be avoided rather than a prescription for a workable solution, Prescott has succeeded in changing the conversation. His thoughtful, reasonable tone acknowledges the complexity of the problem of abolition. No solution will come without cost—in time, in wealth, in lives.

One hazard of allegory is that its interpretation quickly escapes the control of its author. Prescott's readers located themselves on so many points of the political compass that they pulled an astounding variety of morals from his work.[91] They were no less able to draw connections between his discussion of ancient times and their own—some of which Prescott might have endorsed though he clearly had not anticipated them. For example, shortly after the discovery of gold in California, the *Boston Daily Advertiser* drew prophetic parallels between Prescott's description of the mad rush to Peru in the sixteenth century and the exodus to San Francisco three hundred years later. As had been the case with the Spanish, farmers abandoned fields and debtors fled from creditors with little foresight. "They thought to dig for gold; but they dug only their graves," Prescott had written, to which the *Advertiser* added bitterly, "Men will not grow wiser by experience, at least by any other experience than their own."[92]

Other readers drew their own conclusions about comparative slavery using evidence Prescott supplied. According to Northern Whigs, the supposed savages of ancient Mexico had practiced a milder form of slavery than that which prevailed in the nineteenth-century United States. The *Berkshire County Whig* cited Prescott's remark that no one was born into slavery in Mexico; further, slaves could own property, their families were recognized, and they were allowed to marry freemen. "If our 'glorious republic' would copy this law from the statues of these barbarians, slavery would soon be extinguished," concluded the *Whig*.[93]

In 1847, the year of the publication of *The Conquest of Peru*, the U.S. War with Mexico suggested other parallels some readers could not ignore. *The Utica Whig* likened the atrocities of "Pizarro and his lawless band of land pirates and buccaneers" to "Mr. Polk's military satraps and proconsuls in the Mexican provinces of which they have taken possession." Like the Spanish, the United States had seized property on slender pretexts and trumped-up charges, held hasty trials, and executed merciless judgments. In both cases, a weaker people was victimized by a stronger in the name of progress.[94] Albert Gallatin, the eighty-six-year-old former secretary of the treasury and an outspoken opponent of the war, wrote in the pamphlet *Peace with Mexico*, "I have faith in our institutions and in the people; and I will now ask them whether this was their mission? and whether they were placed by Providence on this continent for the purpose of cultivating false glory, and of sinking to the level of those vulgar conquerors who have at all times desolated the earth."[95]

The precedent of the Conquest could serve as a warning to a headstrong United States. In a funeral oration for an officer in the U.S. War with Mexico in July 1848, the Reverend Francis Vinton did not hesitate to condemn the cause for which the soldier died. Wars on foreign soil, Vinton argued, are de facto wars of aggression and cannot be justified. "What has our country to gain by aggressive war?" demanded the preacher. "What is she to acquire by conquests? What but the *curse*?" The Spanish, he pointed out, had waged a war of conquest against the Mexicans, who themselves had conquered their neighbors, and the evil cycle still continued. If the past was a clue to the future, the United States could expect its populace, addicted to luxury, to fall prey to military dictators.[96] Two days after printing the funeral oration, the *Brooklyn Eagle* castigated Vinton for his "very great and absurd errors."[97]

But although Prescott's troubled perspectives on slavery and territorial expansion stand out in plain sight, *The Conquest of Mexico* was also beloved of supporters of the War with Mexico, who turned the book into a blueprint, a guidebook, a how-to manual. In 1846, every ship in the U.S. Navy had a copy of Prescott's history in its library.[98] Soldiers marched off to battle using *The History of the Conquest of Mexico* as a traveler's guide, even writing to assure its author that the descriptions of the landscape he had based entirely on secondary sources were reliable.[99] "Comparing my own observations with Mr. Prescott's descriptions, I cannot but be astonished at the accuracy of the latter," reflected Marine surgeon Richard McSherry.[100] Prescott's panoramic presentation of landscape, viewed through the eyes of the conquerors from assorted eminences, was prelude to possession of the land. Seeing and seizing were related enterprises.[101] Nathaniel Lyon, a Connecticut-born captain, wrote from Mexico City on April 5, 1848, "[Trist's treaty] is rather a hard bargain for Uncle Sam inasmuch as we already owned by right of conquest all this Territory and even more & Mexico should have considered herself fortunate that we take no more & pay her nothing."[102]

Cortés himself furnished a role model for latter-day conquerors. When the war began to bog down in late 1846, Commanding General Winfield Scott urged President Polk to approve his plan to follow Cortés's route from Vera Cruz into the heart of Mexico.[103] Further invoking the precedent of the Conqueror, Scott wrote Secretary of War William Marcy, "Like Cortez, finding myself isolated and abandoned; and again like him, always afraid that the next ship or messenger might recall or further cripple me—I resolved no longer to depend on Vera Cruz or home, but to render my little army *'a self-sustaining machine.'* "[104] Naval lieutenant Raphael Semmes referred to Cortés as "our great predecessor, whose descendants we had come to destroy."[105] But latter-day U.S. conquistadores were not simply following Spanish footsteps and repeating flawed actions; they interpreted their mission in the context of a more enlightened age. "I trust a better day is about to dawn on this benighted region and that another generation under a better government may abandon their idleness and popish idolatry," Captain E. Kirby Smith, a career officer from Litchfield, Connecticut, wrote his wife.[106]

Prescott had so popularized the idea of Mexico as a nation for conquest, linking the two words so inextricably in the imagination of his readers, that Americans of the time acknowledged almost casually the cold reality of what the United States was doing, presenting the justification as if manifest: "The [Mexican] race is perfectly accustomed to being conquered, and the only new lesson we shall teach is that our victories will give liberty, safety, and prosperity to the vanquished . . . Well may the Mexican nation, whose great masses have never yet tasted liberty, prattle over their lost phantom of nationality," declared the *New York Sun* dismissively.[107] "We can conquer Mexico," stated Samuel Houston on the floor of the Senate in 1847.[108] "You seem to have, while describing so eloquently the *past* Conquest of Mexico, foretold the *future* one," remarked Count Adolph de Circourt in a letter to Prescott in 1847.[109] If the Conquest was the type, the War with Mexico was the antitype: "Nor the chronicles of ancient wars, nor the prowess of modern achievements, furnish a parallel to the second conquest of Mexico, while the lustre that hung around the name of Cortés and his hardy adventurers, burnished by the glowing description of Prescott, becomes dimmed by the deeds of these latter days," announced George Wilkins Kendall in one of a series of letters written home from the war.[110]

For the most gung-ho of the war's supporters, the tricky question of amalgamation presented no obstacle: "Then pursue the conquest," advised the *Philadelphia Public Ledger*: "a good stiff authority will keep down its tyrants. Gen. Scott is the very fellow for the head of such a government. Our Yankee young fellows and the pretty senoritas will do the rest of the annexation, and Mexico will soon be Anglo-Saxonized, and prepared for the confederacy."[111] H. Judge Moore, a volunteer from Greenville, South Carolina, similarly conflated the impulses for both sexual and territorial conquest in a diary entry of February 19, 1847: "I long to see a Mexican Donna. I have been in sight of their shores so long, that I am getting very impatient for a nearer peep. I should like to go over if I could claim the promise made to Abraham that my seed should possess the land."[112]

At the same time, enthusiastic supporters of the war not infrequently protested that conquest was not their purpose. "It has never been contemplated by me, as an object of the war, to make a permanent conquest of the republic of Mexico," declared James Polk.[113] Even John C. Calhoun, anxious about the potential assimilation of Mexicans into the American republic and no friend of Polk, acknowledged, "Since the commencement of the war until this time, the President has continually disavowed the intention of conquering Mexico and subjecting her to our control."[114] The cover of George Lippard's lurid potboiler *Legends of Mexico* (1847) featured a misquotation from Thomas Paine's 1777 *The Crisis*: "We fight not to enslave, nor for conquest; but to make room upon the earth for honest men to live in."[115]

Prescott's own private memoranda and correspondence use the conquest analogy to reflect this anxiety. He was not above acknowledging the connection between his own labors and those of his subjects. Urging himself to give up his "loafing vagaries," he admonished himself, "the gold of Peru is not to be won by idle hands."[116] But more often he wrote out of a gnawing sense of uneasiness about a second Conquest. "I am sick of our domestic troubles, brought on us by unparalleled folly. And I take refuge from them in Peruvian hills, where the devildoms I read of—black enough—have at least no reference to ourselves," complained Prescott wearily to George Sumner in May, 1846.[117] The distance between the two situations was shrinking, and shrinking because of the vivid and immediate manner in which Prescott portrayed his subject. Prescott watched developments in Texas and Mexico with increasing distaste between 1845 and 1848. Noting the analogy of the military and literary conquests, he wrote in April 1847: "I have been carrying on the Conquest of Peru while the Government have [sic] been making the Conquest of Mexico. But mine is the best of the two, since it cost only the shedding of ink instead of blood; and if I ever get so little fame by it that is better than the dirty superfluous acres which we shall get by the other Conquest, and the still more barren glory."[118] As Eric Wertheimer writes, Prescott's ambivalence exemplifies the "contradiction between the fascination for imperial conquest and the rational political argument that found the Mexican War and Texas annexation abhorrent."[119]

One way Prescott sought to resolve this conflict in his own mind was by making distinctions among Americans based on geography or class. He connected the assumed "destiny to overrun this wide continent, and swell the dimensions of a territory already too vast for a republic,"[120] to Southern Democrats: "The Texas project is very distasteful to most of us in the North, and the party to which I belong view it with unqualified detestation," he wrote apologetically to the Mexican politician and historian Lúcas Alamán in 1845.[121] He referred slightingly to "Brother Jonathan," a braggart whose appetite for land is insatiable, using the caricature as English visitor Frances Trollope used it in 1832, to refer to the swearing, spitting members of the rabble who go around insisting on their rights.[122] As early as 1846 Prescott elided section and party, with the North guided by worthy elites and the South in the hands of the great unwashed: "The Southern and Western men have a free and open bearing that contrasts with the more prim and cautious manners of the North, which still retains a slight savor of the original Puritan stock, but with more really good stuff in its composition than is to be found in any other quarter of the country,—and much more cultivation."[123] Prescott's analysis proved accurate to the degree that he claimed the war with Mexico exacerbated sectional tensions.[124]

Despite such regional condescension, Prescott made room in his worldview for new people, new enterprises, and the new opportunities they presented. Certainly some of these attitudes reflect Yankee pragmatism. Whatever their prejudices about the shortcomings of the West, Prescott and his father considered a purchase of stock in a Cincinnati or Louisville bank in 1833, when Prescott wrote to George Bancroft for his counsel.[125] Catholics bought books, and there was no harm in an endorsement from Bishop John Hughes, whom Prescott met in New York in 1844 and who thanked him for his respectful treatment of Catholicism.[126] Prescott's attitudes might cynically be put down to some combination of Yankee shrewdness and commonplace upper-class courtesy, the roots of which did not penetrate too deep. Yet neither is Prescott's tolerance to be taken for granted. A suggestion of just how threatening Prescott's ideas could be is found in two responses to him, one written six years after the publication of *The Conquest of Mexico* and the other shortly before Prescott's death in 1859. For both of these angry critics, Prescott's empathy did not extend far enough. What offended them shows just how far Prescott pushed popular opinion from unquestioned assumptions of superiority to a greater complexity if not a greater tolerance of people outside the Anglo-Saxon majority.

Generally reviews of Prescott's works ran a narrow gamut from glowing to ecstatic. But *The Conquest of Mexico* received one outright pan published in, of all places, a hometown journal, the *Massachusetts Quarterly Review*.[127] The review—along with an earlier analysis of Prescott's shortcomings as a historian—was published anonymously, but was written by the fiery antislavery sectionalist Theodore Parker, who, along with Ralph Waldo Emerson, was one of the journal's founders. Parker desired to reappropriate the New England past that was increasingly applied to a national agenda that served the South. He believed that Prescott, by spinning a romantic fable of the Conquest, lulled the North into supporting the ill-advised adventures of the Polk administration.[128]

Prescott had said that it was necessary for the historian to judge not by the standards of the present but by the realities of the past, to imagine ignorance of future progress. A different moral standard had prevailed in the sixteenth century.[129] It is easy to condemn the sins of the past in the light shed by the revelation of days to come, but the people of the past stumbled about in darkness. The historian must judge accordingly. In an essay titled "Character of Mr. Prescott as an Historian," Parker countered that the historian's duty is far more profound: he must judge by absolute standards, which are not bound by time. While acknowledging "the spirit of the age . . . it is also the Historian's duty to criticize that spirit, and when a superior man rises, he must not be judged merely by the low standard of his age, but the absolute standard of all ages," wrote Parker.[130] Writing history is moral education; the historian must praise the just and condemn the wicked.

And to Parker, the conquistadores were wicked. How did Prescott dare to excuse the actions of the conquerors? First Parker endeavored to damn the Spanish for their seizure of the natives' land while exculpating the English. His logic was not particularly convincing.[131] But he was more successful in incriminating the conquistadores for cloaking their avarice in the guise of religious zeal, in effect making their converts pay for the privilege of conversion by surrendering gold and gemstones. Parker himself learned from Prescott's appeal to the present: "Imagine, oh gentle or simple readers, imagine the American board of foreign missionaries sending out their servants to China with such instructions, asking for 'comfortable presents' of silks, and Sycee silver, and tea!"[132] Parker was no less affronted by what he considered Prescott's lack of sympathy for his Indian subjects.[133] According to Parker, wherever the Spanish and the Aztecs come into conflict, however equivalent their cruelties, Prescott always sides with the Spanish: "the Spirit of Chivalry is mightier with him than the Spirit of Humanity."[134]

Neither do Prescott's remarks about slavery go far enough for Parker. Indeed, he takes no notice of the historian's measured homilies. For Parker, the facts are simple: native slavery paled beside the institution introduced by the "civilized" Spanish and justified by their learned divines, and Prescott tolerates their hypocrisy. Like the Massachusetts radicals who would the next year howl against Daniel Webster's accommodation to the Compromise of 1850, Parker demands, "Can it be that the commercial atmosphere of Boston had stifled the natural and nobler breath of the historian?"[135]

In 1849 Parker castigated Prescott for insufficient sympathy toward the Indians; ten years later Robert Anderson Wilson accused him of an excess of admiration. Wilson, a native of Cooperstown, New York, and "late judge of Sacramento District, California," wrote two books based on the experience of his residency in Mexico between 1851 and 1854: *Mexico and its Religion* (reissued a year later as *Mexico: Its Peasants and Priests*) and *A New History of the Conquest of Mexico in which Las Casas' Denunciations of the Popular Historians of that War are Fully Vindicated* (1859).[136] While both of his books are a confused mishmash of received opinion, secondhand description, paranoia, and screed, the former book is written as a travel narrative and the latter more particularly as a corrective to Prescott.

Wilson confessedly based his work less on scholarly historical research than on firsthand observation of contemporary Mexicans, whom he compared to his recollections of the Iroquois in his native New York. He concluded that Indians of North and South America were the same people—and both were improvident, shiftless, and incompetent. What to make, then, of the surviving Spanish chronicles describing the works of the Aztecs and Incas in awed admiration? Clearly, Wilson decided, they were fabrications: "I have presumed to doubt that water ever ran up hill, that navigable canals were ever fed by 'back water,' that pyramids (*teocalli*) could rest on a foundation of soft earth, that a canal twelve feet broad by twelve feet deep, mostly below the water level, was ever dug by Indians with their rude implements."[137] (Wilson proposed that the few ancient remains of skill and beauty that could not be written off were relics of an earlier race of white people, the Phoenicians this time.) The only talent the Spanish possessed was that of lying, as they recounted extravagant tales of their own accomplishments to burnish their reputations. Their deceit was in turn protected by the rigorous censorship of the Holy Office of the Inquisition, which maintained a vast conspiracy of misinformation.

But when compared to Prescott's level-headed generosity, Wilson's knee-jerk chauvinism in the absence of any actual scholarship was more difficult to take seriously. (Wilson also played into the hands of his critics by displaying a limited command of punctuation, grammar, and composition.[138]) "It is hardly necessary for us to characterize this whole theory of Mr. Wilson's as one of the most fantastic and absurd that was ever devised," scoffed *The New Englander*.[139] His glaring errors and the disrespect he demonstrated toward Prescott pushed the *Atlantic* so far as to defend the Spanish and condemn Wilson's anti-Catholicism. Wilson might "[enlist] the sympathies of a class in whom hatred of Romanism preponderates over knowledge and judgment," but readers exposed to Prescott would demand evidence. George Ticknor presented "Papers Discussing the Comparative Merits of Prescott's and Wilson's Histories, Pro. and Con." before the Massachusetts Historical Society in 1861.[140] Not surprisingly, Ticknor sided with his late friend Prescott.

Modern critics charge that Prescott was inclined to see the hand of destiny in the triumph of the conquerors and to estimate the achievements of the Aztecs accordingly. For all his weighing of evidence, he did not read his sources as critically as twenty-first-century scholars do, and he was unequipped with the tools of ethnohistory that might have supplied evidence where textual sources are lacking. Nonetheless, Prescott earned his place in the pantheon of American historiography. To no inconsiderable extent, his felicitous prose, his extraordinary organization, his ability to sustain suspense and to foreshadow doom and triumph compel attention. "[E]ven today's readers, conditioned by fast-paced drama and powerful visual imagery, are still likely to be gripped by the excitement of the story," notes J. H. Elliott.[141] Beyond considerations of style, however, Prescott managed to discuss vexing issues with contemporary overtones—notably slavery—and to question prevailing assumptions without promoting controversy. Although Parker faulted Prescott for not raising his voice against human bondage, Prescott did express an explicit critique of slavery that could not easily be dismissed as cant or fanaticism. His grace and tact expressed the thoughts of an open mind. His nuanced, sympathetic portrait of the people of the past challenged his readers to think more inclusively about the strangers on their borders and in their midst.

It would seem sacrilegious, then, or at least anticlimactic, to mention *The History of the Conquest of Mexico* in the same breath with two pieces of pulp fiction of the same period, George Lippard's novelette *Legends of Mexico* (1847) and Ned Buntline's *The Volunteer, or, the Maid of Monterey* (1847). Primitive in composition, sensational and sometimes quasi-pornographic in appeal, these texts, intended for a mass audience, seem to belong not to another category of literature but another universe. Their authors could not have been more dissimilar from the historian. Prescott labored for years in obtaining and interpreting obscure sources; Lippard and Buntline worked quickly, their research a matter of scanning the latest war news. Both Lippard and Buntline were Democrats—in Lippard's case a radical Democrat who looked for the righteous vindication of the workers—very much in contrast to Prescott's Whiggish conservatism.[142] Prescott paid considerable attention to the physical appearance of his masterworks, fretting over broken type, leading, binding specifications, and paper weights in order to assure the most pleasing and harmonious effect.[143] Lippard and Buntline, on the other hand, published in a world of wood pulp and mass production. Taking advantage of innovations in printing and distributing technologies, their fictional works (along with pamphlets, song sheets, and story papers), using newspaper accounts for background and stock characters and situations for structure, were produced with a frantic immediacy and sold for pennies.[144]

Yet on second glance these works intersect in subtle ways. Prescott wrote history influenced by the conventions of romantic fiction; Lippard and Buntline wrote accessible fiction grounded in recent history. All three authors traded in national pride. All three may have appealed to the same taste for thrills and violence. Lippard's and Buntline's audience almost certainly overlapped with Prescott's. All three authors benefited from—and took advantage of—a vast reading public thirsting for news from Mexico and eager for tales of heroism and adventure. However much he despised it, Prescott profited from the war with Mexico, both in terms of the new market it produced for his work and the access to formerly unobtainable sources it allowed him. Always a canny businessman, Prescott produced abridged versions of his own work when pirated abridgements threatened to eat into his market share. Despite his correspondence with a titled readership, ordinary middle-class readers clearly made up much of his audience. Parker damned his perspective with these words: "Mr. Prescott writes with the average Sense of mankind, with their average of Conscience—and his judgment, the average judgment of a trading town, is readily accepted by the average of men, and popular with them."[145] Lippard gained renown by appealing to just this "average" audience. Writing at nobody's invitation, he imagined *Legends of Mexico*, which he subtitled *The Battles of Taylor*, as part of a series of historical works that would stretch back to the struggle for the Aztec Empire.[146] Lippard's lurid and phenomenally popular *Quaker City* (1845) sold nearly 200,000 copies by the end of 1850, and he was proclaimed "unquestionably the most popular writer of the day" by *Godey's Lady's Book*.[147] If it was Prescott that soldiers carried with them into Mexico as a Baedecker, it was Lippard they turned to for entertainment around the dull campfire of the army bivouac: one volunteer recalled listening as a fellow soldier, sitting on a cannon, read from one of Lippard's romances about Washington and the Revolution.[148]

Born in Pennsylvania in 1822, Lippard had no very fine conception of the kind of historical research necessary for undertaking such a project, but he did have what Parker called a philosophy of history, one not so very far from Prescott's. What generally passes for history, Lippard writes, deals too much with "Kings and blood, Revolutions and Battles, Murderers by wholesale, but not a word . . . of that of Home-life of nations," Lippard insisted, ". . . History to speak to the heart, should not lie to us by wholesale, nor deal in vague generalities . . . It should, in narrating the records of an event or age, make us live with the people, fight by them in battle, sit with them at the table, make love, hate, fear, and triumph with them."[149] To this end Lippard presents a pageant of the U.S. War with Mexico, or, perhaps more accurately, a panorama. Like the narrator of one of these nineteenth-century presentations, he commands his audience to look at a series of scenes: a half-clad young woman on her couch, a Mexican general next to his "voluptuous bed," noble Zachary Taylor on his rude cot.[150] In *Legends of Mexico*, his narrative has no more connective tissue than that linking a series of articles in a newspaper. A volunteer listening to this material read aloud by a fellow soldier perched on a cannon could be called away to guard duty and return the next night without suffering any loss of comprehension.

A cursory glance at Lippard's style suggests that he had little more at stake than producing work quickly and selling it in prodigious quantities. A typical page from his oeuvre is a putrid mixture of awkward, pretentious writing, exaggerated patriotism, and queasy suggestions of incest, rape, and torture (Lippard typically promises to reveal more than he actually describes, which makes his literary striptease all the more meretricious). Yet recent scholarship has demonstrated that Lippard had more on his mind than simply selling novelettes at ten cents a copy.[151] In the late 1840s he formed an anticapitalist labor organization called the Brotherhood of the Union that within four years boasted 150 branches in twenty-four states.[152] Although he presented a United States entirely in the right ("We are the American People. Our lineage is from God"), he condemned "those gamblers in fraud, those grey-beards in falsehood, termed politicians, [who] have ursurped control of the Nation."[153] In his own day, Prescott's scrupulous critic Parker was inclined to take Lippard seriously, noting that although he was clearly writing from "an inferior motive," he always demonstrated "the interest of mankind, showing a ready sympathy with justice, mercy, and unaffected trust in God" (recall that it was the absence of sympathy for the Indians for which Parker took Prescott to task).¹⁵⁴ Lippard was hard to dismiss, either in his time or our own.

By far the most conspicuous part of *The Legends of Mexico* is the recounting of battle scenes. Here, perhaps surprisingly, Lippard betrays his debt to Prescott. "Did you ever read of Montezuma?" inquires Lippard; "you have read it all."¹⁵⁵ Again and again Lippard reproduces the improbability of Cortés's victory in the reality of his outnumbered forces. "Taylor, the Conqueror of the New Conquest of Mexico," constantly triumphs over impossible odds: two thousand to six thousand at Palo Alto; sixteen hundred against nine thousand at Resaca de la Palma; four thousand to twenty thousand at Buena Vista.¹⁵⁶

In observance of his stated purpose of letting history speak to the heart, he leaves no battlefield without inspecting every body lacerated, mutilated, drenched in gore. A widow holds the severed head of her husband in her lap and fends off hovering vultures; a bayonet pierces a soldier's skull, entering his mouth and emerging behind his ear.¹⁵⁷ Prescott himself was not above retailing this kind of gruesome image as *The Conquest of Mexico* shifts from romanticism to the gothic.¹⁵⁸ Up until the return of the conquistadores to Tenochtitlan after the *Noche Triste*, Prescott maintains a certain judicious circumspection about the mechanics of human sacrifice and cannibalism. But when the Spanish return to the city for its final conquest and destruction, heads literally roll, and in profusion. Literature scholar Jesse Alemán suggests that this shift has something to do with Prescott's own latent racial anxiety: "the romance of indigenous adversaries darkens as their terrifying resistance inspires the gothic in the romantic historian whose greatest fear in the 1840s may very well be collective racial rebellion to Anglo imperialism."¹⁵⁹

More significantly, Lippard partakes of Prescott's toleration.¹⁶⁰ He dismisses the idea that Americans are all of one origin. "We are no Anglo-Saxon People. No! All Europe sent its exiles to our shores. From all the nations of Northern Europe, we were formed. Germany and Sweden and Ireland and Scotland and Wales and England, aye and glorious France, all sent their oppressed to us, and we grew into a new race."¹⁶¹ Lippard makes clear that in the crucible of war this mass is fused into one people. The United States bestrides slavish Canada and pusillanimous Mexico, but Lippard imagines a future in which these foreign sovereignties are absorbed rather than simply conquered. The "mongrel" race of the south, consisting of both Spanish and Indian blood, will likewise "melt into, and be ruled by" the people of the United States.[162] To demonstrate exactly how this will happen, Lippard both opens and closes the novel with scenes of American soldiers taking Mexican women as wives—in both cases after facing their brides' fathers in battle.[163]

Like Lippard, pulp novelist Buntline—the pseudonym of Edward Zane Carroll Judson—emerged from the journalistic tradition and was responsible for helping to instigate the 1849 Astor Place Riot in New York.[164] Buntline's *The Volunteer; or, The Maid of Monterey: A Story of the Mexican War* (1847) is, like *Legends of Mexico*, a hastily composed dime novel, although composed along more conventional novelistic lines. The titular character is George Blakey, a vigorous young Kentuckian who raises a company of volunteers and goes to Mexico. Among Blakey's other accomplishments, notes Buntline, he is well informed about current events and well read in current literature despite his lack of formal education—the result, Buntline writes, of regular reading of two or three newspapers in his rural isolation.[165]

Blakey is in effect a cut-rate, Polk era Francis Berrian. Yet his mission to Mexico is not to free a neighboring country from oppression but (ostensibly) to defend the honor of his own. When he arrives south of the border, nothing is as it seems. Early in his military career Blakey makes prisoner of a Mexican officer. "He" turns out to be a woman, Edwina Canales, sister of a notorious guerilla chief, who speaks surprisingly good English. Edwina is as loyal to her country's cause as Blakey is to his, but Blakey frees her since "Americans never war upon women!"[166] One of Blakey's fellow volunteers, the Texan Ranger Gorin, recognizes the trousered Edwina Canales: she is Helen Vicars, a half-American, half-Mexican woman who had been "born in the province of Texas, while the Mexican flag waved over its soil. Yet when the province revolted," she adds, "we joined not with the Mexican arms. We became Texans in the true sense of the word."[167] The brutish Gorin, having been discouraged in his improper advances to the virtuous Edwina/Helen, had assembled a party of "Regulators" who murdered her parents; now he makes repeated attempts on her life.

Just as Prescott breathed life into his Indian characters, the tragic Montezuma and the hapless Atahualpa, Buntline peoples his narrative with individuated black and Mexican characters as well as white ones. Gorin has a slave described as so lazy as to appear narcoleptic.[168] On the other hand, Edwina's brother the guerilla leader has a statuesque black body servant "with a step wondrously light and agile for one of his bulk and build" whose son, "having a face expressive of great intelligence," acts as a spy on his own recognizance.[169] Blakey employs a Mexican guide "who, recreant to all feelings of honor or principles of patriotism, was serving his country's foe for gold."[170] Gorin hires a Mexican spy, too, although his is actually a double agent who serves Edwina/Helen and her brother.[171] This individuation of nonwhite characters is precisely what will seem so groundbreaking in *Uncle Tom's Cabin* five years later.

Buntline's flag-waving story makes patriotism the supreme good and betrayal of country an unpardonable offense, creating rather a problem when it is time to give his fictional lovers the requisite happy ending. His novel was published while the war still continued: as Edwina's brother acknowledges, in words that recall the lengths to which Cortés was brought in his determination to subdue the country: "My countrymen are as stubborn as mules. They will struggle, even though defeated on every hand; you must crush, nay extirpate, before you can conquer them!"[172] Buntline's plot calls for Blakey rescuing his lover on three separate occasions, with her returning the favor almost as often. The obligations that the lovers owe each other ultimately seem to trump those they owe their respective countries.

On each side family members doubt the appropriateness of the union: Blakey's mother complains that "blue eyes are prettier than black ones, any day!" and Edwina/Helen's brother laments that she has taken up with someone of Saxon blood, but his fiancée insists that Blakey's deeds are more indicative of his character than his descent.[173] When Blakey's tour of duty is over, Edwina/Helen's brother gives his blessing: "We give you our deepest treasure, noble American; we know that you will guard and cherish her. You have won her by your own prowess. Take her, and God bless you!"[174]

Buntline follows the precedent of earlier writers who used Latin American settings to present North American realities. But in *The Volunteer* the characters are themselves almost all American. The transplanted United States society of the U.S. War with Mexico allows for the kind of interactions among classes and races often apparent during times of armed conflict, when fraternization with sympathetic soldiers and brave people of color is possible.[175] Love can blossom with a Mexican who turns out to be Helen Vicars—not so very foreign after all.

Lippard and Buntline are more unambiguous in their celebration of the war's aims and the ambitions of the United States than is Prescott. But like him they are willing to "make room upon the earth" for difference; to acknowledge people on the margins and in border areas; to admit that the boundaries that separate nations and races are sometimes transgressed and that these transgressions are not always apparent. Their compromises were ones that proslavery advocates in the South, looking at slavery in Cuba and Brazil, steadfastly refused to make.

Chapter 5

An Even More Peculiar Institution

By almost any measure, the 1850s in the United States were marked by less national reticence on the subject of slavery than the decades that preceded them. But in public and private, Americans continued to complain bitterly that they were not free to speak out. Both political parties, declared Charles Sumner of Massachusetts in his 1852 "Freedom National; Slavery Sectional" speech in the Senate, insisted that the topic of slavery be evaded: "On a subject which for years has agitated the public mind; which yet palpitates in every heart and burns on every tongue; which in its immeasurable importance, dwarfs all other subjects; which, by its constant and gigantic presence, throws a shadow across these Halls; which at this very time calls for appropriations to meet extraordinary expenses it has caused, they impose the rule of silence. According to them, sir, we may speak of every-thing except that alone, which is most present in all our minds."[1] Four years later one of his opponents made sure Sumner's voice would be stilled in Congress. Representative Preston Brooks of South Carolina came up behind him in the Senate and beat him unconscious with his cane. The attack roused many previously reserved citizens to respond. His friend William Hickling Prescott wrote to him, "There are few in old Massachusetts, I can assure you, who do not feel that every blow on your cranium was a blow on them."[2]

The problem posed by the disposition of the former Mexican territory—its division into states slave or free, and the authority entitled to determine that division—quickly entered the national discourse. The Compromise of 1850, the implications of the Fugitive Slave Act, the Pottawatomie Massacre and the riots in Bleeding Kansas, the Supreme Court's *Dred Scott* decision and John Brown's raid on Harpers Ferry all acted as catalysts that impelled people to speak up and choose sides. Politics provided sides to join beginning in the 1840s: the Liberty Party, the Free Soil

Figure 9. Southerners were wary of drawing close connections between U.S. slavery and that of Brazil. As these illustrations from Thomas Ewbank's *Life in Brazil; or, a Journal of a Visit to the Land of the Cocoa and the Palm* (New York: Harper & Brothers, 1856) suggest, urban slaves took the place of modern infrastructure in Brazilian cities: in the absence of omnibuses, slaves ferried passengers in sedan chairs; yoked to massive trucks like oxen, they drew freight through the city streets.

Party, and ultimately the Republican Party addressed the issue of slavery more directly, even as the Whig Party, which had muted discussion in order to gather both North and South under its big tent, collapsed. "I have always hated slavery, I think as much as any Abolitionist,—I have been an old-line Whig,—I have always hated it, but I have always been quiet about it until this new era of the introduction of the Nebraska bill began," declared Abraham Lincoln in 1858.[3]

The breaking of that long-maintained silence was apparent even to foreign visitors. The Swedish writer Fredrika Bremer noted that in 1850 the question of slavery was no longer "forbidden, on pain of death, in Congress."[4] A few days after his arrival in New York in 1856, Edwin L. Godkin, the Irish journalist and future editor of the *Nation*, recalled, "I became aware that themes were under popular discussion which had never before been so discussed—the rights and wrongs of slavery, the equality of man, the provisions of the written Constitution, the position of leading public men on questions which were half moral and only half political or legal."[5] The constraints that had led a canny politician like Lincoln to hold his tongue were presumably different from those governing the "popular discussion" Godkin mentioned, but heightened awareness of slavery as a problem brought the issue into the open in the 1850s.

Uncle Tom's Cabin swept away the dam that had blocked representations of slavery in U.S. fiction, and the subject was now treated forthrightly:

ENTRANCE TO A COFFEE ESTATE.

Figure 10. This Cuban coffee estate from "Three Weeks in Cuba, by an Artist," *Harper's New Monthly Magazine* 6, no. 22 (January 1853): 172 is depicted in a manner that emphasizes its exoticism, and possibly its decadence. Some Southerners worried that Cuba was another Haiti in the making. Image courtesy of Butler Library, Columbia University in the City of New York.

for example, in Caroline Lee Hentz's *The Planter's Northern Bride* (1854), a slaveholder about to marry an abolitionist's daughter pleads for the cessation of his future father-in-law's incendiary activities: "You are blowing the flames of insurrection, and no language can convey the faintest conception of the horrors that may ensue."[6] The paranoia of hysterical Southerners suddenly appeared justified to some, while the erstwhile fanaticism of Northern abolitionists seemed less extreme to others. The middle ground of silence, where people spoke in whispers or through metaphor to avoid giving offense, did not disappear entirely, but it was shrinking.

The case of New England-born George William Gordon illustrates the greater willingness of formerly cautious politicians of the 1850s to identify themselves with a once-extreme cause. As the U.S. consul to Rio de Janeiro in the early 1840s, Gordon did much to expose the illegal trade in slaves between Rio and the coast of Africa. He kept meticulous records of the slave ships, the ports where they were registered, and the names of their owners—compiling a catalogue that revealed that many of them came from Boston, Portland, New York, Philadelphia, and Salem.[7] In 1846 abolitionist Lewis Tappan wrote to him, "Are you willing to prepare a work for the press—telling all you know? A great service might be done the cause of humanity."[8] Evidently Gordon was not willing. But in 1856, now running as the American Party candidate for Massachusetts governor, Gordon was more inclined to publicize his antislavery activities. In support of his candidacy appeared a pamphlet mincing no words and outlining in detail "The Slave Trade at Rio de Janeiro—Seizure of Slave Vessels—Conviction of Slave Dealers, Personal Liberation of Slaves, &c." The pamphlet contained the testimony of two African teenagers whose evidence of the inhumanity of the trade provided ammunition to "lovers of freedom."[9]

And yet talking about slavery often lobbed the apple of discord into polite conversation with the impact of a hand grenade. The subject still possessed the power to sour a business deal or end a friendship. Wise men and women looked for ways to discuss it indirectly. Miner and bookkeeper Charles Ballou wrote to his sister Almira from the rough gold-rush settlement of Shaw's Flat, California, in 1856, a town he described as the nation in microcosm, with transplants from all over the country and a wide variety of responses to current political issues, particularly slavery extension. Tension was often held in check through distraction: "in their burning desires to 'serve their country' [politicians] are making every effort to banish the subject [of slavery] from the public's mind, by talking about, 'Nationality,' war with 'England,' and 'Americans ruling America,' t'is all in vain." Ballou predicted, "The line between North and South, is being rapidly drawn, and some events which have lately taken place here, have served to make it more distinct."[10]

Furthermore, overt discussion of U.S. slavery was not the only context in which U.S. slavery was discussed. As historian David Potter wrote memorably of the "impending crisis" period, "Questions of tariff policy, of banking policy, of public land policy, of subsidy to railroads—all loomed large and engendered strong feelings. Such questions were not necessarily sectional, and on their face they seemed unrelated to slavery, but they tended to get translated into terms of sectional conflict, with slavery somehow involved."[11] To Potter's list might be added the way Latin America was talked about in the 1850s: it continued to serve as a context for what could not be said overtly. For Southerners, it even allowed the expression of a very particular manifestation of the proslavery argument.

The more clearly drawn were the battle lines, the less people felt comfortable speaking up when they held opinions contrary to their neighbors or associates. As its proslavery rhetoric became increasingly inflexible, the South represented itself as a world apart. Stifling Northern criticism was proving impossible, but at least internal dissent must be proscribed. In such a climate, Latin America served as a useful metaphor in sectional, rather than national, conversation to engage issues that might otherwise be considered treasonous. U.S. Southerners in particular used critiques of Cuba and Brazil as a way of disguising their own anxieties about slavery, to vent the possibility that there might be flaws in a slave society. Although they felt increasingly beleaguered by a world that was setting bond people free, they refrained from holding Cuba and Brazil up as exemplars of how bondage could be adapted to a variety of circumstances or how it could thrive in foreign cultures. They shared many perspectives and goals with Latin American slaveowners.[12] But when U.S. slaveholders analyzed the practical workings of slavery in Brazil and Cuba, when they publicly compared themselves to their Latin American counterparts, they found more basis for contrast than for community.

In this cautious conversation, Cuba and Brazil were slave systems that Southerners defined themselves against, rather than peers that might aid them in their defense of slavery. They pounced on data about Cuba and Brazil not for offshore evidence of slavery's superiority to other labor systems, but for proof that their own version of the peculiar institution was in fact unique. Rather than glorifying slavery in the abstract, U.S. Southerners carefully framed their observations of Cuban and Brazilian slavery to particularize their celebration of slavery in the United States. By estranging Cuba and Brazil, U.S. slaveholders hoped to credibly attribute to Latin Americans the very qualities antislavery writers heaped on them—cruelty and inhumanity. In the process, they reassured themselves that they were not heirs to the errors that had doomed slavery in Haiti and the West Indies, whose echoes they identified in their Latin American neighbors. The denigration and belittling of a failed competitor as a way of reassuring an uncertain population echoes the situation in Cuba itself half a century earlier: in the wake of the Haitian Revolution, Cuban planters saw an opportunity. Once Haitian sugar production lay in ruins, Cuba chose to fill the void by expanding its output. At the same time, Cuban planters emphasized all the ways they would avoid the errors of the French in their irresponsible administrative policies. The ratio of Spanish colonists to African slaves promised safety in Cuba. As the number of slave imports rose precipitously in the nineteenth century, however, those arguments became harder to sustain.[13]

In the South of the 1850s, what could be said about U.S. slavery—and by whom it could be proclaimed—was rigorously policed. Hinton Rowan Helper, a Southern writer of polemics warning of disasters to come, recalled that in 1855 a Virginia editor would not release a book he had written without excising certain passages, making him realize that there was not "any medium of the press through which thought could be disseminated, save only where the thinking, honest or dishonest, had been done with a view to the more positive security and aggrandizement of slavery."[14] As the 1850s proceeded, editor James Dunwoody Brownson DeBow found it increasingly difficult to republish the work from Northern publications in his eponymous *Review* without a disclaimer; otherwise readers accused him of being an abolitionist.[15]

Private conversations were also monitored for potential subversion. "There is a terrorism at work in the Southern States which effectually keeps down every open expression of dissent from the prevailing orthodox creed of slavery," noted British visitor James Stirling in 1857.[16] Indiscreet visitors to the South were warned about the inadvisability of asking too many questions about the conditions they observed. Jane Cazneau, a fierce advocate of expansionism and a journalist who had worked as a war correspondent during the U.S. War with Mexico, met a British abolitionist aboard a steamboat bound for Texas in 1850. She found him a little too eager to point out that "Political equality and social amalgamation are twin sisters."[17] She sternly warned "the stalwart *negrophilo*,—to borrow a word the Cubans have lately coined,—not to be rash in his arguments, for they might be misunderstood at the south, where it was a stringent necessity of self-preservation to suppress all discussions that could tend to unbridle the tiger that sleeps by their hearths."[18] Self-censorship was effective, too. "[H]owever politicians may talk at Washington, to frighten the doughfaces, there is a class among the slaveholders, who realize the evils of their position," remarked a character in Mary Pike's antislavery novel *Caste* (1856): "They watch silently, however, for no body dares say openly what would offend the multitude."[19]

In a climate of unyielding defense of slavery, honest discussion about how to reform obvious abuses or address developing problems appeared disloyal. Journalist Frederick Law Olmsted, on a trip through Alabama and Mississippi in 1860, pointed out that while Southerners were eager to probe the disadvantages of the Northern free-labor system (a conversation in which Northern reformers were not shy about participating), they refused to entertain any examination of the possible shortcomings of the slave-labor economy. "Why, if their system has such tangible evidence of its advantages within the personal knowledge of any citizen, do they object to its alleged disadvantages being set forth for consideration, and, if it should happen, discussion?" he asked.[20] But many problems had far-reaching implications. For example, white Southerners preferred not to publicly air the eternal problem of fugitives. Despite the evidence of thousands of advertisements for the return of runaway slaves, Southern periodicals offered little advice about how to effectively prevent the escape of slave owners' human property or how to recover their lost bondmen. Acknowledging the extent of the problem meant admitting that slaves were kept in bondage only under duress, and articles addressing plantation management skirted the issue.[21]

The most consistently boosterish texts were books and periodicals—like *DeBow's Review, Southern Literary Messenger,* and *Southern Quarterly Review*—that presumed to speak for the whole South, and articulated the shared concerns of the region long before secession. Southern intellectuals, many of whom knew and corresponded with each other, made a conscious effort to supply answers to the difficult questions posed by abolitionists in the 1850s about the brutality and backwardness of an economic system that seemed increasingly antiquated.[22] They also showed a particular sensitivity to Northern attacks on slavery in particular and the Southern way of life in general, and supplied extensive, tightly structured replies. Spooked by what they saw as Northern aggression, Southerners were more successful in circling the wagons in defense of slavery than were Northerners unilateral in condemnation of it.[23] Whether or not every proslavery text spoke for the entire South, this confident literature enjoyed a respectability not matched by the antislavery publications of the North.[24] When Richmond and New Orleans spoke for themselves they quickly disabused the image of a monolithic South. Their understandings of Rio and Havana were as various and unique as their positions on any other issue. But when they spoke for the South to defend slavery, geographically separate regions spoke with one voice, and that voice disparaged Rio and Havana—even though plenty of individual planters enjoyed cordial and close relations with their counterparts south of the border. In defending slavery, the South was learning to sound like a nation long before secession.

One cannot proceed far in the perusal of these texts without sensing that a great variety of material shares but one agenda. *DeBow's Review* provides a good example of proslavery's most myopic lens. Superficially a business journal that ran articles and statistical overviews that would not be entirely out of place in a modern commercial publication, the July 1857 issue included features on "The Wealth, Resources, and Hopes of Virginia," "The Industrial Resources of Delaware," shipping, patents, and the national budget.[25] At the same time, editor James Dunwoody Brownson DeBow's eclectic tastes (or perhaps the limitations on available material for publication) permitted the inclusion of notices of new books, an article by George Fitzhugh about the modern relevance of Aristophanes's "Ecclesiazusæ," a piece on anthropology, and an exposé of exploited Chinese workers brought to the West Indies.

Yet each of these topics quickly turns into a defense of white Southern superiority or a justification for slavery. Thus, Fitzhugh's reading of Aristophanes remarked that "the Athenian dames were but a little behind the modern free-love and infidel Amazonide who fight shoulder to shoulder with the free negroes and Black Republicans of the North."[26] "The Industrial Resources of Delaware" noted that the state still held three thousand slaves in bondage and was therefore a "sister State" to the South.[27] The hypocrisy of both England and the abolitionist North was manifest in the former case by the use of "coolies" to grow sugar in Mauritius and in the latter by the provisioning of slave trading vessels in Long Island to make the voyage between Africa and Cuba.[28] "The Earth and its Indigenous Races," a capsule discussion of an 1857 book edited by surgeon and scientist Josiah Nott, suggested that "there were many creations, in different zones of the habitable earth"; thus the ancestors of the Europeans and of the Africans had no common origin.[29] A short piece on agricultural patents poked fun at the idea that beet sugar would ever eclipse "slave-made sugar."[30] A book review of *White Oak Farm* cast a skeptical glance at the novel's moralizing on the subject of slavery. The work's theme, that "the slave is our fellow-creature" might be just as easily thrown back in the faces of Northern capitalists.[31]

Juxtaposed beside this literature of apparent consensus, however, newspaper accounts provide more localized perspectives suggesting considerable regional, political, economic, and cultural variation. Geography, class, and political affiliation strongly influenced Southern priorities.[32] Many people in the older states of the Upper South could foresee a not-distant day when slavery in their region would be no more. In the Deep South, on the other hand, expansionists kept audible the drumbeat of further Latin American conquest up to the Civil War. Yeomen farmers were less committed to slavery than were plantation nabobs and some of them actively opposed the Slave Power's claims to the most productive land. Coastal cities had a different take on the importance of slavery than did land-bound planta-tions, and residents of Charleston thought differently about slavery than did those of New Orleans.

The historian David Donald concluded that in an increasingly modern world the proslavery project was an exercise in nostalgia, "not so much defending slavery-as-it-was as . . . dreaming of the South-as-it-might-have-been."[33] Yet Donald's evocation of the Lost Cause *avant la lettre* does not quite explain the exertion that writers applied to their task. More convinc-ing is historian James Oakes's allusion to fear: "While the slave economy was being transformed from within, its importance outside the South was waning. Corresponding declines in the South's demographic predominance and political authority were brought into sharp relief by the increasing vol-ume of Northern antislavery rhetoric."[34] Southerners were keenly conscious of abolitionist attacks against them, and able to perceive the statistics that backed up Northern arguments in a rapidly changing world. Proslavery discourse attempted to rebut abolitionist charges point for point. But it was also evidently intended to remind Southerners why they were right, to strengthen their resolve and dispel their doubts.[35]

It can legitimately be asked for how large a constituency this material spoke. "Did the intellectuals discussed here have much influence? Did they, as it were, speak for their people, in particular the slaveholders?" asks histo-rian Eugene Genovese at the beginning of *Slaveholders' Dilemma: Freedom and Progress in Southern Conservative Thought, 1820–1860*. "The answer to both questions is yes."[36] Even when the proslavery propagandists did not speak for everyone, they often spoke the loudest, and their opponents kept quiet.[37] Ordinary people justified slavery with some of the same arguments, albeit in their own words. Mary Ann Waterman of Clear Branch, Virginia, wrote a series of letters to her cousin Lucretia Sibley in Providence, Rhode Island, in the 1840s and 1850s. Waterman often sounded apologetic when she talked about slavery—"I do not like a slave state," she admitted in one letter. She herself employed a variety of hired-out slaves, "bound girls," and free women to help with her extensive housework. But at the possibility of making a match between her cousin and an eligible slaveholding widower, she echoed points made by the proslavery press:

I suppose this thing of slavery will rise up as a mighty bugbear, to fright you from a comfortable home. But it need not. The poor creatures are here, and if you are a good calvinist, you must believe it is necessarily so, as God foreordained whatsoever comes to pass, and that agreeable to his immutable decree, as slavery does exist, could not be otherwise. I do not subscribe to that doctrine myself, but I do believe that thousands will praise God through vast eternity that they were ever brought under the sound of the gospel, though it was by the chains of slavery. . . . You had no hand in bringing them into a state of bondage and if you consent to place yourself in a situation to make their lives more comfortable and pleasant I cannot see that you will be doing wrong. They are a good conditioned set of servants, and having a predilection for you, would I believe give you less trouble than anyone else.[38]

Waterman's defense—that slaveholders lived in circumstances not of their making, that slavery was compatible with the Gospel and in fact a benefit to the erstwhile heathen, and finally that slave labor was often superior to paid labor—were pillars of the proslavery position.

At the same time, it should be kept in mind that behind the public face of proslavery apologetics lurked private doubts and misgivings. In their diaries and in letters to friends, Southerners confided fears of slave insurrections and questions about the absolute rightness of slavery that they dared not admit in public. "I wonder if it be a sin to think slavery a curse to any land," plantation mistress Mary Boykin Miller Chesnut brooded in her diary just before the start of the Civil War. "[Abolitionist Charles] Sumner said not one word of this hated institution which is not true." She went on to describe the humiliation of living "surrounded by prostitutes." The paternity of every half-white child on a plantation was perfectly obvious to every female neighbor; only the wife of the master pretended blissful ignorance. "Who thinks any worse of a Negro or Mulatto woman for being *a thing we can't name*." (The editor notes that these words were written over an "unrecoverable erasure." Apparently Chesnut could not name the thing even in the privacy of her diary.)[39]

Cuba and Brazil became safe spaces in which these self-censoring white Southerners could air potentially seditious views about slavery. In their examinations they drew upon the same sources to which latter-day historians have referred, namely, export and census statistics and travel accounts, and they sometimes deplored the inherent biases of this material. "The progress and present condition of this empire [Brazil], so rich in nature's choicest gifts, are then to us matters worthy of investigation. Unfortunately, at the outset, we encounter the difficulty of obtaining information, and it becomes necessary to draw one's inference from works written either by Northerners or Europeans," complained one article.[40] But the attitudes these writings reflected would not necessarily have offended proslavery sentiments. Typical accounts of travel in Cuba and Brazil, even when offering firsthand observations by Northerners, traded in a finite vocabulary of stereotypes that fit perfectly into Southern publications.

In many of their considerations of Cuba and Brazil, proslavery writers focused on the landscape rather than the sometimes radically different deployment of slave labor. Indeed, in many analyses, these foreign slave systems are almost incidental: what interested U.S. slaveholders was the land itself, rich with unexploited potential. Many Southern accounts of these regions read like real estate prospectuses, descriptions of places that might alternately be colonized by North American knowhow or used to contain the unnecessary overflow of natural slave increase. That slavery thrived in these regions was not insignificant: U.S. Southerners recognized that there were only certain geographic regions where a plantation-based, agriculturally intensive economy proved viable, and many doubted that slave labor could be effectively used in contexts other than physical work requiring little judgment or initiative.[41] But overt comparisons with alternate slave societies were not the point of these geographical assessments. Instead, they offered extensive catalogues of agricultural and mineral resources, assembling figures on exports and human capital with almost proprietary interest. Although Southerners expressed doubts about the way the Spanish Americans and Portuguese Americans developed these resources and deployed labor, they fairly salivated in describing the wealth of Cuba and Brazil, measuring harbors and calculating profits on potential harvests as if they expected to take immediate possession. This territory contained infinite possibilities for the expansion of U.S. influence and sometimes U.S. control.

Southerners expressed frustration about the difficulty of obtaining information about these tempting regions. Oceanographer Matthew Fontaine Maury of Virginia, one of the first Americans to survey Brazil, bristled with indignation about the "Japanese-like policy which has been observed with regard to scientific explorations of La Plata and its tributaries [and] has kept the world in the dark as to many parts of that valley."[42] But descriptions of Cuba provide a clue about why the Brazilians had reason to be secretive. A report published in 1854, at the height of the filibuster period, listed, besides the usual statistics on population, climate, and natural resources, an extensive survey of the military force of the island along with the ships in the navy and the number of guns borne by each.[43] Clearly conquest was a constant subtext.

The issue of territorial acquisition was the subject of much regional variation in the South in the 1850s. Even when most Southerners gave apparent support to plans of expansion, competing motivations lurked behind their impulses—to provide more proslavery legislators in Congress, to mark territory and check the spread of free labor, to have a place to banish unnecessary blacks.[44] New Orleans had economic reasons for supporting U.S. expansion into the Caribbean: city leaders could see that the railroads of the North were intercepting more and more of the freight that had formerly passed down the Mississippi to the Crescent City, and they hoped to restore their market share of the nation's trade.[45] The Upper South, on the other hand, was more lukewarm about annexing more of Latin America, except to exile surplus slaves. This attitude concerned some in the Deep South. If the demand for laborers in the proposed tropical regions of the U.S. drained the old seacoast states of its bondmen so quickly that the political bona fides of even such proslavery stalwarts as Maryland and Virginia were in question, what would happen to the fragile sectional balance in Congress?[46] "It is not generally known, *yet it is nevertheless true that two-thirds of the people of Virginia are open and undisguised advocates of ridding the State of Slavery*," warned the *Augusta Chronicle*.[47]

Southern acquisitive impulses typically focused more on Cuba, a nearby colony of a worn-out European power, rather than on Brazil, a faraway, independent empire. Throughout the 1850s, Spain's grip on its ever-faithful isle seemed conspicuously tenuous. Two potential dangers argued strongly in favor of Cuban annexation by the United States. First, an independent Cuba, without Spanish control, might prove easy prey for British or French colonization. Second, given the high black population, it might as easily proceed down the road already trodden by Haiti and become a black republic. In either case, slavery would end in Cuba. England or France would emancipate the slaves as much out of a desire to eliminate a competing source of cheap, slave-grown sugar as any misplaced humanitarian impulse.[48] Recalling the precedent of Saint Domingue, Southerners feared that the well-publicized success of foreign slaves winning their freedom could inspire slaves in the United States.

The Gulf states in particular favored seizing Cuba out of fear of the effects of Cuban emancipation on their slaves at home: "such an event would entail upon us a struggle with the negro communities upon our Southern borders, resulting, perhaps, in a war of extermination against four millions of free blacks," raved the *New Orleans Times Picayune* in 1854.[49] In the Senate, Judah P. Benjamin of Louisiana, possibly remembering the goad to slave insurrection thought to have come from the Haitian revolt, deplored the "pernicious influence upon the social, commercial, and political interests and institutions of the United States" that would result from the abolition of Cuban slavery.[50] The *New Orleans Delta* urged private citizens to come forward "with the sinews of war" in the absence of officially sanctioned U.S. government action.[51]

But what effect would Cuba's entry into the union have on the economy of the existing sugar-growing areas of the United States? Once under the stewardship of more efficient U.S. planters, the fertile lands of the Caribbean might produce such a surplus that they would drive planters in Louisiana to destitution. And the Cuban slaves, once reproducing at capacity because of the beneficent treatment of their new masters, would render superfluous the slaves of the Upper South, whose value depended upon their being commodities that could be sold to the new cotton-growing regions.[52] DeBow himself tried to paper over this danger with reassuring promises. "It is not saying too much to say that if we hold Cuba, in the next fifty years we will hold the destiny of the richest and most increased commerce that ever dazzled the cupidity of man. And with that commerce we can control the power of the world."[53] The U.S. possession of Cuba did not necessarily entail the ruin of Louisiana: Cuban sugar was kept cheap by the illegal importation of African slaves, which would cease under U.S. law.[54] Further, with the price of sugar equalized, the United States might use its influence to reduce the tariffs on imported sugar in foreign markets, producing a vastly increased demand for the product.[55]

Expansionist projects were time sensitive, waxing and waning as the probability of the U.S. possession of Cuba appeared proximate or remote and as the Civil War approached. As important were mutually beneficial opportunities for trade between regions that shared certain assumptions. Dreams of further expansion fired the imagination of J. D. B. DeBow in 1848. "The North Americans *will* spread out far beyond their present

bounds. They *will* encroach again and again on their neighbors. New territories *will* be planted, declare their independence, and be annexed! We have
New Mexico and California! We *will* have Old Mexico and Cuba! The Isthmus cannot arrest—nor even the Saint Lawrence!! Time has all of this in
her womb."[56]

Cuba, temptingly close to Florida, was the focus of imperialist lust. But
the acquisition of "the Gem of the Antilles" proved surprisingly elusive.
Spain refused an offer by President Polk to purchase Cuba for one hundred
million dollars, and a bungled second attempt to buy the island led to the
scandal of the Ostend Manifesto in 1854. Between these years, filibusters led
by Narciso Lopéz and backed by John Quitman, governor of Mississippi,
attempted to seize Cuba by force.[57] Spain hinted it was contemplating the
emancipation of Cuban slaves—a poison pill intended to deter the filibusters, but a threat that turned some Southerners wild with impatience, determined not to see the formation of a black republic ninety miles from
American shores.[58]

The passage of the Kansas-Nebraska Act in 1854, effectively disembow-
eling the provisions of the Missouri Compromise, cost Southerners much
of the political capital they might have needed to secure support from their
northern allies in order to annex Cuba.[59] In the event, however, the failure
of Kansas to enter the Union as a slave state offered slavery expansionists
another incentive for the acquisition of Spain's prize possession. Unlike
the Western territories of the continental United States, where introducing
slavery was at best a questionable proposition, Cuba was territory with an
existing, and a flourishing, slave economy. The incorporation of Cuba into
the Union would be a comparatively easy way to increase proslavery representation in the U.S. Senate.[60]

The exposure of the Ostend Manifesto and subsequent embarrassment
to the administration of Franklin Pierce suppressed schemes to acquire
Cuba until James Buchanan became president in 1857. His interest in the
island reached a crescendo in 1859, when Congress considered a bill appropriating three hundred million dollars for the purchase.[61] Once again, however, Spain proved uncooperative, refusing to part with what the rhetoric
of the time referred to as the last remaining jewel in its empire. The decade's
last serious attempt to gain Cuba foundered.[62]

The 1850s saw the fluorescence of further filibustering projects undertaken by William Walker and others who saw the Caribbean as an American
Mediterranean. Some still dreamed of seizing even more of Mexico.[63] Yet

these schemes won neither the official support of the federal government nor the U.S. military.[64] Under the 1818 Neutrality Act they were illegal.[65] The 1850 Clayton-Bulwer Treaty with Great Britain further stymied U.S. expansion into Central America and prevented official sanction of many filibustering attempts.[66] These projects neither drew exclusively Southern participants, nor were they overtly disunionist. But promoters certainly used benefits to the slave interest as a selling point in the South.[67] Unlike the Mexican war, which won the grudging acquiescence, if not the support, of many of its detractors, even those from the North, the filibusters never garnered anything like widespread approval. Perpetual outliers, they recruited deadbeats, criminals, and soldiers of fortune with vouchers for future glory and prosperity.

Ultimately, the lack of unanimity in the Southern effort to make Cuba part of the United States contributed to these missteps.[68] By the 1850s the porous borders of the Upper South, where abolitionists reached out to extend a helping hand to escaping fugitives, became a greater threat to slavery than the failure to acquire Cuba or more of Mexico. Southern politicians applied their energies to keeping Kansas open to slavery not because it offered ideal growing conditions for plantation agriculture but because it served as a buffer between Missouri and freedom.[69]

But the ultimate reason for the hesitation with which Southerners embraced the possibility of further conquest of contiguous Latin American territory may have been its population of slaves and Spaniards, which no amount of rhetorical bleaching would make entirely white. Filibuster attempts to annex Mexico, Honduras, and Ecuador similarly collapsed under the challenge of making citizens of people who had been so effectively vilified. Although Baltimore native Anna Ella Carroll commended William Walker for his takeover of Nicaragua in 1855 in *A Star of the West*, she expressed her conviction that Mexico's "population of ignorant paupers and criminals . . . could never appreciate our Anglo-American liberty, under the aegis of American laws."[70]

In regard to Cuba, General Felix Huston insisted in a letter to the *Mississippian*, "They are a full blooded white race, and not mongrels, like the Mexicans," but his was a minority view.[71] Even DeBow came to temper his expansionism by the early 1850s, publishing articles that admitted that grave hazards might attend Cuba's annexation. The island offered little open territory for footloose Southerners; it was already densely populated, and populated with people who were "different from us in nearly every respect, and would not easily coalesce with us. . . . Cuba is now, and will perhaps always be, in the hands of the Spanish race, which can never be assimilated to our own."[72] Legislators drawn from such a population were sure to be corrupt.[73] Spanish Cubans would be more likely to migrate to the continental United States than would U.S. Southerners be drawn to Cuba.[74] Were Cuba added to the Union, *DeBow's* predicted, the North would demand the annexation of Canada, a territory so vast it would quickly undo any temporary representational advantage to be gained.[75]

The territory of Brazil offered another attraction, one only increased by its distance from the United States and the unlikelihood of its incorporation into the Union. By the 1840s whites in the Upper South beheld areas where the soil was exhausted and slaves were superfluous. They foresaw a time when slaves would become a positive burden.[76] In such an instance the South would follow the example of the North, which had banished its free-men after abolition—or sold them beforehand—rather than incorporating them into civil society.[77] At such time, declared *DeBow's* with apparently no conscious irony, the valley of the Amazon offered blacks a "last resting-place upon this continent."[78] Brazil thus would provide what Cuba, because of its overpopulation, could not supply, in a term used with increasing frequency during the 1850s, "the safety-valve of the Union."[79] Exiling unwanted slaves to Brazil, where the undiscriminating Portuguese had not the finer feeling necessary to exhibit prejudice against these black immigrants, would be a blessing to all concerned. "Let the young, the vigorous and healthy of both sexes, the source of future increase, be the sole adventurers selected for this expedition," proposed the *Southern Literary Messenger*, "and the others left to finish their days in the land of their birth and sojourn."[80]

The so-called diffusion argument, the idea that spreading the area of slavery would "dilute the evil," dates at least to Thomas Jefferson, who in an 1820 letter to Lafayette included the amelioration of slave misery among the benefits of spreading human bondage over a greater area.[81] Where slaves were a lower proportion of the population, they would be more valuable and thus better treated. During the Missouri Compromise debates, other Southerners added a sinister component to this argument by suggesting that the risk to be avoided by reducing the concentration of slaves was the possibility of insurrection.[82] But when thirty years later in the wake of Texas annexation some Southerners proposed reopening the African slave trade because of the insufficiency of domestic bondmen, they exposed the fallacy of the "Texas-outlet logic."[83]

Alternately, as was also suggested, an independent Brazil uninfluenced by North American abolitionism would provide a viable getaway for frustrated slaveholders in the event of a U.S. regime unfriendly to slavery.[84] In comparison with Cuba, with its hobbling restrictions imposed by its despotic European colonizer, Brazil was autonomous and relatively tolerant. According to C. S. Stewart, author of *Brazil and La Plata: The Personal Record of a Cruise*, Brazil's progress resulted from the 1808 immigration into Rio de Janeiro of the Portuguese court and twenty thousand followers fleeing Napoleon's advancing army. In an instant, according to Stewart, the transplanted Europeans introduced active commerce, vibrant arts and culture, and a modern press.[85] Though Brazil was governed with a modern parliamentary system, the presence of a royal sovereign in the person of the emperor, Dom Pedro, assured stability and succession.[86] A monarchy might respect the rights of slaveholders that were imperiled in the U.S. democracy that was easily swayed by abolitionist sentiment. If abolition passed from threat to reality in the United States, the region of the Amazon basin would provide a fertile home for the perpetuation of slavery, predicted *DeBow's Review* in 1854.[87] After the Civil War, defeated Confederates—known as *Confederados*—did indeed follow this prescription and decamped for Brazil.[88]

The benefits provided by Cuba and Brazil as territories did not have to involve their susceptibility to U.S. domination. The United States already enjoyed a profitable trade with Cuba, which would be increased if the island won its independence and Spain forfeited the duties the mother country imposed on imports.[89] Even more might be gained by increased trade with the fabulous and unexploited wealth of Brazil, a country that was not held up as the object of imperial takeover. "The 'policy of commerce,' and not the 'policy of conquest,' is the policy of the United States," insisted Matthew Fontaine Maury. But Brazil refused to yield its riches. "Has diplomacy no arts, commerce no charms, by which this policy may be broken up: by which its rivers may be opened to navigation, its forests to settlement, its pampas to cultivation?"[90]

However attractive the real estate, though, U.S. Southerners drew few positive lessons from the slave systems that thrived in the enviable territory of Cuba and Brazil. They preferred to hold up their own version of human bondage as a paragon rather than to admit they might be schooled by their Latin American counterparts. In spite of the fact slavery advocates in the United States used Southern journals to discuss more progressive ways of extracting labor from their bondmen and -women; more cost-effective ways of feeding, clothing, and housing them; more scientific ways of caring for them in sickness; and more efficacious means of punishing them; they avoided drawing productive lessons from the markedly different deployment of slaves in Cuba and especially in Brazil.[91]

What might they have learned? To take one example, the diverse occupations of slaves in the cities of Latin America might have offered a model for a more urbanized and commercial South: the traveler was sure to notice the variety of employments of slaves in Rio, noted one account.[92] In Cuba, while Africans off the boat were sent to the fields, second-generation slaves were generally selected "for city labor, becoming postilions, house-servants, draymen, laborers on the wharves, and the like."[93] Slaves might thus have had a role in the modernizing South championed by *DeBow's Review*, which employed the occasional tagline "Commerce is King."[94] In accounting for the decision not to cite Cuba and Brazil as exemplars, historian Michael O'Brien declares flatly that "the Old South shared this sense of relevance very little. It was its misfortune mostly to look towards Europe for its comparative cultural understandings, not Brazil or Cuba, with which it shared many experiences."[95]

But to learn from these societies would be to acknowledge weaknesses in the inviolability of the proslavery defense, and Southerners showed no hesitation in asserting that U.S. slavery was superior to every other system, ancient and modern.[96] "Domestic slavery in the Southern States has produced the same results in elevating the character of the master that it did in Greece and Rome. He is lofty and independent in his sentiments, generous, affectionate, brave and eloquent; he is superior to the Northerner in every thing but the arts of thrift," declared Fitzhugh. And for the slave, bondage secured the benefits falsely promised by the up-to-date "beau ideal of Communism; it [the Southern farm] is a joint concern, in which the slave consumes more than the master, of the coarse products, and is far happier, because although the concern may fail, he is always sure of a support; he is only transferred to another master to participate in the profits of another concern."[97] Since the ideology of U.S. slavery had a ready response to every objection, a retort to every attack, it could only undermine its own perfection by borrowing from and thus putting itself in the ideological debt of its poorer relations.

In two areas only were North American proslavery advocates willing to make even half-hearted associations with Cuba and Brazil. They insisted that it was owing to slavery that Cuba and Brazil were, after them, the most prosperous economies in the New World. They pointed out that, like them, Cuba and Brazil had fewer incidents of crime and social unrest. But beyond this, they did not use these societies to buttress their defense of slavery.

According to *DeBow's Review*, the leading journals in Europe acknowledged the contrast between the prosperity and contentment of Cuba, Brazil, and the U.S. South and the degradation, poverty, and barbarism of Central and South America and the English and French colonies in the West Indies where slavery had ended.[98] Slavery brought civilization: lacking the peculiar institution, New World societies easily slipped into savagery. But slavery put the U.S. in rather oddly assorted company. "The civilized world does not condemn [slavery]," insisted Henry Bedinger, U.S. minister plenipotentiary to Denmark, in a conversation with British Admiral Sir Charles Napier, "for the United States, Spain, Brazil, Russia, and Turkey (as civilized as some Christian countries I could name) form a considerable part of the civilized world."[99] How were Southern readers expected to understand "civilization" in this context? Specific attributes of Southern progress were more often assumed than enumerated. The South lagged in railroads and manufactures; its citizens had to go North or abroad for education. But defining civilization too loosely drew the United States into an undesired identification with Brazil and Cuba, which were noted for many qualities from which Southerners wished to distance themselves.

Both *DeBow's Review* and *Southern Quarterly Review* found a happy characteristic of civilization in economic prosperity, which could be quantified. According to author David Christy (of Cincinnati, but cited approvingly in proslavery literature), civilization was advanced through the cultivation of cotton, which "may be seen freighting every vessel, from Christian nations, that traverses the seas of the globe; and filling the warehouses and shelves of the merchants of two-thirds of the world," promoting industry and clothing mankind.[100] Likewise, frequent tables of exports showed the soaring production of sugar in Cuba, coffee in Brazil.[101] Clearly it was slave labor that made possible this output; free labor would not cultivate these resources on the scale possible under slavery, and, without compulsion, black laborers would be content to tend modest garden patches, sustaining no one but themselves.[102] "Without the institution of slavery the great staple products of the South would cease to be grown, and the immense annual results which are distributed among every class of the community, and which give life to every branch of industry, would cease.

... Brazil, whose slave population nearly equals our own, is the only South American state which has prospered. Cuba, by her slave labor, showers wealth upon old Spain."[103]

The corollary to this equation of civilization with productivity was the charge that, after emancipation, the West Indies slipped back into chaos. "Now, Mexico and South America (except Brazil) are barbarous, because they have abolished slavery—and even Northern and Western Europe would starve or become barbarous if they were not fed, clothed and sustained by the profits of trade with slave countries," wrote slavery advocate Fitzhugh (to which A. Hogeboom of New York responded acidly, "Were Mexico and South America ever *less* barbarous than they are now? How, then, has the abolition of slavery made them *more* barbarous?").[104] The rate of exports plummeted after the abolition of slavery, with shipment of "less than half the sugar, rum or ginger; less than one-third the coffee; less than one-tenth the molasses; and nearly two millions of pounds less of pimento, than during the three years which preceded the Emancipation Act."[105] Vast, once-productive estates were overgrown with weeds, their fine houses in disrepair, their labor force, now freed of discipline, "sunk to the ears in pumpkin, imbibing saccharine juices" while unharvested crops rotted in the fields.[106] The ease with which the veneer of civilization could be stripped away was evidently a potent threat for Southerners, one that could only be maintained by the application of force.

The lack of crime and the presence of social stability were other measures of societal health that flattered the South. Like "civilization," "crime" and "stability" had to be defined in specific ways. Crimes perpetrated by masters against slaves—cruel and unusual punishments, sexual exploitation—fell outside the definition. Acts of slave resistance did not count. What Southerners apparently meant by crime was burglary, assault, pickpocketing, prostitution, and riot, vices associated with the dense and diverse population of urban areas, of which the South had few. "While the South has been so much more secure than the North, in life and property, from individual crime, it has been at least equally exempt from social disturbance. The apprehensions of danger from the dissimilarity of its white and black population, have not been realized," wrote one Elwood Fisher in 1849. "Even in Brazil, where this proportion is reversed, where there are two blacks to one white, tranquility has reigned for a quarter of a century."[107] What should slaves gain by crime? Their wants were provided for, their security assured. They had no fear of poverty and no opportunity for drunkenness.[108] Since slaves were the property of the master, and therefore an extension of him, it was in his interest to treat them generously; for the slaveholder, labor was capital, and thus there could be no conflict between the two.[109]

Again, the example of emancipated societies provided evidence of how near at hand was chaos, exposing the propensity for disorder as pronounced in "free" Latin America as it was in the North of the United States: out of attempts to establish political equality among the races in Spanish America grew instability, anarchy, and want.[110] But the prime counterpoint to Southern rural stability was the urban, industrial North, where an unpredictable immigrant population imported dangerous "isms" that threatened civil society. In the South, where the African slave trade had been discontinued in 1808, no dangerous foreign ideas were imported.

But too close an identification with the purported civilization and order of Cuba and Brazil posed problems for U.S. Southerners. By many measures, these Latin American societies hardly constituted models of stability and advance. Conditions in Brazil and Cuba, however "civilized," too often appeared shockingly primitive. In his 1856 *Life in Brazil* Thomas Ewbank described the city of Rio substituting human labor for municipal infrastructure: lacking water and sewer pipes, slaves hauled water from common wells and made nightly forays to dump wastes into the bay; in the absence of omnibuses, slaves ferried passengers through the streets in sedan chairs. Slaves waded some fifty feet from the docks to where ships were anchored and returned with one-hundred-and-sixty-pound sacks of lime or coal or coffee on their heads. Yoked to massive trucks like oxen, they drew freight through the cities: why could there not be at least rails laid along the streets, even wooden ones, to make their progress more efficient, Ewbank mused.[111]

Cuba was similarly in a rudimentary state of civilization by most indices. A colony unable to escape the "febrile grasp" of its corrupt and worn-out European oppressor, Cuba was bled dry by restrictive policies proscribing the local production of both flour and wine, stifling industry, and strictly regulating foreign trade.[112] Richard Henry Dana reported that the general education of most of the population was limited, its prospects for self-government dim.[113] For entertainment there was no art or music save the gaudy excesses of Roman Catholicism; for sport there were cockfights and bullfights.[114] Street crime there may not have been, but the Presidio and Grand Carcel of Havana was a prison of shocking brutality, with political offenders in solitary confinement.[115] Money poured in from the sugar industry, but there was little diversification of agriculture and less development of the island's mineral resources.[116]

Though Southerners believed that slavery assisted in the civilizing process, its presence alone was not proof that a given society was in an absolute state of civilization. Southerners were civilized because of their bloodlines and their gentle breeding; they were well read in the classics and conversant with modern science and politics. When Southerners discussed Latin American nations, civilization was relative: "With equal advantages of soil and climate, the inferiority of the Spanish and Creole character tend to place the countries inhabited and administered by them, even under the best systems, very far behind those in which the Anglo-Saxon element is allowed to operate."[117] Cuba and Brazil remained ignorant, indolent, and benighted by superstition; only in comparison with their neighbors were they far advanced.

As the sectionalism of the 1850s intensified, proslavery writings supplied Southerners with ready-made arguments with which to resist Northern attacks. Beyond specific criticisms of slavery, Northerners stereotyped Southerners with all the expected slurs: Southerners were idle and improvident, barbaric in their cruelty and lascivious in their sexuality. A consistent vocabulary of pejorative images of outsiders appears across cultures.[118] Consequently, it is not surprising that Southerners turned around and applied to Latin Americans many of the same stereotypes that Northerners applied to them. In particular, they focused on three factors that prevented them from expressing anything but the most cursory and expedient identification with Cuba and Brazil: religion, race, and slave management practice. Each of these factors reveals something essential about Southern understandings of self-identity. In comparison with their Latin American counterparts, Southern slaveholders were decorous and God-fearing but also independent and up-to-date; they were racially pure—scrupulously so; and as masters they were benign and considerate, but always firmly in control.

The first major obstacle to identification was the fact that both the Spanish in Cuba and the Portuguese in Brazil were Roman Catholics. Significantly, for Southerners the influences of Catholicism had little or nothing to do with the workings of slavery per se. Historians Frank Tannenbaum and Stanley Elkins argued that the Roman Catholic faith of the Spanish and Portuguese slaveholders acted as a check on their cruelty: it subjected them to oversight from the clergy and forced them to regularize marriages and proscribe labor on Sundays and holydays.[119] Elkins also located in the Church the power to interpose itself between master and slave: a slave could apply to a clergyman for redress of wrongs perpetrated by the master.[120]

But if Southern commentators ever noted such phenomena, they did not remark on them. Rather, their enmity to Catholicism seems reflexive and unselfconscious. Observance of the Sabbath was disgraceful, with Sunday ceremonials displaying the splendid costumes and "intoxicating perfumes" of a pageant and the "*Evangel*, *Kyrie*, and *Credo* . . . recited to the music of Trovatore and Traviata."[121] Exiting these stimulating exercises, worshipers thronged the streets and the open stores, attended cockfights, and purchased lottery tickets.[122] In their prejudice, the attitudes of Southerners resembled their Northern neighbors more than might have been expected: in the North of the 1850s, after all, Know Nothings linked "Slavery and Priestcraft": "one denies the right of a man to his body, and the other the right of a man to his soul."[123] But as historian James Oakes writes, "Slaveholders, like other white Americans, indulged in most of the popular prejudices of their day. It did not matter in the least that most of the groups the slaveholders disdained were represented in their own class. They did not like Catholics."[124]

From the Southern perspective, Roman Catholicism bred flaws particularly dangerous to slaveholders: credulity, deference, venality. Unlike Southerners, who professed a sober devotion to the tenets of American Protestantism, independent Cubans and Brazilians winked at religious authority because its agents fell so obviously short of its professed ideal.[125] The clergy's dereliction was a serious matter because the church hierarchy provided no check to the baser impulses of their flocks. Moreover, Roman Catholicism emphasized tradition over the literal reading of scripture. U.S. Southerners found some of their favorite defenses of slavery in the Bible; the history of slave codes in Catholic countries that stretched back to St. Paul and Justinian complicated Southerners' elaborately worked out scriptural arguments.[126]

But the effect of Catholicism scarred slaves more than masters. Southerners most deplored the syncretic character of Roman Catholicism. The absorption and channeling of paganism into acceptable practice has historically been both a key to Catholic missionary success and a stumbling block to more rigid, and less effective, Protestants.[127] In Cuba and Brazil, pagan rites from Africa were sometimes cloaked in Catholic symbolism, from which they were nearly indistinguishable.[128] "I could have imagined myself in a heathen temple sooner than in a Christian Church," remarked one Southern visitor to the cathedral in Havana.[129] Because the conversion of Africans from paganism to Christianity was an important element in the justification of U.S. slavery, Christianity of the Catholic variety, which could be enthusiastic in its liturgy and superstitious in its popular practice, was not far enough removed from paganism to give evidence of "civilization." While Protestant Christianity could be a powerful tool in the management of slaves, especially when under the direction of a wise master, the hybrid devotions of Roman Catholicism allowed slaves to retain too much autonomy.

Second, North American travelers observed relations between the races in Cuba and Brazil that differed markedly from their own. In the United States, elaborate disquisitions sought to establish the permanent inferiority of the African and the error of elevating him to anything like equal status. "[T]he negro was created essentially to be a slave, and finds his highest development in that condition," declared *DeBow's*.[130] Proslavery author Samuel Cartwright went so far as to insist that "the species of the genus homo are not a unity, but a plurality, each essentially different from the others . . . [the negro is] more like the monkey tribes and the lower order of animals than any other species of the genus man."[131] In the United States, "the distinction of races has been invariably preserved; or viciously violated by concubinage; and in vice, the loftiest prince and the meanest savage occupy one level."[132] Persons of mixed race were firmly classified as black.[133]

The racial order of Latin America differed sharply from the U.S. taxonomy. Not only was the proportion of blacks to whites noticeably greater; mixed race people passed easily into the white society of Cuba and Brazil. "The number of negroes and persons of mixed blood within the territory [of Brazil] is estimated as bearing the proportion of five to one of the white population. All of these are not slaves; the bond being estimated as only two-fifths of the whole. The number of free negroes, mulattoes, &c., is hence very considerable," wrote Thomas R. R. Cobb, whose work concerned legal issues related to slavery. "There is probably no state in the world where there is less 'prejudice of color' than in Brazil, though a slave-holding state. At court, in the army, in the haunts of business, everywhere may be found freely mingling together persons of every hue."[134]

Cuba was still more willing to incorporate mixed-race people. As Thomas C. Reynolds wrote in 1850, "Free persons of mixed blood in Cuba are ambitious of classing themselves with the whites; the policy of the government, its laws, the customs of the white creoles themselves, and the almost entire absence, among the Spanish officials, of prejudices on the subject of color, afford facilities for their quiet admission into the class of whites." Like Cobb in his remarks about Brazil, Reynolds did not admire what he described: "These circumstances, and, in some cases, the real difficulty in deciding claims based on shades of color and questions of genealogy, as well as the leaning of the ecclesiastical authorities toward the assumption, that every child brought to the baptismal font is white, unless the contrary be notorious, have doubtless operated so as to throw into the class of whites, in the census, many who would, in most of the southern States of our Union, be considered 'free people of color.' "[135] Significantly, this tacit acknowledgment of the higher rate of manumission in Latin America was not understood by U.S. Southerners as indicative of a milder form of slavery; the large number of free people, and their easy transition into white society, signified a kind of blindness, the inability to distinguish very dissimilar racial groups.

Thomas Dew, a professor at the College of William and Mary, insisted that the skewing of population ratios in favor of the Africans presented no threat to well-ordered slave societies: more slaves meant more wealth, and more wealth meant more public services including, if necessary, a police force to control restive slaves.[136] But more often Southerners expressed the sentiment that the proportion of blacks to whites was a delicate matter indeed. In 1854 Stephen Mallory, senator from Florida, introduced a resolution in Congress condemning Spain for the "Africanization" of Cuba, importing so many illegal blacks onto the island as to produce a volatile tipping point. The importation of African slaves was a conscious provocation of the U.S. government, Mallory argued, a known formula for producing instability on an island only a few hours away from American soil.[137]

Mallory's horror of Africanization referred to a conspiracy attributed to Spain as a way to keep its colony in check. Maturin M. Ballou, the author of *History of Cuba* published in Boston at the height of the filibuster period, posited an infernal alliance between Spain and England to allow the importation of Africans into the island in an attempt to maintain a high ratio of blacks to Europeans and a cynical policy of enrolling blacks as regular troops in the army. "[T]he Spanish authorities have . . . constantly endeavored to weaken the bonds of attachment between master and slave, and to ferment the unnatural hatred of races with fearful design of preparing another St. Domingo for the Cubans, should they dare to strike a strenuous blow for freedom."[138] Outnumbered by the armed blacks, the white creoles, understanding their own vulnerability, would not dare to rebel against Spanish tyranny. Five years after Mallory's resolution, when the acquisition of Cuba was again being debated in the Senate, Judah P. Benjamin warned that because of the Spanish policy of arming former slaves, "the bayonets of the black race threaten . . . an exterminating war of races."[139]

Once a slave won his freedom in Latin America, observers noted few barriers to hold back his advance. Travel writer John Esaias Warren's 1851 *Para; or, Scenes and Adventures on the Banks of the Amazon*, described how Brazilian slaves, after completing the comparatively little labor required of them each day, were allowed to work gainfully and save money against their own emancipation. One enterprising black whom Warren met had been loaned money to purchase his freedom, which he repaid by starting his own business hiring out laborers in the loading and unloading of freight.[140] Blacks formed a significant presence in the armies of both Cuba and Brazil. In his work on Cuba, Maturin Ballou anticipated that free blacks would soon be admitted to holy orders and Stewart reported that freedmen were already members of the clergy.[141] The same civil rights and rights of property applied to free members of both races in Cuba.[142] Daniel Kidder and J. C. Fletcher pointed out that in Brazil there were few checks to the social advance of a freed slave and concluded that the consequent collapse of slavery there was imminent.[143]

Yet this toleration and colorblindness had the immediate result that the races were clearly mixed. George M. Colvocoresses, who wrote an account called *Four Years in the Government Exploring Expedition*, claimed that the population of Rio was "perhaps more mixed than that of any other city in the world" and Julia Ward Howe made a similar claim for Cuba, adding that mixed blood ran in the veins of even the wealthiest and most important families there.[144] Clearly it was less the presence of mixed-race people than their access to agency and even power in society that presented the real threat to Southern order. But some Southerners managed a remarkable nearsightedness when it came to recognizing the products of racial mixing in their own neighborhoods. "Shall the white and black races in America abandon all distinctions of color, and unite, socially and politically as one people?" demanded *De Bow's Review* rhetorically in 1860. In a sentence that is a marvel of understatement the author admitted that the "black and white races have now been commingling, to a certain extent, in the Southern States during six or eight generations" but otherwise demonstrated remarkably little curiosity about where mixed-race people came from.[145]

What is critical to recognize, of course, is that for Southerners this absence of racial prejudice indicated not tolerance but moral carelessness. "Amalgamation, to any great extent, is a moral impossibility," stated Cobb.[146] The sloppy decision to let standards slip could have dangerous consequences. Slavery seemed secure in Brazil; it was inextricably bound up with the commercial success of the nation. But the racial composition of the population was anything but auspicious: "A race which has so large an admixture of caste has not the essential qualities of progressive development; hence ignorance, superstition, and social and political inharmoniousness; and with all these, worst of all, licensed amalgamation, the raising up a hybrid race with titles to rule and govern—a nation who, as a people, never had, or never can have either a history or a literature."[147]

The promiscuous mingling of the races that Southern observers noted in Latin America set Cuba and Brazil apart from the U.S. South, where such congress was not acknowledged. But more threatening was the Latin American practice of allowing mixed-race people to pass as white. Over the centuries colonial Spain had developed a process by which births to unmarried parents could be legitimated with the stroke of a pen. More strikingly, "impurity of blood"—whether because of Jewish, Moorish, African, or Native American ancestors—could be "cleansed" through a similar bureaucratic mechanism, a certificate of whiteness (cédula de gracias al sacar). The legacy of these transformations appeared in the nineteenth-century nations as people of mixed-race were able to move into white society provided they had the necessary social and financial backing.[148] In Brazil, marveled Daniel Kidder and J. C. Fletcher, "if a man have freedom, money, and merit, no matter how black may be his skin, no place in society is refused him."[149] Southerners scarcely acknowledged that the supposed absence of the problem in the United States was the result of a contrary legal fiction—classing mixed-race people as black no matter how indistinguishable might be the evidence. U.S. Southerners were capable of splitting hairs much finer than that, even among white people of English extraction: New Englanders, explained more than one article, were descended from the intolerant Saxons who had come to America to practice their inflexible Puritanism; Southerners claimed kin with the gentle and cultivated Normans.[150] In comparison with such razor-thin distinctions, the Latin American practice of allowing an inclusive definition of "white" stood out in sharp contrast.

Finally, North American slaveholders drew a firm line between their own compassionate and solicitous treatment of their slaves and that of masters in Latin America. Here again some distinction should be noted between Cuba and Brazil, with Spanish Cuba—the extant example of the Black Legend of Spanish cruelty—coming in for more frequent criticism. *The Southern Literary Messenger* declared that imputations of Spanish inhumanity were well known throughout the world.[151] A poem published in the *Southern Literary Messenger* in 1860 began,

> Isle of the ocean! jeweled on the breast
> Of waters fragrant with thy tropic breath,
> Thou seem'st alike some happy dream at rest
> In the calm sea of mind! But underneath
> Those clear, blue skies there lurks despair and death.[152]

The apparent expendability of slave lives in areas where the slave trade was still countenanced—as it was in both Cuba and Brazil—explained a valid demographic observation: while the black population of the North American South in the antebellum period was growing through natural increase, an illegal transatlantic trade was necessary to replenish the slave supply in the sugar-growing regions of Cuba and Brazil. Thomas Reynolds—quoted above—reasoned that in Cuba the proclivity for freeing mixed race offspring of Africans and Europeans and classifying them as white must be part of the key to the declining number of slaves. But he, as well as many other authors, declared that that the infinite need for new immigrants was owing to the mistreatment and cruelty of Latin American slaveholders. "[S]o long as the slave was made cheap by the trade, the master's pecuniary interest was more operative than his sympathies. In Brazil now, (as in Louisiana before her annexation,) it costs less to buy an adult negro from Africa than to rear an infant," noted *Southern Quarterly Review*.[153]

It is possible to detect in this discourse a hint of envy for the ability of the Spanish and the Brazilians to routinely flout international regulations against the slave trade. But since the suppression of trade with Africa affected different parts of the South in different ways—a boon for the Upper South, from whence excess labor could be sold, but a handicap for the Lower South, which might have benefited from prices lowered through imports—publications aiming for a wide audience tended to make a virtue of the necessity of the ban. Calling the Portuguese and Spanish traders pirates allowed U.S. Southerners to claim the moral high ground.

Southern slaveholders did not consider that the comparatively large birthrate among their bondmen might be due to anything (the rigors of sugar cultivation as opposed to cotton growing; the ratio of women to men) besides superior care; indeed, pointed out one article, the population growth of North American slaves neatly exploded the myth that slaves were overworked, while calling into question the conditions of free workers in Europe, whose increase was less.[154] In comparison to the Southern United States, which prided itself on the care it took of its elderly and infirm slaves, Brazilian masters of urban slaves sent their elderly bondmen into the streets to work, and expected them to beg if they failed.[155] Proslavery novelist Charles Jacobs Peterson compared the fate of a white victim of Northern capitalism to a mistreated Cuban slave: "He was foully murdered, more folly than if he had been worked to death, as they say negroes are in Cuba."[156]

Kindly treatment maintained the security of the Southern United States. "Having been generally well-treated, the slaves have never exhibited that disposition to revolt so frequently seen in the West Indies. No Maroons have infested our mountains; no wars of the Maroons stain our annals," wrote Cobb.[157] What fear should the Southern slaveholder have of his contented bondmen, indignantly demanded Southern Quarterly Review. "How ignorant, people at a distance are, of the little antagonism that really exists between master and slave." The English abolitionists who dwelt among a starving and desperate laboring class had comparatively more to fear. When one English critic imagined Southerners suffered amid "fearful firesides and nightly alarm of massacre," Southern Quarterly Review claimed that he himself lived "in constant insecurity, in the metropolis of the British Empire, amidst elements as combustible and dangerous as the powder magazine at Woolwich."[158]

Accusing Latin American slavery of greater cruelty served to deflect abolitionist interference while implicating Northerners in the very enterprise they condemned: "the illegal African slave-trade, of the most cruel and murderous character, (and with many of the slave vessels fitted out in Northern cities and by Northern capital,) continued to add to the number of slaves, and by such additions to increase the sufferings of all. . . . Yet scarcely have the Northern abolitionists noticed the horrors of Cuban and Brazilian slavery, while all their denunciations and hostility have been reserved for the milder slavery in the Southern States," declared fire-eater Edmund Ruffin in 1857.[159]

The South's felt need to defend itself against charges of brutality increased after the 1852 publication of Stowe's *Uncle Tom's Cabin,* an event that all three Southern journals and not a few pamphlets and tracts noted with anger stoked by its fantastic popularity.[160] The depictions of sadism in Stowe's novel hit a particular nerve with Southern audiences. "Her argument is a description of scenes such as we have never seen or heard of, but which, of course, we cannot undertake to deny," wrote Edward Pringle in a proslavery pamphlet. "It is always easy to attack an institution by dwelling with emphasis upon its abuses."[161] According to Southern critics, Stowe erred by confusing extreme and isolated incidents for the general rule. In consequence, particularly after 1852, U.S. slaveholders took care to distance themselves from the legendary barbarism of Latin American slavery.

Comparing North American to Spanish systems of slave governance spoke not only to the beneficence of masters in the United States, but to their superior understanding of the relations between the races, with one intended by God to rule and the other to serve. Latin American ambivalence made masters by turns weak administrators and vicious tyrants. Brazilian mistresses, neither able to think of sufficient work to assign their female slaves nor possessing effective means of managing them, wore out their health in futile scolding.[162] The consequences of Cuban incompetence in slave management were more serious. "When in Cuba, I was surprised to see overseers carrying a broad-sword into the field instead of a whip, and relying upon blood-hounds to catch and hold resisting negroes, instead of negroes themselves," wrote Samuel Cartwright in 1861. "The Spaniards have never made anything profitable out of negroes, because they govern them on the same principles that white slaves are governed, instead of governing them by moral powers, applicable to them, but not to the white man."[163]

U.S. Southerners were better masters because they felt so deeply their own superiority. As Cobb wrote, "Born to command, and habituated to rule, they frequently commend themselves to the nation by their firmness, their independence, and their fearlessness."[164] Conversely, the lack of distance between the Spanish and Portuguese slaveholders and their bondmen caused doubt about their aptitude for leadership. Allowing the possibility that the incidence of violence was indeed greater on Cuban plantations, Southern critiques did not acknowledge other factors that might contribute to the disparity. (On the other hand, New Yorker William Cullen Bryant, who visited Cuba in 1849, speculated that slaves born in Africa, of which Cuba had a higher proportion than the United States, might draw more punishment down upon themselves through their resistance than American-born slaves who had been better schooled in acquiescence.[165]) The public insistence that U.S. slavery was not cruel, that "*mutual affection between* the owners and the owned" prevailed in the South, offered a whistling-past-the-graveyard reassurance that the specter of bloody uprising did not haunt the United States.[166]

For the Latin American master, the possession of slaves was a license to loaf rather than an opportunity to engage in more productive work. The Spanish plantation owner exhibited no inclination to "improvement of his mind or preparation of philanthropic plans for the amelioration of his servant's lot." Without colleges and learned societies, uninterested in the news of the world, Spanish slaveholders were sunk in indulgence and avarice.[167] "The Brazilian, feeling himself above all the drudgery of life, is a man of leisure, and looks down in perfect contempt upon the foreigner, who is always grumbling, fretting, and busy."[168] Once free, a Brazilian slave, who in theory had the prerogative to become a prime minister, followed the example of the whites he observed and became, "instead of a producer, an idle and perhaps dangerous consumer."[169]

Because U.S. slavery advocates were aware that even the most irreproachable slave systems could succumb to decay, they defended the particularity of U.S. slavery. Ancient Israel had practiced slavery—in fact, provided scriptural justification for the peculiar institution—but had not prospered. David and Solomon brutalized the state slaves who built the temple.[170] Disconcertingly, even the unassailable slaveholding paragons of Greece and Rome collapsed: Rome, Southerners argued, weakened its once glorious race through amalgamation.[171] Some slavery advocates went so far as to acknowledge that, among societies of lesser men, slavery could indeed be a curse. The *Southern Literary Messenger* recoiled at "the manifest injustice in which a similitude is asserted between the American and Egyptian systems of slavery. . . . *there is no resemblance* . . . in the land we are describing, slavery is marked by everything loathsome and revolting, where obscurity of mind and filthiness of body distinguish the slave; and indifference or cruelty, the master."[172]

Latin America offered nearby examples of what happened or might happen to slave societies that were irresolute. The fact that Cuba and Brazil stopped short of total commitment to the absolute rightness of slavery made them suspect: as Elizabeth Fox-Genovese and Eugene Genovese write, unlike U.S. Southerners, "The Brazilian and Cuban slaveholders who defended slavery as a positive institution for blacks and whites did not celebrate slavery as the best foundation for all social order and as the wave of the future."[173] What would be their fate if their commitment to slavery wavered? Cuba and Brazil edged alarmingly close to their unfortunate neighbors: "Plunge Brazil into a political revolution, and destroy the present Imperial government, and her army, composed for the best part of free negroes, will soon dictate its terms of emancipation to the nation, and the empire be converted into another Venezuela," warned one article.[174] A close reading of the history of failed slave societies both maintained the uniqueness of U.S. slavery and enabled its defenders to avoid repeating the mistakes of lesser societies.

The coming of the Civil War effected a sharp break with the nascent Confederacy's previous policy of keeping political distance from the inferior slave systems farther south. By 1861, the year of secession, the value of Cuba and Brazil as allies—or buffer zones—and the benefits of their possession by sympathetic foreign powers, was belatedly acknowledged.[175] *DeBow's* pointed out, "Spain, Brazil, and the South, are the only slaveholding countries. If Cuba were detached from Spain, the cause of slavery would be weakened, not only by the loss of one of the great powers of Europe as its friend, but still more, by converting that rising nation into its irreconcilable enemy."[176] Fitzhugh went so far as to suggest that the Monroe Doctrine be disregarded by the Confederacy and France invited to repossess its former colony of Haiti, strengthening the balance of power among the areas surrounding the South and supplying a viable rival to the United States.[177] By the beginning of the Civil War, maintaining Cuba and Brazil as slave societies—and reestablishing slavery where it had been eradicated—became more critical than ever.

Even without the elaborate defenses and justifications fabricated by U.S. slavery advocates, slavery ended up continuing longer in both Cuba and Brazil than it did in the United States. Abolition came to Cuba only in 1886 and to Brazil two years later. Yet despite the earlier ending of slavery in the U.S. South, it is possible to see some truth in historian Frank Tannenbaum's formulation that emancipation freed the slaves from their bondage but could not free whites of their racism.[178] Examining Southern attitudes to Cuba and Brazil reveals how consciously Southerners constructed that racism, how painstakingly they fitted it together, and how carefully they polished it.

Some U.S. Southerners understood that, in the abstract, slavery linked their interests with those of Cuba and Brazil. "To succeed with cotton, and every other Southern product in British Asia and New Holland [cultivated by free labor], it is foreseen that nothing stands in the way but the associated or slave-labor of the United States, Brazil, and Cuba," declared DeBow's Review in 1851.[179] But the 1850s saw the definition of U.S. slavery as an exclusive institution, distinguished by its coherence. Not even by reaching far back in history—to the inviolate precedent of Hebrew slavery, to the glory of imperial Rome—could one find its equal. Nowhere else in the modern world was slavery an institution of such integrity, spreading the benefits of Christianity and civilization to a benighted race, preserving labor from dissatisfaction and hunger and crime. Southern society shunned the amalgamation that weakened other races; it was impervious to corruption as a diamond. The rate of manumission in Cuba and Brazil, and the comparative lack of racial prejudice, revealed the wavering and uncertain commitment these regions demonstrated to a system the U.S. South found perfect.

"[T]he condition of the negro slave in the United States is preeminently superior to that of the free negro in any part of the earth, and . . . the negro's greatest happiness and greatest usefulness are best secured under our system of domestic servitude," asserted Florida's Stephen Mallory in the Senate in 1859.[180] Comparisons with the slave systems of other nations only served to provide Southerners with evidence of their own industrious efficiency, gentle firmness, and racial purity. Acknowledging the shared interests of slaveholders in a world that organized labor in new ways involved compromises Southerners were unwilling to make. Defending their own superiority over Latin American slaveholders weighed more heavily than finding mutual agendas.

But the implications of such imperious exclusivity were not reassuring. "The Southern people, now, are fused into a common mass," asserted DeBow's Review on the very eve of the Civil War. Arguing against the acquisition of Cuba by the United States, it continued, "[In the United States,] all speak the same language, have the same manners and customs, the same moral notions, the same political opinions; emphatically, they are one people. Disturb not this harmony by introducing a foreign element. Harmony constitutes national strength: discord begets dissension, civil broils, and national weakness. Peoples of different national descent cannot live peaceably under one government, unless the one people be slaves to the other. We do not propose to make the Cubans slaves, and yet know not how they might get along as our co-equals."[181] This quotation cuts to the heart of the inconsistency with which Southern expansionists regarded the acquisition of Cuba during the 1850s: the nearer they approached, the more clearly they divined the impossibility of absorbing such a foreign culture into American society. Assuredly, this article affirmed the conservative extreme of the proslavery position, but it was part of an ideology that had no mechanism for incorporating outsiders and no intention of tolerating difference. If the successful slave society depended upon such an inflexible set of assumptions, its survival must be precarious. If it required exactly the correct ethnic composition of masters, precisely the right proportion of blacks to whites, exactly the right roles assigned to slaves, it rested on a delicate balance indeed: its foundations were insecure. The irony of the preoccupation with the security of the Southern system was that it depended upon stasis and must necessarily resist change. Such a perfect system could easily breed conservatism, suspicion, and hostility to outsiders at a time when the North was finding ways to accommodate and even welcome new ideas, new technologies, and new politics.

An unabashedly proslavery and pro-filibustering novel published in the wake of *Uncle Tom's Cabin* exposes the way the South was held back by its inflexibility and blind to the kind of change that might be growing within the system itself. In 1854, under the pseudonym M. H. Hardimann, Southerner Lucy Holcombe (1832–1899) published a short novel called *The Free Flag of Cuba; or, The Martyrdom of Lopez*. Within a typical novelistic plot that introduces, separates, and finally unites two sets of lovers, *The Free Flag of Cuba* unabashedly raises the banner of its particular politics: Holcombe's heroes are American filibusters in the legacy of Timothy Flint's Francis Berrian, hero of the first filibustering novel of 1826.[182] Written when its author was only nineteen, the short fiction was inspired by Holcombe's 1851 meeting with the revolutionary Narciso Lopéz at the home of John Quitman (whose term as governor of Mississippi was interrupted by his need to respond to charges relating to his own freebooting activities).[183] Holcombe locates the failure of Cuba's independence movement in the official policy of the United States toward its unfortunate neighbor. She directs her icy condemnation toward President Millard Fillmore's refusal to protect U.S. citizens who left the country as soldiers of fortune.

Holcombe's narrative embrace of the filibusters did not speak for all Southerners, who, as the citations from the Southern journals above demonstrate, were of two minds about the incorporation of Cuba into the American republic. But her outspoken views did not make her a pariah. To the contrary, in 1858 she married the eligible, much older Francis W. Pickens, whom she met at Sweet Springs, Virginia. ("The lady may feel proud of her conquest," remarked a gossipy correspondent of the *Charleston Courier*.[184]) Two years later, Pickens was the governor of South Carolina when the state seceded from the Union. Charming and clever, Lucy Holcombe (now Lucy Holcombe Pickens) was the only woman whose likeness appeared on Confederate currency and was known as the "uncrowned Queen" of the Confederacy.[185]

In *The Free Flag of Cuba*, Holcombe leaves open-ended the goal of the proposed Cuban revolution, whether for outright independence or annexation by the United States. (In fact, the historical Lopéz was equally unclear about his intentions for "free" Cuba.[186]) But as historian Orville Vernon Burton and Georganne B. Burton point out in their introduction to a 2002 reissue of the novel, Holcombe had spent part of her youth in Texas and would have been familiar with the precedent of an independent republic choosing to be annexed to the United States. Holcombe decidedly has no doubts about the goal of the filibuster cause. The U.S. revolutionaries come "not for conquest," Holcombe repeats more than once; rather, they are assisting Lopéz in his attempt to liberate his people from their tyrannous mistress, the Queen of Spain.[187] The author situates their struggle as the last in a line of noble battles that begins with Washington, Lafayette, and the American Revolution. And in the tradition of eighteenth-century revolution, the Cubans are "slaves" to Spanish tyranny. At his last desperate stand, with the Spanish army in sight of their depleted forces, Lopéz attempts to rouse his men: "Soldiers! you have fought to free slaves; you will not bear yourselves less bravely now that the slave of slaves gloats on the butchered forms of freemen. Stand firmly to your arms, and trust the God of truth for victory."[188]

In a manner that curiously anticipates the post-Civil War Lost Cause tradition, Holcombe paints the struggle as all the holier for its ultimate failure.[189] The blood of martyrs and the tears of suffering women cleanse every human error and frailty from the doomed enterprise. Yet with her constant identification of the white Cubans as slaves, Holcombe has unconsciously done something extraordinary. What she has depicted is nothing more or less than a slave rebellion.

Perhaps it goes without saying that Holcombe assumes her readers will understand that this slave rebellion is open to whites only. The "slaves" in question cannot and can never be African; without irony or even apparent consciousness, she considers the possibility of emancipation a perversion. Freeing Cuba's African slaves is a filthy trick of the Spanish, who might resort to anything to keep their colony from falling into U.S. hands. López explains: "rather than this silver-set gem which nature so much loves, should shine amid the stars of the Columbian flag, rather than she should stand in the self-sustaining life of her own republicanism, the Spaniard would cast upon her the undying stain of African equality. He would bid the Cuban clasp his slave as a brother, and together kneel before a crown whose pollution, fiends might blush to wear."[190]

Within the setting of Cuba and the U.S. South, however, Holcombe cannot entirely avoid acknowledging the presence of blacks, both slave and free. Ostensibly, the black slaves in Holcombe's story prefer bondage to freedom. When Ralph Dudley, one of López's American allies, proposes granting freedom to his faithful slave, the slave retorts angrily that the master has insulted him and the memory of Dudley's father.[191]

Yet these are slaves who, in the disruption of war, manage to tailor their enslavement to their own specifications. Their direct or vicarious encounters with life in both Mexico (where one of the white characters also served as a soldier) and in Cuba allow them a wider perspective and a less deferential manner. The reader senses that beyond a certain point, Holcombe's black characters are out of her control, and her narrative cannot quite suppress their resilience, resourcefulness, and independence. The novel's hero, the headstrong, improvident Ralph Dudley, invests his fortune in the attempt to free Cuba and loses everything. He returns home, determined to sell his estate and all its slaves, when he is intercepted by Marmion, his oldest retainer.[192] Rather than being bereft by the prospect of the coming sale, Marmion quickly schools his master in some home truths, patiently explaining how mortgages work, how creditors can be put off, how a few years' relocation to "Callyforny" will enable the neighbors to forget the shame of the family's indebtedness. Dudley takes Marmion's advice. "You must control me," Dudley tells his slave, though it is evident Marmion hardly needs Dudley's permission to do so.[193]

Scipio, Dudley's body servant, takes an even more active role in Dudley's welfare, and is even more determined to keep from escaping the grasp of a master he can easily manipulate. Having already accompanied Dudley to Mexico in the war of the previous decade, he knows what to expect from combat in a Latin American country. When a Spaniard is about to kill the sleeping Dudley, Scipio pops out of the shadows and dispatches the assassin.[194] Although Dudley attempts to leave Scipio behind when he sets out to restore his fortunes in California, the slave stows away onboard the vessel. Confronted by the flummoxed Dudley, Scipio fires back, "You can't *nuver* lef me, Marse Ralph; you need n't try to more, tain no use."

"Well, sir, we will see which will be master," Dudley retorts, but it is already clear to both Holcombe and the reader that the master is Scipio. He points out that once in California he could pass himself off for free, but he has no intention of doing so. "I gwine foller arter you to de 'other side of Jurden,'" he tells Dudley, in words which, if they were not clearly intended to be delivered as sassy backtalk, could easily sound like a threat.[195] Both Marmion and Scipio are loyal and devoted, but were their powers of calculation and perseverance applied to escape—or revolt—they would be formidable antagonists indeed.[196]

One publisher to whom Holcombe submitted the manuscript rejected it as too provocative, faulting its incendiary overtones in words usually applied to the instigation of slave rebellion: "He said its principles were dangerous—its fillibustering [sic] tendency rendered it inflammable, and he had conscientious scruples which prevented him from giving to the American public a work which contained such elements of agitation," Holcombe complained in a letter to Quitman.[197] The black characters in *The Free Flag of Cuba* do not appear poised on the edge of revolt. Rather, seemingly beyond the power of their own author's governance, they appear to have found a less dangerous way of seizing control. Like the slaves in W. E. B. Du Bois's *Black Reconstruction*, who eschew active deeds of violence in favor of passive strategies of resistance as a safer, smarter method of achieving their goals, Holcombe's Marmion and Scipio cleverly conceal the upper hand they clearly possess.[198]

No less than Holcombe's white characters who foresee the possibility of freedom transcending national boundaries, both fictional and actual African Americans were capable of seeing both slavery and freedom in hemispheric terms. Like Henry Blake, the hero of Martin Delany's abolitionist novel *Blake, or, The Huts of America* of just a few years later, Marmion and

Scipio live in a world where they can cross lines with relative ease.[199] Where proslavery Southerners insisted that borders, properly guarded, would protect their institution, these characters understand how porous and easily breached those boundaries are. This vision of the hemispheric—indeed, the global—implications of slavery contrast markedly with the borders outlined by proslavery Southerners, who insisted on their own exceptionalism and maintained—publicly, at least—that what happened in slave societies outside of the South affected them in minimal ways. Against the white Southern insistence on the superiority of the peculiar institution in the United States, these black characters see U.S. slavery as mutable, capable of being undermined, and not so peculiar after all.

Epilogue. 1861 and After

In his fourth annual message, December 3, 1860, lame-duck president James Buchanan laid the blame for Southern secession at the doorstep of the antislavery North. If only the fanatics had stifled their "abolition sermons and lectures," their "violent speeches" and appeals, and kept their mouths shut! The people of the North, scolded Buchanan, "have no more right to interfere, than with similar institutions in Russia or in Brazil."[1] Buchanan's words were an odd acknowledgment that the South had become a foreign country.

During the Civil War the process of estranging the South continued in earnest. When a series of military losses threatened Northern morale, Abraham Lincoln called a national day of fasting on September 26, 1861. The *New York Evening Post* reported that the city's banks and businesses were closed and churches were full.[2] At Trinity Church, the Reverend Francis Vinton—who thirteen years earlier had delivered a funeral oration in honor of a soldier killed in the U.S. War with Mexico, in which he called all foreign wars indefensible—now preached a sermon citing a text from the first letter of John in which John compared renegade Christians to the anti-Christ: "They went out from us because they were not of us, for if they had been of us they would no doubt have continued with us: but they went out that it might be more manifest that they were not all of us."[3] What Vinton was doing—as the entire United States found it necessary to do—was to characterize Southerners, formerly U.S. citizens, as aliens and strangers.[4]

Southern nationalists similarly identified the Union as Other. The *Richmond Whig*, for its part, explained what made the Confederate fighting forces prevail over the U.S. Army: Southern troops belonged to the "master race" which, according to the *Whig*, exhibited "superior manhood to the mongrel and many-tongued enemy."[5] The amalgamation of foreigners into the North had adulterated its racial purity.

Civil wars, as William Hickling Prescott noted, are second only to wars of religion in savagery and horror. Former familiarity breeds a sense of bitterness and betrayal. How can one abruptly understand as antagonists a people with a common origin, language, form of government? Combatants must learn to cast friends as sworn enemies, to make foes of people among whom they traveled and lived and studied, with whom they entered business and invested money, with whom they shared a past. History must be rewritten to foreshadow the ultimate divide.

Yet in this project of defamiliarizing the familiar, people in the Union and the Confederacy had considerable practice in their understanding of Latin America. At the time of the Spanish-American wars of independence, citizens of the United States needed little encouragement to see these Hispanic republicans as their counterparts. Differences of religion and language did not guarantee their being regarded as inferiors. However much the United States and its Southern neighbors emerged from different backgrounds, their shared characteristics could not easily be overlooked: their colonial past, their conflation of European, African, and indigenous racial stock, their constitutions. The Latin American aspiration to the type of government pioneered by the United States might have been the prelude to a close association of nations. Instead, in 1826 the door closed on this type of community, and race and slavery became the point at which the United States and Latin America were seen to diverge.

The need to make Latin Americans into strangers arose out of both cupidity and fear. However much citizens of the United States affected to disparage the people south of the border, with their superstition and inefficiency, the United States admired, desired, and acquired the territory those people occupied. Latin Americans had to be identified as unworthy possessors of land that the people of the United States could turn to better account. Admiration for Latin America in the post-Panama Congress period emphasized the region's ancient history and its valuable land and resources. Its contemporary situation, on the other hand, was held up for contempt. Expressions of U.S. superiority focused on racial difference.

The particular circumstances of the Second Party System also served the interest of casting the United States' southern neighbors as inferiors rather than allies. Popular politics put a premium of whiteness at the very moment when the Panama Congress debates broadcast the racial amalgamation of Latin America. The felt need of Southerners to defend U.S. slavery against all criticism benefitted from a region of difference where fears and critiques could be displaced. Manifest Destiny's imperatives of conquest and possession were justified by insisting on the unworthiness of Spanish-American claims.

In Latin America, the people of the United States were also forced to see a reflection of themselves with troubling weaknesses. Here the republican form of government appeared a sickly, fragile thing, easily bruised, ailing under cures prescribed by quack doctors. Here ideals of racial equality were pushed to extremes. The tenuous compromise the United States had drawn between slavery and freedom appeared not simply precarious but potentially explosive. Belittling their Latin American counterparts made U.S. nationalists feel more confident about their own union even as it was falling apart.

All these expressions of difference made possible the use of Latin America as a context in which to talk about slavery, the most intractable and provocative problem of the antebellum period. Northerners could speak without offending their neighbors in the slave states—or their neighbors down the street who profited from human bondage. Southerners discovered an opportunity to criticize, to brood over, and to express doubt about an institution whose weaknesses they could not otherwise admit. Latin America proved more valuable as a foil than as an ally.

During the Civil War, domestic strife distracted Americans from international affairs. So occupied was the Union with its struggle that it did little when European powers installed an emperor in Mexico in 1864. In a speech accepting the nomination for the vice presidency in the fall of that year, Andrew Johnson vowed that "we will attend to this Mexican affair," but put off this threat until after "the Rebellion will be put down."[6] Yet even after the Union victory the United States hung fire: "Our unconcern comes from our conviction that no such thing is possible as the permanent establishment of an imperial dynasty in Mexico; and that it is not worth while to go to war about it," asserted the *New York Times*. Then, with a backhanded compliment tossed off with characteristic disdain, the *Times* added, "With all their ignorance, the Mexican people are as thoroughly democratic in all their feelings as the people of our own republic."[7]

The North identified a role for Latin America to play in the postwar future. Further colonization efforts might yet have a purpose, one that both looked backward to early nineteenth-century outposts in Africa and forward to late nineteenth-century imperialism in the Caribbean and the Pacific. A day before signing the Emancipation Proclamation, Abraham Lincoln approved a contract to transport five thousand slaves to Ile à Vache, a tiny Caribbean island.[8] The project echoed other efforts of members of the Republican Party to relocate free American blacks to Central America during the 1850s in hopes of both blocking Southern attempts to expand slavery southward and discouraging freed slaves from settling in the North. With outrageous arrogance, Republicans further expected these black Americans in exile to represent U.S. commercial and political interests in an area eyed by European imperialists. Black refugees, not desirable for residence among the white citizens of the United States, would be superior to the natives of Latin America.[9] In the event, black leaders like Martin Delany, who during the 1850s had looked to Central America as a welcoming retreat from U.S. racism, saw opportunities for meaningful U.S. citizenship during and after the Civil War and did not decamp en masse for regions farther south.

During the war, the Confederacy fought to protect its own territory, not to make further conquests.[10] Southern journals focused on fostering patriotism through articles like "Commercial Importance and Future of the South" and "Southern Individuality."[11] Articles on Cuba and Brazil disappeared, and then the journals themselves disappeared—*DeBow's Review* ceased publication in 1862 and the *Southern Literary Messenger* in 1864 (*Southern Quarterly Review* had printed its last issue in 1857).[12] Southern interest in Latin America now focused on its potential as an escape hatch for slaveholders, a sovereign territory where a languishing way of life might be nursed back to health. Some white Southerners, refusing to surrender their reliance on an enslaved workforce, retreated to the few south-of-the-border regions that still allowed slavery. Sharon Hartman Strom and Frederick Stirton Weaver estimate that between eight and ten thousand disaffected whites left the South for Latin America after the Civil War.[13] Some sought refuge in Mexico and Brazil.[14]

As before the war, few Southerners looked to Latin America for useful lessons. Use of nominally free Asian laborers in the Caribbean offered a possibility for cultivating the cane fields of Louisiana.[15] But repeated assertions of superiority left the South few reasons to look to Latin America for models of how to deal with an emancipated labor force. Matthew Pratt Guterl wrote that "if the wide and troubling sweep of Caribbean history had served as an encyclopedic guidebook of sorts for the slaveholding antebellum South, there were precious few positive lessons to be learned when the subject therein turned to emancipation."[16] Though in 1826 the United States celebrated as it observed Latin America imitating its example of republicanism, it found fewer causes for festivity now that it discovered itself in the position of following a Latin American precedent and seeing its slaves set free.[17] If anything, Latin American parallels made Americans anxious they were not so different from their troubled, unstable neighbors after all.

Latin America continued to figure as a metonym for governmental instability and ineptitude in the wartime and postwar period. Visiting the United States in 1862, Anthony Trollope, son of Frances Trollope, whose caustic *Domestic Manners of the Americans* had caused such consternation thirty years earlier, predicted that Southern secession would ultimately succeed, but that the Confederate states would "stand something higher in the world than Mexico and the republics of Central America"—hardly high praise.[18] Southerners shared some of his doubts. What assurance did the Confederacy have, asked a character in Augusta Evans Wilson's 1864 novel *Macaria; or, Altars of Sacrifice*, that "so soon as the common dangers of war, which for a time cemented you so closely, are over, entire disintegration will not ensue and all your boasts end in some dozen anarchical pseudo-republics, like those of South America and Mexico?"[19] After the war, the fragility of the republican ideal in Latin America continued to haunt the United States, when the collapse of the Union suggested to some Cassandras that the U.S. great experiment might yet be doomed to ultimate failure.[20]

In many ways, slavery was no easier to talk about in 1865 than it had been ten years earlier. Attempts to dodge or deny the extent to which the problem of slavery caused the Civil War began during the conflict and continue to the present day. Lincoln himself engaged in discursive soft-pedalling as late as 1865. His second inaugural address, for example, contains this assessment of the role of slavery in the collapse of the Union: "These slaves constituted a peculiar and powerful interest. All knew that this interest was somehow the cause of the war."[21] Even he could not resist the qualifier "somehow." During and after Reconstruction, efforts to reconcile the two belligerents focused on muting the importance of slavery as the central issue of the conflict, a process that reached a climax in the early twentieth century. Historians from W. E. B. Du Bois to David Blight have exposed this laborious obfuscation.[22] Slavery remains a subject that is difficult to talk about.

Yet it was also true, as James McPherson pointed out, that the "American Civil War could not end with a negotiated peace because the issues over which it was fought—Union versus Disunion, Freedom versus Slavery—proved to be non-negotiable."[23] The Civil War marked the termination of the problem that had caused Americans so much difficulty in discussing it openly. With the war's conclusion and the passage of the Thirteenth Amendment to the Constitution, the United States achieved the abolition of slavery, a consummation won forty years earlier among many of its southern neighbors. Just as 1826 marked the waning of dreams of Pan-American community, the events of 1861, in turn, ended the rhetorical function of Latin America as a useful proxy for discussions of U.S. slavery. In the roar of battle there was little need for metaphor.

Notes

Preface. Creatures of Silence

1. George M. Fredrickson, *Race: A Short History* (Princeton, N.J.: Princeton University Press, 2002), 68–80.

2. Theodore Dwight Weld, quoted in James Oliver Horton and Lois E. Horton, *In Hope of Liberty: Culture, Community, and Protest Among Northern Free Blacks, 1700–1860* (New York: Oxford University Press, 1997), 220; italics in original.

3. Supreme Court of the United States, December Term 1856, *Dred Scott v. John F. A. Sandford*, 11.

4. Ralph Waldo Emerson, "An Address . . . on . . . The Emancipation of the Negroes in the British West Indies" (1 August 1844) *Emerson's Antislavery Writings*, ed. Len Gougeon and Joel Myerson (New Haven, Conn.: Yale University Press, 1995), 21.

5. Amos A. Phelps, "Address to Clergymen," in *Lectures on Slavery and Its Remedy* (Boston: New-England Anti-Slavery Society, 1834), 22–23.

Introduction. Surrounded by Mirrors

1. [Julia Ward Howe], "A Trip to Cuba," *Atlantic Monthly* 3, 19 (May 1859): 604; Howe, *A Trip to Cuba* (Boston: Ticknor & Fields, 1860), 12, 13. The French antislavery writer Victor Schoelcher expressed similar disappointment with the progress of free blacks on a trip to Haiti in 1841, but was more sympathetic than Howe. Laurent Dubois, *Haiti: The Aftershocks of History* (New York: Metropolitan Books, 2012), 112–13.

2. George Fitzhugh, "Southern Thought," *DeBow's Review* 23, 4 (October 1857): 339.

3. Quoted by C. Vann Woodward in the introduction to George Fitzhugh, *Cannibals All! or Slaves Without Masters* (Cambridge, Mass.: Belknap Press of Harvard University Press, 1960), xvii.

4. See Joshua D. Rothman, *Flush Times and Fever Dreams: A Story of Capitalism and Slavery in the Age of Jackson* (Athens: University of Georgia Press, 2012) and Walter Johnson, *River of Dark Dreams: Slavery and Empire in the Cotton Kingdom* (Cambridge, Mass.: Belknap Press of Harvard University Press, 2013).

5. Aaron Hulin to Samuel Hunter, December 24, 1835, Beinecke Rare Book and Manuscript Library, Yale University.

6. James Stirling, *Letters from the Slave States* (London: John W. Parker and Son, 1857), 200.

7. For a recent study of children's literature that subverted contemporary politics, see *Inside the Rainbow: Russian Children's Literature 1920–35: Beautiful Books, Terrible Times*, ed.

Julian Rothenstein and Olga Budashevskaya (London: Redstone, 2013). Sharona Ben-Tov considers how science fiction expresses national anxieties about technology in *The Artificial Paradise: Science Fiction and American Reality* (Ann Arbor: University of Michigan Press, 1995).

8. These themes suggest the career of the historiography of the post-1831 period in a nutshell. Alice Dana Adams's *The Neglected Period of Anti-Slavery in America* (Boston: Ginn and Co., 1908) attributes to the charged rhetoric of William Lloyd Garrison the galvanizing of abolitionist thought and the provocation of the proslavery response. Later historians more attuned to issues of slave agency like Drew Gilpin Faust in *The Ideology of Slavery: Proslavery Thought in the Antebellum South, 1830–1860* (Baton Rouge: Louisiana State University Press, 1981) have suggested the primacy of the Nat Turner revolt and subsequent Virginia debates that led to the hardening of proslavery attitudes. The recent transnational turn exemplified by Edward Bartlett Rugemer in *The Problem of Emancipation: The Caribbean Roots of the American Civil War* (Baton Rouge: Louisiana State University Press, 2008) demonstrates that the United States did not exist in a vacuum; Americans watched and reacted to events in Haiti and the British colonies of the West Indies. In *The Transformation of American Abolitionism: Fighting Slavery in the Early Republic* (Chapel Hill: University of North Carolina Press, 2002), Richard S. Newman cites the Second Great Awakening, "egalitarian rhetoric," and the redefining of women's roles in the public sphere as some of the causes of this newly vocal phase of post-1831 abolitionism (14). Finally, Robert Pierce Forbes in *The Missouri Compromise and Its Aftermath: Slavery and the Meaning of America* (Chapel Hill: University of North Carolina Press, 2007) and *Contesting Slavery: The Politics of Bondage and Freedom in the New American Republic*, ed. John Craig Hammond and Matthew Mason (Charlottesville: University of Virginia Press, 2011) argue that Adams's "neglected period" was a time of vigorous debate.

9. Frederick Douglass, "Slavery in the Pulpit of the Evangelical Alliance: An Address Delivered in London, England, on September 14, 1846," *The Frederick Douglass Papers: Series One—Speeches, Debates, and Interviews*, ed. John Blassingame et al. (New Haven, Conn.: Yale University Press, 1979), 1: 407.

10. For a discussion of the "contingency and instability of the value of rational argument" and the "tensions and fault lines within the concept of rational public argument itself," see Kimberly K. Smith, *The Dominion of Voice: Riot, Reason, and Romance in Antebellum Politics* (Lawrence: University Press of Kansas, 1999), 8.

11. Amos A. Phelps, *Lectures on Slavery and Its Remedy* (Boston: New-England Anti-Slavery Society, 1834), 22.

12. David Grimsted, *American Mobbing, 1828–1861* (New York: Oxford University Press, 1998), viii–ix. Indeed, as Michel-Rolph Trouillot wrote, the expression of resistance forces an acknowledgment that there is something wrong with the system itself; the roots of silence are structural. Michel-Rolph Trouillot, *Silencing the Past: Power and the Production of History* (Boston: Beacon Press, 1995), 84, 106.

13. Matthew Clavin, *Toussaint Louverture and the American Civil War: The Promise and Peril of a Second American Revolution* (Philadelphia: University of Pennsylvania Press, 2010).

14. "Revolutions in Haiti," *Littell's Living Age* 2, 14 (August 17, 1844): 65.

15. Rugemer, *Emancipation*; Matthew Pratt Guterl, "An American Mediterranean: Haiti, Cuba, and the American South," in *Hemispheric American Studies*, ed. Caroline F. Levander and Robert S. Levine (New Brunswick, N.J.: Rutgers University Press, 2008), 104–11; Matthew

Pratt Guterl, *American Mediterranean: Slaveholders in the Age of Emancipation* (Cambridge, Mass.: Harvard University Press, 2008), 36; Richard Henry Dana, *To Cuba and Back* (London: Smith, Elder and Co., 1859), 238.

16. See, for example, Timothy Patrick McCarthy and John Stauffer, eds., *Prophets of Protest: Reconsidering the History of American Abolitionism* (New York: New Press, 2006); Newman, *Transformation*; Lacy K. Ford, *Deliver Us from Evil: The Slavery Question in the Old South* (Oxford: Oxford University Press, 2009); Paul Finkelman, *Defending Proslavery Thought in the Old South: A Brief History with Documents* (Boston: Bedford/St. Martin's, 2003); Betty L. Fladeland, "Revisionists vs. Abolitionists: The Historiographical Cold War of the 1930s and 1940s," *Journal of the Early Republic* 6, 1 (Spring 1986): 1–21.

17. Dwight Lowell Dumond, *Antislavery Origins of the Civil War in the United States* (Ann Arbor: University of Michigan Press, 1939); Russell Nye, *Fettered Freedom: Civil Liberties and the Slavery Controversy, 1830–1860* (East Lansing: Michigan State College Press, 1949).

18. Frank L. Owsley, *"Freedom of Thought in the Old South"* [review], *Journal of Southern History* 6, 4 (Nov. 1940): 559.

19. Clement Eaton, "Preface to the Torchbook Edition," *The Freedom-of-Thought Struggle in the Old South* (New York: Harper Torchbooks, 1964), vi–vii. That same year a Birmingham lawyer named Charles Morgan, Jr., published a book implicating the passivity of white people in failing to resist the violence directed against the civil rights movement—*A Time to Speak* (New York: Harper & Row, 1964).

20. Leonard L. Richards, *"Gentlemen of Property and Standing": Anti-Abolition Mobs in Jacksonian America* (London: Oxford University Press, 1970); William Lee Miller, *Arguing about Slavery: The Great Battle in the United States Congress* (New York: Knopf, 1996); Michael T. Gilmore, *The War on Words: Slavery, Race and Free Speech in American Literature* (Chicago: University of Chicago Press, 2010).

21. Carolyn L. Karcher, "Censorship, American Style: The Case of Lydia Maria Child," *Studies in the American Renaissance* (1986): 285.

22. Richard Kielbowicz plays devil's advocate for communities that invoked common-law justifications for mob activity by citing concerns for public safety, the common welfare, and curtailment of public nuisance. Richard B. Kielbowicz, "The Law and Mob Law in Attacks on Antislavery Newspapers, 1833–1860," *Law and History Review* 24, 3 (Fall 2006): 559–600.

23. Carl Schurz, "The Doom of Slavery," *Speeches of Carl Schurz* (Philadelphia: Lippincott, 1865), 125.

24. George M. Weston, *The Progress of Slavery in the United States* (Washington, D.C., 1857), 176–89.

25. Newman, 8–15.

26. William Lloyd Garrison, *The Liberator*, January 1, 1831. One defense of antislavery activities from this period neatly turns the rhetoric of slavery's advocates against them: "The agitators are those who are endeavouring, by deception and fraud, to subvert the constitution, and change the settled policy of this country. These fanatics, by means of their incendiary meetings and publications, have long been laboring to inflame the public mind against the abolitionists, by misrepresenting their sentiments and designs": "Defensor," in *The Enemies of the Constitution Discovered: or, An Inquiry into the Origin and Tendency of Popular Violence* (New York: Leavitt, Lord, & Co.: 1835), iii.

27. Edwin G. Burrows and Mike Wallace, *Gotham: A History of New York City to 1898* (New York: Oxford University Press, 2000), 559.

28. Rothman, *Flush Times*, esp. 91–117.

29. Frederick Douglass at the Rochester Ladies Anti-Slavery Society in 1855, quoted in Amy Reynolds, "The Impact of *Walker's Appeal* on Northern and Southern Conceptions of Free Speech in the Nineteenth Century," *Communication Law and Policy* 9, 1 (Winter 2004): 76.

30. [William Drayton], *The South Vindicated from the Treason and Fanaticism of the Northern Abolitionists* (Philadelphia: H. Manly, 1836), 174.

31. Richard R. John, *Spreading the News: The American Postal System from Franklin to Morse* (Cambridge, Mass. Harvard University Press, 1995), 268.

32. [Drayton], 308.

33. Ibid., 310.

34. For a consideration of the gag rule, see Miller, *Arguing About Slavery*; Richard P. Kollen, "The House Gag Rule Debate: The Wedge Dividing North and South," *OAH Magazine of History* 12, 4 (Summer 1998): 55–63; Robert Ludlum, "The Antislavery 'Gag-Rule': History and Argument," *The Journal of Negro History* 26, 2 (April 1941): 203–43. In " 'The Only Mode of Avoiding Everlasting Debate': The Overlooked Senate Gag Rule for Antislavery Petitions," *Journal of the Early Republic* 27, 1 (Spring 2007): 115–38, Daniel Wirls points out that although the House of Representatives' prohibitions on the discussion of slavery was eroded by 1844, in the Senate the "gag rule" only met its demise in 1850.

35. *Register of Debates in Congress*, 24th Cong., 1st Sess., March 1, 1836, 672.

36. Richards, 81–82.

37. On the decline of suppression in the 1840s, see Newman, 149–51, and Richards, 156–65. For more furious anti-abolitionist activity in the Old Northwest in the 1840s, see Dana Elizabeth Weiner, *Race and Rights: Fighting Slavery and Prejudice in the Old Northwest, 1830–1870* (DeKalb: Northern Illinois Press, 2013), 76, 134–38.

38. Charles Sumner, *The Crime Against Kansas* (Boston: John P. Jewett & Co., 1856), 9.

39. "Our Special Contributors: Silence Must Be Nationalized," *The Independent*, June 12, 1856, 1.

40. Michael Kent Curtis, "The Crisis over *The Impending Crisis*: Free Speech, Slavery, and the Fourteenth Amendment," in *Slavery and the Law*, ed. Paul Finkelman (Madison: Madison House, 1997), 161–205.

41. Vernon Louis Parrington, *Main Currents in American Thought, Volume Two, 1800–1860: The Romantic Revolution in America* (New York: Harcourt, Brace, 1927; 1954 Harvest Book Edition), 237; *Appendix to the Congressional Globe*, 36th Cong., 1st Sess., April 5, 1860, 205.

42. *Congressional Globe*, 36th Cong., 1st Sess., January 16, 1860, 448.

43. Ibid., January 23, 1860, 558.

44. Gilmore, 20.

45. Zelotus Holmes to his cousin, February 1, 1840, Zelotus Lee Holmes papers, 1820–1888, South Caroliniana Library, University of South Carolina.

46. Angelina Grimké to Sarah Grimké, September 27, 1835, Slavery Collection, MS569, Series 5, New-York Historical Society.

47. Daniel Rood, "Bogs of Death: Slavery, the Brazilian Flour Trade, and the Mystery of the Vanishing Millpond in Antebellum Virginia," *Journal of the American Republic* 101, 1 (June 2014): 19–43.

48. Matthew Pratt Guterl, *American Mediterranean: Southern Slaveholders in the Age of Emancipation* (Cambridge, Mass.: Harvard University Press, 2008); Gerald Horne, *The Deepest South: The United States, Brazil, and the African Slave Trade* (New York: New York University Press, 2007).

49. Peter Kolchin, *A Sphinx on the American Land: The Nineteenth Century South in Comparative Perspective* (Baton Rouge: Louisiana State University Press, 2003), 39–73; Matthew Mason, "The Maine and Missouri Crisis: Competing Priorities and Northern Slavery Politics in the Early Republic," *Journal of the Early Republic* 33, 4 (Winter 2013): 698–99.

50. Terence Whalen, *Edgar Allan Poe and the Masses: The Political Economy of Literature in Antebellum America* (Princeton, N.J.: Princeton University Press, 1999), 111–12.

51. Slavery found potent defenders in the North in the 1830s. See Larry E. Tise, *Proslavery: A History of the Defense of Slavery in America, 1701–1840* (Athens: University of Georgia Press, 1987), esp. chapters 9 and 10.

52. See Michael O'Brien, *Conjectures of Order: Intellectual Life and the American South, 1810–1860* (Chapel Hill: University of North Carolina Press, 2004), 27 ff.

53. "Cora Montgomery" (Jane Cazneau), *The Eagle Pass; or, Life on the Border* (New York: Putnam, 1852), 24.

54. Tillson Harris to Samuel Harris, October 1, 1856, and January 12, 1857, Samuel Harris Correspondence [SC001], Historical Society of Pennsylvania.

55. Among the antiabolitionists of the North, wrote Lydia Maria Child, "you will find that some manufacture negro cloths for the South—some have sons who sell those cloths—some have daughters married to slave-holders—some have plantations and slaves mortgaged to them—some have ships employed in Southern commerce—and some candidates for political offices would bow until their back-bones were broken, to obtain or preserve Southern influence" (Mrs. [Lydia Maria] Child, *Anti-Slavery Catechism* (Newburyport, Mass.: Charles Whipple, 1839), 35.

56. Anne Farrow, Joel Lang, and Jenifer Frank, *Complicity: How the North Promoted, Prolonged, and Profited from Slavery* (New York: Ballantine, 2005), 4, 7.

57. Edward Neufville Tailer Diaries, MS2495, October 22, 1852; September 22, 1852; February 16, 1854; March 30, 1854; December 19, 1854; quote from December 22, 1859; New-York Historical Society.

58. William Freehling includes a particularly resonant discussion of the private hypocrisies—and torments—of Southerners who were unwavering proslavery advocates in public. See William W. Freehling, *The Road to Disunion*, vol. 2, *Secessionists Triumphant, 1854–1861* (New York: Oxford University Press, 2007), 27–58.

59. Ford, 357.

60. Sven Beckert, *Empire of Cotton: A Global History* (New York: Knopf. 2014), 122.

61. David Reynolds, *Waking Giant: America in the Age of Jackson* (New York: HarperCollins, 2008), 91–92.

62. In *A Republic of Righteousness*, Jonathan Sassi states, "No issue proved more divisive to the clergy's public Christianity than that of slavery." Jonathan D. Sassi, *A Republic of Righteousness: The Public Christianity of the Post-Revolutionary New England Clergy* (Oxford: Oxford University Press, 2001), 199.

63. Kenneth M. Stampp, *America in 1857: A Nation on the Brink* (New York: Oxford University Press, 1990), 114.

64. Quoted in Constance Mayfield Rourke, *Trumpets of Jubilee* (New York: Harcourt, Brace, 1927), 59.

65. Julie Roy Jeffrey, *The Great Silent Army of Abolitionism: Ordinary Women in the Antislavery Movement* (Chapel Hill: University of North Carolina Press, 1998), 138–41.

66. Diary, Anna Quincy Thaxter Cushing Papers, 1816–1918, American Antiquarian Society, Worchester, Massachusetts.

67. Harriet Beecher Stowe, "Introduction to the New Edition," *Uncle Tom's Cabin; or, Life Among the Lowly* (Boston: Houghton Mifflin, 1890 [1878]), x.

68. Noting incidentally that "the greatest improvement that could possibly be effected in the condition of the human race [was] the total abolition of slavery on earth," Adams interpreted Congress's refusal to hear a petition from a hundred and fifty women as "calumny [against] a class of citizens as pure and virtuous as the inhabitants of any section of the Union." "They were, many of them, sisters and mothers of his constituents. Every member of the House (said Mr. A.) has, or had, a mother . . . do they say that they will not even listen to a petition coming from such a source?" (*Register of Debates in Congress*, 24th Cong., 2nd Sess., January 9, 1837, 1314–15). Adams's biographer Paul C. Nagel calls him "mischievous" and "fiendishly clever in presenting petitions from abolitionists and from Peace Society members." Paul C. Nagel, *John Quincy Adams: A Public Life, a Private Life* (New York: Knopf, 1997), 356, 364.

69. Nagel, 379–81.

70. Quoted in Fred Kaplan, *John Quincy Adams, American Visionary* (New York: Harper-Collins, 2014), 481. Adams published an essay on *Othello* in the *New England Magazine* in December 1835. In the Georgetown *Metropolitan* of December 28, 1835, S. D. Langtree and J. L. O'Sullivan criticized Adams for not distinguishing between an "*African negro*" and "one of the chivalrous race of *Moors*." See William Jerry MacLean, "Othello Scorned: The Racial Thought of John Quincy Adams," *Journal of the Early Republic* 4, 2 (Summer 1984): 148–49; italics in original.

71. Quoted in Annette Gordon-Reed, *The Hemingses of Monticello: An American Family* (New York: Norton, 2008), 196.

72. And "events soon demonstrated that the Republican threat to slavery was far from imaginary." James Oakes, *Freedom National: The Destruction of Slavery in the United States, 1861–1865* (New York: Norton, 2013), xii–xiii.

73. James Oakes, *The Radical and the Republican: Frederick Douglass, Abraham Lincoln, and the Triumph of Antislavery Politics* (New York: Norton, 2007), 119–20. In *Lincoln and Race*, Richard Striner concludes after reviewing much supposed evidence for Lincoln's racism, particularly in quotations taken out of context, that the "preponderance of evidence suggests in all probability Lincoln had no racial bias." Richard Striner, *Lincoln and Race* (Carbondale: Southern Illinois University Press, 2012), 70. "Like any politician," writes Eric Foner, "he said things for strategic reasons." Eric Foner, *The Fiery Trial: Abraham Lincoln and American Slavery* (New York: Norton, 2010), xvi; see also 117–23.

74. Exactly the opposite situation exists today. The most avowed racist is unlikely to champion the return of slavery because of its improbability. But the same racist, in a situation where he or she is unsure of the reception of forthright expressions of intolerance, is apt to resort to coded language and circumlocutions about "crime," the "middle class," "nice" neighborhoods that "changed," and "urban" problems.

75. A twenty-first-century subject similarly vexed in its implications and impact might be abortion, which engages issues of health, privacy, feminism, class, geography, religious identity, and political affiliation.

76. Elizabeth Palmer Peabody, September 25, [1847], via typed transcript, original missing. Gage Family, Additional Papers, American Antiquarian Society, Worcester, Mass.

77. Eric Foner, *Free Soil, Free Labor, Free Men: The Ideology of the Republican Party Before the Civil War* (New York: Oxford University Press, 1970), 40–41.

78. Foner, *Free Soil*, 262–65.

79. Peter Williams, "To the Citizens of New York," *New York Daily Advertiser*, July 17, 1834, 2.

80. Maria Dubois to Mary Ann Blount, June 29, 1848, AHMC-Dubois, Maria, MS2958, New-York Historical Society.

81. A. Sydney Southworth to George Shepard Burleigh, March 6, 1839, John Hay Library, Brown University Library.

82. Gertrude, "No. 64," *Water-Cure Journal* 19 (March 1855): 65.

83. John Humphrey Noyes, *Slavery and Marriage: A Dialogue* (1850), 14.

84. William R. Taylor, *Cavalier and Yankee: The Old South and the American National Character* (Garden City, N.Y.: Anchor, 1963 [1957]), xix.

85. Andrew W. Robertson, "'Look on this Picture . . . And on This!' Nationalism, Localism, and Partisan Images of Otherness in the United States, 1787–1820," *American Historical Review* 106, 4 (October 2001): 1263–80, passim.

86. Foreign *visitors* exercised a freedom of speech not always permitted to foreigners who hoped to settle permanently in the South. See Dennis C. Rousey, "Friends and Foes of Slavery: Foreigners and Northerners in the Old South," *Journal of Social History* 35, 2 (Winter 2001): 373–96.

87. "Slavery," *North American Review* 41, 88 (July 1835): 185. This article echoes one written in the thick of the Missouri Crisis: "The existence of slavery in this country may be regarded as affecting our character abroad, and our condition at home. . . . we cannot divest ourselves of a secret and distressing consciousness of the glaring inconsistency of our professions and our practice. "Slavery and the Missouri Question," *North American Review* 10, 26 (January 1820): 137–38.

88. Alexis de Tocqueville, *Democracy in America*, trans., ed., and intro. Harvey C. Mansfield and Delba Winthrop (Chicago: University of Chicago Press, 2000), 1: 244.

89. Charles Dickens, *The Life and Adventures of Martin Chuzzlewit* (London: Chapman and Hall, 1844), 209.

90. Frances Trollope, *Domestic Manners of the Americans*, ed. Donald Smalley (New York: Knopf, 1949 [1832]), 354.

91. Lieutenant E. T. Coke, quoted in Smalley, "Introduction," Trollope, ix.

92. Fredrika Bremer, *The Homes of the New World: Impressions of America*, trans. Mary Howitt (New York: Harper & Brothers, 1853), 1: 254.

93. For a good example of deflection and finger-pointing, see "Blackwood's Magazine," *United States Democratic Review* 32, 4 (April 1853): 289–324; quote from 311.

94. By contrast, Ashli White demonstrates that much of what Americans in the 1790s and early 1810s understood about Saint Domingue they learned much more directly from refugees fleeing the Haitian Revolution and seeking sanctuary in the United States. Americans

began defining their national character against a Haitian foil and argued for their own exceptionalism. Ashli White, *Encountering Revolution: Haiti and the Making of the Early Republic*
(Baltimore: Johns Hopkins University Press, 2010), 3–7.

95. Mary Gardner Lowell, *New Year in Cuba: Mary Gardner Lowell's Travel Diary, 1831–
1832*, ed, and intro. Karen Robert (Boston: Massachusetts Historical Society, Northeastern
University Press, 2003), 38, 51.

96. In *One Drop of Blood*, Scott L. Malcomson suggests that "race unhinged the American
mind by about 1820," leading to the currency of three ideas among white people: slavery was
not the fault of the Americans, but an institution imposed on them by their colonial oppres-
sors; black people are essentially different from white people; removal of nonwhite people
from the nation would solve the problems caused by their presence. Scott L. Malcomson, *One
Drop of Blood: The American Misadventure of Race* (New York: Farrar, Straus, and Giroux,
2001), 190–91.

97. Thomas Jefferson to Archibald Stuart, January 25, 1786, quoted in John Kukla, *A
Wilderness So Immense: The Louisiana Purchase and the Destiny of America* (New York: Knopf,
2003), 6.

98. Fisher Ames in *New-England Palladium*, quoted in Kukla, *A Wilderness So Immense*,
293.

99. Peter J. Kastor, *The Nation's Crucible: The Louisiana Purchase and the Creation of
America* (New Haven, Conn.: Yale University Press, 2004).

100. William W. Freehling, "The Louisiana Purchase and the Coming of the Civil War,"
in *The Louisiana Purchase and American Expansion, 1803–1898*, ed. Sanford Levinson and
Bartholomew H. Sparrow (Lanham, Md.: Rowman & Littlefield, 2005), 73.

101. Sanford Levinson and Bartholomew H. Sparrow, "Introduction," in *The Louisiana
Purchase and American Expansion*, 7.

102. See Lawrence W. Levine's discussion of heterogeneous early nineteenth-century
audiences and the jumble of cultural productions they enjoyed in *Highbrow/Lowbrow: The
Emergence of Cultural Hierarchy in America* (Cambridge, Mass. Harvard University Press,
1988).

103. See, for example, Thomas Hietala, *Manifest Design: Anxious Aggrandizement in Late
Jacksonian America* (Ithaca, N.Y.: Cornell University Press, 1985), 263.

104. "The Americans, in Their Moral, Social, and Political Relations" (review), *North
American Review* 46, 98 (January 1838): 106–7.

Chapter 1. Never So Drunk with New-Born Liberty

1. *Register of Debates in Congress*, 19th Cong., 1st Sess., March 2, 1826, 117.

2. David Johnson, *John Randolph of Roanoke* (Baton Rouge: Louisiana State University
Press, 2012), 2–5, 207; George Dangerfield, *The Era of Good Feelings* (New York: Harcourt,
Brace & World, 1952), 354.

3. Robert Pierce Forbes, *The Missouri Compromise and Its Aftermath: Slavery and the
Meaning of America* (Chapel Hill: University of North Carolina Press, 2007).

4. Jeremy D. Popkin, *You Are All Free: The Haitian Revolution and the Abolition of Slavery*
(Cambridge: Cambridge University Press, 2010), 297.

5. Anthony E. Kaye, "The Second Slavery: Modernity in the Nineteenth-Century South
and the Atlantic World," *Journal of Southern History* 75, 3 (August 2009): 627–50.

6. James Lewis, Jr., *The American Union and the Problem of Neighborhood: The United States and the Collapse of the Spanish Empire, 1783–1829* (Chapel Hill: University of North Carolina Press, 1998); Mark G. Jaede, "Brothers at a Distance: Race, Religion, Culture and U.S. Views of Spanish America, 1800–1830" (Ph.D. dissertation, State University of New York at Buffalo, 2001); John J. Johnson, *A Hemisphere Apart: The Foundations of United States Policy Toward Latin America* (Baltimore: Johns Hopkins University Press, 1990); Lester D. Langley, *The Americas in the Age of Revolution, 1750–1850* (New Haven, Conn.: Yale University Press, 1996); Light T. Cummins, "John Quincy Adams and Latin American Nationalism," *Revista de Historia America* 86 (July–December 1978): 226.

7. Caitlin A. Fitz, "Our Sister Republics: The United States in an Age of American Revolutions," (Ph.D. dissertation, Yale University, 2010); Sarah Cornell, "An American Revolution: Southern Views of Mexican Independence," paper presented at the Annual Meeting of the Society for Historians of the Early American Republic, Philadelphia, July 15, 2011.

8. See, for example, Andrew R. L. Cayton, "The Debate over the Panama Congress and the Origins of the Second American Party System," *Historian* 47, 2 (February 1985): 219–38; Lewis, *American Union*; Jeffrey J. Malanson, "The Congressional Debate over U.S. Participation in the Congress of Panama, 1825–1826: Washington's Farewell Address, Monroe's Doctrine, and the Fundamental Principles of U.S. Foreign Policy," *Diplomatic History* 30, 5 (November 2006): 813–37.

9. Thomas Hart Benton, *Thirty Years' View; or, A History of the Working of the American Government for Thirty Years, from 1820 to 1850* (Boston: Frederick Parker, 1854), 66 ("abortion"); 65.

10. Piero Gleijeses, "The Limits of Sympathy: The United States and the Independence of Spanish America," *Journal of Latin American Studies* 24, 3 (October 1992): 495, n.66.

11. Andrew Burstein, *America's Jubilee* (New York: Knopf, 2001).

12. For his part, Lafayette exclaimed the same thing upon meeting the aged Adams: "That was not the John Adams I remember!" quoted in Burstein, 14.

13. "Zero," "For the Fourth of July, 1826," *National Intelligencer*, July 4, 1826, 3.

14. "The Jubilee of Liberty," *Richmond Enquirer*, July 4, 1826, 3.

15. Jaede, 41–62, 187–90. David Waldstreicher's *In the Midst of Perpetual Fetes: The Making of American Nationalism 1776–1820* (Chapel Hill: Published for Omohundro Institute of Early American History and Culture by the University of North Carolina Press, 1997) demonstrated the value of toasts in revealing popular attitudes in the early republic.

16. Caitlin A. Fitz, "A White Republic in a Hemisphere of Color: The Inter-American Origins of the Democratic Party," paper presented at the Annual Meeting of the Society for Historians of the Early American Republic, Philadelphia, July 15, 2011.

17. Caitlin A. Fitz, "The Problem of Slavery in a Hemisphere of Republics: The United States and Spanish American Emancipation," paper presented to the McNeil Center for Early American Studies Seminar Series, The Library Company of Philadelphia, November 12, 2010.

18. Rufus King, quoted in Ronald Angelo Johnson, *Diplomacy in Black and White: John Adams, Toussaint Louverture, and Their Atlantic World Alliance* (Athens: University of Georgia Press, 2014), 44.

19. Don E. Fehrenbacher, *The Slaveholding Republic: An Account of the United States Government's Relations to Slavery*, completed and ed. Ward M. McAfee (Oxford: Oxford University Press, 2001), 366.

20. Laurent Dubois, *Haiti: The Aftershocks of History* (New York: Metropolitan, 2012), 137–38; Donald R. Hickey, "America's Response to the Slave Revolt in Haiti, 1791–1806," *Journal of the Early Republic* 2, 4 (Winter 1982): 361–79.

21. For a discussion of Southern fears of Haitian-inspired revolts, see Robert Alderson, "Charleston's Rumored Slave Revolt of 1793," in *The Impact of the Haitian Revolution in the Atlantic World*, ed. David P. Geggus (Columbia: University of South Carolina Press, 2001), 93–111.

22. Ronald Angelo Johnson, *Diplomacy in Black and White: John Adams, Toussaint Louverture, and Their Atlantic World Alliance* (Athens: University of Georgia Press, 2014), 173–74.

23. Fehrenbacher, 111–18.

24. Jay Kinsbruner, *Independence in Spanish America: Civil Wars, Revolutions, and Underdevelopment* (Albuquerque: University of New Mexico Press, 1994), 102–3.

25. *Register of Debates in Congress*, 19th Cong., 1st Sess., March 1826, 330.

26. Daniel Rasmussen, *American Uprising: The Untold Story of America's Largest Slave Revolt* (New York: HarperCollins, 2011).

27. Alfred N. Hunt, *Haiti's Influence on Antebellum America: Slumbering Volcano in the Caribbean* (Baton Rouge: Louisiana State University Press, 1988), chap. 4.

28. *Register of Debates in Congress*, 19th Cong., 1st Sess., March 1826, 330.

29. See Tom Nairn, *Faces of Nationalism: Janus Revisited* (London: Verso, 1997), 75ff.

30. Jaede, 79.

31. Maurice G. Baxter, *Henry Clay and the American System* (Lexington: University Press of Kentucky, 1995), 56–59.

32. Manuel Torres, "An Exposition of the Commerce of Spanish America; with Some Observations upon its Importance to the United States" (Philadelphia: G. Palmer, 1816), 11.

33. Henry Clay, *The Speeches of Henry Clay: Delivered in the Congress of the United States* (Philadelphia: H. C. Carey & I. Lea, 1827), 226. Similar passages are quoted in Randolph B. Campbell, "The Spanish American Aspect of Henry Clay's American System," *Americas* 24, 1 (July 1967): 3, 6, 7.

34. Lindsey Apple, *The Family Legacy of Henry Clay: In the Shadow of a Kentucky Patriarch* (Lexington: University Press of Kentucky, 2011), 87.

35. *Register of Debates in Congress*, 19th Cong., 1st Sess., March 30, 1826, 395. The almost giddy pleasure taken in scurrilous caricature is classic Randolph.

36. Richard C. Anderson to Beaufort Taylor Watts, July 24, 1825, Beaufort Taylor Watts Papers, 1822–1879, South Caroliniana Library, University of South Carolina.

37. Fred Kaplan, *John Quincy Adams, American Visionary* (New York: HarperCollins, 2014), 401–2.

38. Adams mentioned the proposed participation in the Panama Congress in his first message to Congress on December 6, 1825; subsequently he sent messages to the Senate, December 26, 1825 and to the House of Representatives, January 15 and March 15, 1826.

39. *Register of Debates in Congress*, 19th Cong., 1st Sess., January 25, 1826, 1117.

40. Ibid., April 13, 1826, 2243.

41. Ibid., 2251.

42. Ibid., April 12, 1826, 2224.

43. John Quincy Adams, Message of the President of the United States to the Senate, Relative to the Panama Mission, *Register of Debates in Congress* (Appendix), 19th Cong., 1st Sess., December 26, 1825, 48.

44. *Register of Debates in Congress,* 19th Cong., 1st Sess., February 2, 1826, 1240.

45. Ibid., March 1826, 183.

46. Ibid., April 14, 1826, 2276.

47. See, for example, Robert V. Remini, *Martin Van Buren and the Making of the Democratic Party* (New York: Columbia University Press, 1951), esp. 104–13. His *Henry Clay: Statesman for the Union* (New York: Norton, 1991) similarly retails his thesis, 290–95. Two recent iterations of his argument appear in Malanson, "The Congressional Debate," 813–38, and in Forbes, *Missouri Compromise.*

48. Sean Wilentz, *The Rise of American Democracy: Jefferson to Lincoln* (New York: Norton, 2005), 295–96; Donald B. Cole, *Martin Van Buren and the American Political System* (Princeton, N.J.: Princeton University Press, 1984), 147–49.

49. Salma Hale ("Algernon Sidney"), "The Administration and the Opposition" (Concord, Mass. 1826), 13.

50. Brian Loveman, *The Constitution of Tyranny: Regimes of Exception in Spanish America* (Pittsburgh: University of Pittsburgh Press, 1993).

51. Ada Ferrer, "Haiti, Free Soil, and Antislavery in the Revolutionary Atlantic," *American Historical Review* 117 no. 1 (February 2012): 40–66.

52. *Register of Debates in Congress,* 19th Cong., 1st Sess., March 1826, 325.

53. Ibid., April 10, 1826, 2164.

54. Ibid., March 1826, 275.

55. Ibid., March 1, 1826, 112.

56. Ibid., March 1826, 291.

57. Forbes, *Missouri Compromise,* 36.

58. *Register of Debates in Congress,* 18th Cong., 2nd Sess., February 28, 1825, 696–97.

59. *Register of Debates in Congress,* 19th Cong., 1st Sess., January 31, 1826, 1214. Italics in original.

60. Ibid., April 10, 1826, 2153.

61. Manisha Sinha, *The Counterrevolution of Slavery: Politics and Ideology in Antebellum South Carolina* (Chapel Hill: University of North Carolina Press, 2000), 15.

62. *Register of Debates in Congress,* 19th Cong., 1st Sess., April 6, 1826, 2062; italics in original.

63. Ibid., April 6, 1826, 2962.

64. Ibid., March 1826, 285; italics original.

65. Ibid.

66. Message of the President of the United States to the House of Representatives, *Register of Debates in Congress* (Appendix), 19th Cong., 1st Sess., March 15, 1826, 71.

67. Ibid., February 2, 1826, 1258.

68. Ibid., April 11, 1826, 2169.

69. Ibid., April 11, 1829, 2179.

70. Ibid., April 11, 1826, 2180.

71. Ibid., March 1826, 207–8.

72. Ibid., March 1826, 208, 210.

73. Ibid., March 1826, 165–66; italics in original. John Sergeant was the individual in question.

74. Ibid., April 10, 1826, 2149–50.

75. Ibid., January 31, 1826, 1215.

76. Remini, *Martin Van Buren*, 106, 115.

77. Jaede, 162.

78. Jaede, 190.

79. Simon Bolivar Hulbert, *One Battle Too Many* (Gaithersburg, Md.: Olde Soldier's Book, 1987).

80. "The Following Volunteer Toasts Were Drunk," *Richmond Enquirer*, September 25, 1826, 2; "Celebration by the Richmond Volunteers of the Fiftieth Anniversary of American Independence," *Richmond Enquirer*, July 7, 1826, 3.

81. Henry Clay to Charles Hammond, April 19, 1826, in *The Papers of Henry Clay*, ed. James F. Hopkins and Mary W. M. Hargreaves (Lexington: University Press of Kentucky, 1973), 253.

82. "The Panama Mission," *New-York Evening Post*, February 7, 1826, 2; "Panama Mission," *New-York Evening Post*, February 10, 1826, 2; "The Panama Mission! The Panama Mission!" *New-York Evening Post*, April 6, 1826, 2. The exclamation points in the last headline do not signal the importance of the subject but exasperation at constant coverage of the debates.

83. "The Panama Debate Concluded," *New-York Evening Post*, February 14, 1826, 2.

84. "The Congress at Panama," *Liberty Hall and Cincinnati Gazette*, February 17, 1826, 3.

85. "Negro Slavery," *Liberty Hall and Cincinnati Gazette*, April 11, 1826, 3.

86. "Cuba," *Liberty Hall and Cincinnati Gazette*, January 20, 1826, 2.

87. Ibid., April 14, 1826, 3.

88. (No title), *Louisiana State Gazette*, March 3, 1826, 2.

89. (No title), *Louisiana State Gazette*, April 15, 1826, 2.

90. (No title), *Louisiana State Gazette*, April 20, 1826, 2.

91. "P. Henry," "Panama," *Richmond Enquirer*, April 4, 1826, 3.

92. Ibid. Bracketed material in original.

93. Cayton, 236–37.

94. Ibid., 237.

95. Gleijeses, 505.

96. Caitlin Fitz suggests that individual Americans in Latin America sometimes displayed more "selfless and ideological motives" in their behavior than the national policy of the United States dictated. Caitlin Fitz, "'A Stalwart Motor of Revolutions': An American Merchant in Pernambuco, 1817–1825," *Americas* 65, 1 (July 2008): 54.

97. "Philantropos" (William Ladd), *Essays on Peace & War, Which First Appeared in the Christian Mirror, Printed at Portland, Me.* (Portland, Maine: A. Shirley, 1827).

98. "Philanthropos," 83–84.

99. Ibid., 85.

100. Ibid., 89.

101. Dangerfield, *The Era of Good Feelings*, 365–66; Cayton, 236.

102. Joel Poinsett to George Frick, October 25, 1828, Joel Roberts Poinsett Papers, 1804–1851, South Caroliniana Library, University of South Carolina.

103. Amy S. Greenberg, *A Wicked War: Polk, Clay, Lincoln and the 1846 U.S. Invasion of Mexico* (New York: Knopf, 2012), 57.

104. Francis Baylies to Gulian C. Verplanck, July 26, 1832, Verplanck Papers, MS656, New-York Historical Society. My thanks to Brendan O'Malley for bringing this material to my attention.

105. The independence movements themselves generated demand for American-made weapons. Andrew Fagan and Edward Pompeian, "Contracted Weaponry: The Law of Nations and the U.S.-Latin American Arms Trade, 1793–1818," paper presented at Annual Meeting of the Society of Historians of the Early American Republic, Philadelphia, July 19, 2014.

106. A typical example appears in the *Louisiana State Gazette*, April 11, 1826, 2.

107. Cayton, 236.

108. "Interior Trade with Mexico," *National Intelligencer*, December 3, 1825 (supplement), 2.

109. Appendix to *Congressional Globe*, 27th Cong., 2nd Sess., April 13, 1842, 513–14.

110. Adrian R. Terry, M.D., *Travels in the Equatorial Regions of South America, in 1832* (Hartford, Conn.: Cooke & Co., 1834), 284–85.

111. Seth Rockman, "Implements Correspondingly Peculiar: Slavery, Plantation Goods, and the Politics of Design in Antebellum America," Bard Graduate Center Lecture, New York City, October 19, 2011.

112. William J. Cooper, Jr., *The South and the Politics of Slavery, 1828–1856* (Baton Rouge: Louisiana State University Press, 1978), 8–9.

113. Loring Moody, *A History of the Mexican War, or, Facts of the People, Showing the Relation of the U.S. Government to Slavery* (Boston: Bela Marsh, 1848), 40.

114. Timothy Flint, *Francis Berrian, or, The Mexican Patriot*, vol. 1 (Boston: Cummings, Hilliard, and Company, 1826), 2.

115. Frederick S. Stimson, " 'Francis Berrian': Hispanic Influence on American Romanticism," *Hispania* 42, no. 4 (December 1959): 511; John T. Flanagan and Raymond L. Grismer, "Mexico in American Fiction Prior to 1850," *Hispania* 23, 4 (December 1940): 309.

116. Timothy Flint's own biography reflected his hero's background: he was also a Massachusetts transplant to the West, and he explored some, though not all, of the wild country he described in *Francis Berrian*.

117. Both *North American Review* and *United States Review and Quarterly Gazette* took issue with the improbability of Flint's fictional hero playing such a leading role among actual historical figures. "Critical Notices: *Francis Berrian*," *North American Review* 24, 54 (January 1827): 210–11; *United States Review and Literary Gazette* (November 1826): 1, 2; 94. But Flint based his character on the historical Henry Adams Bullard, the "patriotic soldier of fortune" to whom he dedicated his novel (Flint, *Francis Berrian* 1: 3). Joel Poinsett, later U.S. minister to Mexico, took a similarly active, if less central, role in Chilean independence. Fred Rippy, *The Rivalry of the United States and Great Britain over Latin America, 1808–1830* (Baltimore: Johns Hopkins University Press, 1929), 10.

118. Keri Holt points out that Berrian "discovers that he must change his own views rather than try to alter the people and places he meets" Keri Holt, "Double-Crossings: The Trans-American Patriotism of Francis Berrian," *Western American Literature* 44, 4 (Winter 2010): 320–21.

119. Flint, *Francis Berrian* 1, 55.

120. Ibid., 68.

121. Flint, *Francis Berrian* 2, 23.

122. Flint, *Francis Berrian* 1, 283.

123. Ibid., 150.

124. Ibid., 152.

125. Ibid..

126. Flint, *Francis Berrian* 2, 271.

127. Ibid., 274.

128. Ibid., 275.

129. Ibid., 276.

130. Flint, *Francis Berrian* 1, 151.

131. Martha Menchaca, *Recovering History, Constructing Race: The Indian, Black, and White Roots of Mexican Americans* (Austin: University of Texas Press, 2001), 161–63.

132. Robert Montgomery Bird, *The Infidel; or, The Fall of Mexico: A Romance* (Philadelphia: Carey, Lea & Blanchard, 1835), 1: 57.

133. Jenny Davidson, *Breeding: A Partial History of the Eighteenth Century* (New York: Columbia University Press, 2009), 2: 164.

134. Davidson, *Breeding*, 200.

135. Ralph Bauer, "The Hemispheric Genealogies of 'Race': Creolization and the Cultural Geography of Colonial Difference across the Eighteenth-Century Americas," *Hemispheric American Studies*, ed. Caroline F. Levander and Robert S. Levine (New Brunswick, N.J.: Rutgers University Press, 2008), 42, 53.

136. Davidson, *Breeding*, 90–91.

137. Timothy Flint, "Owen's Concluding Speech," *Western Monthly Review* (September 1829): 142–43.

138. Timothy Flint, "Paulina, or the Cataract of Tequendama," *Western Monthly Review* (March 1830): 469.

Chapter 2. "Our" Aborigines

1. A similar whitening process was administered by white American archaeologists to the ancient Egyptians, and rebutted by African Americans. See Bruce Dain, *A Hideous Monster of the Mind: American Race Theory in the Early Republic* (Cambridge, Mass.: Harvard University Press, 2002). For another instance of whitening the national past, see Michael Harkin, "Performing Paradox: Narrativity and the Lost Colony of Roanoke," in *Myth and Memory: Stories of Indigenous-European Contact*, ed. John Sutton Lutz (Vancouver: University of British Columbia Press, 2007), 103–17.

2. *Congressional Globe*, 29th Cong., 1st Sess., May 28, 1846, 918. "The oldest" race to which Benton refers is the people of Asia.

3. John Greenleaf Whittier, "Stanzas for the Times," 1835, in *Anti-Slavery Poems: Songs of Labor and Reform* (Boston: Houghton Mifflin, 1894), 35–36.

4. In *History's Shadow: Native Americans and Historical Consciousness in the Nineteenth Century* (Chicago: University of Chicago Press, 2004), Steven Conn argues that midcentury Americans needed the Mound Builders to be a separate people from the Indians they knew in the present. Once archaeologists like John Wesley Powell presented convincing evidence that the Mound Builders were in fact the ancestors of modern Indians, nineteenth-century Americans lost interest in them (120–35).

5. Robert Silverberg's *Mound Builders of Ancient America: The Archaeology of a Myth* (Greenwich, Conn.: New York Graphic Society, 1973) remains an excellent resource about the discovery and changing perceptions of the mounds by white Americans in the eighteenth and nineteenth centuries. Barbara Alice Mann's *Native Americans, Archaeologists, and the Mounds* (New York: Peter Lang, 2003) considers the history of the mounds, their despoilation

and attempted Native American reclamation from her perspective as a Seneca-descended scholar.

6. The Spanish historian Clavigero repeated the theory that the Toltecs had emigrated from the north, where they had built cities surrounded by earthen walls. See Samuel F. Haven, *Santa Anna* (Washington, D.C.: Smithsonian Institution, 1856), 31.

7. The presentation of historical landscapes for political purposes, omitting all mention of some groups or presenting inequality as natural, continues in the present day. Paul A. Shackel, "Public Memory and the Search for Power in American Historical Archaeology," *American Anthropologist* 103, 3 (September 2001): 655–70.

8. Sven Beckert, *Empire of Cotton: A Global History* (New York: Knopf. 2014), xv–xvi, 107.

9. Ibid., 108.

10. Ibid., 131.

11. Alice Beck Kehoe argues that early archaeologists "found support from organizations promoting national identity, using archaeology to establish a preconquest past crying out for the technological breakthroughs brought to the continent by the superior race now dominating the hemisphere." Alice Beck Kehoe, *The Land of Prehistory: A Critical History of American Archaeology* (New York: Routledge, 1998), xii.

12. In *The Ruling Race*, James Oakes writes, "Few slaveholders ever bothered to offer a coherent racial defense of bondage in their letters or diaries. So ingrained were their racist assumptions that slaveholders were most likely to reveal themselves by recoiling in shock from the mere hint of racial egalitarianism or antislavery sentiment." James Oakes, *The Ruling Race: A History of American Slaveholders* (New York: Knopf, 1982), 131.

13. The United States was not exceptional in this endeavor. See Philip L. Kohl, "Nationalism and Archaeology: On the Constructions of Nations and the Reconstructions of the Remote Past," *Annual Review of Anthropology* 27, 1 (1998): 223–46, and Don D. Fowler, "Uses of the Past: Archaeology in the Service of the State," *American Antiquity* 52, 2 (April 1987): 229–48.

14. See Adam Rothman, *Slave Country: American Expansion and the Origin of the Deep South* (Cambridge, Mass.: Harvard University Press, 2005).

15. Edward Baptist, *The Half Has Never Been Told: Slavery and the Making of American Capitalism* (New York: Basic, 2014), xxii–xxiii.

16. Appendix to the Congressional Globe, 28th Cong., 2nd Sess., January 1854, 126.

17. Sean Wilentz, *The Rise of American Democracy: Jefferson to Lincoln* (New York: Norton, 2005), 322–29.

18. Theodore Sedgwick, *Thoughts on the Annexation of Texas* (New York, 1844), 38, quoted in Stephen Harnett, "Senator Robert Walker's 1844 *Letter on Texas Annexation*: The Rhetorical 'Logic' of Imperialism," *American Studies* 38, 1 (Spring 1997): 41.

19. Isaac C. Kenyon, [Untitled], *North Star*, January 7, 1848, 2.

20. See, for example, Baptist, *The Half Has Never Been Told*; Daniel Brett Rood, "Plantation Technocrats: A Social History of Knowledge in the Slaveholding Atlantic World, 1830–1865" (Ph.D. dissertation, University of California at Irvine, 2010); Walter Johnson, *River of Dark Dreams: Slavery and Empire in the Cotton Kingdom* (Cambridge, Mass.: Belknap Press of Harvard University Press, 2013); James Oakes, *Freedom National: The Destruction of Slavery in the United States, 1861–1865* (New York: Norton, 2013); and Steven Deyle, *Carry Me Back: The Domestic Slave Trade in American Life* (Oxford: Oxford University Press, 2005), chap. 4.

21. Ralph Waldo Emerson, "'Address to the Citizens of Concord' on the Fugitive Slave Law," May 3, 1851, *Emerson's Antislavery Writings*, ed. Len Gougeon and Joel Myerson (New Haven, Conn.: Yale University Press, 1995), 69.

22. Daniel Walker Howe, *What Hath God Wrought: The Transformation of America, 1815–1848* (New York: Oxford University Press, 2009), 342.

23. Laird W. Bergad, *Comparative Histories of Slavery in Brazil, Cuba, and the United States* (New York: Cambridge University Press, 2007), 116–30.

24. Albert Gallatin Brown, "Remarks, in the House of Representatives, January 3, 1853, on the Cuba Question," *Speeches, Messages, and Other Writings of The Hon. Albert G. Brown* (Philadelphia: Jas. B. Smith, 1859), 324.

25. John Craig Hammond, "'Uncontrollable Necessity': The Local Politics, Geopolitics, and Sectional Politics of Slavery Expansion," in *Contesting Slavery: The Politics of Bondage and Freedom in the New American Republic*, ed. John Craig Hammond and Matthew Mason (Charlottesville: University of Virginia Press, 2011), 138–60; Amy S. Greenberg, *A Wicked War: Polk, Clay, Lincoln, and the 1846 U.S. Invasion of Mexico* (New York: Knopf, 2012), 196. Even foreign visitors understood: "It is especially in the interests of slavery and slave-extension that Cuba and Central America are coveted," wrote James Stirling, *Letters from the Slave States* (London: John W. Parker and Son, 1857), 128.

26. Thomas Hietala sees the white preoccupation with "racial homogeneity" as the rationale for much early national expansionism. Thomas Hietala, *Manifest Design: Anxious Aggrandizement in Late Jacksonian America* (Ithaca, N.Y.: Cornell University Press, 1985).

27. "American Antiquities," *The Knickerbocker; or New York Monthly Magazine* 10, 1 (July 1837): 5.

28. "Letter of Mr. Walker, of Mississippi, Relative to the Reannexation of Texas" (Philadelphia: Mifflin and Parry, 1844), 9.

29. "The President's Message: Splendid Government!" *Richmond Enquirer*, December 8, 1825, 3.

30. Howe, *What Hath God Wrought*, 544–45; James Brewer Stewart, "The Emergence of Racial Modernity and the Rise of the White North, 1790–1840," *Journal of the Early Republic* 18, 2 (Summer 1998): 181–217.

31. Stewart.

32. That the expanded democracy is essentially a cover for white supremacy is one of the themes of Howe's *What Hath God Wrought*; see, for example, 357, 440–43, 497, 852. See also Leonard L. Richards, *The Slave Power: The Free North and Southern Domination* (Baton Rouge: Louisiana State University Press, 2000), 116–17. William Stanton's *The Leopard's Spots: Scientific Attitudes Toward Race in America, 1815–1859* (Chicago: University of Chicago Press, 1960) remains a compelling analysis of scientific racism. The construction of Anglo-Saxonism as a justification for the policies of Manifest Destiny is considered in Reginald Horsman's *Race and Manifest Destiny: Origins of American Racial Anglo-Saxonism* (Cambridge, Mass.: Harvard University Press, 1981). For the emergence of the "positive good" proslavery argument, see Elizabeth Fox-Genovese and Eugene D. Genovese, *The Mind of the Master Class: History and Faith in the Southern Slaveholders' Worldview* (Cambridge: Cambridge University Press, 2005), 110; also Howe, 478–80.

33. William E. Lenz, *Ruins, Revolution, and Manifest Destiny: John Lloyd Stephens Creates the Maya* (New York: Peter Lang, 2013), 56.

34. Anthony F. C. Wallace describes the politics of Indian Removal in *The Long, Bitter Trail: Andrew Jackson and the Indians* (New York: Hill and Wang, 1993). See also Robert Remini, *The Legacy of Andrew Jackson: Essays on Democracy, Indian Removal, and Slavery* (Baton Rouge: Louisiana State University Press, 1988) and *Andrew Jackson and his Indian Wars* (Harmondsworth: Penguin, 2002).

35. See "Speeches on the Indian Bill," *North American Review* 31, 69 (October 1830): 396ff.

36. Andrew Jackson, Message of the President of the United States to Both Houses of Congress. *Register of Debates in Congress* (Appendix), 21st Cong., 2nd Sess., December 6, 1830, x.

37. Ibid.

38. My thanks to David Spanagel of the Worcester Polytechnic Institute who pointed this out to me at the Annual Meeting of the Society for Historians of the Early American Republic in Rochester, New York, July 25, 2010.

39. Caleb Atwater to Andrew Jackson, June 24, 1824, *The Papers of Andrew Jackson*, vol. 5, *1821–1824*, ed. Harold D. Moser, David R. Hoth, and George H. Hoemann (Knoxville: University of Tennessee Press, 1996), 421.

40. In fact, in *Views of the Cordilleras* Alexander von Humbolt was cautious about drawing conclusions that suggested the direct influence of one Old World race upon the New World, predicting that the ultimate history of humanity pointed to one common origin. However widely scattered and differentiated by circumstance, all the world's people expressed themselves with a similar vocabulary of symbols, told similar stories, and sought to preserve their own histories. Alexander von Humboldt, *Views of the Cordilleras and Monuments of the Indigenous Peoples of the Americas: A Critical Edition* (Chicago: University of Chicago Press, 2012), 6, 83, 341.

41. Caleb Atwater, *Writings of Caleb Atwater* (Columbus: Published by Caleb Atwater; Printed by Scott and Wright. 1833), 150.

42. Jackson, Message, December 6, 1830, x.

43. Robert E. May, *Slavery, Race, and Conquest in the Tropics: Lincoln, Douglas, and the Future of Latin America* (New York: Cambridge University Press, 2013), 13.

44. William Henry Harrison, *A Discourse on the Aborigines of the Valley of the Ohio: To Which Are Prefixed Some Remarks on the Study of History* (Cincinnati; printed at the Cincinnati Express), 1838; *Transactions of the Historical and Philosophical Society of Ohio* 2, vol. 1 (Cincinnati: Geo. W. Bradbury, 1939), 217–67; William Henry Harrison, *A Discourse on the Aborigines of the Valley of the Ohio* (Boston: William D. Ticknor, 1840); William Henry Harrison, *A Discourse on the Aborigines of the Ohio Valley* (Chicago: Fergus, 1883); William Henry Harrison, *The Mound Builders of the Ohio Valley: An Extract from a Discourse on the Aborigines of the Valley of Ohio, Before the Historical and Philosophical Society of Ohio, Published in the Transactions of the Society, 1839* (Boston: Old South Meeting House, 1890).

45. Robert M. Owens's *Mr. Jefferson's Hammer: William Henry Harrison and the Origins of American Indian Policy* (Norman: University of Oklahoma Press, 2007) argues that an examination of Harrison's policies as governor of Indiana prefigure the perspectives that would shape the policy of Indian removal later in the nineteenth century.

46. Gail Collins, *William Henry Harrison* (New York: Times Books/Henry Holt, 2012), 66–69.

47. *Transactions*, 222.

48. Ibid., 223–24.

49. Ibid., 225.

50. Ibid., 226–27, 226.

51. Ibid., 230; italics mine.

52. Another politician who speculated about Indian origins and made connections between North and South America was Thomas Loraine McKenney, appointed superintendent of Indian trade by James Madison in 1816 and serving as superintendent for Indian Affairs from 1824 to 1830, when he was fired by Andrew Jackson. McKenney believed the Indians of America were descended from the Tartars of Asia, having traveled across "Behring's Straits." But when these migrants advanced into North America, they found a people already living there. "I believe them to have been MEXICANS, or Peruvians, or both" (vol. 2, 43). Thomas L. McKenney, *Memoirs Official and Personal; With Sketches of Travels Among the Northern and Southern Indians* (New York: Paine & Burgess, 1846).

53. Funding for research was notoriously limited and unpredictable. Brian Dippie, *Catlin and His Contemporaries: The Politics of Patronage* (Lincoln: University of Nebraska Press, 1990), 161.

54. Horsman, 115, passim; Stanton, passim.

55. *Testimonial of Respect of the Bar of New York to the Memory of Alexander W. Bradford, Esq.* (New York: Baker & Godwin, 1868), 5–6, 12, 18; *The Writings of Herman Melville: Correspondence*, ed. Lynn Horth (Evanston, Ill.: Northwestern University Press, 1993), 37.

56. Alexander W. Bradford, *American Antiquities and Researches into the Origin and History of the Red Race* (New York: Wiley & Putnam, 1843 [1841]).

57. Josiah Priest, *American Antiquities and Discoveries in the West* (Albany, N.Y.: Hoffman and White, 1837), 44.

58. Priest, 47–48.

59. Priest, title page.

60. Brian Fagan, *Elusive Treasure: The Story of Early Archaeologists in the Americas* (New York: Charles Scribner's Sons, 1977), 115.

61. Josiah Priest, *Bible Defence of Slavery; or, The Origins, History and Fortunes of the Negro Race* (Glasgow, Ky.: Rev. W.S. Brown, 1853 [sixth stereotype edition]), x.

62. In *Mapping the Nation: History and Cartography in Nineteenth-Century America* (Chicago: University of Chicago Press, 2012), Susan Schulten considers how new kinds of maps that presented information in graphic form helped form Americans' understanding of their nation.

63. As Stephanie M. H. Camp notes, what Edward Said refers to as "rival geography" describes the way two groups of people understand and use space. In her work with the way slaves imaginatively mapped their plantation worlds, rival geography could serve as a form of resistance. See Stephanie M. H. Camp, *Closer to Freedom: Enslaved Women and Everyday Resistance in the Plantation South* (Chapel Hill: University of North Carolina Press, 2004). Interestingly, in the case of the Manifest Destiny-era United States, it was the more powerful white Americans who found utility in borrowing the spatial conceptions of their Indian predecessors.

64. Benjamin Smith Barton, born in Philadelphia in 1766 and educated in Scotland, was one of the first to speculate that the builders of the Ohio Valley mounds (who he suspected

had come from Denmark) had later migrated to Mexico (Silverberg, 30–32). See also Benjamin Smith Barton, "Some Observations and Conjectures concerning Certain Articles which were Taken out of an Ancient Tumulus, or Grave, at Cincinnati," *Transactions of the American Philosophical Society* 4 (1799): 181–215.

65. Fagan, 119–28.

66. A very cursory catalogue of articles about ancient Americans might include the two-part series "Aborigines in America," *American Monthly Magazine* 1, 1 and 2 (April and May 1829); the five-part series "American Antiquities," *Knickerbocker* 10, nos. 1, 2, 4, 6, and 11, no. 2 (July August, October, December 1837, February 1838); Francisco Corroy, "American Antiquities" *Knickerbocker* 2, 5 (November 1833); "Mexican Antiquities," *United States Democratic Review* (October 1837) and countless feature-length articles based on the works of Josiah Priest, John Delafield, Samuel Morton, John Lloyd Stephens, and Ephraim Squier.

67. Stephen Jay Gould, "Fall in the House of Ussher," *Natural History* 100 (November 1991): 12–21.

68. Ham is popularly supposed to be the father of African people, Shem the father of Asian people, and Japeth the father of European people.

69. See Stanton.

70. Quoted in Haven, 76.

71. Dr. Wyman, "Memoir of Dr. Warren, read to the Society of Natural History in December, 1856," in Edward Warren, M.D., *The Life of John Collins Warren, M.D.* (Boston: Ticknor and Fields, 1860), 329.

72. Samuel George Morton, *Crania Americana; or, A Comparative View of the Skulls of Various Aboriginal Nations of North and South America* (Philadelphia: J. Dobson, 1839), 244.

73. Charles D. Meigs, M.D., *A Memoir of Samuel George Morton, M.D.* (Philadelphia: T.K. & P.G. Collins, 1851); Stanton, *The Leopard's Spots*, 24–44.

74. Morton, 1, 3.

75. As Ann Fabian points out, Morton did not support slavery, but neither did he support racial equality. As a U.S. native, he seems to have had certain unexamined racial prejudices that surprised his European colleague George Combe. Fabian, *Skull Collectors: Race, Science, and America's Unburied Dead* (Chicago: University of Chicago Press, 2010), 113, 97.

76. Morton, 230.

77. Ibid., 5.

78. Ibid., 84.

79. See, for example, Samuel Forry, "The Mosaic Account of the Unity of the Human Race, Confirmed by the Natural History of the American Aborigines," *American Biblical Repository* 10, 1 (July 1843): 29ff.

80. In the late twentieth century Stephen Jay Gould attempted to duplicate some of Morton's studies and found his methods sloppy and irregular even on their own terms. Stephen Jay Gould, *The Mismeasure of Man* (New York: Norton, 1981). Morton himself acknowledged that the size of his sample was not always ideal: whereas he had a hundred Peruvian crania to measure, he based his study of the Mound Builders on the examination of only eight skulls (Morton, 97, 228). The Mexican skulls in his collection were hardly ancient, dating only from the time of the Conquest (144).

81. Fabian, 93; Stanton, 52.

82. Mrs. [Lydia Maria] Child, *Anti-Slavery Catechism* (Newburyport, Mass.: Charles Whipple, 1839), 35.

83. Eran Shalev, *American Zion: The Old Testament as a Political Text from the Revolution to the Civil War* (New Haven, Conn.: Yale University Press, 2013), 100, 154.

84. Shalev, 8.

85. Quoted in Terence Whalen, *Edgar Allan Poe and the Masses: The Political Economy of Literature in Antebellum America* (Princeton: Princeton University Press, 1999), 136.

86. William Gilmore Simms, "The White Man,—Northman or Irish,—in America," *Views and Reviews in American Literature, History and Fiction* (New York: Wiley and Putnam, 1845), 77.

87. Fanny Bristol Murdock to her sister, December 10, 1847, Fanny Bristol Murdock and Sarah Bristol Family Papers 1836–1866, Series I, Box 1, Folder 9, University of Chicago Library; Harvey Lindsly, M.D., "Differences in the Intellectual Character of the Several Varieties of the Human Race," *Southern Literary Messenger* 5, 9 (September 1839): 617. Lindsly concludes, surprisingly, that the inferiority of the dark races does not automatically justify their involuntary slavery.

88. Dana Elizabeth Weiner, *Race and Rights: Fighting Slavery and Prejudice in the Old Northwest, 1830–1870* (DeKalb: Northern Illinois Press, 2013), 34–75.

89. "Put simply, scientific anthropology bestialized slavery; adamic theology sanctified it." David N. Livingstone, *Adam's Ancestors: Race, Religion, and the Politics of Human Origins* (Baltimore: Johns Hopkins University Press, 2008), 182.

90. On the other hand, Robert Taylor Conrad in a poem called "The Sons of the Wilderness: Reflections Beside an Indian Mound," *Graham's Magazine* 23, 1 (July 1843): 39–47 inquired who had extinguished the race that built a "death-fill'd mound" beside a "cotter's window" and predicted that "history will say / That we . . . Robb'd them of home, and drove them to the wild . . ." Conrad went on to annotate his 37-verse poem with six pages of footnotes cataloguing white betrayals of the Indians.

91. A similar effort is Henry Wadsworth Longfellow's "The Skeleton in Armor," which appeared in *Knickerbocker* 17, 1 (January 1841): 52–54. It describes the imagined career of a soldier whose armed skeleton was disinterred in Fall River, Massachusetts, in 1832. "I was a Viking old!" declares the spirit of the remains.

92. Edward L. Widmer, *Young America: The Flowering of Democracy in New York City* (New York: Oxford University Press, 1999), 57; "M" [Cornelius Mathews], "Our Illustrious Predecessors," *Arcturus, A Journal of Books and Opinions* 1, 3 (February 1841). Mathews's authorship is confirmed by the appearance of this article in a collection of his work, *The Various Writings of Cornelius Mathews* (New York: Harper & Brothers, 1863), 346.

93. *Various Writings of Cornelius Mathews,* 348.

94. Mathews also attempted a short novel imagining the life of the ancient American people in *Behemoth: A Legend of the Mound-Builders* (1839). The incidence of sixteen occurrences of the words "nation" or "national" when describing this "great race that preceded the red men as the possessors of our continent" in a work of only twenty-five dense (and, unfortunately, tiresome) pages suggest that, if Mathews was not constructing an allegory of the future American republic, he was at least presenting a case for his characters as forerunners of U.S. citizens. Cornelius Mathews, *Behemoth: A Legend of the Mound-Builders* (1839) in *The Various Writings of Cornelius Mathews* (New York: Harper & Brothers, 1863).

95. "Lisette" [Louisa Currier], "The Western Antiquities," *Lowell Offering* 2, 1 (May 1841): 46.

96. "Lisette," 45–46.

97. Fawn M. Brodie, *No Man Knows My History: The Life of Joseph Smith, the Mormon Prophet* (New York: Knopf, 1957), 34.

98. Randall H. McGuire, "Archeology and the First Americans," *American Anthropologist* 94, no. 4 (December 1992): 816–36. In *History's Shadow: Native Americans and Historical Consciousness in the Nineteenth Century* (Chicago: University of Chicago, 2004), Steven Conn argues that consigning the study of Native American history to the discipline of archaeology further distances and estranges it from the narrative of the United States nation (146–51).

99. The story of the Israelite emigrants is recounted in Joseph Smith, Jr., translator, *The Book of Mormon: An Account Written by the Hand of Mormon, Upon Plates Taken from the Plates of Nephi* (Palmyra, N.Y.: E.B. Grandin, 1830), 1 Nephi.

100. Book of Mormon, 1 Nephi 19: 23; 2 Nephi 5: 21.

101. Shalev, 137.

102. Richard Lyman Bushman with the assistance of Jed Woodworth, *Joseph Smith: Rough Stone Rolling* (New York: Knopf, 2006), 94.

103. Brodie, 35.

104. Book of Mormon, 2 Nephi 5: 21; 3 Nephi 3: 15.

105. Brodie, 149; Bushman, 240–41.

106. Fagan, 138–49.

107. R. Tripp Evans, *Romancing the Maya: Mexican Antiquity in the American Imagination, 1520–1915* (Austin: University of Texas Press, 2004), 49–60.

108. Stephens claims to have explored forty-four ancient cities. John Lloyd Stephens, *Incidents of Travel in Yucatan* (New York: Harper & Brothers, 1843), 2: 444.

109. Fagan, 186.

110. "Literary Notices: *Incidents of Travel in Central America, Chiapas, and Yucatan*," *Knickerbocker* 18, no. 1 (July 1841): 71.

111. John Lloyd Stephens, *Incidents of Travel in Central America, Chiapas, and Yucatan* (New York: Harper & Brothers, 1841), 1: 102.

112. Stephens, *Central America*, 1: 115.

113. Stephens, *Yucatan*, 1: 43.

114. "The Rotunda in Prince street, N.Y., erected for the exhibition of Catherwood's admirable Panoramas, was consumed by fire on Friday night, 29th ult. The manner in which it took fire is yet a mystery," "General Intelligence: A Great Loss," *New York Evangelist*, August 4, 1842, 123.

115. As Robert D. Aguirre writes in *Informal Empire: Mexico and Central America in Victorian Culture* (Minneapolis: University of Minnesota Press, 2005), 101: "writing and looking are frequently inseparable from desire, despoliation, and appropriation."

116. In a study of amateur anthropologist John Perkins Barratt, an English transplant to South Carolina, Lester D. Stephens writes, "Barratt had formed an opinion of black people long before he became interested in natural history, and science became for him a way of confirming his stereotype of the human races." Lester D. Stephens, "Centers of Creation: John Perkins Barratt, "Biogeographical Theory of Racial Origins," *Journal of Southern History* 80, 2 (May 2014): 270.) See also Horsman, *Race and Manifest Destiny*, 114–15.

117. David Hurst Thomas, *Skull Wars: Kennewick Man, Archaeology, and the Battle for Native American Identity* (New York: Basic, 2000), 42–43.

118. Julia King suggests that modern historical archaeology, while more scrupulously drawing on factual evidence, similarly reflects the desires and anxieties of our own time. Julia A. King, *Archaeology, Narrative, and the Politics of the Past: The View from Southern Maryland* (Knoxville: University of Tennessee Press, 2012), 91, 177.

119. U.S. ministers also strove to prevent fugitive slaves and even free blacks from achieving legal status in Mexico itself. Sarah E. Cornell, "Citizens of Nowhere: Fugitive Slaves and Free African Americans in Mexico, 1833–1857," *Journal of American History* 100, 2 (September 2013): 351–74.

120. "Summary: Slavery in Mexico . . . Slavery at Home," *Freedom's Journal*, September 25, 1828, 3.

121. Timothy J. Henderson, *A Glorious Defeat: Mexico and Its War with the United States* (New York: Hill and Wang, 2007), 60.

122. Quoted in Andres Resendez, "National Identity on a Shifting Border: Texas and New Mexico in the Age of Transition, 1821–1848," *Journal of American History* 86, 2 (September 1999): 681.

123. Horsman, 213.

124. David S. Reynolds, *Waking Giant: America in the Age of Jackson* (New York: Harper-Collins, 2008), 117–18; Anders Stephanson, *Manifest Destiny: American Expansionism and the Empire of Right* (New York: Hill and Wang, 1995), 33.

125. Henderson, 123–27.

126. Charles Blancher Thompson, *Evidence in Proof of the Book of Mormon* (Batavia, N.Y.: C. B. Thompson, 1841), 101, cited in Evans, 99.

127. *Times and Seasons*, October 1, 1842, 927, cited in Evans, 99.

128. Leonard J. Arrington, *Brigham Young: American Moses* (Urbana: University of Illinois Press, 1986).

129. Joseph F. O'Callaghan, *Reconquest and Crusade in Medieval Spain* (Philadelphia: University of Pennsylvania Press, 2003), 3–5.

130. William Montgomery Meigs, *The Life of Thomas Hart Benton* (Philadelphia: Lippincott, 1904), 340–41.

131. "Letter of Mr. Walker, of Mississippi, Relative to the Reannexation of Texas" (Philadelphia: Mifflin and Parry, 1844).

132. Asked to explain to a Cincinnati group his views on Texas early in his campaign, Polk replied that he favored "immediate re-annexation" of Texas on April 23, 1844. Charles Sellers, *James K. Polk: Continentalist, 1843–1846* (Princeton, N.J.: Princeton University Press, 1966), 67.

133. Stephanson, 44.

134. Greenberg, 95–96, 196.

135. Brian DeLay, *War of a Thousand Deserts: Indian Raids and the U.S.-Mexican War* (New Haven, Conn.: Yale University Press, 2008), 229–35.

136. Paul Foos, *A Short, Offhand, Killing Affair: Soldiers and Social Conflict during the Mexican-American War* (Chapel Hill: University of North Carolina Press, 2002), 113–37.

137. "One of the People," "The Past and Future—No. 1," *Brooklyn Eagle*, July 13, 1848, 2.

138. Stephens, *Central America*, 2, 442–43.

139. Stephens, *Yucatan*, 2: 244–55.

140. Jennifer L. Roberts, "Landscapes of Indifference: Robert Smithson and John Lloyd Stephens in Yucatan," *Art Bulletin* 82, 3 (September, 2000): 550.

141. "Stephens' Central America," *Arcturus* 2, 9 (August 1841): 152ff.

142. See, for example, Haven, *Archaeology*, and Henry R. Schoolcraft, *Information Respecting the History, Condition, and Prospects of the Indian Tribes of the United States* (Philadelphia: Lippincott, 1857).

143. Wisconsin Indian trader William Pidgeon's *Traditions of De-Coo-Dah* (1852), which purported to be an account of the "Tortoise Mounds" provided by a ninety-year-old descendant of the tribe that had built them, belongs in the category of Josiah Priest's *American Antiquities*. Although Pidgeon's work was unquestionably popular—it went through three printings—Henry Rowe Schoolcraft, in the sixth annual report of the Smithsonian Institution, declared it dubious (Dippie, 252).

144. Barbara Alice Mann, *Native Americans, Archaeologists, and the Mounds* (New York: Peter Lang, 2003); Silverberg, 173.

145. Silverberg, 97.

146. Dippie, 237–63.

147. Angela Miller, "'The Soil of an Unknown America;' New World Lost Empires and the Debate over Cultural Origins," *American Art* (Summer/Fall 1994): 10.

148. Joshua Brown's *Beyond the Lines: Pictorial Reporting, Everyday Life, and the Crisis of Gilded Age America* (Berkeley: University of California Press, 2006) provides a good overview of the transformation effected by the spread of graphic images through nineteenth-century magazines.

149. Dippie, 219, 253.

150. John Russell Bartlett, *Personal Narrative of Explorations and Incidents in Texas, New Mexico, California, Sonora, and Chihuahua*, vol. 2 (New York: D. Appleton, 1854), 283.

151. According to Robert Silverberg, "the legend of the Mound Builders achieved its apotheosis when a major religious creed was founded upon it by Joseph Smith and made lasting by his successor, Brigham Young" (Silverberg, 96).

152. For resistance to U.S. participation in the Mexican War, see Robert Johannsen, *To the Halls of the Montezumas: The Mexican War in the American Imagination* (New York: Oxford University Press, 1985), 270–300.

153. William King to his mother, quoted in John C. Pinheiro, *Missionaries of Republicanism: A Religious History of the Mexican-American War* (Oxford: Oxford University Press, 2014), 112.

154. *Congressional Globe* (Appendix), 28th Cong., 1st. Sess., 557.

155. Pinheiro, 43.

156. Milton P. Braman, The Mexican War: A Discourse Delivered on the Annual Fast, 1847 (Danvers, Mass.: Printed at the Courier Office, 1847), 18.

157. Braman, 19–20.

158. Christopher Childers, *The Failure of Popular Sovereignty: Slavery, Manifest Destiny, and the Radicalization of Southern Politics* (Lawrence: University Press of Kansas, 2012), 109. See also Eldon Kenworthy, *America/Américas: Myth in the Making of U.S. Policy Toward Latin America* (University Park: Pennsylvania State University Press, 1995), 27.

159. John C. Calhoun, "Speech of Mr. Calhoun, of South Carolina, on His Resolutions in Reference to the War with Mexico, Delivered in the Senate of the United States, January 4, 1848" (Washington, D.C.: John T. Towers, 1848), 9–10. Calhoun says Brazil has, like the United States, so far escaped the error of "placing the colored race on an equality with the white."

160. Thomas Hietala (134) argues that because expansionism was so implicated in the project of purging the United States of nonwhite people, it waned in Mexico and Cuba where amalgamation and racial conflict appeared inevitable.

161. Greenberg, *Wicked War*, 260–63.

162. Henry Highland Garnet, *The Past and the Present Condition, and the Destiny, of the Colored Race: A Discourse Delivered at the Fifteenth Anniversary of the Female Benevolent Society of Troy, NY, February 14, 1848* (Troy, N.Y.: Steam Press of J. C. Kneeland and Co., 1848), 21.

163. Charles Sealsfield, *Tokeah, or, the White Rose* (Philadelphia: Carey, Lea & Carey, 1829).

164. Glen E. Lich, "Postl, Carl Anton," The Handbook of Texas Online, http://www.tshaonline.org/handbook/online/articles/PP/fonds_print.html; accessed April 18, 2009; John T. Krumpelmann, "Tokeah, The First English-Language Novel in Our Southwest," *South Central Bulletin* 28, 4 (Winter 1968): 142–43; Wulf Koepke, "Charles Sealsfield's Place in Literary History," *South Central Review* 1, 1/2 (Spring/Summer 1984): 52–66.

165. Bernhard Alexander Uhlendorf, "Charles Sealsfield: Ethnic Elements and National Problems in his Works" (Ph.D. Thesis, University of Illinois, 1920), 26; Albert B. Faust, *Charles Sealsfield: Materials for a Biography* (Baltimore: Press of Friedenwald, 1892).

166. Sealsfield, *Tokeah* 1: 23.

167. Ibid., 106.

168. Ibid., 178.

169. "*Tokeah; or the White Rose*" (review), *The Critic: A Weekly Review of Literature, Fine Arts, and the Drama* 7 (March 1829): 285.

170. Sherry Sullivan, "A Redder Shade of Pale: The Indianization of Heroes and Heroines in Nineteenth-Century American Fiction," *Journal of the Midwest Modern Language Association* 20, 1 (Spring 1987): 57.

171. Sealsfield, *Tokeah* 1, 115–16.

172. Sealsfield, *Tokeah* 2, 165–66.

173. Ibid., 163–64.

174. Ibid., 188.

175. Ibid., 189.

176. "Original Notices: *Tokeah, or the White Rose*," *Ariel: A Semimonthly Literary and Miscellaneous Gazette* 3, 1 (2 May 1829): 4.

177. Lich, "Postl, Carl Anton."

Chapter 3. The Problem of Slavery

1. Sarah Josepha Hale, *Northwood; A Tale of New England* (Boston: Bowles and Dearborn, 1827), 25–26.

2. "I do not think it is quite right to say that antebellum writers stayed silent about slavery, but when they did approach the subject, they—even Melville—did so obliquely," writes Andrew Delbanco in *The Abolitionist Imagination* (Cambridge, Mass.: Harvard University Press, 2012), 24–35. Jean Fagan Yellin notes that despite the "lively" antislavery literature written for the abolitionist marketplace in the 1830s and 1840s, it took the "unheard-of popularity" of *Uncle Tom's Cabin* to spur "publishers who had shunned the slavery issue for fear of losing 'the southern market'" to unleash a torrent of fictional responses. Jean Fagan Yellin, "*The Bondwoman's Narrative* and *Uncle Tom's Cabin*," in *In Search of Hannah Crafts*, ed. Henry Louis Gates, Jr., and Hollis Robbins (New York: Basic, 2004), 106. Michael T.

Gilmore explores the way both "external force" and "self-regulating apprehension" (1) restrained and shaped nineteenth-century American literature in *The War on Words: Slavery, Race, and Free Speech in American Literature* (Chicago: University of Chicago Press, 2010).

3. Jane Tompkins, *Sensational Designs: The Cultural Work of American Fiction, 1790–1860* (New York: Oxford University Press, 1985), 200.

4. George Eliot said Stowe "*invented* the Negro novel," quoted in Sarah Meer, *Uncle Tom Mania: Slavery, Minstrelsy, and Transatlantic Culture in the 1850s* (Athens: University of Georgia Press, 2005), 48. Meer suggests that *Uncle Tom's Cabin* reconfigured the plantation novel to make slave characters central (83). David S. Reynolds's *Mightier than the Sword: Uncle Tom's Cabin and the Battle for America* (New York: Norton, 2011) shows how Stowe drew from many traditions in composing her bestseller. Lucinda H. MacKethan's essay "Domesticity in Dixie: The Plantation Novel and *Uncle Tom's Cabin*" concisely explains some of the reasons *Uncle Tom's Cabin* was so revolutionary, in *Haunted Bodies: Gender and Southern Texts*, ed. Anne Goodwyn Jones and Susan Van D'Elden Donaldson (Charlottesville: University Press of Virginia, 1997), 223–42.

5. John Pendleton Kennedy, *Swallow Barn; or, A Sojourn in the Old Dominion* (Philadelphia: Carey & Lea, 1832). William Taylor explains that after the first blush of plantation fiction in the 1830s "there was a lull in literary planting and there was nothing quite like this first intense interest in Southern life until the eighteen fifties when *Uncle Tom's Cabin* was followed not only by a rash of 'answers' but also by a great mass of nostalgic writing about the South which was seemingly unrelated to the slavery issue." William R. Taylor, *Cavalier and Yankee: The Old South and the American National Character* (Garden City, N.Y.: Anchor, 1963 (1957)), 127–28; Karen Sánchez-Eppler, *Touching Liberty: Abolition, Feminism, and the Politics of the Body from the Sentimental to the Lyric* (Berkeley: University of California Press, 1993), 24–25. According to Jennifer Rae Greeson, abolitionist literature became more outspoken about the depravity and brutality of slavery during this period. Jennifer Rae Greeson, *Our South: Geographic Fantasy and the Rise of National Literature* (Cambridge, Mass.: Harvard University Press, 2010), 118.

6. Sydney Smith, *Edinburgh Review* 65 (January 1820): 79–80.

7. Similarly, Andrew Cayton pondered the way American readers made sense of their Revolution through their reading of fiction. Andrew R. L. Cayton, "The Authority of the Imagination in an Age of Wonder," Presidential Address, Conference of the Society of Historians of the Early American Republic, Baltimore, July 21, 2012.

8. Stephen Douglas complained that English literature polluted its American readership with "lurking and insidious slanders and libels upon the character of our people and the institutions and policy of our Government." Britain did not even have need of composing this material: "millions are being expended to distribute 'Uncle Tom's Cabin' throughout the world, with the view of combining the fanaticism, ignorance, and hatred of all the nations of the earth in a common crusade against the peculiar institutions of the States." *Appendix to the Congressional Globe*, 32nd Cong., 2nd Sess., March 16, 1853, 275–76.

9. "Blackwood's Magazine," *The United States Review* 32, 4 (April 1853): 299.

10. In the United States, Stowe's *Uncle Tom's Cabin* is perhaps the ultimate type of the social problem novel, of which the works of Charles Dickens, Charlotte Brontë, and Elizabeth Gaskell provide just a few British examples. U.S. theater also provided a venue for the exploration of the targets of antebellum social reform: consider, for example, the melodramas *Ten*

Nights in a Bar Room (Timothy Shay Arthur, 1854) and *The Poor of New York* (Dion Bouci-cault, 1857).

11. Edwin Hubbell Chapin, "Anti Slavery Society," n.d., John Hay Library, Brown University Library. References to the "tragedies of Southampton and St. Domingo" and the attempt to prevent "the scholars of Miss Crandall from attending divine worship" suggest composition during the early 1830s.

12. Daniel R. Vollaro, "Lincoln, Stowe, and the 'Little Woman/Great War' Story: The Making, and Breaking, of a Great American Anecdote," *Journal of the Abraham Lincoln Association* 30, 1 (Winter 2009): 18.

13. Thomas Jefferson, *Notes on the State of Virginia* (Richmond, Va.: J.W. Randolph, 1853 [1787]), 70. This quote of Abbé Raynal is known almost exclusively from Jefferson's citation to a particular edition of *L'Histoire philosophique et politique*. As a matter of fact, Jefferson acknowledges in a footnote that in later editions Raynal "removed his censure from that part of the new world inhabited by the Federo-Americans" (72). But apparently Jefferson's indignation outlived Raynal's repudiation of the slur.

14. William Gilmore Simms, "Americanism in Literature," in *Views and Reviews in American Literature: History and Fiction* (New York: Wiley and Putnam, 1845), 6.

15. Daniel Walker Howe's *What Hath God Wrought: The Transformation of America, 1815–1848* (Oxford: Oxford University Press, 2007), 635; Edward L. Widmer, *Young America: The Flowering of Democracy in New York City* (New York: Oxford University Press, 1999), 99. See also William St. Clair, *The Reading Nation in the Romantic Period* (Cambridge: Cambridge University Press, 2004), 382–93.

16. Pirated American literature was also abridged without the authors' consent and presented in low-cost paperback editions in England. *The Novel Newspaper*, Vol. 5 was "exclusively composed of the works of transatlantic authors, and those of no mean reputation" (n.p.) and included works by Charles Brockden Brown, James Kirke Paulding, and Robert Montgomery Bird, *Novel Newspaper*, vol. 5 (London: J. Cunningham, 1840).

17. As it happens, many moved into politics. Robert Montgomery Bird, who had outlined a series of eight novels on Latin American themes, abandoned writing, first seeking the Whig nomination to Congress as a representative of Delaware in 1842 and then angling for a post with the Smithsonian Institution. Other literary figures like Washington Irving, Herman Melville, Nathaniel Hawthorne, and James Russell Lowell turned up in government positions that ranged from ambassadorships to humble office jobs. Meanwhile, a partisan press flourished, rewarding loyal editors and writers. Curtis Dahl, *Robert Montgomery Bird* (New York: Twayne, 1963), 29–31; Howe, 635; Widmer, *Young America*, 72, 76.

18. Among many other examples that could be cited of the influence of Scott in American culture of this period, Frederick Douglass notes that after his escape from slavery he called himself Frederick Johnson. "But when I got to New Bedford, I found it was necessary again to change my name. . . . Mr. Johnson had just been reading the 'Lady of the Lake,' and at once suggested that my name be 'Douglass'." Frederick Douglass, *Narrative of the Life of Frederick Douglass* (New York: Dover, 1995 (1845)), 66. "The Lady of the Lake" also has the dubious distinction of introducing some Americans to the practice of cross-burning.

19. Robert Montgomery Bird to James Lawson, June 4, 1835, James Lawson Papers, 1826–1890, South Caroliniana Library, University of South Carolina.

20. George Dekker, *The American Historical Romance* (Cambridge: Cambridge University Press, 1987), 8; 35.

21. For an analysis of this period as one of wrenching disruption and anxiety, see John Lauritz Larson, *The Market Revolution in America: Liberty, Ambition, and the Eclipse of the Common Good* (Cambridge: Cambridge University Press, 2010).

22. Dekker, 34.

23. W. H. Gardiner, "*The Spy, a Tale of the Neutral Ground*" (review), *The North American Review* 15, no. 36 (July 1822): 252–23.

24. "*Calavar: or the Knight of the Conquest*," *North American Review* 40, 86 (January 1835): 233.

25. "*Calavar; or, the Knight of the Conquest*," *American Quarterly Review* 32 (December, 1834): 380. Actually, Robert Charles Sands (1799–1832), an early associate of William Cullen Bryant, had chosen a Latin American setting for a masterful short story called "Boyuca" six years earlier. Appearing in a collection called *The Talisman* in 1828, "Boyuca" evokes a credible horror-story atmosphere and engages issues of the ethics of human intervention into the mechanics of destiny. In this story Ponce De Leon and a younger conquistador, Perez, arrange with a witch to take them to the fountain of youth. The characters' errancy into the wilderness, through a landscape alive with snares and predators, anticipates the blundering progress of characters from Hawthorne's Young Goodman Brown to Conrad's Marlow into an ethical terrain they cannot possibly understand. Despite its obscurity, Sands's tale is a neglected jewel. Robert C. Sands, *The Writings of Robert C. Sands in Prose and Verse, with a Memoir of the Author* (New York: Harper & Brothers, 1835), 1: 20.

26. *Novel Newspaper*, vol. 5, n.p.

27. Robert Montgomery Bird, *Calavar; or, The Knight of the Conquest: A Romance of Mexico* (Philadelphia: Carey, Lea & Blanchard, 1834), 1: 216; italics original.

28. Ibid. 223.

29. "*Calavar*," *North American Review*, 232. This review cites Scott directly on 255. Among other reviews making explicit comparisons with Scott, see "Literary Notices: *Calavar*," *Knickerbocker* 4, 6 (December 1834): 489, and Poe, "*Calavar*," *Southern Literary Messenger* 1, 6 (February 1835): 315.

30. "All that I have [done] has been poured to waste in Charleston, which has never smiled on any of my labors, which has steadily ignored my claims, which has disparaged me to the last, has been the last place to give me its adhesion, to which I owe no favor, having never received an office, or a compliment, or a dollar at her hands," he confided in a private memorandum; quoted in William P. Trent, *William Gilmore Simms* (Boston: Houghton Mifflin, 1892), 239. John Caldwell Guilds faults Trent's biography of Simms for erroneously portraying Simms as the victim of a "benighted, self-centered society incapable of aesthetic nurturing or appreciation." John Caldwell Guilds, " 'Long Years of Neglect': Atonement at Last?" in *"Long Years of Neglect": The Work and Reputation of William Gilmore Simms* (Fayetteville: University of Arkansas Press, 1988), 3–4. Rather, Guilds argues, Simms was generally lionized (14). The fact remains, however, that Simms evidently did not feel himself appreciated in his native place.

31. Vernon Louis Parrington, *Main Currents in American Thought*, vol. 2: *The Romantic Revolution in America* (New York: Harcourt, Brace & World, Inc., 1927), 119–30.

32. Simms, "Americanism," 2; William Gilmore Simms, "The Epochs and Events of American History, as Suited to the Purposes Art in Fiction," in *Views and Reviews*, 36.

33. Edgar Allan Poe in *Broadway Journal* (October 4, 1845) cited in John Caldwell Guilds, Introduction, William Gilmore Simms, *The Simms Reader* (Charlottesville: University Press of Virginia, 2001), 26.

34. William Gilmore Simms, *The Damsel of Darien* (Philadelphia: Lea and Blanchard, 1839), 1: 61.

35. Simms, *Damsel*, 1: 67.

36. Ibid., 192.

37. Ibid., 184.

38. David Reynolds argues that the scene in which the slaves Sam and Andy thwart the pursuit of Eliza through their supposed incompetence is far more subversive than it appears. "This portrait of a group rebellion, in which two blacks are in partnership with a white woman [their mistress, Mrs. Shelby], ventured toward dangerous territory, but Stowe made it palatable by using the accepted techniques of minstrelsy." Reynolds, *Mightier Than the Sword*, 78.

39. Charles S. Watson, *From Nationalism to Secessionism: The Changing Fiction of William Gilmore Simms* (Westport, Conn.: Greenwood, 1993).

40. Simms, *Damsel* 1: 13–14.

41. Ibid., 16, 61.

42. *Lucas de Ayllon: A Historical Nouvellette* appears in W. Gilmore Simms, *The Wigwam and the Cabin* (New York: Redfield, 1859). John Caldwell Guilds and Charles Hudson date it to 1842 in *An Early and Strong Sympathy: The Indian Writings of William Gilmore Simms* (Columbia: University of South Carolina Press, 2003).

43. Guilds, *The Simms Reader*, 22. For a historical contextualization of *Benito Cereno*, see Greg Grandin, *The Empire of Necessity: Slavery, Freedom, and Deception in the New World* (New York: Metropolitan Books, 2014).

44. Simms, *Lucas de Ayllon*, 453.

45. Ibid., 468.

46. Ibid., 430.

47. Another example occurs in V. V. Vide's "The Aztec Princess." Offered a reward for rescuing Montezuma's daughter from a viper, her enslaved nursemaid pleads, "Give me, O give me freedom" (V. V. Vide, "The Aztec Princess," in *American Tableaux No. 1: Sketches of Aboriginal Life* (New York: Buckland and Sumner, 1846), 22.

48. Robert W. Weathersby, II, "Joseph Holt Ingraham," in *Lives of Mississippi Authors, 1817–1967*, ed. James B. Lloyd (Jackson: University Press of Mississippi, 1981), 249–52.

49. Robert Johannsen, *To the Halls of the Montezumas: The Mexican War in the American Imagination* (New York: Oxford University Press, 1985), 182; [Joseph Holt Ingraham], "A Legend of the Mountain of the Burning Stone: A Story of the First Montezuma," *Southern Literary Messenger* 5, 12 (December 1830): 781–87; [Joseph Holt Ingraham], *Montezuma, the Serf; or, The Revolt of the Mexitili: A Tale of the Last Days of the Aztec Dynasty* (Boston: H.L. Williams, 1845).

50. Ingraham, *Montezuma*, 25.

51. Ibid., 784.

52. [Joseph Holt Ingraham], *The Quadroone; or, St. Michael's Day* (New York: Harper & Brothers, 1841). The quoted material is not Ingraham, but is taken from the epigraph by William Cutter.

53. Ezra Tawil, *The Making of Racial Sentiment: Slavery and the Birth of the Frontier Romance* (Cambridge: Cambridge University Press, 2006), 94.

54. "Varieties," *The Critic: A Weekly Review of Literature, Fine Arts, and the Drama*, November 22, 1828, 4.

55. "Edwin Forrest, the American Tragedian," *New-York Mirror* 4, 31 (February 24, 1827): 245.

56. *The Encyclopedia of New York City*, ed. Kenneth T. Jackson (New Haven, Conn.: Yale University Press; New York: New-York Historical Society, 1995), 1007.

57. Bruce A. McConachie, *Melodramatic Formations: American Theatre & Society, 1820–1870* (Iowa City: University of Iowa Press, 1992), 69–118.

58. Richard Moody, *Edwin Forrest: First Star of the American Stage* (New York: Knopf, 1960), 234.

59. "Literary Notices: Oralloossa," *New-York Mirror* 10, 14 (6 October 1832): 106.

60. The review of Bird's script in "Literary Notices: Oralloossa" in the October 6, 1832 *New-York Mirror* is particularly enthusiastic. The *Mirror* was somewhat more measured in its review of the production two months later ("Park Theatre," *New-York Mirror* 10, no. 24 [December 15, 1832], 190); John Frost, *The American Speaker* (Philadelphia: Thomas, Cowpertwait, & Co., 1845), 426–31. Bird wrote a second play with a Spanish American setting, *The Broker of Bogota* (1834) whose situations seem contrived today. Setting the play in colonial Bogota seems an arbitrary decision made to allow for stilted dialogue in free verse. As tragedy, it is a bore. In comparison, *Oralloossa* has a kind of crazy grandeur.

61. Moody, *Edwin Forrest*, 60, 64.

62. Richard Brinsley Sheridan, *Pizarro; A Tragedy in Five Acts* (London: James Ridgway, 1799), III iii; I i.

63. Julie A. Carlson, "Trying Sheridan's 'Pizarro,'" *Texas Studies in Literature and Language* (Fall-Winter 1996), 359; Michael Caine, "Sheridan's 'Pizarro,'" *Times Literary Supplement* 26 July 2006.

64. Jeremy Ravi Mumford, "The Inca Priest on the Mormon Stage: A Native American Melodrama and a New American Religion," www.common-place.org 5, no. 4 (July 2005). It was also performed in the governor's palace in Santa Fe during the U.S. War with Mexico on November 21, 1846 with $150 worth of tickets sold. Elvira was played by "*Miss* Edward W. Shands, and Cora by *Miss* William Jameison, both of the Rangers." Richard Smith Elliott, *The Mexican War Correspondence of Richard Smith Elliott*, ed. and annotated Mark L. Gardner (Norman: University of Oklahoma Press, 1997), 117; italics original.

65. See Jill Lepore, *In the Name of War: King Philip's War and the Origins of American Identity* (New York: Knopf, 1998). Forrest's other great role was Metamora in the hit play of the same title by John Augustus Stone.

66. Robert Montgomery Bird, *Oralloossa*, IV iii, in *The Life and Dramatic Works of Robert Montgomery Bird*, ed. Clement E. Foust (New York: Knickerbocker Press, 1919).

67. Bird, *Oralloossa*, I i; italics in original.

68. Richard Harris, "A Young Dramatist's Diary: The *Secret Records* of R. M. Bird," *Library Chronicle: University of Pennsylvania* 25 (Winter 1959): 16–17. Quoted in Brent D. Shaw, *Spartacus and the Slave Wars: A Brief History with Documents* (Boston: Bedford/St. Martin's, 2001), 22–23.

69. Bird, *Oralloossa* III iv.

70. Robert Montgomery Bird, Ms. Collection 108, box 6, folders 187 and 189, Robert Montgomery Bird Papers, University of Pennsylvania, Rare Book and Manuscript Library, Philadelphia.

71. Bird, *Oralloossa* II i.

72. The gunpowder, despite its appearance in Act I, does not explode in Act III. It certainly seems possible that Bird had read Thomas Gray's *The Confessions of Nat Turner* (Richmond, Va.: Thomas Gray, 1832), 6.

73. Bird, *Oralloossa* V ii.

74. Ibid., V viii.

75. James Shapiro, *Shakespeare in America: An Anthology from the Revolution to Now* (New York: Library of America, 2014).

76. Shapiro.

77. "Communication: Chesnut Street Theatre," *U.S. Gazette*, October 12, 1832: n.p., Robert Montgomery Bird, Robert Montgomery Bird Papers, Ms. Collection 108, box 7, folder 200, University of Pennsylvania, Rare Book and Manuscript Library, Philadelphia.

78. "Theatrical," reprinted from the *Boston Commercial Gazette* in *The Pennsylvanian* (?), n.d., n.p., Robert Montgomery Bird, Robert Montgomery Bird Papers, Ms. Collection 108, box 7, folder 200, University of Pennsylvania, Rare Book and Manuscript Library, Philadelphia.

79. See, for example, Shaw, *Spartacus and the Slave Wars*, 22–23.

80. Bird is best known for his novel *Nick of the Woods*, about an apparently peaceful Quaker who, like some perverse white supremacist superhero, disguises himself as a vengeful Indian hunter at night. See Richard Drinnon, *Facing West: The Metaphysics of Indian-Hating & Empire-Building* (Norman: University of Oklahoma Press, 1980), 147–51.

81. Bird, "The Secret Records," transcribed in Richard Harris, "A Young Dramatist's Diary: *The Secret Records* of R. M. Bird," *Library Chronicle* (University of Pennsylvania) (Winter 1959): 16–17.

82. Charles Sellers, *The Market Revolution: Jacksonian America, 1815–1846* (New York and Oxford, 1991), 375.

83. See, for example, Vivien M. Green, "Hiram Powers's 'Greek Slave:' Emblem of Freedom," *American Art Journal* 14, 4 (Autumn 1982): 31–39.

84. Walt Whitman, "The Gladiator," *Brooklyn Eagle*, December 26, 1846, 2.

85. My thanks to Beate Hein Bennett for bringing Ira Aldridge to my attention.

86. Bernth Lindfors, *Ira Aldridge* (Rochester, N.Y.: University of Rochester Press, 2011), 1: 325 n. 28; Jonathan Dewberry, "The African Grove Theatre and Company," *Black American Literature Forum* 16, 4 (Winter 1982): 131.

87. Herbert Marshall and Mildred Stock, *Ira Aldridge: The Negro Tragedian* (New York: Macmillan, 1958), 39.

88. In England Aldridge was not made to appear on segregated stages; he performed at Covent Garden and Sadler's Wells as well as now-obscure theatres like the Royalty, the Coburg, and the Surrey. See "An African Roscius," *National Era* 6, 266 (February 5, 1852): 21.

89. McConachie, 69–118.

90. Ginger Strand makes a similar argument about Oralloossa as a noble patriot hero in "'My Noble Spartacus': Edwin Forrest and Masculinity on the Nineteenth-Century Stage," *Passing Performances: Queer Readings of Leading Performers in American Theater History*, ed. Robert A. Schanke and Kim Marra (Ann Arbor: University of Michigan Press, 1998), 22.

91. Bird, *Oralloossa* IV, i.

92. David Walker, *Walker's Appeal, in Four Articles: Together with a Preamble, to the Coloured Citizens of the World, but in Particular, and Very Expressly, to Those of the United States of America* (1830), Preamble.

93. Walker, Article III.

94. Ibid., Preamble.

95. [John Greenleaf Whittier], "Toussaint L'Ouverture," *New-England Magazine* 5, 5 (November 1833): 368–73.

96. Jean Fagan Yellin, *The Intricate Knot: Black Figures in American Literature, 1776–1863* (New York: New York University Press, 1972), 16.

97. See "Literary Notices: *The Hour and the Man*," *Knickerbocker* 17, no. 2 (February 1841): 160–62; "Miss Martineau's Later Writings," *Christian Examiner* 32 (May 1842): 190–204. See also Susan Belasco, "Harriet Martineau's Black Hero and the American Antislavery Movement," *Nineteenth Century Literature* 55, 2 (September 2000): 157–94.

98. Two fascinating exceptions—as it happens, by Bird and Simms—discuss American slave revolt but employ other strategies to distance the possibility from the realities of the present day. Bird's surreal *Sheppard Lee*, an experimental novel of 1836, concerns a human soul that migrates into a variety of human bodies including a slave named Tom involved in a revolt he comes to regret. Simms's *Mellichampe* (also 1836) is set at the time of the American Revolution, includes a scene in which a slave's excited narration of his murder of his master's attacker is misunderstood as an account of his murder of his master. See Sarah Nelson Roth, "Rebels and Martyrs: The Debate over Slavery in American Popular Culture, 1822–1865" (Ph.D. dissertation, University of Virginia, 2002), 96–109. Note that these works are from 1836, after which texts considered incendiary were subject to even greater scrutiny.

99. [Richard Hildreth], *The Slave: Or Memoirs of Archy Moore* (Boston: Bela Marsh, 1848), 2: 84. The plot synopsis is from Evan Brandstadter, "Uncle Tom and Archy Moore: The Antislavery Novel as Ideological Symbol, *American Quarterly* 26, 2 (May, 1974): 174.

100. Brandstadter, 168, 167.

101. From the review in the *Boston Atlas*, quoted in Brandstadter, 168.

102. Robert H. Abzug, "The Influence of Garrisonian Abolitionists' Fears of Slave Violence on the Antislavery Argument, 1829–40," *Journal of Negro History* 55, 1 (January 1970): 15–28.

103. William Lloyd Garrison, "The Insurrection," *Liberator*, September 3, 1831.

104. William Birney, *James G. Birney and His Times* (New York: D. Appleton, 1890), 125–28.

105. *The Cincinnati Republican*, July 21, 1836, quoted in *Narrative of the Late Riotous Proceedings Against the Liberty of the Press in Cincinnati* (Cincinnati, 1836), 19; italics original.

106. *Narrative of the Late Riotous Proceedings*, 36.

107. Parrington, *Main Currents*, 2: 237.

108. Elizabeth R. Varon, *Disunion! The Coming of the American Civil War, 1789–1859* (Chapel Hill: University of North Carolina Press, 2008), 133–34.

109. Even in abolitionist literature as late as 1860, referring to recent violence was problematic, and historical distance was useful. In *The Slave's Rebellion* Adeleke Adeeko notes that Harriet Jacobs had wanted to include John Brown's raid in her slave narrative *Incidents in the Life of a Slave Girl* (1860), but her editor, Lydia Maria Child, considered the incident too fresh. Child suggested she replace it with her memories of the repercussions of the more historically remote Nat Turner rebellion in her North Carolina community. Adeleke Adeeko, *The Slave's Rebellion: Literature, History, Orature* (Bloomington: Indiana University Press, 2005), 24.

110. In "The Romance Ferment after *Waverley*," G. Harrison Orians says, "The romance ferment may be said to have died down after 1833, although the active faith of novelists and short story writers was for years little affected." G. Harrison Orians, "The Romance Ferment after *Waverley*," *American Literature* 3, 4 (January, 1932): 431.

111. The classic study of this period remains F. O. Matthiessen's *American Renaissance: Art and Expression in the Age of Emerson and Whitman* (London: Oxford University Press, 1941). See also Perry Miller's *The Raven and the Whale: The War of Words and Wits in the Era of Poe and Melville* (New York: Harcourt, Brace & World, 1956). For a more recent study, see Widmer's *Young America*.

112. Beaufort Taylor Watts to General W. Thompson, May17, 1841, Beaufort Taylor Watts Papers, 1822–1879, South Caroliniana Library, University of South Carolina.

113. Allen Cadwallader Izard to Lucy Heyward, April 16, 1852, and Allen Cadwallader Izard to Mary C. Izard, January 25, 1852, Allen Cadwallader Izard Papers, 1834–1943, South Caroliniana Library, University of South Carolina.

114. Herman Melville, *Moby-Dick, or, The Whale* (Evanston, Ill.: Northwestern University Press and Newberry Library, 1988), 249. My thanks to Mark Noonan for pointing out this reference.

115. Edward Neufville Tailer Diaries, MS2495, November 29, 1849, New-York Historical Society.

116. Rosamond Culbertson, *Rosamond: or, a Narrative of the Captivity and Sufferings of an American Female under the Popish Priests, with a Full Disclosure of their Manners and Customs, in the Island of Cuba* (New York: Leavitt, Lord & Co., 1836).

117. David S. Reynolds, *Faith in Fiction: The Emergence of Religious Literature in America* (Cambridge, Mass.: Harvard University Press, 1981), 180; Marie Anne Pagliarini, "The Pure American Woman and the Wicked Catholic Priest: An Analysis of Anti-Catholic Literature in Antebellum America," *Religion and American Culture* 9, 1 (Winter 1999): 97–128.

118. Richard Hofstadter, *The Paranoid Style in American Politics and Other Essays* (New York: Knopf, 1965), 19–21.

119. Hofstadter, 22; 1852 marked the publication of Stowe's *Uncle Tom's Cabin*, which overturned all previous publishing records.

120. Susan Griffin, "Awful Disclosures: Women's Evidence in the Escaped Nun's Tale," *PMLA* (January 1996): 93.

121. Culbertson, 7.

122. Ibid., 68.

123. Ibid., 68.

124. Ibid., 97; italics in original. "Beard" would seem to be a more apt slang term describing this man's function.

125. Culbertson, 188–89.

126. For a discussion of this relationship, see Evan Haefeli and Kevin Sweeney, "'The Redeemed Captive' as Recurrent Seller: Politics and Publication, 1707–1853," *New England Quarterly* 77, 3 (September 2004): 341–67.

127. Heather Nathans, *Slavery and Sentiment on the Nation's Stage, 1787–1861: Lifting the Veil of Black* (Cambridge: Cambridge University Press, 2009), 70.

128. Marcus Rediker, *The Amistad Rebellion: An Atlantic Odyssey of Slavery and Freedom* (New York: Viking, 2012), 114–18.

129. Playbill from the Bowery Theatre (New York), September 4, 1839 (Courtesy of the Harvard Theatre Collection) http://amistad.mysticseaport.org/library/misc/hvd.bowery.html accessed November 10, 2009. Iyunolu Folayan Osagie says definitively that "Like other Amistad performances of the nineteenth century, the play has not survived." Iyunolu Folayan Osagie, *The Amistad Revolt: Memory, Slavery, and the Politics of Identity in the United States and Sierra Leone* (Athens: University of Georgia Press, 2000), 72.

130. Frank Luther Mott, *A History of American Magazines, 1741–1850* (Cambridge, Mass.: Harvard University Press, 1930), 544–55.

131. *The Slaver: A Tale of Our Own Times*, by a Son of the Late Dr. John D. Godman, *Graham's Magazine* 31, 1 (July 1847): 7.

132. *The Slaver*, 8.

133. Ibid., 9.

134. John D. Godman, *American Natural History* (Philadelphia: Carey and Lea, 1826); Thomas Sewall, "Memoir of Dr. Godman," *North American Review* 40, 86 (January 1835): 87–99. Godman's first name was variously spelled "Stuart" (on the title page of his 1852 novel *The Ocean-Born*), "Stewart" (in a profile that appeared in *Graham's* in 1852), and "Steuart" (in his obituary in *Southern Literary Messenger* in 1853).

135. "*The Ocean Born*" (review), *Graham's Magazine* 42, 3 (March 1853): 362; Charlton H. Wells, M.D., "Eminent Young Men.—No. II: Stewart Adair Godman," *Graham's Magazine* 40, no. 5 (May 1852): 467; "Editor's Table," *Southern Literary Messenger* 19, 8 (August 1853): 518.

136. *The Slaver*, 6.

137. "Editor's Table," *Graham's Magazine* 36, 6 (June 1850): 418. Here Godman is identified as "T. A. Godman."

138. Herman Melville, *Benito Cereno, Putnam's Monthly* 9 (1855): 353–67, 459–73, 633–44. For excellent analyses of *Benito Cereno*, see Eric J. Sundquist, *To Wake the Nations: Race in the Making of American Literature* (Cambridge, Mass.: Belknap Press of Harvard University Press, 1993) and Grandin, *The Empire of Necessity*.

139. See Joy Jordan-Lake, *Whitewashing Uncle Tom's Cabin: Nineteenth-Century Women Novelists Respond to Stowe* (Nashville: Vanderbilt University Press, 2005), xvii.

140. For an abolitionist response to the charge that " 'Uncle Tom has done us a world of mischief abroad,' " see [Gamaliel Bailey], "Uncle Tom Abroad," in *National Era*, March 24, 1853: "there is nothing in the work itself calculated to do harm to *American* character or institutions, and . . . we can see no indications in any quarter that our country has fallen in the estimation of the people of the Old World."

141. "Critical Notices: The Memoir of Pierre Toussaint," *Southern Quarterly Review*, 9, no. 18 (April 1854): 543. Pierre Toussaint worked as a hairdresser to the New York *haute monde* and came to the attention of Hannah Farnham Sawyer Lee, who told his story in *Memoir of Pierre Toussaint, Born a Slave in St. Domingo* (Boston: Crosby, Nichols, and Company, 1854).

142. Katherine Emma Manthorne, *Tropical Renaissance: North American Artists Exploring Latin America, 1839–1879* (Washington, D.C.: Smithsonian Institution Press, 1989), 34. The phrase comes originally from Edward W. Said, *Orientalism* (New York: Vintage, 1979), 3.

143. William Gilmore Simms, *The Social Principle: The True Source of National Permanence, An Oration, Delivered before the Erosophic Society of the University of Alabama, at Its Twelfth Anniversary, December 13, 1842* (Tuscaloosa, Ala.: Published by the Society, 1843).

144. "The University of Alabama: History of UA," http://www.ua.edu/history.html, accessed December 5, 2009; C. Watson, *From Nationalism to Secessionism*, 31.

145. Simms, *Social Principle*, 15.

146. Ibid., 15.

147. Ibid., 15.

148. Ibid., 10.

149. Ibid., 18; italics in original.

150. Ibid., 13.

151. "*The Social Principle; the True Source of National Permanence*," *Southern Quarterly Review* 4, 7 (July 1843): 242.

152. C. Watson, *From Nationalism to Secessionism*, 55.

153. William Gilmore Simms, "The Morals of Slavery" in *The Pro-Slavery Argument; As Maintained by the Most Distinguished Writers of the Southern States* (Charleston: Walker, Richards & Company, 1852), 282. See also Ritchie Devon Watson, *Normans and Saxons: A Southern Race Mythology and Intellectual History of the American Civil War* (Baton Rouge: Louisiana State University Press, 2008).

154. Generations of American school children were subjected to the 1825 oration as an exercise in public speaking. See, for example, Mabel F. McKee, "Three Examples of Motivation," *English Journal* 9, no. 8 (October 1920): 459.

155. Daniel Webster, "The Completion of the Bunker Hill Monument," *Washington's Farewell Address and Webster's Bunker Hill Orations* (New York: Macmillan, 1915), 78.

156. "Liberty *and* Union, now and for ever, one and inseparable!" *Register of Debates in Congress*, 21st Cong., 1st Sess., January 27, 1830, 80.

157. Webster, "The Completion of the Bunker Hill Monument," 85.

158. Ibid., 87, 89.

159. Ibid., 91.

160. Ibid., 96.

161. Webster, "Bunker Hill Oration," *Washington's Farewell Address*, 62.

162. Webster, "The Completion of the Bunker Hill Monument," 96–97.

Chapter 4. *Conquest* and Reconquest

1. Edward Maturin, *Montezuma: The Last of the Aztecs: A Romance* (New York: Paine & Burgess, 1845).

2. As the *Knickerbocker* reported in its review, in the character of Montezuma, "the spirit of resistance . . . is mingled [with] a superstitious fear that the gods of Anahuac have decreed the destruction of his people, and the subversion of his throne to the white gods. This consciousness, acting upon his religious fears, palsies every effort of his mind, and renders him the willing slave to a designing priest, who, cloaking his deep-laid plans under the holy robe of religion, by supernatural omens and dark prophecies, which as the High Priest he alone can read," "Literary Record—'*Montezuma, the Last of the Aztecs*'," *Knickerbocker* 26, 6 (December 1845): 588. Maturin's novel can be read as an allegory for a country in the thrall of Rome. Substitute "Pope" for "High Priest" in the quote above, and one quickly perceives an expression of the nativist fear of Catholics who control access to Holy Writ among the faithful.

3. Maturin, *Montezuma*, iv.

4. See also "Notices of New Books: *Montezuma, the Last of the Atzecs* [sic]," *Democratic Review* 48, 91 (January, 1846): 76.

5. "*Montezuma, the Last of the Aztecs: An Historical Romance on the Conquests of Mexico*," (review), *The American Review: A Whig Journal of Politics, Literature, Art* 3, 2 (February 1846): 224; italics in original.

6. Evert A. Duyckinck and George L. Duyckinck, *Cyclopaedia of American Literature,* (New York: Charles Scribner, 1856), 1: 286.

7. See, for example, the issue of January 7, 1843.

8. "Yes, more, more, more! . . . till our national destiny is fulfilled . . . and the whole boundless continent is ours." Quoted in Edward L. Widmer, *Young America: The Flowering of Democracy in New York City* (New York: Oxford University Press, 1999), 51.

9. "*Montezuma*, the Last of the Aztecs," 224. Amy Greenberg analyzes two kinds of conquest in gendered terms. Amy S. Greenberg, *Manifest Manhood and the Antebellum American Empire* (Cambridge: Cambridge University Press, 2005), 11ff.

10. For a useful discussion of this overlap, see Kirsten Silva Gruesz, *Ambassadors of Culture: The Transamerican Origins of Latino Writing* (Princeton, N.J.: Princeton University Press, 2002), chap. 3.

11. This characterization, memorably expressed by John Quincy Adams, who said Prescott was the ideal historian, "who should be apparently without country and without religion," was exploded by William Charvat in 1942. William Charvat, "Prescott's Political and Social Attitudes," *American Literature* 13, 4 [January, 1942]: 320.

12. George Ticknor, *Life of William Hickling Prescott* (Boston: Ticknor and Fields, 1864), 358.

13. Ibid., 359.

14. The quote is a paraphrase of Prescott from his friend George Ticknor in his 1864 biography. Ticknor, *Life of William Hickling Prescott*, 335.

15. William Hickling Prescott to Lady Mary Lyell, May 12, 1852, William Hickling Prescott Papers, Massachusetts Historical Society, Boston. The letter goes on, "It gives a lively picture of our lawless manner in the Far West, and though there is a good deal too much negro talk in the volumes, I suppose both you & your mother, as well as your brother—now that he is an ex-minister—may read them with interest.—You know you belong to the Abolitionist party."

16. The failure of the Whig Party to take a stand on slavery contributed to its collapse, but was not solely responsible for it. It was similarly hobbled by its inability to resolve the tensions between immigrant Catholics and native Protestants. See David M. Potter, *The Impending Crisis, 1848–1861* (New York: Harper & Row, 1976), 225–65.

17. During his lifetime, Prescott took his success to the bank. C. Harvey Gardiner estimates that he grossed $100,000 from his books during his lifetime. C. Harvey Gardiner, *Prescott and His Publishers* (Carbondale: Southern Illinois University Press, 1959), 243. Gardiner also speculates that the sale of four thousand copies of *Mexico* between its debut in December 1843 and April 1844 "possibly represented the larges sale of an historical work in the United States in an interval of four months." C. Harvey Gardiner, *William Hickling Prescott: A Biography* (Austin: University of Texas Press, 1969), 214.

18. John E. Eipper, "The Canonizer De-Canonized: The Case of William H. Prescott," *Hispania* 83, 3 (September 2000): 416, 423.

19. J. H. Elliott, "An Epic in Prose," *Times Literary Supplement*, July 31, 2009, 15. This article is an edited version of Elliott's introduction to Prescott's *History of the Conquest of Mexico*.

20. Elliott, 15.

21. David Levin argues that all the Romantic historians "agreed on the vitality of the middle class, on defining progress as movement toward popular liberty." The role of great men was to embody the people. David Levin, *History as Romantic Art: Bancroft, Prescott, Motley, and Parkman* (Stanford, Calif.: Stanford University Press, 1959), 49. See, for example, William Hickling Prescott, *The History of the Conquest of Mexico and The History of the Conquest of Peru* (New York: Modern Library, 1936 [1843, 1847]), 369.

22. The first books of *The Conquest of Mexico* and *The Conquest of Peru* are entirely devoted to surveys of the native civilizations at the time of the Conquest. Prescott even gives Montezuma an internal monologue in *Mexico*, 289. He indicates that Bernardino de Sahagun, his best source for the perspective of the Aztecs, ends his narrative before Prescott is finished with his history (Prescott, *Mexico*, 619). For the role of Spanish women in the Conquest, see *Mexico*, 584. For the role of Indian women, see *Mexico*, 593.

23. From Prescott's *Literary Memoranda*, quoted in Gardiner, *William Hickling Prescott*, 104.

24. Prescott, *Mexico*, 164, 212, 482: "many a llama was destroyed solely for the sake of the brains,—a dainty morsel, much coveted by the Spaniards. So reckless was the spirit of destruction, says Ondegardo, the wise governor of Cuzco, that in four years more of these animals perished than in four hundred, in the times of the Incas. The flocks, once so numerous over the broad table-lands, were now thinned to a scanty number that sought shelter in the fastnesses of the Andes. The poor Indian, without food, without the warm fleece which furnished him a defense against the cold, now wandered half-starved and naked over the plateau." Prescott, *Peru*, 1121.

25. Eipper, 419.

26. "Prescott's vision fluctuated, but not as some writers suggest. Back and forth, across the years, William's sight generally ranged from good to fair to poor, not from poor to nonexistent. Sentimentalists, prostrating themselves before man's conquest of physical adversity, have commonly selected, as though it were the only evidence, that which exaggerates Prescott's problem with his vision." Gardiner, *William Hickling Prescott*, 86.

27. Edward C. Atwater, M.D., "William Hickling Prescott, 1796–1859: An Early Report of Iritis with Arthritis," *New England Journal of Medicine* 275 (1966): 1228–32.

28. Gardiner, *William Hickling Prescott*, 60.

29. Howard Cline, "Foreword," *William Hickling Prescott: An Annotated Bibliography of Published Works* (Washington, D.C.: Hispanic Foundation, Library of Congress, 1958), iii.

30. William Hickling Prescott, "Literary Memorandum," 1820–1858, January 19, 1826, William Hickling Prescott Papers

31. William Hickling Prescott, *History of the Reign of Ferdinand and Isabella, the Catholic, of Spain* (London: Richard Bentley, 1842), 1: 12.

32. Ibid., 12–13.

33. Gardiner, *William Hickling Prescott*, 304.

34. Ibid., 142. "Had Williams's first title been his *Conquest of Mexico*, instead of *Ferdinand and Isabella*, his initial British reception, like that later accorded Francis Parkman's first book, might have bordered on disaster."

35. Prescott, *Mexico*, 3–4.

36. See, for example, his account of the career of the researches of Sahagun, which were composed as answers to his queries by Tezcucan natives writing in hieroglyphics, translated (by three sets of translators) into "the Mexican tongue," and then translated by Sahagun himself into Spanish in the late sixteenth century. His work was then lost for two centuries, only to be recovered in the late 1700s, Prescott, *Mexico*, 52–53.

37. Ibid., 19.

38. Ibid., 34.

39. Ibid., 35.

40. Ibid., 309.

41. Ibid., 92. "Boturini was eminently qualified, by his enthusiasm and perseverance, for collecting the materials necessary to illustrate the antiquities of the country. It requires a more highly gifted mind to avail itself of them," notes Prescott.

42. Ibid., 140.

43. William Hickling Prescott, "Literary Memorandum," 1820–1858, November 3, 1828, William Hickling Prescott Papers.

44. Fred Lewis Pattee, *The Development of the American Short Story: An Historical Survey* (New York: Harper & Brothers, 1923), 34. Pattee unequivocally credits Washington Irving as being the innovator of the first American short story. Irving wrote early histories of the Conquest (1828ff.) upon which William Gilmore Simms built his romances and against which Prescott wrote his much more nuanced *Conquest of Mexico* and *Conquest of Peru*.

45. William Hickling Prescott, "Literary Memorandum," 1820–1858, May 17, 1830, William Hickling Prescott Papers.

46. Prescott, *Peru*, 727.

47. For example, see the simile in Prescott, *Mexico*, 438. See the catalogue of Cortés's weapons and war materiel, *Mexico*, 549.

48. Gardiner, *William Hickling Prescott*, 103.

49. William Gilmore Simms to James Lawson, December 27, 1839, in *The Letters of William Gilmore Simms*, ed. Mary C. Simms Oliphant, Alfred Taylor Odell, and T. C. Duncan Eaves (Columbia: University of South Carolina Press, 1952), 153. Simms's argument is that the romance concerns the fantastic and sublime; it is not to be judged according to the standards of the novel, which concerns itself with the plausible and the everyday.

50. William Gilmore Simms, "The Epochs and Events of American History, as Suited to the Purposes of Art in Fiction," in *Views and Reviews in American Literature, History, and Fiction*, ed. William Gilmore Simms (New York: Wiley and Putnam, 1845), 26, 27.

51. Prescott, *Mexico*, 6; italics in original.

52. Ibid., 5. On the other hand, in the introduction to a 1934 abridgement for the Junior Literary Guild, Carl Van Doren blithely justifies the excising of the material about the pre-Columbian Indian civilizations: "Although Prescott put as much into his account of Aztec life and customs as anybody in his day knew or could know, so much has since been discovered about them that his first part is no longer so valuable as it was." Carl Van Doren, Introduction to William H. Prescott, *The Conquest of Mexico* (New York: Book League of America, 1934), xiii).

53. Ibid., 5.

54. Ibid., 159.

55. Ibid., 276. He credits the Puritans with attempting to legalize their conquest through legitimate purchase, but casts doubt on the ultimate Protestant justification of higher claims based on cultivation. "Yet it may be thought, as far as improvement of the soil is concerned, that this argument would afford us but an indifferent tenure for much of our own unoccupied and uncultivated territory, far exceeding what is demanded for our present or prospective support" (n. 11).

56. Ibid., 217. Prescott goes on to contrast this painstaking method with the more vigorous and cruel methods of Islam: his tolerance was unfortunately not all-embracing.

57. See, for example, Prescott to Brantz Mayer, July 24, 1844, *The Papers of William Hickling Prescott*, Selected and Edited by C. Harvey Gardiner (Urbana: University of Illinois Press, 1964), 219, and Prescott to Lúcas Alamán, March 30, 1845, *The Correspondence of William Hickling Prescott, 1833–1847*, transcr. and ed. Roger Wolcott (Boston: Houghton Mifflin, 1925), 533.

58. Prescott to Brantz Mayer, July 24, 1844, *Papers of William Hickling Prescott*, 219.

59. Prescott, *Mexico*, 278.

60. Levin, 27ff.

61. William Hickling Prescott to Susan Prescott, April 21, 1828, *Papers of William Hickling Prescott*, 57.

62. Prescott, *Mexico*, 33–34.

63. This is not the only spot Prescott makes this observation. See his Appendix, *Mexico*, 712.

64. Georges Louis Leclerc, Comte de Buffon. *Natural History, General and Particular, by the Count de Buffon*, trans. William Smellie (London: Printed for A. Strahan and T. Cadell, 1791 [originally published in French, 1749–1778]), 7: 394.

65. Ibid., 395–96.

66. Ibid., 398.

67. Quoted in Prescott, *Mexico*, 677.

68. Prescott, *Mexico*, 672; italics in original.

69. Ibid., 678.

70. Quoted by Samuel Eliot Morison, Introduction, William Hickling Prescott, *History of the Conquest of Peru* (New York: Heritage Press, 1957), xiii–ix.

71. Ibid., 1129.

72. Prescott, *Mexico*, 451.

73. Ibid., 463.

74. Ibid., 465.

75. Ibid., 465.

76. Ibid., 681.

77. Pizarro did rely on Cortés as a "captivating model," even when conditions in Peru might have merited a more patient, politic, or accommodating approach. See Prescott, *Peru*, 1094; see also 897, 933 for examples of his imitation of Cortés.

78. Ibid., 1095.

79. Ibid., 771–74.

80. Levin, 26. The "she-philosophers" quip is Francis Parkman's.

81. Prescott, *Peru*, 1120.

82. Ibid., 1037.

83. Ibid., 1037–38.

84. Ibid., 1054–55.

85. Ibid., 1112.

86. "This lofty morality, it will be remembered, was from the lips of a Dominican, in the sixteenth century, one of the order that founded the Inquisition, and in the very country where the fiery tribunal was then in most active operation!" (1123.)

87. Ibid., 1124.

88. Ibid., 1125.

89. Ibid., 1125.

90. Ibid., 1163.

91. For a useful discussion of Prescott's multivariate appeal, see Jenny Franchot, *Roads to Rome: The Antebellum Protestant Encounter with Catholicism* (Berkeley: University of California Press, 1994), 42: "Prescott's narrative stance both entertained proponents of the war and spoke to the war's large opposition, which consisted of an unstable coalition of abolitionists, conservative Whigs, and a significant number of southerners reluctant to assimilate the racially suspect populations of Mexico."

92. Prescott, *Peru*, 1010; From *Boston Daily Advertiser*, reprinted in *Nantucket Inquirer*, January 1, 1849, 2.

93. *Berkshire County Whig*, January 4, 1844, 3; see also *Berkshire County Whig*, June 10, 1847, 2.

94. From *Utica Whig*, reprinted in *Berkshire County Whig*, August 12, 1847, 2.

95. Albert Gallatin, *Peace with Mexico* (New York: Bartlett & Welford, 1847), 24–25.

96. "The Obsequies," *Brooklyn Eagle*, July 15, 1848, 2; italics in original.

97. "Mr. Vinton and the Mexican War," *Brooklyn Eagle*, July 17, 1848, 2.

98. Eipper, 420.

99. Robert Johannsen, *To the Halls of the Montezumas: The Mexican War in the American Imagination* (New York: Oxford University Press, 1985), 246.

100. Richard McSherry, *El Puchero, or, A Mixed Dish from Mexico* (Philadelphia: Lippincott, 1850), 168–69, cited by Eipper.

101. Robert D. Aguirre, *Informal Empire: Mexico and Central America in Victorian Culture* (Minneapolis: University of Minnesota Press, 2005), 48–56.

102. Nathaniel Lyon Papers, 1840–1861, American Antiquarian Society, Worcester, Mass.

103. Allan Peskin, *Volunteers: The Mexican War Journals of Private Richard Coulter and Sergeant Thomas Barclay, Company E, Second Pennsylvania Infantry* (Kent, Ohio: Kent State University Press, 1991), 4–5.

104. Winfield Scott to William Marcy, February 24, 1848, quoted in Allan Peskin, *Winfield Scott and the Profession of Arms* (Kent, Ohio: Kent State University Press, 2003), 174. Italics in original.

105. Lieutenant Raphael Semmes, U.S.N., *Service Afloat and Ashore During the Mexican War* (Cincinnati: William H. Moore & Company, 1851), 393.

106. Captain E. Kirby Smith to Mrs. Smith, November 2, 1846, *To Mexico with Scott: The Letters of Captain E. Kirby Smith to His Wife* (Cambridge, Mass.: Harvard University Press, 1917), 68–69.

107. *New York Sun*, October 22, 1847, quoted in *The War with Mexico: Why Did it Happen?*, ed. Armin Rappaport (New York: Rand McNally, 1964), 45.

108. *Congressional Globe* (Appendix) 29th Cong., 2nd Sess., February 19, 1847, 222.

109. Count Adolph de Circourt to Prescott, June 7, 1847, *Correspondence of William Hickling Prescott*, 645.

110. George Wilkins Kendall, quoted in "Some Very Just Remarks About the New Conquest of Mexico," *Brooklyn Eagle*, November 18, 1847, 2. See also the anonymous pamphlet, "The Conquest of Mexico! An Appeal to the Citizens of the United States, on the Justice and Expediency of the Conquest of Mexico" (Boston: Jordan & Wiley; Hill & Brodhead; Redding & Co.; Waite, Pierce & Co., 1846).

111. From *Philadelphia Public Ledger*, December 11, 1847, cited in *The War with Mexico: Why Did It Happen?* 46–47.

112. Diary of H. Judge Moore of Greenville, SC Fairfield Volunteers, February 19, 1847, Yale Collection of Western Americana, Beinecke Rare Book and Manuscript Library.

113. "Speech of Mr. Calhoun, of S.C.," *Niles Register* 73 (January 15, 1848): 317.

114. *Congressional Globe*, 30th Cong., 1st Sess., January 4, 1848, 50.

115. In the original, the Paine quotation runs, "We fight not to enslave, but to set a country free, and to make room upon the earth for honest men to live in." The misquotation is noted in Shelley Streeby, "American Sensations: Empire, Amnesia, and the US-Mexican War," *American Literary History* 13,1 (2001): 14.

116. Gardiner, *William Hickling Prescott*, 218.

117. Prescott to George Sumner, May 15, 1846, *Correspondence of William Hickling Prescott*, 597.

118. Prescott to Lord Morpeth, April 30, 1847, *Correspondence of William Hickling Prescott*, 634.

119. Eric Wertheimer, *Imagined Empires: Incas, Aztecs, and the New World of American Literature, 1771–1861* (Cambridge: Cambridge University Press, 1999), 131.

120. Prescott to Count Adolphe de Circourt, July 10, 1847, *Correspondence of William Hickling Prescott*, 656.

121. Prescott to Lúcas Alamán, March 30, 1845, *Correspondence of William Hickling Prescott*, 533.

122. See, for example, Prescott to George Sumner, August 14, 1845, *Correspondence of William Hickling Prescott*, 550. Frances Trollope wrote: "Jonathan will be a fine gentleman, but it must be in his own way. Is he not a free-born American?" Frances Trollope, *Domestic Manners of the Americans* (London: Printed for Whittaker, Treacher, & Co., 1832), 1: 57.

123. Prescott to Pascual de Gayanos, April 30, 1846, *Correspondence of William Hickling Prescott*, 595. Similarly, see Prescott to George Summer, May 15, 1846: "The South and West seem to be overrun with a dare-devil war spirit that one might expect to meet with in France, but not in a money-making democracy. . . . One would suppose that the millions of uncultivated acres inviting settlement and the hand of civilization that lie within our present limits might satisfy the most craving cupidity. And so it would have at the North, where we have sober business-like habits and the steadiness of one somewhat advanced in years. But in the Far West we are wedded to a brisk young helpmate who is like to give us enough of our gambols and who most unhappily has the control of brother Jonathan's ménage—for the present" (597).

124. Susan Mary Grant, *North Over South: Northern Nationalists and American Identity in the Antebellum Era* (Lawrence: University Press of Kansas, 2000), 72–73.

125. Gardiner, *William Hickling Prescott*, 120.

126. Ibid., 214.

127. [Theodore Parker], *History of the Conquest of Mexico* [review], *Massachusetts Quarterly Review* 8 (September 1849): 437–70.

128. Paul E. Teed, "The Politics of Sectional Memory: Theodore Parker and *Massachusetts Quarterly Review*, 1847–1850," *Journal of the Early Republic* 21, 2 (Summer 2001): 302, 312.

129. Prescott, *Mexico*, 6.

130. [Theodore Parker], "Character of Mr. Prescott as an Historian," *Massachusetts Quarterly Review* 2, no. 5 (March 1849): 235.

131. [Parker], "*Conquest*," 455–57.

132. Ibid., 458.

133. Ibid., 465.

134. Ibid., 466.

135. Ibid., 469.

136. Robert A. Wilson, *Mexico: Its Peasants and Priests* (New York: Harper & Brothers, 1856), i; t.p.

137. Ibid., iii–iv.

138. "The number, the novelty, and the variety of his blunders have given us a very favorable impression of his ingenuity, and have afforded us constant entertainment in what we feared was to be a drudgery and a task." "Reviews and Literary Notices: *A New History of the Conquest of Mexico* [Second Notice]," *Atlantic* 3, 9 (May 1859): 633.

139. "Notices of Books: *Wilson's New History of the Conquest of Mexico*," *New Englander* 42, 66 (May 1859): 546.

140. George Ticknor, "Papers Discussing the Comparative Merits of Prescott's and Wilson's Histories, Pro. and Con.: As Laid Before the Massachusetts Historical Society" (Boston?: s.n, 1861).

141. Elliott, 15.

142. David Reynolds, *Beneath the American Renaissance: The Subversive Imagination in the Age of Emerson and Melville* (New York: Knopf, 1988), 206.

143. Gardiner, *William Hickling Prescott*, 258.

144. Streeby, 2–3.

145. [Parker], "Character," 248.

146. Johannsen, 199.

147. Reynolds, *Beneath the American Renaissance*, 207.

148. Johannsen, 61.

149. George Lippard, *Legends of Mexico* (Philadelphia: T.B. Peterson, 1847), 27.

150. Lippard, *Legends*, 28, 22, 23.

151. See particularly Streeby, *American Sensations*, and Reynolds, *Beneath the American Renaissance*.

152. Mark A. Lause, *A Secret Society History of the Civil War* (Urbana: University of Illinois Press, 2011), 21–36; David S. Reynolds, *The Quaker City* (Introduction) (Amherst: University of Massachusetts Press, 1995), xvii–xviii.

153. Lippard, *Legends*, 16, 103.

154. [Theodore Parker], "Washington and his Generals; or, Legends of the Revolution," (review), *Massachusetts Quarterly Review* 1, 1 (December 1847): 125.

155. Lippard, *Legends*, 33.

156. Lippard, *Legends*, 27, 60, 81, 136.

157. Lippard, *Legends*, 54–55, 91.

158. Jesse Alemán, "The Other Country: Mexico, the United States, and the Gothic History of Conquest," *American Literary History* (2006): 418.

159. Alemán, 418.

160. Jenna Gibbs notes that Lippard's oeuvre is noticeably "racially inclusive." Jenna Gibbs, *Performing the Temple of Liberty: Slavery, Theater, and Popular Culture in London and Philadelphia, 1760–1850* (Baltimore: Johns Hopkins University Press, 2014), 233.

161. Lippard, *Legends*, 16. Tyler V. Johnson makes the argument that this acknowledgment of immigrant volunteers—many of whom were presumably Catholic—proving their patriotism in a battle against a Catholic foe is a significant step in their admission to the American mainstream. Tyler V. Johnson, *Devotion to the Adopted Country: U.S. Immigrant Volunteers in the Mexican War* (Columbia: University of Missouri Press, 2012), 2–8, 122.

162. Lippard, *Legends*, 15.

163. But this union is not quite the marriage of equals imagined by Timothy Flint. Streeby notes that Lippard "attempts to turn force into consent and symbolic rape into marriage" (Streeby, 73).

164. Prescott unsuccessfully attempted to arrange a dinner for Macready in the early 1840s; he was more successful in 1848, an occasion the actor recalled as "*very elegant*" Gardiner, *William Hickling Prescott*, 164, 283; italics in original.

165. Ned Buntline [Edward Zane Carroll Judson], *The Volunteer; or, the Maid of Monterey: A Story of the Mexican War* (Boston: Elliott, Thomes & Talbot: 1847), 5.

166. Ibid., 10.

167. Ibid., 57.

168. Ibid., 42.

169. Ibid., 28–29.

170. Ibid., 31.

171. Ibid., 22.

172. Ibid., 111.

173. Ibid., 105, 88.

174. Buntline, *Volunteer*, 115. As with her discussion of *Legends of Mexico*, Streeby rightly points out that there is something unsettling about this scene. Edwina/Helen's brother "gives" her to Blakely, and in the process Buntline "strives to turn force/invasion into consent/marriage through a guarded imperialist rhetoric of international romance" (Streeby, 144–45).

175. Jaime Javier Rodriguez characterizes the border zone between the United States and Mexico as it is depicted in this fiction as a "troubled but nevertheless energizing and creative region of loss and disruption. Jaime Javier Rodriguez, *The Literatures of the U.S.-Mexican War: Narrative, Time, and Identity* (Austin: University of Texas Press, 2010), xiii.

Chapter 5. An Even More Peculiar Institution

1. Charles Sumner, "Freedom National; Slavery Sectional: Speech of Hon. Charles Sumner of Massachusetts, on his Motion to Repeal the Fugitive Slave Bill, in the Senate of the United States, August 26, 1852" (Boston: Ticknor, Reed, and Fields, 1852), 10–11.

2. William Hickling Prescott to Charles Sumner, quoted in Rollo Ogden, *William Hickling Prescott* (Boston: Houghton, Mifflin, 1904), 199.

3. Abraham Lincoln, "Lincoln's Reply to Judge Douglas at Chicago on Popular Sovereignty, the Nebraska Bill, etc., July 10, 1858," *Speeches and Letters of Abraham Lincoln, 1832–1865*, ed. Merwin Roe (London: J.M. Dent, 1907), 83–84.

4. Fredrika Bremer, *The Homes of the New World: Impressions of America*, trans. Mary Howitt (New York: Harper & Brothers, 1853), 1: 477.

5. Edwin L, Godkin, *Life and Letters of Edwin Lawrence Godkin*, ed. Rollo Ogden (New York: Macmillan, 1907), 1: 112.

6. The slaveowner continues: "You know not what you are doing. The time will come when waves of blood may roll over the land—and where will Eulalia be? Can my single arm hold her up above the crimson billows, my single breast shield her from the unimaginable horrors of servile warfare?" But even here the Spanish precedent serves a dramatic function. When the future father-in-law proposes to call off the wedding, the slaveowner protests, "I never will submit to this wanton trifling with my hopes and affections. Why, it is worse than the tortures of the Inquisition!" Caroline Lee Hentz, *The Planter's Northern Bride* (Philadelphia: A. Hart, 1854), 1: 166–67.

7. George William Gordon Papers, Manuscripts and Archives Division, New York Public Library, Astor, Lenox and Tilden Foundations. Gerald Horne points out that U.S. involvement in the Brazilian slave trade was hardly a secret; the illegal activities of U.S. nationals were reported in major newspapers. Gerald Horne, *Deepest South: The United States, Brazil, and the African Slave Trade* (New York: New York University Press, 2007), 33–35.

8. Lewis Tappan to George William Gordon, September 24, 1856, Gordon Papers.

9. "The Record of George Wm. Gordon. The Slave Trade at Rio de Janeiro—Seizure of Slave Vessels—Conviction of Slave Dealers, Personal Liberation of Slaves, &c." (Boston: Published at the American Head-Quarters, 1856).

10. Charles Ballou to his sister, April 13, 1856, Ballou Family Papers, 1849–83, American Antiquarian Society, Worcester, Massachusetts.

11. David M. Potter, *The Impending Crisis: 1848–1861*, ed. and completed by Don E. Fehrenbacher (New York: Harper and Row, 1976), 145.

12. Matthew Pratt Guterl, *American Mediterranean: Southern Slaveholders in the Age of Emancipation* (Cambridge, Mass.: Harvard University Press, 2008).

13. Ada Ferrer, "Speaking of Haiti: Slavery, Revolution and Freedom in Cuban Slave Testimony," *The World of the Haitian Revolution*, ed. David Patrick Geggus and Norman Fiering (Bloomington: Indiana University Press, 2009), 223–47.

14. Hinton Rowan Helper, *Noonday Exigencies in America* (New York: Bible Brothers, 1871), 161.

15. John F. Kvach, *De Bow's Review: The Antebellum Vision of a New South* (Lexington: University Press of Kentucky, 2013), 79.

16. James Stirling, *Letters from the Slave States* (London: John W. Parker and Son, 1857), 89.

17. Linda S. Hudson, *Mistress of Manifest Destiny: A Biography of Jane McManus Storm Cazneau, 1807–1878* (Austin: Texas State Historical Association, 2001), 6, 26.

18. "Cora Montgomery" (Jane Cazneau), *The Eagle Pass; or, Life on the Border* (New York: G.P. Putnam & Company, 1852), 26.

19. Sydney A. Story, Jr. [Mary Pike], *Caste: A Story of Republican Equality* (Boston: Phillips, Sampson, and Company, 1856), 371–72.

20. Frederick Law Olmsted, *A Journey in the Back Country* (New York: Mason Brothers, 1863), 388–89.

21. John Hope Franklin and Loren Schweninger, *Runaway Slaves: Rebels on the Plantation* (New York: Oxford University Press, 1999), 262.

22. Drew Gilpin Faust inserts a chart that maps the interpersonal connections among the most prominent politicians, novelists, scientists, and clergymen who defended slavery in "A Southern Stewardship: The Intellectual and the Proslavery Argument," *American Quarterly* 31, 1 (Spring 1979): 68.

23. For one perspective on the origins of this unity, see Robert Pierce Forbes, *The Missouri Compromise and Its Aftermath* (Chapel Hill: University of North Carolina Press, 2007), 106ff. Similarly, as Leonard L. Richards points out, time after time doughface Democrats caved in to Southern demands and helped push many proslavery measures through Congress in the antebellum period. See Leonard L. Richards, *The Slave Power: The Free North and Southern Domination, 1780–1860* (Baton Rouge: Louisiana State University Press, 2000), 112–33.

24. William E. Dodd recalled the primacy of these three journals in influencing attitudes among the Southern elites: "In the great house there . . . were quarterly reviews on the library tables . . . Of course, New England periodicals gave place to the *Southern Review*, published in the sacred Carolina city, to *De Bow's Review* of New Orleans, and especially to the *Southern Literary Messenger*, which always brought with it something of the atmosphere of Richmond and was hardly less dear to the Southern heart than Charleston itself." William E. Dodd, *The Cotton Kingdom: A Chronicle of the Old South* (New Haven, Conn.: Yale University Press, 1919], 79–80.

25. *DeBow's Review* 23, 1 (July 1857).

26. George Fitzhugh, "Black Republicanism in Ancient Athens," *DeBow's Review* 23, 1 (July 1857): 24.

27. "The Industrial Resources of Delaware," *DeBow's Review* 23, 1 (July 1857): 27.

28. "The Coolie Trade," *DeBow's Review* 23, 1 (July 1857): 31; "The African Slave Trade," *DeBow's Review* 23, 1 (July 1857): 51.

29. J. D. B. DeBow, "The Earth and Its Indigenous Races," *DeBow's Review* 23, 1 (July 1857): 71.

30. M. Gross, "The Agricultural Bureau of the Patent Office—Its Operations and Reports," *DeBow's Review* 23, 1 (July 1857): 84.

31. "Editorial—Book Notices, Etc.," *DeBow's Review* 23, 1 (July 1857): 108.

32. Peter Kolchin, *A Sphinx on the American Land: The Nineteenth-Century South in Comparative Perspective* (Baton Rouge: Louisiana State University Press, 2003), 39–73.

33. David Donald, "The Proslavery Argument Reconsidered," *Journal of Southern History* 37, 1 (February 1971): 17.

34. James Oakes, *The Ruling Race: A History of American Slaveholders* (New York: Knopf, 1982), 228.

35. So surmises Stirling in *Letters from the Slave States*, 123: "His creed, like many other creeds, is reiterated all the oftener and the more loudly from a lurking doubt. The slave-owner defends his position ostensibly against the Abolitionist; but in reality against his inner self."

36. Eugene Genovese, *Slaveholders' Dilemma: Freedom and Progress in Southern Conservative Thought, 1820–1860* (Columbia: University of South Carolina Press, 1992), 1.

37. As William Freehling writes, "Embattled minorities' power over sleepy majorities . . . repeatedly drove the drama." William W. Freehling, *The Road to Disunion*, vol. 2, *Secessionists Triumphant, 1854–1861* (New York: Oxford University Press, 2007), 532.

38. Lucretia Carter Sibley Correspondence, 1841–76, American Antiquarian Society, Worcester, Massachusetts.

39. Entry for March 18, 1861, Mary Boykin Miller Chesnut, *The Private Mary Chesnut: The Unpublished Civil War Diaries*, ed. C. Vann Woodward and Elisabeth Muhlenfeld (New York: Oxford University Press, 1984), 42; italics mine. For other expressions of anxiety, see *The Secret Eye: The Journal of Ella Gertrude Clanton Thomas, 1848–1889*, ed. Virginia Ingraham Burr (Chapel Hill: University of North Carolina Press, 1990). In the introduction Nell Irwin Painter raises her suspicion that Thomas's repeated citing of a line of poetry, "There are some thoughts we utter not . . ." alludes to her knowledge of her husband's liaison with an enslaved woman.

40. "Slavery in Brazil—The Past and Future," *DeBow's Review* 28, 4 (October 1860): 479.

41. Thomas R. R. Cobb, *An Inquiry into the Law of Negro Slavery in the United States of America* (Philadelphia: T & J.W. Johnson & Company, 1858), ccxvii.

42. Matthew Fontaine Maury, "Valley of the Amazon," *DeBow's Review* 14, 5 (May 1853): 453.

43. "Cuba as It Is in 1854," *DeBow's Review* 17, 3 (September 1854): 223–24.

44. See, for example, *The Ruling Race*, 148–49.

45. Freehling, *Disunion* 2, 151.

46. Ibid., 155.

47. "A Sectional War," *Augusta Chronicle*, June 23, 1848, 4; italics in original.

48. Ashbel Smith, "Our Relations with Cuba," *DeBow's Review* 7, 6 (December, 1849): 538.

49. "Purchase of Cuba," *New Orleans Times Picayune*, June 2, 1854, 2.

50. *Congressional Globe*, 33rd Congress, 1st Sess., May 24, 1854, 1298. For a discussion of the effect of the Haitian Revolution that whites in the Southern U.S. feared among their slaves, see Alfred N. Hunt, *Haiti's Influence on Antebellum America: Slumbering Volcano in the Caribbean* (Baton Rouge: Louisiana State University Press, 1988).

51. *New Orleans Delta*, quoted in "Cuba—A Perilous Inaction," *San Antonio Ledger*, June 8, 1854, 1.

52. "The Cuba Question," *DeBow's Review* 7, 6 (December 1849): 540.

53. "Destiny of the Slave States," *DeBow's Review* 17, 3 (September 1854): 281.

54. J. S. Thrasher, "Cuba and the United States: How the Interests of Louisiana Would be Affected by Annexation," *DeBow's Review* 17 2 (August 1854): 46.

55. Thrasher, 48.

56. "The South American States," *DeBow's Review* 6, 1 (July 1848): 9; italics in original.

57. Robert E. May, *The Southern Dream of a Caribbean Empire, 1854–1861* (Baton Rouge: Louisiana State University Press, 1973), 23–30.

58. May, 34; see also *Congressional Globe*, 33rd Cong., 1st Sess., May 24, 1854, 1299.

59. Edward E. Baptist, *The Half Has Never Been Told: Slavery and the Making of American Capitalism* (New York: Basic, 2014), 373–74.

60. May, 36–37.

61. May, 171–72.

62. May, 184.

63. Rachel St. John, *Line in the Sand: A History of the Western U.S.-Mexico Border* (Princeton, N.J.: Princeton University Press, 2011), 40–50.

64. Mark A. Lause, *A Secret Society History of the Civil War* (Urbana: University of Illinois Press, 2011), 66.

65. Walter Johnson, *River of Dark Dreams: Slavery and Empire in the Cotton Kingdom* (Cambridge, Mass.: Belknap Press of Harvard University Press, 2013), 323.

66. Robert E. May, *Slavery, Race, and Conquest in the Tropics: Lincoln, Douglas, and the Future of Latin America* (New York: Cambridge University Press, 2013), 89.

67. Robert E. May, *Manifest Destiny's Underworld: Filibustering in Antebellum America* (Chapel Hill: University of North Carolina Press, 2002), 252–54.

68. Even in a city like New Orleans opinion was divided: The *Louisiana Courier* and *La Union* both discouraged filibustering projects, while the *Delta* favored them. See Johnson, 333–35.

69. William W. Freehling, "The Complex Career of Slaveholder Expansionism," *The Reintegration of American History: Slavery and the Civil War* (New York: Oxford University Press, 1994), 169–73.

70. Anna Ella Carroll, *The Star of the West; or, National Men and National Measures* (Boston: James French and Company, 1856), 172–93, 347. See also Robert E. May, "Reconsidering Antebellum U.S. Women's History: Gender, Filibustering, and America's Quest for Empire" *American Quarterly* 57, 4 (December 2005): 1170–73.

71. Felix Huston, "Cuba—Freesoilism at the North," from the *Mississippian*, reprinted in *Texas State Gazette*, October 21, 1854, 68.

72. "Cuba and the United States: The Policy of Annexation Discussed," *DeBow's Review* 14, 1 (January 1853): 65.

73. "Cuba Question," 540.

74. "Independence of Cuba," *Debow's Review* 14, 5 (May 1853): 421.

75. "Cuba and the United States," 65.

76. "Southern Slavery and Its Assailants," *DeBow's Review* 16, 1 (January 1854): 58.

77. "Direct Foreign Trade of the South," *DeBow's Review* 12, 2 (February, 1852): 145.

78. "Direct Foreign Trade," 144.

79. "Cuba and the United States," 64; "Direct Foreign Trade," 147.

80. "The Black Race in North America: Why Was Their Introduction Permitted?" *Southern Literary Messenger* 21, 11 (November 1855): 682.

81. Thomas Jefferson, *The Writings of Thomas Jefferson*, vol. 7, ed. H. A. Washington (New York: Derby & Jackson, 1859), 194.

82. Forbes, *Missouri Compromise*, 48.

83. William W. Freehling, "The Complex Career of Slaveholder Expansionism," *The Reintegration of American History: Slavery and the Civil War* (New York: Oxford University Press, 1994), 167.

84. Horne, *Deepest South*.

85. C. S. Stewart, *Brazil and La Plata: The Personal Record of a Cruise* (New York: G.P. Putnam, 1856).

86. Stewart, 110–11.

87. "Southern Slavery and Its Assailants," 58.

88. See Cyrus B. Dawsey and James M. Dawsey, eds., *The Confederados: Old South Immigrants in Brazil* (Tuscaloosa: University of Alabama Press, 1995). See also Horne, *Deepest South.*

89. "The Independence of Cuba," *DeBow's Review* 14, 5 (May 1853): 420.

90. Maury, "Valley of the Amazon," 449, 450.

91. See, for example, "The Management of Negroes upon Southern Estates," *DeBow's Review* 10, 6 (June 1851): 621–27; "The Management of Negroes," *DeBow's Review* 11, 4 (October–November 1851): 369–72; "Management of Slaves," *DeBow's Review* 17, 4 (October 1854): 421–26; "Management of a Southern Plantation—Rules Enforced on the Rice Estate of P. C. Weston, Esq., of South Carolina," *DeBow's Review* 22, 1 (January, 1857): 38–44; "Domestic Treatment of Slaves," *DeBow's Review* 24, 1 (January, 1858): 63–64.

92. Stewart, 72.

93. Maturin M. Ballou, *History of Cuba; or, Notes of a Traveller in the Tropics* (Boston: Phillips, Sampson, 1854), 181.

94. For example, see *DeBow's Review* 23, 1 (July 1857): 1. John F. Kvach argues that DeBow envisioned an economically diverse future for the South and drew much of his subscription base from an urban, professional readership that shared his vision. John F. Kvach, *De Bow's Review: The Antebellum Vision of a New South* (Lexington: University Press of Kentucky, 2013).

95. Michael O'Brien, *Conjectures of Order: Intellectual Life and the American South, 1810–1860* (Chapel Hill: University of North Carolina Press, 2004), 192.

96. John Ashworth, *Slavery, Capitalism and Politics in the Antebellum Republic, Volume I: Commerce and Compromise, 1820–1850* (Cambridge: Cambridge University Press, 2004), 194.

97. [George Fitzhugh], *Slavery Justified; by a Southerner* (Fredericksburg, Va.: Recorder Printing Office, 1850), 9.

98. "Cuba: The March of Empire and the Course of Trade," *DeBow's Review* 30, 1 (January 1861): 33.

99. "Interview between a British Admiral and an American Diplomat," *Daily Picayune* (New Orleans), May 26, 1854, 1.

100. David Christy, "Cotton is King; or, Slavery in the Sight of Political Economy" in *Cotton is King, and Pro-Slavery Arguments*, ed. E. N. Elliott (Augusta, Ga.: Pritchard, Abbot & Loomis, 1860), 55.

101. Christy continues (57), "The principal articles demanded by this increasing commerce have been coffee, sugar, and cotton, in the production of which slave labor has greatly predominated. Since the enlargement of manufactures, cotton has entered more extensively into commerce than coffee and sugar, though the demand for all three has advanced with the greatest rapidity." For Cuban production, see, among many others, "Cuba and Our Relations with Her" *DeBow's Review* 26, 5 (May, 1859): 589–90. For Brazil, see, among others, "The South American States," 16.

102. "The coercion of slavery alone is adequate to form man to habits of labor. Without it, there can be no accumulation of property, no providence for the future, no tastes for comfort or elegancies, which are the characteristics and essentials of civilization. He who has obtained the command of another's labor, first begins to accumulate and provide for the future, and the foundations of civilization are laid." Chancellor Harper, "Slavery in the Light of Social Ethics," in *Cotton Is King*, 552.

103. "The Non-Slaveholders of the South" *DeBow's Review* 30, 1 (January 1861): 75.

104. George Fitzhugh and A. Hogeboom in *A Controversy on Slavery Between George Fitzhugh and A. Hogeboom* (Oneida, N.Y.: Printed at the "Oneida Sachem" Office, 1857), 5, 17–18.

105. "Emancipation in the British West Indies," *Southern Quarterly Review* 23 (April 1853): 426.

106. Thomas Carlyle, "Carlyle on West India Emancipation," *DeBow's Review* 8, 6 (June 1850): 530.

107. Elwood Fisher, "The North and the South, Part III" *DeBow's Review* 7, 4 (October 1849): 310.

108. Cobb, ccxiv; Fisher, 310.

109. Cobb, ccxiv.

110. Fisher, 310.

111. Thomas Ewbank, *Life in Brazil; or, a Journal of a Visit to the Land of the Cocoa and the Palm* (New York: Harper & Brothers, 1856), 93, 91, 112, 85.

112. Ballou, 14; Julia Ward Howe, *A Trip to Cuba* (Boston: Ticknor & Fields, 1860), 225–26; Ballou, 216.

113. Richard Henry Dana, *To Cuba and Back* (Carbondale: Southern Illinois University Press, 1966), 130, 12.

114. Ibid., 109, 96–101.

115. Ibid., 93.

116. Ibid., 128–29.

117. "South American States," 8.

118. Frederick B. Pike, *The United States and Latin America: Myths and Stereotypes of Civilization and Nature* (Austin: University of Texas Press, 1992), 44ff.; Ashli White, *Encountering Revolution: Haiti and the Making of the Early Republic* (Baltimore: Johns Hopkins University Press, 2010), 54.

119. Frank Tannenbaum, *Slave and Citizen: The Negro in the Americas* (New York: Knopf, 1946); Stanley M. Elkins, *Slavery: A Problem in American Institutional and Intellectual Life* (Chicago: University of Chicago Press, 1976).

120. Elkins, 67–80.

121. Ballou, 80–81; Howe, 143; italics in original.

122. Ballou, 83.

123. Anson Burlingame, Massachusetts Congressman, in 1854, quoted in Tyler Anbinder, *Nativism and Slavery: The Northern Know Nothings and the Politics of the 1850s* (New York: Oxford University Press, 1992), 45.

124. Oakes, *Ruling Race*, 130.

125. Tenella [Mary Bayard Devereux Clarke], "Some Farther Reminiscences of Cuba" *Southern Literary Messenger* 21, 12 (December, 1855): 745.

126. See Mark Noll, *America's God: From Jonathan Edwards to Abraham Lincoln* (Oxford: Oxford University Press, 2002), 367–421.

127. For example, in *The Invasion Within: The Contest of Cultures in Colonial North America* (New York: Oxford University Press, 1985), James Axtell compares the conversion rate of the French Jesuits in Canada with that of the English Protestants in New England and finds the latter wanting in sympathy for their "heathen" subjects.

128. Stewart, 293–94.

129. Clarke, 745.

130. "The West India Islands," *DeBow's Review* 5, 6 (June, 1848): 487.

131. Samuel Cartwright, "The Prognathous Species of Mankind," in *Slavery Defended: The Views of the Old South,* ed. Eric L. McKitrick (Englewood Cliffs, N.J.: Prentice-Hall, 1963), 139.

132. "Amalgamation," *DeBow's Review* 29, 1 (July, 1860): 2. Southerners were not the only ones to deny "amalgamation" in the United States. In 1846 James Gordon Bennett attributed the "imbecility and degradation of the Mexican people" to "the amalgamation of races," which "has been always abhorrent to the Anglo-Saxon race on this continent," quoted in Thomas Hietala, *Manifest Design: Anxious Aggrandizement in Late Jacksonian America* (Ithaca, N.Y.: Cornell University Press, 1985), 155.

133. While Brazil was no paradise of colorblindness, other considerations could trump race. According to a Brazilian axiom, "Money whitens" (George M. Fredrickson, *The Arrogance of Race: Historical Perspectives on Slavery, Racism, and Social Inequality* [Middletown, Conn.: Wesleyan University Press, 1988], 190). As Ann Twinam notes, in Spanish America from the late colonial period into the nineteenth century the state could officially permit individuals to change race even if the private reality was quite different. Ann Twinam, *Public Lives, Private Secrets: Gender, Honor, Sexuality and Illegitimacy in Colonial Spanish America* (Stanford, Calif.: Stanford University Press, 1999), 25, 336–41. See also Carl N. Degler, *Neither Black Nor White: Slavery and Race Relations in Brazil and the United States* (Madison: University of Wisconsin Press, 1986).

134. Cobb, ccvi. A similar observation is made by Charles Wilkes in *Voyage Round the World: Embracing the Principal Events of the Narrative of the United States Exploring Expedition* (Philadelphia: Geo. W. Gorton, 1849), 17.

135. Thomas C. Reynolds, "Cuba—Its Position, Dimensions and Population," *DeBow's Review* 8, 4 (April 1850): 315.

136. Thomas R. Dew, "Professor Dew on Slavery," *The Pro-Slavery Argument; As Maintained by the Most Distinguished Writers of the Southern States* (Charleston: Walker, Richards, 1852), 470.

137. *Congressional Globe,* 33rd Cong., 1st Sess., May 16, 1854, 1194.

138. Ballou, 189–90.

139. *Congressional Globe,* 35th Cong., 2nd Sess., February 12, 1859, 962.

140. John Esaias Warren, *Para; or, Scenes and Adventures on the Banks of the Amazon* (New York: G. P. Putnam, 1851), 65–66.

141. Ballou, 60; Stewart, 72.

142. Dana, 121–22.

143. Rev. D. P. Kidder and Rev. J. C. Fletcher, *Brazil and the Brazilians* (Philadelphia: Childs & Peterson, 1857), 138.

144. George M. Colvocoresses, *Four Years in the Government Exploring Expedition* (New York: J. M. Fairchild & Company, 1855), 216.

145. W. W. Wright, "Amalgamation," *DeBow's Review* 29, 1 (July 1860): 2, 4.

146. Cobb, ccxxi.

147. "Slavery in Brazil—The Past and Future," 480.

148. Ann Twinam, *Public Lives, Private Secrets.*

149. Rev. D. P. Kidder and Rev. J. C. Fletcher, *Brazil and the Brazilians* (Philadelphia: Childs & Peterson, 1857), 133.

150. For a further explication of this remarkable idea, see "The Difference of Race Between the Northern and Southern People," *Southern Literary Messenger* 30, 6 (June 1860): 401–9; "The True Question: A Contest for the Supremacy of Race, as between the Saxon Puritans of the North, and the Normans of the South," *Southern Literary Messenger* 33, 1 (July 1861): 19–27; William Gilmore Simms, "The Morals of Slavery," *The Pro-Slavery Argument*, 282; [George Fitzhugh], "Superiority of Southern Races—Review of Count de Gobineau's Work, *DeBow's Review* 31, 4–5 (October–November 1861): 369–81.

151. "Twenty Months in the Andes," *Southern Literary Messenger* 24, 5 (May 1857): 373.

152. Reynolds, "Cuba," 313–23; "Cuba," *Southern Literary Messenger* 31, 4 (October 1860): 256.

153. "Christian Missions and African Colonization," *Southern Quarterly Review* 2, 2 (February 1857): 294.

154. "That their bondage has been mild is evidenced by their great and rapid increase. For about 333,000 slaves imported, there are now more than 4,000,000" (Cobb, ccxii.) On the other hand, "Negroes from Africa were first introduced into Cuba in 1524; but, from causes other than climatic, the multiplication of the race has never corresponded with what might have been reasonably expected. The race has, according to most accounts—though this is steadily denied by the Spaniards—been greatly diminished by the masters. Be this as it may, it is certain that millions of negroes have been introduced into the island as slaves from Africa since 1524, and that now its slave population is only little more than half a million" ("Cuba as It Is in 1854," 220); "British and American Slavery," *Southern Quarterly Review* 8, 16 (October 1853): 386.

155. Kidder, 128.

156. J. Thornton Randolph [Charles Jacobs Peterson], *The Cabin and Parlor; or, Slaves and Masters* (Philadelphia: T.B. Peterson, 1852), 245.

157. Cobb, ccxi.

158. "British and American Slavery," 397–99.

159. Edmund Ruffin, "Consequences of Abolition Agitation (Concluded)," *DeBow's Review* 23, 6 (December 1857): 602.

160. See, for example, "Notices of New Works," *Southern Literary Messenger* 18, 10 (October 1852): 630–38; "Uncle Tom's Cabin," *Southern Literary Messenger* 18, 12 (December 1852): 721–31; "Uncle Tom's Cabin," *Southern Quarterly Review* 7, 13 (January 1853): 81–120; "The Queen's Dream—A Sequel to 'Uncle Tom's Cabin,'" *DeBow's Review* 15, 1 (July 1853): 95–105. For a discussion of the way responses to Stowe mobilized the forces of Southern literary nationalism, see Coleman Hutchison, *Apples and Ashes: Literature, Nationalism, and the Confederate States of America* (Athens: University of Georgia Press, 2012), 43–53.

161. [Edward J. Pringle], *Slavery in the Southern States by a Carolinian* (Cambridge, Mass.: John Bartlett, 1852), 8.

162. "The Empire of Brazil," 11.

163. "Editorial Miscellany," *DeBow's Review* 30, 4 (April 1861): 504–5.

164. Cobb, ccxiv.

165. William Cullen Bryant, "Sketches of Travel," [22 April 1849] *Prose Writings of William Cullen Bryant*, (New York: Appleton, 1884), 2: 142.

166. "En Route: or, Notes of the Overland Journey to the East," *Southern Literary Messenger* 20, 2 (February 1854): 106; italics in original.

167. Brantz Mayer, *Mexico: Aztec, Spanish and Republican* (Hartford, Conn.: S. Drake & Company, 1853), 35.

168. Kidder, quoted in "The Empire of Brazil," 12.

169. "Slavery in Brazil—The Past and Future," 480.

170. Eugene D. Genovese, "King Solomon's Dilemma—and the Confederacy's," *Southern Cultures* (Winter 2004): 61.

171. [Fitzhugh], "Superiority of Southern Races," 380.

172. "En Route," 106; italics in original.

173. Fox-Genovese and Genovese, 77.

174. "Slavery in Brazil—The Past and Future," 480.

175. Robert F. Durden, "J. D. B. DeBow: Convolutions of a Slavery Expansionist," *Journal of Southern History* 17, 4 (November, 1951): 460.

176. "Cuba: The March of Empire and the Course of Trade," 33.

177. George Fitzhugh, "Hayti and the Monroe Doctrine," *DeBow's Review* 31, 2 (August 1861): 131.

178. Frank Tannenbaum, *Slave and Citizen: The Negro in the Americas* (New York: Knopf, 1946), 42. In an early attempt to compare slavery in Brazil and the United States, Tannenbaum suggested that Europeans in Cuba and Brazil never equated people of African descent with permanent servitude as they did in North America.

179. "How to Save the Republic, and the Position of the South in the Union," *DeBow's Review* 11, 2 (August 1851): 190.

180. *Congressional Globe*, 35th Cong., 2nd Sess., February 25, 1859, 1828.

181. "Cuba: The March of Empire and the Course of Trade," 34.

182. That the first filibustering novel is Flint's 1826 *Francis Berrian* is pointed out in Orville Vernon Burton and Georganne B. Burton, Introduction, *The Free Flag of Cuba: The Lost Novel of Lucy Holcombe Pickens* (Baton Rouge: Louisiana State University Press, 2002), 3.

183. Elizabeth Wittenmyer Lewis, *Queen of the Confederacy: The Innocent Deceits of Lucy Holcombe Pickens* (Denton: University of North Texas Press, 2002), 39–40.

184. "Life at the White Sulfur," *Charleston Courier*, August 15, 1857, reprinted, with commentary, in "Fashionable Gossip at the Southern Springs," *New York Herald*, September 6, 1857, 2.

185. Lewis, vii; John Lowe, "'Calypso Magnolia': The Caribbean Side of the South," *South Central Review* 22, 1 (Spring 2005): 58.

186. Burton and Burton, Introduction, *The Free Flag of Cuba*, 10.

187. Holcombe Pickens, *The Free Flag of Cuba*, 118; see also 59, 124.

188. Ibid., 157.

189. Burton and Burton, Introduction, *The Free Flag of Cuba*, 4.

190. Holcombe Pickens, *The Free Flag of Cuba*, 173.

191. Ibid., 100.

192. Marmion's name recalls the hero of an 1808 epic poem by Sir Walter Scott.

193. Holcombe Pickens, *The Free Flag of Cuba*, 202.

194. Ibid., 186.

195. Ibid., 205.

196. Pushed just a little further, Marmion and Scipio would resemble Babo in Melville's *Benito Cereno*, published in *Putnam's Monthly* in 1855. Apparently the slave of a sea captain encountered by the American Amasa Delano, Babo has in fact led a successful slave revolt and uses the captain as a puppet to conceal his own autonomy. Babo's performance of solicitude and devotion—he never leaves his master unattended—masks the reality that he never permits his supposed master the freedom of revealing the true state of affairs.

197. Georganne B. Burton and Orville Vernon Burton, "Lucy Holcombe Pickens, Southern Writer," *South Carolina Historical Magazine* 103, 4 (October 2002): 306.

198. W. E. B. Du Bois, *Black Reconstruction in America: An Essay Toward a History of the Part Which Black Folk Played in the Attempt to Reconstruct Democracy in America, 1860–1880* (Oxford: Oxford University Press, 2007), 53.

199. Martin R. Delany, *Blake; or, the Huts of America*, intro. Floyd Miller (Boston: Beacon, 1970). Delany published the first twenty-six chapters in *Anglo-African Magazine* in 1859; the entire novel was published in *The Weekly Anglo-African* in 1861 and 1862.

Epilogue. 1861 and After

1. James Buchanan, Fourth Annual Message, December 3, 1860, *The Works of James Buchanan*, ed. and collected John Bassett Moore (New York: Antiquarian Press, 1960), 11: 8.

2. "National Fast-Day," *New York Evening Post*, September 27, 1861, 1.

3. 1 John 2:19. The sermon was reported in "National Fast-Day," *New York Evening Post*, September 27, 1861, 1.

4. Francis Vinton played a third act on the historical stage when in 1862 he supposedly won the unchurched Lincoln to Christianity. The episode of Lincoln's purported conversion is told, among other places, in William Jackson Johnstone, *Abraham Lincoln: The Christian* (New York: Eaton and Mains, 1913), 82–84 with all the requisite sentimental stops pulled out: "Mr. Lincoln threw his arm around Dr. Vinton's neck, laid his head upon his breast, and sobbed aloud."

5. *Richmond Whig*, June 25, 1862, quoted in "'The Master Race,'" *New York Evening Post*, July 8, 1862, 2.

6. Andrew Johnson, quoted in John Savage, *The Life and Public Services of Andrew Johnson: Including His State Papers* (New York: Derby & Miller, 1866), 297.

7. "The Mexican Question," *New York Times*, June 8, 1865, 4.

8. Michael Vorenberg, "Abraham Lincoln and the Politics of Black Colonization," *Journal of the Abraham Lincoln Association* 14, 2 (Summer 1993): 23–45.

9. Eric Foner, *Free Soil Free Labor, Free Men: The Ideology of the Republican Party Before the Civil War* (New York: Oxford University Press, 1970), 267–80.

10. The Confederacy did make an unsuccessful attempt to poach U.S. territory at the beginning of the war. See Donald S. Frazier, *Blood and Treasure: Confederate Empire in the Southwest* (College Station: Texas A & M University Press, 1995).

11. "Commercial Importance and Future of the South," *DeBow's Review* 32, 1 and 2 (Jan.-Feb. 1862): 120–34; "Sigma," "Southern Individuality," *Southern Literary Messenger* 38, 6 (June 1864): 369–73.

12. *DeBow's* resumed publication in 1866 and expired in 1869.

13. Sharon Hartman Strom and Frederick Stirton Weaver, *Confederates in the Tropics: Charles Swett's Travelogue of 1868* (Jackson: University Press of Mississippi, 2011), 4.

14. Matthew Pratt Guterl, "Refugee Planters: Henry Watkins Allen and the Hemispheric South," *American Literary History* 23, 4 (Winter 2011): 724–50; Andrew F. Rolle, *The Lost Cause: The Confederate Exodus to Mexico* (Norman: University of Oklahoma Press, 1965).

15. Moon-Ho Jung, *Coolies and Cane: Race, Labor, and Sugar in the Age of Emancipation* (Baltimore: Johns Hopkins University Press, 2006).

16. Guterl, *American Mediterranean*, 77.

17. Seymour Drescher, *Abolition: A History of Slavery and Antislavery* (Cambridge: Cambridge University Press, 2009), 329.

18. Anthony Trollope, *North America* (New York: Harper & Brothers, 1862), 353.

19. [Augusta Evans Wilson], *Macaria; or, Altars of Sacrifice* (Richmond, Va.: West & Johnston, 1864), 162.

20. Gregory P. Downs, "The Mexicanization of American Politics: The United States' Transnational Path from Civil War to Stabilization," *American Historical Review* 117, 2 (April 2012): 387–409.

21. Abraham Lincoln, *Abraham Lincoln: His Speeches and Writings*, ed. Roy P. Basler (Cambridge, Mass.: Da Capo Press, 2001), 792.

22. W. E. B. Du Bois, *Black Reconstruction in America: An Essay toward a History of the Part Which Black Folk Played in the Attempt to Reconstruct Democracy in America, 1860–1880* (New York: Oxford University Press, 2007 [1934]); David Blight, *Race and Reunion: The Civil War in American Memory* (Cambridge, Mass.: Belknap Press of Harvard University Press, 2001).

23. James M. McPherson, "No Peace Without Victory, 1861–1865," *American Historical Review* 109, 1 (February 2004): 1.

Index

Acknowledgments

I am indeed fortunate to have been engaged for so long on a project I have found so enjoyable, and to have had the support and assistance of many extraordinary people. James Oakes can convey more substance in a few well-considered words than generally can be communicated with whole disquisitions. It was he who taught me what it is to be a historian and made me believe I might be one. This project grew out of a wonderful comparative slavery class he taught in the spring of 2005 that led me to study the antebellum period.

CUNY boasts many skilled and challenging historians. Herman Bennett, Gregory Downs, Andrew Robertson, and Jonathan Sassi were generous with time and suggestions. Martin Burke and Dagmar Herzog presided over excellent seminars in which I developed early drafts of this project. Tim Alborn offered wise advice as I began my teaching career. The inestimable assistance of Betty Einerman in the history office smoothed many potential rough spots of my work. I am very grateful to CUNY for the support I received in the form of University Fellowships that gave me the opportunity to work with Joshua Freeman and Thomas Kessner. The Benjamin Altman Fellowship provided most welcome assistance and a dose of encouragement as I worked on the project in the midst of a recessionary economy.

To Michael Zuckerman at the University of Pennsylvania I owe a particular debt of gratitude. Mike took the time to read the manuscript and offered insightful criticism and abundant encouragement. He sets a most generous example of building communities of scholars. Not the least of his kind offices was introducing me to Robert Lockhart, my thoughtful and meticulous editor at the University of Pennsylvania Press. Thanks also to Andrew Burstein and an anonymous reviewer for their perceptive suggestions about an early draft of this book.

Portions of the first, second, and third chapters of this book were presented at the Barnes Conference at Temple University in Philadelphia, the

Society for Historians of the Early American Republic Conference in Rochester, and the Southern Historical Association Conference in Mobile, and I extend my gratitude for the valuable suggestions of the respondents.

I particularly want to thank the librarians and archivists at the American Antiquarian Society; the American Philosophical Society; the Beinecke Library at Yale University; the Historical Society of Pennsylvania; the Massachusetts Historical Society; the New-York Historical Society; the New York Public Library; the Rare Book and Manuscript Library at Columbia University; the Rare Book Room in the Public Library of Cincinnati and Hamilton County; the South Caroliniana Library at the University of South Carolina; and the University of Pennsylvania Rare Book Library.

My parents, Paul William and Mary Reed Naish, instilled in me my interest in history. One of the great blessings of having older parents is that the past always seems remarkably proximate. My parents' recollections—repeated with new details and new emphases as I grew up—taught me about how the telling of history can change depending on its audience and the circumstances in which it is told.

My colleagues Evan Friss, Gwynneth Malin, Thomas Harbison, and Carl Lindskoog provided invaluable feedback over a series of peanut butter sandwiches and pizza dinners. David Gary, who keeps up with the current literature with a formidable zeal, sent me numerous citations for new books I needed to read. Jim McGrath and Kate Mazza provided comments and encouragement.

While working on this project I also worked at Hines, a real estate development and management company with high standards of quality. My coworkers there were especially accommodating in allowing me a schedule flexible enough to take classes and teach. I am grateful to them all, but must particularly acknowledge Jenny Dharamsey, Ken Hubbard, and Emily Lopez.

I am blessed with wonderful friends who have enriched my life in ways they cannot imagine. From my years in Cincinnati I thank Jim Downie, Greg Fedroff, Dick and Janet Neidhard, Michael Schmidt and Laurie Hoppenjans, Kevin Shoemaker, and Sister Mary Timothea, R.S.M. Through my undergraduate years at Yale I am fortunate to count as friends Betta and Tom Fisher-York, Lenny Picker and Chana Thompson Shor, Arnie Sheetz and Jessica Bienstock, Jane and Cary Siegel, and Lengko Valsamis. From my years in New York I appreciate the friendship of Dorothy Chansky and Terry Bennett, Katrina Jeffries, Dan Opler and Yamuna Bhaskaran, Stacey

Pramer, Eileen Lally Ross, and Ilyse Shechtel. That there are many others—in fact, more friends than I can count—is truly a source of wonder to me. I am sure I am neglecting many who should be included here.

When I was halfway through the third chapter, my brother, Matthew John Naish, died unexpectedly. I owe a particular debt of gratitude to Kelli Adamczak, who took upon herself the task of settling his affairs, allowing me to proceed with this project.

The opportunity to teach at Lehman College, City College, and Guttman Community College enriched this project immeasurably. My students read some of the primary sources considered here (even acting out scenes from some of American literature's most obscure plays). Their sharp responses helped me see things I would otherwise have missed. Their perspectives—often so different from mine, but tenaciously held and vigorously defended—helped me to recognize assumptions and prejudices in myself of which I had not been aware. As historians, we work with the materials of the past—but my students always remind me that history belongs to the present, and the future.